masters of the WIRED WORLD

'O, wonder!
How many goodly creatures are there here!
How beauteous mankind is! O brave new world
That has such people in't!'

Miranda in *The Tempest*, Act 5, Scene 1, William Shakespeare

masters of the
WIRED WORLD
cyberspace speaks out

Edited by
Anne Leer

Foreword by
The Rt Hon Tony Blair
Prime Minister of the United Kingdom

FINANCIAL TIMES
PITMAN PUBLISHING

FINANCIAL TIMES

MANAGEMENT

LONDON · SAN FRANCISCO
KUALA LUMPUR · JOHANNESBURG

*Financial Times Management delivers the knowledge,
skills and understanding that enable students,
managers and organisations to achieve their ambitions,
whatever their needs, wherever they are.*

London Office:
128 Long Acre, London WC2E 9AN
Tel: +44 (0)171 447 2000
Fax: +44 (0)171 240 5771
Website: www.ftmanagement.com

An imprint of Pearson Education Limited

————————————

First published in Great Britain 1999

ISBN 0 273 63559 X

British Library Cataloguing in Publication Data
A CIP catalogue record for this book can be obtained from the British Library

10 9 8 7 6 5 4 3 2

Typeset by Pantek Arts, Maidstone, Kent
Printed and bound in Great Britain by Redwood Books, Trowbridge, Wiltshire

The Publishers' policy is to use paper manufactured from sustainable forests.

Publisher   Pradeep Jethi
Project editor   Elizabeth Truran
Copy editor   Michelle Clark
Text design   Colin Reed
Cover design   Ian Roberts

————————————

contents

4 CONTENT

5 TECHNOLOGY

6 ELECTRONIC COMMERCE

7 THE NETWORKED ECONOMY

8 WIRED ORGANIZATIONS

9 PUBLIC SERVICES

10 PEOPLE

foreword

by The Rt Hon Tony Blair

Prime Minister of the United Kingdom

The world's economy is undergoing a process of change as fundamental as the shift from agrarian to industrial production: the emergence of the knowledge-driven economy, the digital economy.

In the next century, the source of sustainable competitiveness will be the ability to create, disseminate and rapidly exploit knowledge. Knowledge has, of course, always been of vital economic importance, but the scale of the knowledge revolution we are now witnessing marks out the new economy as something different in kind from anything that has gone before. That revolution is being fuelled by three key drivers. First, the explosion of scientific and technical knowledge. Second, the success of the international community in opening up the global market, allowing knowledge – and the capital and skills needed to exploit it – to flow freely across borders. Third, the ability, through modern technologies, to codify that knowledge in a common digital language that can be manipulated, assessed and communicated at high speed. The last of these drivers is the focus of this valuable and timely book.

The digital revolution will transform the way we live and work. Some of the changes are with us now. Electronic commerce has the potential to revolutionize the way we do business even more than it has done already. Remote working will enable us to reshape our lives, and developments such as telemedicine mean traditional services can be carried out in new ways. However, the process of change has only just begun. We do not know exactly where it will take us or how quickly, but we do know that change will come, and that it will bring a vast array of new products and services, delivered in new ways we cannot yet imagine.

One thing is clear. The changes flowing from the digital revolution have not been, and will not be, planned by governments – the massive, sprawling growth of the Internet is testament to that. However, I believe governments can play a vital role –

not in directing, but in enabling change. In the UK, we have been creating our strategy for meeting this challenge. Our goal is an inclusive Information Age that doesn't divide society into information 'haves' and 'have nots'. We are encouraging the use of information and communication technologies in school education and more widely for lifelong learning. We are taking IT into communities, for example through libraries, enabling it to be accessed by people in society who might not otherwise have the opportunity, including the elderly, unemployed and disabled. Also, we are promoting the use of IT by businesses, fostering competitiveness and the development of new products and services, and planning legislation on secure electronic commerce to increase business and consumer confidence in electronic transactions.

However, the digital revolution is a global phenomenon. International action is crucial if we are all to benefit – for example, to ensure that electronic commerce becomes a powerful agent for global economic growth. The UK will continue to play a leading role nationally and internationally. Our goal is to ensure that every country, every business, every individual, can benefit from the new digital economy – ensuring that we can all be 'Masters of the Wired World'.

Tony Blair

September 1998

about the editor

ANNE LEER

Presently Strategy Planner at Oxford University Press, Anne Leer has worked in publishing, television and media for many years. Her academic background is multidisciplinary (B.Sc./MA/MBA). She is a specialist in strategy and multiple media management. In addition to her corporate role, she also acts as a senior advisor to governments and intergovernmental organizations on media and communication industries. She has particular expertise in the field of intellectual property, media and telecommunication regulations, policy development for markets subject to globalization and industry convergence, strategic issues to do with public service provision of broadcasting, education and culture, and business development in fast-changing media markets.

Anne Leer has extensive international experience working at a senior level in a highly competitive environment in the UK, Europe, Scandinavia and the US. She also has an interest in the emerging economies in Asia, China and Africa. In 1993 she joined Oxford University Press, a company with more than 500 years of history and with operations in 62 countries around the world. Anne Leer is also on the British Library's Advisory Committee on Research and Innovation. She is a frequent public speaker and also lectures at business schools and universities. She contributes articles regularly to the newspaper press as well as to trade journals. She is the author of several reports and books, most recently, *Welcome to the Wired World,* the companion volume to this title, also published by Financial Times Pitman Publishing.

preface

by Anne Leer

I am your tour guide on this fascinating journey into the Wired World. I promise it will be a worth-while trip and one to remember and re-visit over the years to come.

I have had the great privilege of doing the route planning for this book and in doing so I gath-ered the key thinkers who I believe will make our journey meaningful and exciting. I went hunting for the Masters who could help us make sense of this fast-changing chaotic world. And I found quite a few scattered around our globe. This is not a coincidental selection; all the contributors in this book have been carefully selected to fill in a particular part of the Wired World picture. No doubt the picture is incomplete, and there are many more perspectives and other thinkers we should seek to include to extend our knowledge-map of the Wired World. In our hearts and minds we need to travel beyond our own culture and reality if we want to build a truly Global Information Society. Only then will we comprehend the global potential of the Wired World and what it means to individual people and organizations on the local level.

However, for this book and for this single journey, I bring you the most wonderful collection of premium local experts who will introduce you to their respective fields of knowledge. We will visit lots of sites of global relevance. We will look at high-level policy development and the changing geo-political order of the world. We will examine the emerging knowledge-based economy and the fast-moving technology underpinning it all. We will identify the impact on legal and regulatory regimes. We will explore the changing market environment and opportunities for business devel-opment. We will look at what this could mean for you and me, and for people around the world.

I will take you to visit the minds of our political leaders as well as leading representatives from the marketplace and different industries. We will be exposed to some of the twentieth-century great visionaries and social commentators. We will also meet inventors, ambitious politicians, successful business leaders and dedicated humanitarians. They are all Masters of the Wired World in their own particular way.

They will share their expertise and experience, their thoughts and visions for the Wired World and the future ahead. Together they paint a rich landscape of our New World. I hope this book will provide you with a useful overview and some essential food for thought to stimulate you in your own life, wherever you may be. Enjoy – and have a good journey!

Anne Leer

acknowledgements

This book would not have been written had it not been for the generous support and commitment of all the contributors involved and their staff who made so much effort in spite of the considerable demands on their time. Together we have managed to create what in many respects is a snapshot of history at the turn of the century and a new millennium.

Also, this book would not have materialized without the support of the publishing team at Financial Times Management whose professional skills I greatly appreciate. It has been a pleasure working with you.

Last, but not least, I would like to extend my gratitude to my family and special friends whose positive encouragement was so wonderful – and a special thanks to Michelle Leer for all her support. I could not have done it without you all behind me – thanks!

VISIONS OF THE WIRED WORLD

contributors

Vice President Al Gore was inaugurated as the 45th Vice President of the United States on 20 January 1993. President Clinton and Vice President Gore were re-elected to a second term in 1996, and Vice President Gore was sworn in again on 20 January 1997. Throughout the years that they have worked together, President Clinton and Vice President Gore have formed an unprecedented partnership to lead the United States into a period of sustained economic growth. Vice President Gore serves as an advisor to President Clinton, a Cabinet member, President of the US Senate, member of the National Security Council, and head of a wide range of administrative initiatives.

Vice President Gore's environmental record is unparalleled. He is the author of the best-seller, *Earth in the Balance* (Earthscan, 1992) and he leads the Administration's initiatives to develop a new generation of vehicles, stabilize climate change, increase sustainable development, and promote environmental technologies. Vice President Gore has taken the lead on the Administration's education technology initiative to ensure classrooms and libraries get connected to the Internet. He also heads the National Partnership for Reinventing Government, an initiative to help create federal government that works better and costs less.

Vice President Gore received a degree in government with honours from Harvard University in 1969. He enlisted in the US Army and served in Vietnam. He began his career in public service in 1976 when he was elected to represent Tennessee in the US House of Representatives. He was a candidate for the Democratic nomination for President in 1988 and won over three million votes and Democratic contests in seven states.

Martin Bangemann has been a Member of the European Commission since 1994, responsible for Industrial Policy, Information Technologies, Information Industry and Telecommunication. He is a lawyer by profession and received his doctorate in law from the University of Munich after submission of his dissertation on topics concerning philosophy and law under the direction of Professor Karl Engisch.

Dr Bangemann has been a Member of the FDP (Free Democratic Party) in Germany since 1963 and over the years he has held several leading positions within the party including the Chairmanship of the FDP between 1985–88. Dr Bangemann was a Member of the German Bundestag between 1972–80 and 1986–89. He became a Member of the European Parliament in 1973, until 1984. He has been the Vice Chairman and Chairman of the Liberal and Democratic Group of the European Parliament (1975–84). He was the Federal Minister of Economic Affairs in Germany between 1984–88, before his appointment as Vice President of the Commission of the European Communities 1989–93.

Dr Bangemann is a member of the managing bodies of numerous European foreign affairs and cultural organizations; holds honorary doctorates from the University of Lille II, the University of Sunderland and Salford College; is an honorary professor at Lausanne University; an honorary citizen of Valenciennes; and he was awarded the Federal Cross of Merit with Star of the Order of Merit of the Federal Republic of Germany and the Bavarian Order of Merit. Additionally he has been awarded several decorations in different countries.

contributors

Alvin Toffler – from Silicon Valley and Washington, from Tokyo to Singapore and Seoul, Alvin Toffler's books and lectures have given advance information and powerful new ideas to the change-makers who are defining the early twenty-first century. Together with Heidi Toffler, his co-author and spouse for 46 years, he has published an impressive collection of best-selling works, including such classics as *Future Shock*, (Macmillan, 1991), *The Third Wave* (Collins, 1981), *Powershift* (Bantam, 1990), *War and Anti-War* (Warner, 1995), and most recently *Creating a New Civilization* (Atlanta Turner, 1995).

Closely studied by CEOs and senior financial leaders, as well as by presidents, prime ministers, and top government officials, their work won the McKinsey Foundation Book Award for Contribution to Management Literature, among many other prizes. Political figures ranging from Mikhail Gorbachev to Newt Gingrich and media leaders like Ted Turner, as well as military and management strategists around the world, repeatedly cite Toffler's ideas as they prepare their organizations for the twenty-first century.

As early as the beginning of the 1960s, the Tofflers foretold the explosive rise of the computer. They wrote and lectured about PCs, electronic agents, virtual reality, and today's electronic networks, decades before they appeared in the marketplace. When the forerunner to the Internet had only 700 people on it, the Tofflers were telling the world about it. Alvin and Heidi Toffler have anticipated and influenced many aspects of business and daily life in the nineties too. They lectured about niche markets long before that term was invented. They wrote about acceleration of change, the shift to work-at-home, and temporary help services in 1970. They identified the move to de-massified media as early as 1981.

Alvin Toffler has served as a Visiting Scholar at the Russell Sage Foundation, a Visiting Professor at Cornell University, a faculty member of the New School for Social Research, a White House correspondent, an editor of *Fortune Magazine*, and a business consultant. He holds a number of honorary doctorates in letters, law, science and management science. He is a member of the International Institute for Strategic Studies, and a Fellow of the American Association for the Advancement of Science.

Sir Arthur C. Clarke KBE is probably the world's best known and bestselling science fiction writer. He has won innumerable international awards for both his fiction and science writing. His 1945 article in *Wireless World* signalled a revolution in global communications with his concept of the communications satellite. His collaboration with Stanley Kubrick on *2001: A Space Odyssey* set a new benchmark for science fiction movies. His commentary on the Apollo Moon landing, alongside legendary broadcaster Walter Kronkite, was seen around the globe and he has been closely linked with space exploration ever since. In 1998 he was honoured by his native country with a knighthood. He lives in Sri Lanka and, though an octogenarian, he regularly addresses international conferences and organizations by satellite. He has long been widely regarded as a respected prophet of the space age and its resultant new technologies.

by Anne Leer

POLITICAL PROMISE TO THE TEST

I have organized our journey into the Wired World around themes, major attractions, popular as well as alternative routes of thought. Our first theme is Visions and the listed attractions include visits to the White House in Washington and to the European Commission in Brussels. We will also have two excursions to a beach house in Sri Lanka to find Sir Arthur C. Clarke and to a secret location in America where Alvin Toffler is thinking.

These four visits with the mission to explore visions are quite compelling and should leave you with a sense of urgency fuelled by the knowledge that something of great historic importance is happening. It is awesome, but fascinating – and perhaps like me you will feel a little like a child on Christmas Eve, full of expectation waiting to open those parcels under the Wired World future tree.

Our first stop is Vice President Al Gore – the political number one champion of the Wired World. Gore has been promoting investment in information technology and the development of the so-called National Information Infrastructure (NII) ever since Bill Clinton's presidential campaign back in 1992. It was Gore who originally coined the phrase 'national information infrastructure' and started the political debate about 'Information Superhighways'. In his chapter he sums up the key developments and achievements so far, and he describes the outstanding challenges that remain to be resolved. He draws attention to the need to safeguard the core values of a democratic society if we want to succeed in using technology to build a better world. He calls for a Digital Declaration of Interdependence to enable us to build a brighter future for all.

Next we visit Dr Martin Bangemann at the European Commission who is also a pioneer of the Wired World. It was Bangemann who kick-started the European agenda for the Global Information Society back in the early days in 1993/1994 and he was very much Gore's counterpart in Europe championing the benefits of the Wired World. He too has moved on from a focus on technology to a focus on people, content and quality. He too asks questions about what we want the technology to do for us. Like Gore, he emphasizes the need to find new forms of international collaboration between public and private sectors and similarly calls for an International Charter for a political understanding to fulfil the Global Information Society agenda.

It is comforting that our political leaders no longer seem to rave exclusively about the glory of technology and how wonderful the world would be if only we all could get connected and live happily ever after in that virtual global village green.

Having taken in what Gore and Bangemann write you may feel a little overwhelmed by their expectations of the networked society. Politicians around the world have come up with a long list of big promises. The question is can these promises be delivered or are we perhaps being promised too much? Is the global song about the wonders of the Wired World rooted in reality or is it lacking in substance, flavoured by popular sound bites and too much hype? Is the world really changing so fast and so profoundly as they will have it – let's move on and find out if two of the world's leading visionaries and thinkers can provide some answers.

Both Alvin Toffler and Arthur C. Clarke have dedicated their working lives to understanding societal change and the impact of technology on mankind. Toffler is no longer the great optimist he used to be back in seventies when he first published his bestsellers *Future Shock* and *Third Wave* through which he infected us all with his enthusiasm for what change and new technology could bring. He is now clearly disappointed that it takes people and organizations so long to learn and exploit knowledge already available. In this chapter he reveals his deep concerns about the state of the world and what lies ahead. He believes we are entering the new millennium going into decades of severe turbulence.

If Gore and Bangemann do not manage to convince you about the scale and impact of the Information Revolution, then Toffler will. He demonstrates just how profound the changes are on all levels – from the individual and the family to business and politics. He describes the power shifts in geo-political order of the world and how the new civilization is learning to operate. He has several visions of the Wired World and the future. He challenges us to think in terms of likely futures, probable futures and desirable futures – what are the options, the consequences and the decisions we need to make.

Arthur C. Clarke's razor sharp mind and long-range vision continue to baffle me as he has always done – his ability to imagine and see what is invisible to most is uncanny. You don't have to live in the power centres of this world to be on the leading edge of technology and wisdom. Sir Arthur made his home in Sri Lanka and from there he is wired up and in constant touch with the rest of the world. Now in his eighties, he continues to correct our often distorted and short-term visions of the Wired World. Most people think about the immediate future – Sir Arthur thinks in terms of centuries. He agrees the long-heralded global village is upon us, but he also says it will last for only a flickering moment in the history of mankind. He helps to put it all in a very exciting and positive perspective, which leaves you with the feeling of 'can't wait to be there – in the future'. ■

Al Gore

Vice President of the United States of America

PUTTING PEOPLE FIRST IN THE INFORMATION AGE

The Global Information Infrastructure, a network of networks that transmits messages and images at the speed of light and on every continent, has the potential, ultimately, to link all human knowledge. Its creation is so revolutionary – the changes it has wrought are so vast – that even those of us who have worked on it for years cannot predict its full impact.

For all the stunning capabilities of the Global Information Infrastructure (GII), we must remember that at its heart it is a way to deepen and extend our oldest, and most cherished global values: rising standards of living and literacy; and an ever-widening circle of democracy, freedom, and individual empowerment.

Thanks to the advancement in digital technology, we are taking part in a truly open moment in world history, a moment when we can come together across our communications networks to rediscover and renew our shared values and build the twenty-first century our children deserve.

As a member of Congress and as Vice President of the United States, one of my top priorities has been to promote the development of the National and Global Information Infrastructure. I have long believed that new information and communications technologies will have a dramatic impact on the way that we work, learn, live and interact with each other. That's why I have worked hard to promote global electronic commerce, to connect every child to the Information Superhighway, and to use information technology to 'reinvent government'. And that's why I have posed five great challenges that still remain to be met as we enter the Information Age, a 'Digital Declaration of Interdependence.'

The Information Revolution — happening at the speed of light

The cluster of technologies that make up the GII, including wired and wireless networks, computers and other information appliances, and networked information and applications, has evolved at an astounding rate, becoming more powerful, affordable, useful, and ubiquitous:

■ The Internet, which connected 1.3 million computers in 1993, by 1998 connected almost 37 million computers and an estimated 148 million people worldwide. The World Wide Web, first developed at CERN (the European Laboratory for Particle Physics) in 1990, now grows at a rate of 1.5 million pages per day and doubles in size every 8 months.

■ In the early 1990s, the Internet was used primarily for e-mail and to download files. Today, a broad range of applications have been developed for the Internet, including search engines, electronic payments, on-line catalogues, real-time transmission of audio and video, intelligent agents, digital signatures, software that can translate foreign languages, and secure Extranets that link firms with their customers and suppliers. In the US and around the world, entrepreneurs are starting thousands of companies to create new Internet software.

■ Our ability to transmit, store and process information continues to expand at a dramatic rate, while the cost of doing so plummets. In 1998, $200 video games had more computing power than the $20 million supercomputer available in 1976. Telecommunications companies are deploying networks capable of transmitting the equivalent of the entire Library of Congress coast-to-coast in 20 seconds, and trans-Atlantic links capable of carrying 7 million simultaneous phone calls.

■ Global satellite systems are being developed that will soon allow anytime, anywhere communication and access to information from any spot on the planet. New wireless technologies may allow developing countries to leapfrog developed country investments in a wired telecommunications infrastructure.

As amazing as these developments are, it is important to remember that the Information Revolution is still in its infancy. First of all, we can expect that the enabling technology will continue to improve. At current rates of improvement, a hard drive capable of storing several million books and a lifetime supply of music and movies will be available in 2012 for a few hundred dollars. The semiconductor industry projects that it can continue to stay on the Moore's Law curve for at least the next 15 years, by doubling the number of transistors on an integrated circuit every 18 months. Competition between new and existing telecommunications companies will eventually drive the deployment of broadband networks capable of handling voice, video and data, putting an end to the World Wide Wait. Second, only a third of the world's 1.5 billion households have access to a telephone, let alone the

Internet and advanced telecommunications services. Cyberspace will undoubtedly be substantially different, and much more valuable, as access to it becomes universal.

We should not view information technology (IT) as an end in itself, but as a tool that we can use to create economic opportunity, improve our quality of life, and advance our most basic values. The range of potential benefits and applications of IT is remarkable, and it has already become an important part of our economic and social fabric. In the US, IT has accounted for more than a third of our economic growth over the last three years. More than 7 million Americans are now employed by IT industries or in IT-related occupations at wages that are almost two-thirds higher than the private sector average. Using the Internet, individuals have the ability to express themselves and communicate with people from around the world who share their interests in a way that is not possible using traditional broadcast media. Patients in remote rural towns consult with medical experts thousands of miles away. Citizens can tap into the voting records of their elected representatives, and use community networks to brainstorm solutions to local problems. Farmers use geographical information systems and satellite imagery to increase their crop yields while minimizing their use of pesticides and fertilizers. Museums, galleries and libraries expand their reach by making their collections available on the World Wide Web. People with disabilities can now lead richer and more independent lives, particularly if IT and information services are designed from the beginning to be accessible.

> We should ... view information technology (IT) ... as a tool that we can use to create economic opportunity, improve our quality of life, and advance our most basic values.

Although much of the public discourse on the Information Revolution has tended to focus on the technology, it is my hope that we can devote more intellectual energy to exploring its uses and applications. As the cost of transmitting and processing information continues to plummet, the applications of IT will be limited only by our imagination, creativity, and ability to innovate. Our vision and the goals we set for the use of IT should be shaped by our values. Some commentators subscribe to a simple-minded technological determinism, and believe that technology will drive economic, political, social and cultural developments. I believe that people, not technology, should be in the driver's seat. As Phil Agre, Professor of Communications at the University of California at San Diego, observed, the next generation of Internet heroes may be those who can build bridges between the esoteric world of technical work and the bigger, messier world in which values are argued and chosen. The greatest promise of this electronic and Digital Age lies not in what is *new*, but in the values that are *renewed*. As each breathtaking new development brings us closer together in communication and in common cause – building a true global electronic village – we have the chance to spread a new prosperity, a new literacy, a new love of freedom and democracy, and even a new sense of community to the farthest regions of the world.

As excited as I am about the potential benefits of IT, we must be prepared to confront its risks and downsides as well. IT could create a digital divide between those who have access to Information Age tools and those who do not, not only within developed countries, but between developed and developing countries. Privacy could be eroded as it becomes easier to collect, store and link personally identifiable information. Our infrastructure may become increasingly vulnerable to disruptions from unreliable information systems and malicious attacks. The year 2000 problem could cause serious disruptions of electric power grids, water treatment plants, financial networks, telecommunications systems, and air traffic control systems worldwide.

We can and must take actions to address the potential downside of IT. On privacy, I have been fighting for an 'electronic bill of rights.' People should have the right to choose whether their personal information is disclosed; the right to know how, when, and how much of that information is being used; and the right to see it themselves, to know if it is accurate. In 1998 we made progress on a number of important privacy issues, including new penalties for identity theft, privacy protection for children under 13, and new protections for financial and medical records.

IT could create a digital divide between those who have access to Information Age tools and those who do not.

On the year 2000 problem, we are pursuing a top-priority, high-level initiative to make sure our national government is prepared. President Clinton recently signed legislation that will provide liability protections to promote and encourage greater information-sharing about both experiences and solutions. But in an era of global interdependence, there is a shared global responsibility to meet the challenge. Every single company and nation that has benefitted from global trade has an obligation to help shoulder this critical burden.

Over the past six years, President Clinton and I have worked hard to advance the Information Superhighway. We fought for legislation to promote competition in the telecommunications industry, so that consumers would enjoy more choice, lower prices, and access to advanced telecommunications services. We made it a national goal to connect every classroom and library to the Internet by the year 2000, and to make sure that all of our children have access to educational technology. To sustain the Information Revolution, we invested in long-term research and development projects such as the Next Generation Internet. We established a framework for global electronic commerce that encourages private sector leadership and sets policy in areas such as intellectual property, privacy, and taxation. Although much remains to be done, I believe that we have made a good beginning to preparing America for the Information Age, and to promoting international cooperation on these important issues.

Connecting our children to the future

Information technology, used creatively, has the potential to revolutionize the way teachers teach and students learn. That is why the use of technology in the schools is an important part our broader strategy to ensure that every child in the US gets a world-class education.

In some classrooms in the US, teachers are using the Internet and multimedia computers to keep up with the latest developments in their fields, exchange lesson plans with their peers, and communicate more frequently with parents. Student are taking 'virtual field trips' to the bottom of the ocean, tapping in to the Library of Congress and the National Archives to learn American history from primary source material, and participating in projects with students from all over the world. For example, students and teachers from over 5500 schools in more than 70 countries are working with research scientists to learn more about our planet as part of my Global Learning and Observations to Benefit the Environment (GLOBE) project. Students make environmental observations at or near their school, report their data through the Internet, and are able to download images that help them understand the GLOBE data in a global context. In short, educational technology can allow students to access material that was previously unavailable to them, participate in 'communities of learners' that extend beyond the four walls of the classroom, and engage in more active, hands-on forms of learning. Students can also explore subjects in ways that are tailored to their background, interests, and learning styles.

In order to take advantage of the promise of educational technology, President Clinton and I have set four national goals:

1 Every classroom should be connected to the Internet and other advanced telecommunications services by the year 2000.
2 All children should have access to modern, multimedia computers.
3 All teachers should have the training and support that they need to use technology effectively in the classroom.
4 High-quality educational software and content should be available to support learning in all subjects.

To achieve these goals, the Administration has significantly expanded its investments in educational technology. In our latest budget, we have proposed over $700 million to help states and local communities meet the four national goals, to encourage innovative applications of educational technology in the schools, and to help ensure that all new teachers entering the workforce can use technology effectively. In addition, President Clinton and I have been strong supporters of expanding the definition of 'universal service' to include discounted telecommunications services and Internet access for schools, libraries, and rural healthcare centres. These discounts, known as the 'e-rate,' were authorized by the Telecommunications Act of 1996, and are being implemented by the Federal Communications Commission.

Although some companies and members of Congress have criticized the 'e-rate,' I believe that it is essential if we are to prevent a further polarization of American society into information 'haves' and 'have-nots.' Currently, students in high minority enrolment schools are three times less likely to have Internet access in classrooms than students in predominantly white schools.

Although the programmes that we have launched at the federal level are important, we will not succeed in reaching our national goals without the involvement and participation from states and local communities, companies, educators, and parents. That's why I have been a strong supporter of a variety of grassroots and private-sector activities. For example, on 9 March 1996, President Clinton and I joined tens of thousands of Californians in the first 'NetDay,' a volunteer effort that installed more than 6 million feet of wiring in a single day. Since then, NetDay efforts have sprung up in almost all 50 states, wiring an estimated 30,000 schools and libraries. I also encouraged several high-tech companies to develop an 'Education Dashboard,' software built on open standards that will increase communication between parents and teachers and allow parents to monitor their children's progress in school.

Creating the Global Electronic Marketplace

IT and the rapid growth of electronic commerce are having an impact on virtually every sector of the economy. Investment in computing and communications equipment now accounts for almost half of total investment in business equipment, and business-to-business electronic commerce in the US alone is expected to exceed $300 billion by 2002. Consumers are using the Internet to buy books, groceries, cars, airplane tickets, and financial services. On-line catalogues and electronic markets often provide customers with greater choice, more information, and a greater ability to compare the products and prices of multiple firms. Companies are using IT to increase productivity, forge closer relationships with suppliers, customize products and services to the needs of individual consumers, provide just-in-time training, and leverage the shared knowledge and expertise of their employees.

To promote the growth of the Internet and electronic commerce, President Clinton and I released *The Framework for Global Electronic Commerce* on 1 July 1997. The *Framework* sets forth a number of policy principles, such as the need for private sector leadership, reliance on market forces when possible, and the desirability of international agreements which will create a truly global marketplace. Although government involvement is sometimes necessary, its goal should be to create a predictable, simple legal environment that will allow electronic commerce to flourish.

In the 16 months since the Administration issued the *Framework*, we have made significant progress in implementing these principles at both the national and international level. The US has reached bilateral agreements on electronic commerce with Japan, France, Australia, Ireland, the European Union, and the Netherlands. All 132 members of the World Trade Organization have agreed not to impose customs duties on electronic commerce when digitized information and services are delivered electronically. The US Congress has ratified treaties of the World Intellectual Property Organization which would extend copyright in the digital environment, and has passed legislation that would create a three-year moratorium on certain Internet and electronic commerce taxes.

The private sector is also responding to the Administration's calls for self-regulation and private-sector leadership. An alliance of over 50 companies that generate the majority of the Internet traffic has formed to promote privacy on-line. The members of this alliance are committed to a set of fair information practices that includes:

- notifying consumers what information will be collected and what will be done with the information
- giving consumers the right to opt out and check the accuracy of the information collected
- stopping the collection of data from children without prior parental permission
- submitting to audits and enforcement by a third party.

Companies are also working with child advocates and education groups to make the Internet more family-friendly. Parents and teachers need to have the tools, such as filtering and blocking software, that will prevent children from gaining access to inappropriate material.

Using IT to reinvent government

In 1993, I launched an effort to 'reinvent government,' so that our government will work better, cost less, and get results that Americans care about. Since then, we have reduced the federal workforce by 351,000 employees, saved $137 billion, eliminated 250 programmes and agencies, and established 4000 standards for customer service.

A cornerstone of the National Partnership for Reinventing Government (NPR) is the creative use of IT. The Access America initiative, which I launched in 1997, is encouraging agencies to use IT to make government more productive, open, responsive, and user-friendly. Agencies are using IT in a variety of ways:

Virtual government

Responsibility for carrying a particular function of government is shared by many different agencies. For example, there are over 100 different agencies involved in international trade – collecting statistics, issuing permits for exports, helping businesses in overseas markets and setting trade policy. This can be very frustrating for individuals, firms, and non-profit organizations attempting to navigate through the maze of the federal government. IT can be used to create virtual organizations that reduce duplication and pull together information and services into a user-friendly 'one-stop shop.' These virtual organizations have been, or are being, created to serve businesses, companies engaged in international trade, senior citizens, non-profit organizations and students.

Laboratories of democracy

Much of the innovation for addressing our most pressing economic and social challenges comes from states and local communities. Local innovation is even more valuable if other communities can learn from, and adopt, these 'best practices.' That's why government agencies are now collecting and disseminating best practices on protecting the environment, expanding parental involvement in education, promoting economic development in rural communities, and helping at-risk youth.

Self-service

Rather than wait in line for hours at a government agency, citizens and businesses should be able to access government services on-line, at a time and place that is convenient for them. Many government agencies are moving in this direction. Using America's Job Bank, developed by the Department of Labor, job seekers can search a nationwide database of employment opportunities, post a CV, and learn which occupations are growing rapidly and paying high wages. The Small Business Administration and the Department of Education are developing electronic lending programmes, and the Department of Veterans' Affairs is allowing veterans to apply on-line to enrol in the VA-healthcare system.

> **Right now, 65 per cent of the world's households have no phone service. Half of the world's population has never made a phone call.**

The Digital Declaration of Interdependence

In my address to the International Telecommunications Union on 12 October 1998, I posed five great challenges that still remain to be met. Together, they make up a Digital Declaration of Interdependence that can create a brighter world for us all.

1 We must improve access to technology so everyone on the planet is within walking distance of voice and data telecommunications services within the next decade.

Right now, 65 per cent of the world's households have no phone service. Half of the world's population has never made a phone call. I challenge the business community to create a global business plan – to put data and voice telecommunication within an hour's walk of everybody on the planet by the end of the next decade. This plan should include ways to stimulate demand. It should involve local businesses, expand access to distance learning and telemedicine, and provide hands-on training. We know it can be done, and it must be done.

2 We must overcome our language barriers and develop technology with real-time digital translation so anyone on the planet can talk to anyone else.

Just imagine what it would be like to pick up a phone, call anywhere in the world, and have your voice translated instantly so you could have a conversation without language being a barrier. I can see the day when we have a true digital dialogue around the world – when a universal translator can instantly shatter the language barriers that so often prevent true collaboration.

I challenge the research community to take these discoveries and develop new technology that allows people around the world to communicate with each other, that makes international cooperation easier; and that allows people to participate in our global community without losing their linguistic and cultural heritage.

3 We must create a Global Knowledge Network of people who are working to meet our most important challenges in education, healthcare, agricultural resources, sustainable development, and public safety.

Just imagine what it would be like if a sick child in rural Mongolia could be linked through video conference to the Sydney Children's Hospital. A small sensor could broadcast X-rays or an MRI back to Australia. A blood sample could be put on a slide and scanned for leukaemia. A leading doctor could prescribe treatment – and the tests would be waiting when the child arrived.

Just think if every farmer in Africa could tap into a local weather channel that provides them with the information they need to plant and rotate their crops. And in natural disasters, we know that just an hour's advance warning can save thousands of lives. Some of the most forward-thinking companies are using new 'knowledge management' techniques that share best practices and take advantage of the expertise of their employees. I challenge the education community to use these same techniques to link practitioners, experts, and non-profit organizations that are working on our most pressing social and economic needs. Today, for example, billions of people don't have access to secondary and higher education. If we can create a 'knowledge network' that extends distance learning around the globe, we can quadruple the number of people who have access to higher education and lifelong learning.

4 We must use communications technology to ensure the free flow of ideas and support democracy and free speech.

In 1994 in Buenos Aires, I said that the GII would promote democracy and greatly increase people's participation in decision-making by expanding access to information and allowing greater freedom of expression.

Self-government is built on the assumption that each citizen should have the power to control his or her own life. More than five centuries ago, this concept was alive in Europe – but it didn't become functionally possible until the printing press helped to spread widely a large body of shared civic knowledge to an informed and engaged public.

Just as the printing press delivered that knowledge 500 years ago, I believe the GII can deliver a new wave of civic knowledge that is comprehensive enough to strengthen the capacity for self-government everywhere. The continuing challenge to all of us – governmental and non-governmental organizations alike – is not to tell other nations what to do, or what values to pursue, but rather to empower people to recognize and act on their own choices. We must continue to work to ensure that the GII promotes the free flow of ideas and supports democracy around the globe.

5 We must use communication technology to expand economic opportunity to all families and communities around the globe.

Everyone in every part of the world should have the opportunity to succeed if they are willing to work for it. In a remote farming village near Chincheros, Peru, life has changed more in the past two years than in the previous half century. In 1996, an Internet Service Provider set up a Net-link for 50 peasant families. The village leaders formed an on-line partnership with an international export company, which arranged for its vegetables to be shipped and sold in New York. Before e-mail, the village's income was about $300 a month; in 1998, it jumped to $1500 a month.

Across the globe, micro-enterprise – which often starts with initial loans of as little as $50 – has been a path out of poverty for millions. There are more than 500 million micro-entrepreneurs, like those Peruvian farmers who eke out an existence by selling their wares and service to their immediate communities.

There are countless micro-entrepreneurs whose quality of life and incomes would change dramatically overnight if they had access to the same tools. I challenge the non-profit community to work with development organizations to provide more of these opportunities. These networks will create jobs and enable micro-entrepreneurs to avoid a middleman and keep more of their profits.

Some estimate that global electronic commerce will grow to more than $300 billion per year in just a few years. By the year 2010, we can triple the number of people who are able to support themselves and their families because they are able to reach world markets through the Internet. It will also help give consumers access to a whole new world of goods and services.

This is our Digital Declaration of Interdependence – five challenges that can strengthen our global community for the twenty-first century.

Conclusion

On the eve of a new millennium, we have an unprecedented opportunity to use these powerful new forces of technology to advance our oldest and most cherished values. We have a chance to extend knowledge and prosperity to our most isolated inner cities, to the barrios, the favelas, the colonias, and our most rural villages. We can bring the twenty-first century learning and communication to places that don't even have phone service today; to share specialized medical technology where there are barely enough family doctors today; to strengthen democracy and freedom by putting it on-line, where it is so much harder for it to be suppressed or denied.

As we move into a new century, let us take that same sense of wonder, that same sense of discovery, and that same sense of courage to make real the values that centuries of human experience have aspired to create – to end suffering, to eradicate disease, to promote freedom, to educate our children, and to lift our families and our nations up. We don't have a moment to waste. Because our children and our world are waiting. ∎

Dr Martin Bangemann

Member of the European Commission

THE GLOBAL ON-LINE ECONOMY

Private and public sector co-operation in policy development

The global on-line economy — what does it mean for politics?

The recent information and communications technology revolution significantly boosted the globalization process in many ways. Digitization, dramatic reductions in the cost of computing power – thanks, for example, to the doubling of 'chip capacity' every 18 months – and worldwide telecoms deregulation are the driving forces for innovative, competitive telecommunications services and applications, and the development of electronic commerce. Distance is losing its importance as an economic decision criterion.

In the near future, there will be access possibilities to broadband multimedia communications networks from any point on the planet, and the growing convergence between the telecommunications, media and information technology sectors will give globalization a new dimension.

In parallel to the development of the new information and communications technologies, the progressive 'dematerialization' of the economy – that is, the trend towards the growing importance of services and 'virtual goods' (such as financial flows, transmission of data, sound and images, electronic commerce and so on) – contributes to the rapid expansion of transactions at the global level.

The on-line economy is one of the most far-reaching developments of our time: its borderless nature puts in question many of the fundamental premises on which political, legal and business decisions have been based in the past. We therefore need to develop a political vision to cope with the new dimension that is given to globalization.

Globalization is thus a major challenge for political decision-makers and demands a new concept and method of problem-solving on a global level indeed. Therefore, we must find new forms of international cooperation on the political level, but, as well, at the level of the private sector and between the two levels. We need a new approach of private- and public-sector cooperation in policy development that takes account of the new, complex and interdependent reality.

> **Distance is losing its importance as an economic decision criterion.**

International organizations – such as the UN system, the Bretton Woods institutions, Organisation for Economic Co-operation and Development (OECD), World Trade Organization (WTO), World Intellectual Property Organization (WIPO), International Telecommunications Union (ITU) – are based on structures: they enable economic and political interdependence to be managed under certain rules. These international organizations greatly contribute to global issue-managing and policy-making. However, the coordination between the various organizations sometimes is problematic. Their approach often remains an addition of national/territorial interests and does not sufficiently take into account transnational cooperation and global problems.

So, the main questions today are the following. How to achieve international governance and cooperative issue-management in an environment characterized by global interdependence, the emergence of open electronic networks and rapid technological change?

What are the long-term consequences of the rise of a globally networked economy and society on policy-making in the economic, social and cultural fields?

How can enforceability of national and regional rules or standards be ensured in the on-line world?

The technical possibilities of open networks such as the Internet are already beginning to put legal structures to the test in various fields of existing law (for example, liability in the Internet environment, bypass of labour laws regarding work carried out electronically on a transborder basis).

The information society sector is the top job creator

Finding answers to these questions is pivotal regarding the fact that the Information Society industries are developing with an incomparable speed in terms of market size, investment and employment.

- With an annual rate of more than 3 per cent, the information and communications technology sectors are growing much faster than most of the other sectors of the economy. While, for example, in Germany the gross domestic product only rose by just over 2 per cent in 1997, growth in the telecommunications market was over 13 per cent.

■ Mobile telephony is a true success story of European ICT industry, particularly regarding private use. Between 1996 and 1998, mobile telephony has been growing at rates of 57 per cent in the West and even 126 per cent in Eastern Europe.

■ The impacts on the labour markets are remarkable. During the years 1995 to 1997, a total number of around 300,000 jobs have been created by IS industries in Europe.

These are only very few figures and we are still at the beginning of the Information Society, so the technological, economic and application potential is enormous.

This is the background against which industry and politicians must undertake continuous efforts to support the development of the Information Society. In many respects, this demands a rethinking and new approaches, particularly on the political side. However, the high unemployment rate in Europe obliges us to focus on issues related to the Information Society, whether they be technological, legal, social or cultural ones.

Another aspect we must see very clearly is the international competitiveness. Although Europe has tremendous strengths and competitive advantages (such as mobile telephony, content industry), the US is still the major player in the Information Communication Technologies (ICT) field. In many cases, Europe is 'importing' on-line technology and services with positive effects, particularly on the US labour market.

Although Europe is doing very well indeed, I am convinced that it could do even better! However, this means that the political piecemeal approach to date will have to be replaced by a convergent, visionary, but hands-on approach driven by both the industrial leaders and, most importantly, Europe's political leaders.

The development of a new policy approach

It appears that in the global networked economy, the biggest challenge the private and public sectors are facing is the need to develop a relationship that allows us to keep up with the tremendous speed in technological, and consequential economic and social, developments to the benefit of society as a whole.

... the political piecemeal approach to date will have to be replaced by a convergent, visionary, but hands-on approach.

In order to free the growth and employment potential of this sector, many of the policies, rules and regulations affecting economy and society will have to be checked on the 'on-line' dimension.

A new relationship in which the private sector, governments, interest groups and international organizations cooperate should identify priorities and guiding principles for solutions. This would allow the development of a set of evolving policy tools, such as industry self-regulation, in a multi-jurisdictional environment. A further tool would be a set of non-legally binding guiding principles at an international level, built on consensus.

In such a process, I see the private sector taking a leading role in the identification of potential policy issues and/or legal or other barriers. Governments' responsibility then would be to try to eliminate these barriers and prevent the creation of new barriers to global trade in goods and services over electronic networks on an international scale.

So, a better coordination of current efforts in the large variety of international organizations becomes increasingly essential to avoid 'double work' but also to avoid new bureaucracy. Regarding the institutional aspect, this would mean no new international organisation or institutional body!

To achieve improved coordination of the international agenda, I launched an initiative proposing the adoption – possibly by the end of 1999 – of a political understanding between industries, governments and international organizations that could be framed in an International Charter. Here again, the partnership with the private sector plays an instrumental role.

Representatives of 70 international companies of a wide range of interested sectors (for instance, retail and banking, content providers, information service providers, Internet companies) participated recently in a Round Table discussion in Brussels on the key obstacles to global communications and, in particular, new electronic services.

The main result of this meeting was that there is a common understanding in the private sector that coordination on a global level is necessary to lift obstacles resulting from divergent rules and policies in seven priority areas: taxation, tariffs, intellectual property, encryption, authentication, data protection and liability.

As a first step, industrialists agreed to launch a Global Business Dialogue with governments and international organizations in order to develop a consensus on solutions to these seven priority issues, and on future issues to be identified over time.

The Commission is committed to guaranteeing that this new process of policy-making is successful in order to ensure that the continuing fast technological developments have a positive impact on the economy, job creation, and the social and cultural values of our society. ■

Alvin Toffler

Author

SHOCKS, WAVES AND POWER IN THE DIGITAL AGE

A powerful tide is surging across much of the world today, creating a new, often bizarre, environment in which to work, play, marry, raise children, or retire. In this bewildering context, businessmen swim against highly erratic economic currents.

I, together with my wife and co-author Heidi Toffler, wrote these words in 1980 when we published our book, *The Third Wave* (Collins, 1981), and, if anything, the environment has grown even more bizarre since then. Bizarre and, in parts, chaotic. But not entirely without discernible patterns, which, if detected and understood, can help us navigate.

Heidi and I have spent our professional lives researching, analyzing and writing about change. As we now stand on the edge of the twenty-first century, there is massive evidence that the tidal wave we've been writing, lecturing and consulting about has washed over every shore. It is clear that, directly or indirectly, the global revolution we are witnessing is altering the structure of all societies on every level. Just as the Industrial Revolution forever changed the world and created a new urban civilization based on mass production, mass consumption, mass media and mass education, so today's information/biological revolution is once more creating a new civilization – a new way of life that is highly technological, but may have more in common with certain pre-industrial social forms than with industrial life.

The world fast emerging from the clash of new values and technologies, new geopolitical relationships, new lifestyles and modes of communication, demands wholly new ideas and analogies, classifications and concepts. We cannot cram the embryonic world of tomorrow into yesterday's conventional cubbyholes. A Wired World demands a complete re-think and major re-construction of society from top to bottom.

The dominant change taking place in the advanced economies is a shift from mass societies based on brute force technologies to de-massified societies that, like the new economy, are much more granular, internally differentiated, more complex and fast moving. What lies behind this historic change are many changes – demographic, environmental, political, religious and cultural, but, above all, changes in the knowledge base of society and how it relates to technology, economics and geo-political power.

Power in the new global order

Prior to the emergence of the knowledge-based economy – a 'Third Wave' economy as we call it – power in the world was divided essentially in two. It was bisected, with First Wave or agrarian countries at the bottom and Second Wave or industrial countries on top.

Power in the world today is no longer bisected. We are moving towards a trisected world. Thus, you now have agrarian countries still on the bottom rung of the power ladder, you have mass-manufacturing industrial economies halfway up the power ladder, but you now also have, for the first time, Third Wave information-based economies at least temporarily on top of the power hierarchy. This shift to a trisected global power structure may well be the most destabilizing consequence of the Third Wave – the emergence of societies heavily based on digitalization and networks.

Of course, it is more complicated than this, because many countries are undergoing more than one wave of change simultaneously and, hence, have multiple 'wave-forms' within them. Also, no country is entirely Third Wave as yet – the information/biological revolution is not complete. Nevertheless, the trisection of world power is already very clear.

Today's scientific and technological changes – along with their economic, cultural and political ramifications all in feedback with one another – combine to create a truly new global social and economic structure as we enter the next millennium.

If we examine the global stage prior to the mid-seventeenth century, we discover a hodgepodge of political entities – city states, principalities, leagues of city states, great empires, Papal domains, pirate-run ports – a wide variety of political forms. With the arrival of industrialization, we eventually got the nation state in its 'modern' form. It was only in 1648 with the Treaty of Westphalia that we began to move towards a map of the world that was all neatly divided into red, pink and blue, supposedly sovereign, nations and states, and these have been, for the past 300 years or more, the dominant players on the global stage. It was the interaction of nation states or states bouncing off one another in an almost Newtonian, billiard ball manner that defined what we called international relations.

What is happening now as we move towards a Third Wave global structure is a proliferation of additional significant players. More actors are climbing on to the stage. Nation states are not necessarily going to disappear, but they are clearly losing their ability to maintain airtight boundaries. Their borders are becoming porous. Not only does trade flow back and forth across the borders, but money instantaneously flits back and forth electronically. Smoke spreads from Indonesia to Malaysia and Singapore, polluting their air. Ideas and alien cultures can penetrate almost any part of the globe, whether a government wants them to or not. Refugees osmose illegally across borders. Immigrants arrive, brain drains wax and wane, and so on. All these indicate a diminution of traditional power of sovereign nation states. The result is a much higher level of interdependency.

We are going back again – not, as some have said, to the early twentieth-century or the late nineteenth-century global order, but, in fact, going forwards to a post-industrial global order that is similar to the pre-industrial order, marked by a wide variety of players on the global scene.

Ask yourself 'Who's important on the global stage apart from nations?' To begin with, the great religions are growing in global power. The Catholic Church is a potent contender. Islam, less centrally directed, is, nevertheless, a key player as well. Religious hostility – Muslim–Hindu – has reached the point at which India and Pakistan feel the need for nuclear weapons.

In addition, more and more giant corporations have global interests to advance or defend. Some of them are essentially stateless. In others, their subsidiaries are allied or partnered with subsidiaries of companies based in many different countries. Very few of these giant corporations are strategic instruments of any one country.

Next, you have Inter-Governmental Organizations (IGOs) such as the United Nations (UN), World Trade Organisation (WTO), Organisation for Economic Co-operation and Development (OECD) and many others. Nations are represented in them, fund them and theoretically control them, but they often take on a life of their own.

Then you have Non-Governmental Organizations (NGOs). In 1970, when I testified before the US Senate Foreign Relations Committee on the future of the UN, there were something in the order of 3000 NGOs that were international in character; there are now over 25,000, and they are all Internet-linked and busy forming coalitions and setting up very complicated political relationships. Some, such as Greenpeace, are able to challenge the power of giant companies, as when Shell wanted to sink an obsolete drilling platform into the sea and was forced to drop the plan. Greenpeace is also able to put significant pressure on nations, as it did with its opposition to French nuclear testing in the Pacific.

Still other 'global gladiators', as we have elsewhere termed them, include drug networks, criminal groups such as the Mafia, Yakuza from Japan, Chinese Triads, Russian and Chechnyan mafias – all of which are linking up, some of which have more advanced communications and surveillance technology than the police and intelligence agencies charged with putting them out of business.

In short, a significant degree of global power is draining out of nations and states, as such, and is accruing to different non-national or non-state players. These different 'gladiators' are very different from one another, but they can, and do, work together.

Deep Coalitions

This brings us to a new concept that we have introduced – 'Deep Coalitions'. Traditional geo-political coalitions, until recently, have been largely coalitions of nation states or states – the Allies and the Axis, for example, during World War II. The last obvious one was the US-led coalition that President Bush put together to wage war against Saddam Hussein, who threatened a number of nearby states. The coalition was made up of governments – of nations.

However in the future, I believe you will see 'Deep Coalitions'. These will consist not only of nations and states, but will be multilayered, multilevelled coalitions in which you may have three nations allied with two giant corporations, not to mention Greenpeace and three other civil society entities, backed, say, by the Vatican, and so on and so on.

We are also finding more and more interlinkages between regions, linkages that bypass nation states and, of course, we see the emergence of binational and trinational regions as important economic players. So, the map is changing. Borders are becoming less hermetically sealed than they were in the past. The system is becoming multidimensional and at least multilayered. Nations and states engaged in geo-political power struggles will no longer be able to win in their contests if they ignore the non-national and non-state players.

All this changes the patterns of power and interdependency of countries as we move into the twenty-first century. And this interdependency increases as countries move beyond agrarian and industrial economies to the new information-based economy. You see this dramatically in the case of the US.

> **The map is changing ... The system is becoming multidimensional and at least multilayered.**

In the 1930s, America had 34 treaties and agreements with other countries. By 1968 that number had grown to 282. However, as the US economy moved from a Second Wave to a predominantly Third Wave, information-based economy, the number of treaties and agreements simply exploded. Today, there are over 1000 treaties and literally tens of thousands of agreements.

This reflects America's global role and its geo-political power. However, the irony, the real paradox, of this is that, often, the more power you have, the less free you are to use it. A perfect example of that was seen during the US involvement in Somalia. It was the proverbial war of the flea against the elephant, so to speak. Here was the world's greatest superpower, with support from other countries, going into Somalia. It had the best communications, the most computers and the most digitized military in the world, but it couldn't make a move without checking it out or clearing it politically with Paris and Tokyo and Rome and getting everyone to act together. The adversary, General Aided, leader of a rag tag gang, on the other hand, didn't have to ask anybody. He was free to act quickly, independently, and the elephant had a hard time trying to catch or trample the flea.

Once you form alliances and once you are interdependent with other countries economically, you naturally become politically involved with them as well and you are not a free agent any longer. You can still act alone – as the US did in recent air strikes against Iraq – but go-it-alone policies weaken alliances and make it harder to form them in the future.

These problems are magnified as we move into the Wired World, which is far more complex than the one we're leaving behind. To succeed in this world, companies and countries alike need to understand power better – and the ways that the information revolution is changing it.

Info-Tactics

Power is not merely shifting at the global level, but in societies and in businesses as well. By wiring the world we threaten many entrenched power-holders.

There are essentially three sources of social power. One is force – violence or the threat of it. You don't have to put everybody in prison, but the fact that you can will keep people in line. The army, soldiers, are a source of power. This, though, is a very brute kind of power. The power of violence, real or implied, is not very flexible. With it you can only punish (or threaten to do so).

The second source of power is wealth. If you have wealth, you can not only punish but reward. That's why money is usually so good as a manipulative tool.

The third source of power – knowledge/information – is the best of all. With it, you may get what you want without having to compel others at all. You may find a win–win solution or you may persuade others that what you want is what they wanted in the first place. We need a deeper understanding of how information is used and misused for power purposes.

People often misperceive who has the power. I once had lunch at the White House with one of President Nixon's close advisers. We were talking about power. I said, 'The President is the most powerful man in the world, isn't he?' My host laughed and said, 'On the contrary, President Nixon feels that most of the time he's shouting into the telephone and there's nobody at the other end.' He was frustrated, as most presidents and prime ministers are, by the unresponsiveness of the bureaucracies on which these leaders depend and that they supposedly control.

Except at moments of crisis, much of what a president or prime minister actually does is simply adjudicate between competing bureaucracies that have been unable to reach agreements. The State Department wants this, the Pentagon wants that, and the Commerce Department wants the other thing.

Normally, if contending bureaucracies or ministries can resolve routine disputes among themselves, a president or top leader doesn't have anything to do with it. It's only when they can't reach agreement that the issue is bucked upstairs. At this point, the top leader, in effect, acts as a judge, choosing which bureaucracy's policy to approve. Sometimes these issues are unworthy of top-level attention, but the contending bureaucracies need a tie-breaker.

To explore decision-making at the top level while writing *Powershift*, we decided to talk to the people in the White House, the Kremlin and the Prime Minister's office in Tokyo who controlled the flow of paper to the top man. We spoke to the Secretary for the Cabinet and other officials in the White House, his counterpart in the Japanese government and, after much difficulty, the then Secretary of the Politburo in the former Soviet Union. (He turned out to be Anatoli Lukyanov, the Gorbachev protégé who later masterminded the coup that attempted to oust Gorbachev.)

What we found were certain common methods in all three power centres. All sides in the kind of bureaucratic disputes we are referring to here use conventional 'Info-Tactics' to win. Policy advocates desperately struggle for 'face time' with the decision maker – face-to-face communication. They engage in 'back channel' communication. They withhold information, dribble it out slowly or release it in such a rush that it is too late for careful analysis. Often, they also try to reach their leader via the media, making calculated leaks to the press, 'spinning the news'. In our book *Powershift*, we presented a model describing all sorts of Info-Tactics and how they fit into the power game.

The department or ministry with the best chance to win top-level endorsement is the one armed with the most persuasive arguments, backed by persuasive (though not necessarily accurate) data, showing that its proposed policy will benefit the top leader. However, its advocates have one more hurdle to climb – it must get past the information gatekeepers who are going to summarize the information and boil it down to a so-called 'option paper' – often no more than a one- or two-page memo.

The writing of presidential options is a high literary artform. Those who define the options – frequently three in number, a high, low and medium approach – are themselves skilled at influencing their ultimate boss. True option-artists can tilt the odds in favour of their own personal choice by the way they position it in relation to personal or political payoffs for the leader or his party. So far, all these Info-Tactics are conventional – some, no doubt, have been used since ancient times.

In the digital era, however, new and far more sophisticated, often undetectable tactics are likely to be used. In *Powershift*, we called them 'Meta-Tactics'. As more and more of the information used in decision-making – not only in government, but in business as well – is digitized or based on previously digitized data, opportunities for high-level deception multiply. Arguments become more and more abstract and rarefied, more removed from the everyday life of the ordinary non-specialist. For example, Democrats and Republicans in Washington warred recently over statistical 'imputation' methods used by the Census Bureau, because different methods yielded different counts on which the allocation of seats in the House of Representatives depends.

> Power will increasingly hinge on knowledge – and the most powerful of all will be software about software, knowledge about knowledge.

Environmentalists and their opponents in and out of government argue over the adequacy of global warming models – the variables used and the weights applied to them – issues about which most elected officials have little education and little time to consider. As we rely more on networks and digitalization, political battles may well break out over alternative software used in collecting, analyzing or presenting information and/or misinformation. Power will increasingly hinge on knowledge – and the most powerful of all will be software about software, knowledge about knowledge.

Info-Power in the firm

It comes as no surprise that many of the same tactics apply not only to government bureaucracies, but to business organizations as well. Thus, if we look closely at the relationship of information to decision-making in large corporations, we can find the source of many of today's changes in power relations in the firm. Take the phrase 'employee empowerment'. Why are so many CEOs and companies today striving to push decision-making down the hierarchy to the lowest level possible?

If I am running a company, and I'm churning out 4 million identical widgets a year and I've been doing that for 25 years and the environment around me is not changing very rapidly, I can insist I want things done a certain way. I know my markets and my competitors. I know all the steps involved in widget production. I have standardized, synchronized, maximized – done all the things that make sense for a company operating in a Second Wave economy. I can tell the chain of command, right on down to the worker on the floor, exactly how their jobs should be done.

But change the environment, accelerate the rate of change, intensify competition (which can now strike overnight from some totally unexpected direction), introduce incredibly complex technology and networks, try to keep up with fast-shifting market demands and worry about the stock price and interest changes and, no matter how clever I think I am, I can no longer know everything I need to know to make smart decisions. I'm up there on top, but things are changing so fast down there on the shop floor or in the office that I no longer know the best way to turn out a widget or service customers with their increasingly customized demands. It's not that I don't have information, I've got too much information. It's coming face to face, over the transom, over the digital phone lines, over the fax and in massive amounts via e-mail. I can't read it all, let alone assess its credibility, let alone relate it to my problems, let alone respond to it all. I have more information and, it's true, I can communicate instantly and electronically with the lowliest employee at the bottom of the corporate ladder, but, as we now make hundreds of different products, not just widgets, I no longer know how most of them are actually made or whether or not our billing procedures are efficient or whether or not our marketing model is still appropriate or whether or not a lot of other things, and the phone is ringing constantly. I can't handle it all. I have to let others share the decision load. I need to unload the less important decisions.

In short, the shift towards employee empowerment has occurred not because managers have all gone to sensitivity training and suddenly become lily-livered advocates of human relations theory. It's because there is no way that the people up at the top can understand the actual, newly complex and fast-changing realities that the employees need to cope with at the periphery or out in the field. Management, therefore, has to rely on knowledge down below to a far greater extent than ever before. I can't compete in today's environment unless my employees are skilled and capable of both innovation and intelligent decision-making. For it is the employee closest to the problem who has the finest-grain understanding of the situation, who must be allowed to make many decisions that were so-called 'management prerogatives' in the not-so-distant past. If I don't understand and act on that principle, there's a good chance my competitor will – and will eat my firm for lunch. That's what happens in competitive markets. The information revolution is driving these changes, and shifting some (not all) power downwards.

The power of markets

We are also seeing change in the relative power of governments and the private sector. The globalization of finance, and its increasing digitalization, has meant that investors can respond to changed conditions in a country's economy faster than governments do. Every government action that even remotely has an impact on the economy is immediately scrutinized by financial markets 10,000 miles away. Investors and lenders vote electronically – instantaneously injecting or extracting capital from the economy. For this reason, the relative power of governments is reduced, while that of markets has increased. Moreover, since the end of the Cold War, and for a decade or so before that, we have seen a dramatic spread of market economics around much of the world. We've seen liberalization free up previously paralyzed economies and release a wave of economic development. We've seen a corresponding reduction in State control in economies and, therefore, many other aspects of life.

Liberalization has been on the march. Books such as Francis Fukuyama's *The End of History* (Hamilton, 1992) extrapolated this trend of the 1980s and early 1990s and triumphally announced that the competitive economy was so successful, it would no longer have any competition. However, I do not think much of such straight-line trend projection. The Asian crisis of the late 1990s and the election of new social democratic governments across Europe suggest at least a temporary setback for liberalism's triumphal march. It isn't the end of history, at least not yet.

> **The relative power of governments is reduced, while that of markets has increased.**

Few any longer believe State intervention is the solution to all economic problems. Even the last hold-outs, the North Koreans and the Cubans, have begun to experiment timorously on a small scale with markets. China proclaims its belief in market socialism, though many of its supposedly private enterprises turn out to be owned by the military or by various municipalities or regional governments.

Nevertheless, a backlash is looming, not so much against markets as against what might be called the 'market mullahs' – market purists who believe that markets can accomplish everything and who, even in emergencies, argue against capital controls, infusions of State money into failing banks and other measures to restabilize a shaken economy.

Competitive markets do a fantastic job of generating wealth, and all socialist or communist alternatives have proven themselves better at sharing poverty than eliminating it. However, we do know from history that markets can sometimes break down. Think of it as a computer crash. The computer needs a reset button, and so do market economies. That's where governments come into play. There are brief moments when governments can restart a dead economy and even some of capitalism's most stalwart defenders today accept that fact. Only the fanatic ideologues insist otherwise.

Exactly *how* governments should intervene in a crisis is, however, another story. All too often, a government's emergency intervention is an excuse for large-scale political corruption or for confiscating property or 'buying' it from one set of owners at forced, fire sale prices so it can be turned over to cronies of the government, as was, in fact, the case in Indonesia in 1998. Russia provides many other examples. Moreover, once governments intervene, they do not easily back out and let the market do its work. Nevertheless, even though the competitive market is the most powerful tool for creating wealth, it is a tool and should not be treated as a religion.

Unfortunately, in the great debate about capitalism's virtues and vices, even as we speed into a digital era when all conventional economic bets are off, we have yet to find much fresh thinking by either the market mullahs or their socialist and social democratic adversaries. (The so-called 'Third Way' touted by British Prime Minister Tony Blair and US President Clinton – capitalism, as it were, with compassion – seems little more than a retread of Sweden's 'middle way' that was promoted when we were children and the Digital Age was not yet even a gleam in anyone's eye.)

The race towards digitalization, part of the great Third Wave of history, is, as we've seen, changing power relations inside the firm, inside nations and political entities, and at the global geo-political level as well. It is time for societies that can hurl so much energy and creativity into technological innovation to devote at least a fraction of the same resources to radically rethinking the obsolete economic theories of Left and Right alike, and their effect on societies all across the planet as we move into the next millennium. ■

Sir Arther C. Clarke KBE

Author

TECHNOLOGY AND HUMANITY

The shape of what's to come

I have always maintained that the future should be of great interest to all of us. It's where most of us will have to live. The genre of science fiction has provided an invaluable service by way of an 'early warning system' to humanity. Even so, it seems to me that the technological reality can bring with it implications that can surprise even the most imaginative of us. In 1964, when I was writing *2001: A Space Odyssey* with my good friend Stanley Kubrick, people thought I was really taking things a little too far by proposing a computer capable of such a high level of artificial intelligence as 'HAL'. In retrospect, I have to say that my most obvious error was that of underestimating the extent to which miniaturization would overtake the computer industry.

I am fond of reciting the story of a mayor from a small town in the US who, when confronted with an early demonstration of the telephone, became wildly enthusiastic. He thought it was a marvellous device and ventured a stunning prediction: 'I can see the time,' he said solemnly, 'when every city will have one.' We have now reached the stage when virtually anything we want to do in the field of communications is possible: the constraints are no longer technical, but economic, legal or political.

On the occasion of World Telecommunications Day, 17 May 1983, I was honoured by an invitation to address the General Assembly of the United Nations from its famous podium in its New York Headquarters. The sentiments I expressed in that speech are, to me, even more valid today as we stand on the threshold of the next millennium than they were then. The communications revolution – or perhaps that should be *evolution* – carries with it a promise that is, in the same instant, both exciting and frightening. Which of these alternative 'futures' we realize will depend on how responsibly the human race is able to face its obligations to its fellows.

As I faced that august body in New York I said:

> Communications satellites have created a world without distance and have already had a profound effect on international business, news-gathering and tourism – one of the most important industries of many developing countries. Yet their real impact has scarcely begun: by the end of this century they will have transformed the planet, sweeping away much that is evil, and, unfortunately, not a few things that are good.

The slogan 'A telephone in every village' should remind you of that American mayor so don't laugh. It can be achieved now that millions of kilometres of increasingly scarce copper wire can be replaced by a handful of satellites in stationary orbit. And on the ground we need only a simple, rugged handset with a solar-powered transceiver and antenna, which could be mass-produced for tens rather than hundreds of dollars.

I suggest that the 'Telephone in the village' would be one of the most effective social stimulants in history, because of its implications for health, animal husbandry, weather forecasting, market advice, social integration and human welfare. Each installation would probably pay for itself, in hard cash, within a few months. I would like to see a cost-effectiveness study of rural satellite telephone systems for Africa, Asia and South America. But the financial benefits, important though they undoubtedly would be, might yet be insignificant compared with the social ones.

However, long before the global network of fixed telephones is established, there will be a parallel development, which will eventually bypass it completely – though perhaps not until well into the first century of the dawning millennium. It is starting now, with cellular networks, portable radiophones and paging devices, and will lead ultimately to our old science fiction friend, the wristwatch telephone.

Before we reach that, there will be an intermediate stage. During the coming decade, more and more businessmen, well-heeled tourists and virtually all journalists will be carrying attaché-case-sized units that permit direct two-way communication with their homes or offices, via the most convenient satellite. These will provide voice, telex and video facilities (still photos and, if needed, live TV coverage). As these units become cheaper, smaller and more universal, they will make travellers totally independent of national communications systems.

The implications of this are profound – and not only to media news gatherers who will no longer be at the mercy of censors or inefficient (sometimes non-existent) postal and telegraph services. It means, quite simply, the end of closed societies and will lead ultimately – to repeat a phrase I heard Arnold Toynbee use over 40 years ago – to the unification of the world.

Consider what this means. No government will be able to conceal, at least for very long, evidence of crimes or atrocities – even from its own people. The very existence of a myriad new information channels, operating in real time and across all frontiers, will be a powerful influence for civilized behaviour. If you are arranging a massacre, it will be useless to shoot the cameraman who has so inconveniently appeared on the scene. His pictures will already be safe in the studio 5000 kilometres away; and his final image may hang you.

What I am saying, in fact, is that the debate about the free flow of information which has been going on for so many years will soon be settled – by engineers, not politicians. (Just as physicists, not generals, have now determined the nature of war.)

When I offered these thoughts to the UN's General Assembly more than a decade ago, even I could not have foreseen how vividly my words would be illustrated by actual developments – or how quickly. The world has watched and listened as the communist world crumbled, along with its harshest symbol, the Berlin Wall. Millions, if not billions, around the globe witnessed the Gulf War from the comfort of their living rooms. I am tempted to think

> **The debate about the free flow of information which has been going on for so many years will soon be settled.**

that George Orwell, in his apocryphal *1984* failed to fully appreciate the true impact of new technology. 'Big Brother' is not watching us. We are watching Big Brother – and Big Sister too.

Yet, in spite of continuing demonstrations to the contrary, there are still those in the governments of the world who would seek to control the flow of information by so-called 'permission to receive' laws. To them I would cite the example of a simple experiment in educational TV carried out in 1976 – the Satellite Instructional Television Experiment (SITE). The beam from the ATS-6 satellite was deliberately slanted towards India to give maximum signal strength there. Yet good images were still received in England, a quarter of the way around the globe. Radio waves do not recognize frontiers and it is totally impossible to prevent spill-over. Even if country A did its best to keep its programmes from reaching its neighbour, B, it could not always succeed.

However, this phenomenon itself raises arguments from another quarter. While I share the genuine concerns of those who are anxious to preserve individual cultural heritage, I do lose patience with some of the complaints levelled by patronizing 'worthies' of the West at the effects of such readily available programming on the developing areas of the world. Their hypocrisy was highlighted by my good friend Dr Yash Pal in these words several years ago:

> In the drawing rooms of the large cities you meet people who are concerned with the damage that one is going to cause to the integrity of rural India by exposing her to the world outside. After they have lectured you about the dangers of corrupting this innocent, beautiful mass of humanity, they usually turn around and add: 'Well, now that we have a satellite, when are we going to see some American programmes?' Of course, they themselves are immune to cultural domination or foreign influences.

I am afraid that cocktail-party intellectuals are the same everywhere. Because we suffer from the scourge of information pollution, we find it difficult to imagine its even deadlier opposite – information starvation. I get very annoyed when I hear arguments, usually from those who have been educated beyond their intelligence, about the virtues of keeping happy, backward peoples in ignorance. Such an attitude seems like that of a fat man preaching the benefits of fasting to a starving beggar.

I am not impressed by the attacks on television because of the truly dreadful programmes it often carries. Every TV programme has some educational content. The cathode ray tube (and now the LCD screen) is truly a window on the world – indeed, on many worlds. Often it can be a very murky window, but I have slowly come to the conclusion that, on balance, even bad TV is better than no TV at all.

There are many people who will disagree with this – and I sympathize with them. Electronic cultural imperialism has the potential to sweep away much that is good, as well as much that is bad. Yet it can only accelerate changes that were, in any case, inevitable; and on the credit side, the new media will preserve for future generations the customs, performing arts and ceremonies of our time, in a way that was never possible in any earlier age.

Of course, there are a great many present-day customs that should not be preserved, except as a warning to future generations. Slavery, torture, racial and religious persecution, treatment of women as chattels, mutilation of children because of ancient superstition, cruelty to animals – the list is endless and no country can proclaim total innocence. I wish I could claim that improved communications capabilities would inevitably lead to peace, but the matter is not as simple as that. Such an aspiration requires the use of far more uniquely human qualities, such as empathy, tolerance, understanding. Nevertheless, good communications of every type, and at all levels, are essential if we are ever to establish peace on this planet. As the mathematicians would say, they are necessary, but not sufficient.

In the closing decade of the nineteenth century, an electrical engineer, W. E. Ayrton, was lecturing at London's Imperial Institute about the most modern of communications devices, the submarine telegraph cable. He ended with what must, to all his listeners, have seemed the wildest fantasy:

> There is no doubt that the day will come, maybe when you and I are long forgotten, when copper wires, gutta-percha coverings and iron sheathings will be relegated to the Museum of Antiquities. Then, when a person wants to telegraph a friend, he knows not where, he will call an electromagnetic voice, which will be heard loud by him who has the electromagnetic ear, but will be silent to everyone else. He will call 'Where are you?' and the reply will come 'I am at the bottom of a coal-mine' or 'Crossing the Andes' or 'In the middle of the Pacific': or perhaps no reply will come at all, and he may conclude that his friend is dead.

This astonishing prophecy was made in 1897, long before anyone could imagine how it might be fulfilled. Now, a century later, it is on the verge of realization by means of advances such as the coming Low-Earth-Orbit cellular satellite telephone – and, of course, the wristwatch receiver. If you still believe that such a device is unlikely, ask yourself this question: 'Who could have imagined the personal watch, back in the Middle Ages when the only clocks were clanking, room-sized mechanisms, the pride and joy of a few cathedrals?' For that matter, many of you carry on your wrists miracles of electronics that would have been beyond belief even 30 years ago. The symbols that flicker across those digital displays now merely give time, date and a few calculator functions. Before the new millennium has completed its first century (possibly even its first decade), they will be capable of far more than that. They will offer access to most of the human race, via the invisible networks already girding our planet.

The long-heralded global village is upon us, but it will last for only a flickering moment in the history of mankind. Before we even realize that it is here, it will be superseded – by the global family.

There are, of course, many who are already alarmed by the immense amounts of information available to us even now through the ever-increasing Internet. To them I offer little consolation other than to suggest that they put themselves in the place of their ancestors at the time of the invention of the printing press. 'My God,' they cried, 'now there could be as many as a thousand books. How will we ever read them all?' Strangely, as history has shown, our species survived that sudden deluge of information and, some say, even advanced because of it. I am not so much concerned with the proliferation of information as the purpose for which it is used. Technology carries with it a responsibility that we are obliged to consider.

As the century that saw the birth of both electronics and optronics draws to a close, it would seem that virtually everything we would wish to do in the field of communications is now *technically* possible. The only limitations are financial, legal or political. In time, I am sure, most of these will disappear, leaving us with only the limitations of our own morality. There will always be those who seek to abuse any technology to their own ends, but I can only hope that they will remain, as throughout history, in the minority. In any event, the surest answer to such profiteers is for society to remove the need on which they depend for their survival.

> **I am not so much concerned with the proliferation of information as the purpose for which it is used. Technology carries with it a responsibility.**

I once said that, in my opinion, seeking information from the Internet was rather like a parched man endeavouring to quench his thirst by putting his head into Niagara Falls. The Information Age has opened many doors for our eager minds to explore. Now the question is not so much 'What information do I want?' as 'What information do I *not* want?' Never before in our history have we been able to enjoy such a tremendous amount of that simple human freedom – choice. We are now faced with the responsibility of discernment. Just as our ancestors quickly realized that no one was going to force them to read the entire library of a thousand books, we are now overcoming our initial alarm at the sheer weight of available information and coming to understand that it is not the information itself that determines our future, only the use we can make of it.

The next millennium will be, I am sure, even more amazing than the last. As a species, we are 'hard-wired' to explore our environment and our imagination. We should never underestimate the capacity of our own ingenuity to take us by surprise. New technologies offer new avenues of exploration. I must confess that I had never considered my life incomplete without the ability to enjoy the world's great composers while sitting on my favourite beach – until someone in the Sony Corporation came up with the Walkman.

However, we should not lose sight of the ancient truth that 'quantity is the enemy of quality', and temper our enthusiasm with humanity. There are still those in the world who have never seen a Walkman – and probably never will. I must hope that we are reaching the point in our technological evolution whereby we are able to commit more of our time to solving the huge problems of inequality that still plague the poorer peoples of the earth.

I have described myself as an optimist. I used to believe that the human race had a 51 per cent chance of survival. Since the end of the Cold War, I have revised this estimate to between 60 and 70 per cent. I have great faith in optimism as a philosophy, if only because it offers us the opportunity of self-fulfilling prophecy. The Information Age offers much to mankind, and I would like to think that we will rise to the challenges it presents. Our future generations will take mankind to new levels of consciousness and achievement, particularly if they can always be mindful that *information is not knowledge – and knowledge is not wisdom.* ■

This chapter was developed and written with the support of Brian Thomas who has worked as Arthur C. Clarke's technical editor for many years.

THE GLOBAL INFORMATION INFRASTRUCTURE

contributors

Denis Gilhooly is Telecommunications and Information Infrastructure Adviser, World Bank. Before joining the World Bank Denis Gilhooly was Vice President, Business Development at Teledesic LLC, the 'Internet in the Sky' satellite venture backed by Bill Gates and Craig McCaw. He was also previously Media and Technology Director at *The Wall Street Journal*, as well as founding Publisher and Editor of *Communications Week International* and The Networked Economy Conferences. He is a founding Commissioner of the Global Information Infrastructure Commission and a member of the Irish government's Telecommunications Advisory Committee.

Simon Olswang is Senior Partner, Olswang and has seen the firm he founded in 1981 become one of the UK's leading communications law practices, internationally recognized as pre-eminent in the converging fields of telecommunications, information technology, media and entertainment law. Active in the wider community, Simon is Chairman of Informed Sources, a London-based briefing and consultancy company; he has chaired the convergence policy commit-tees of the British Screen Advisory Council; until August 1997 he was a non-executive Director of the Press Association; he is currently Chairman of the British Library's Advisory Committee on Research and Innovation, and he serves as Chairman of the Governors of Langdon College of Further (Special) Education in Salford.

Brian Kahin is currently Senior Policy Analyst for Information Infrastructure at the Office of Science and Technology Policy in the US Executive Office of the President. He was founding director of the Harvard Information Infrastructure Project and is the editor of many books on information technology and policy (most recently, *Coordinating the Internet*, with James Keller, MIT Press, 1997). He also served as general counsel for the Interactive Multimedia Association from 1987 to 1997.

Dr Peter Cochrane joined BT Laboratories in 1973 as Head of Research. He is on the Advisory Board of CSC Index, a large international management consultancy. Dr Cochrane is a graduate of Trent Polytechnic and Essex Universities. He is a visiting professor at several uni-versities in the UK and the US and is a member of the New York Academy of Sciences. During 1990 he led a team that received the Queen's Award for Innovation and Export. Cochrane has been awarded Honorary Doctorates in 1996 from Essex University and the University of Staffordshire. He has published and lectured around the world on issues to do with technology and the implications of IT. His book *Tips for Time Travellers* was published by Orion Publishing Group in 1998. He is also a frequent contributor in the press including the *Financial Times*, *Guardian* and *Wired* and he has a weekly column in the *Daily Telegraph*.

introduction by Anne Leer

GATEKEEPERS' PARADISE

Visions generate passion and commitment to work for common goals. However, the given structure and context we have to operate within in order to stay alive, let alone succeed, limit the reachability and fulfilment of our visions. There are rules and regulations, there are physical structures and dependent variables, which all make up the reality and determine the soil quality for our grand visions to grow and prosper. In the case of the Wired World this is the Global Information Infrastructure (GII).

The GII is the theme of this section and we will journey into technological, legal, political and commercial camps in order to grasp the key elements which constitute the GII and provide the underlying foundation for the Information Society. As we proceed, it will become apparent that the GII works like a central nervous system for the Wired World and that those who control it are crucial, powerful gatekeepers in the new networked economy.

Denis Gilhooly shows how the emerging electronic networks of the GII challenges established business strategies, market structures, regulatory regimes and notions of sovereignty. He says the traditional communication infrastructure owners – namely the incumbent telecommunication operators – will no longer exclusively control the channels. There are a number of new players and gatekeepers emerging within the GII – network operators, software developers, content providers, system integrators, and others. Gilhooly describes the power struggle between the telecommunication operators, who have so far been the main investors and gatekeepers of the global fibre optic network, and the fast-growing content and IT conglomerates. He warns that the telecommunication industry needs to totally transform its business if it wants to survive. The pricing models and means of service delivery for the emerging GII applications cannot be made profitable based on their old legacy systems. The liberalization of the telecommunication industry and the explosion of new broadband capable networks, mean practically unlimited communication capacity for the market to exploit.

We can argue that the GII, like other infrastructures of the world, lends itself to natural monopolies – for example, there is no need to have more than one power cable in the road or one satellite dish on your rooftop or one operating system on your PC – is there? Of course you can have competition and thank goodness we do, but there is a limit to how much choice the market can sustain. You cannot build, maintain and operate an infrastructure without a critical mass of traffic to support it. And you will not get traffic without compelling content. I am reminded of a statement Robert Allen, the former CEO of AT&T made during a high-level debate in Washington on the subject of funding the GII. He stated that he didn't want to be left holding the 'digital garden hose'. By that he meant that there was no way the telecommunication industry could afford to continue to fund the infrastructure development and maintenance unless they could do more than own the pipes and were able to extend their business to recoup their investments from traffic and content.

Inevitably, this all leads to market concentration and dominance by powerful companies which function as the gatekeepers of the GII. There are good political and commercial reasons to control and regulate those players and their power over the vital veins of the new economy. How, though, remains the subject of much debate both sides of the Atlantic.

Simon Olswang has built up an international law firm specializing in the regulation of the media and communication industry. In his chapter he explains how the regulatory regimes affecting the GII industry have developed and changed over time. He shows how the US and Europe have traditionally adopted fundamentally different approaches to media and communication regulation. In the US regulation has evolved with a minimum of government intervention and the industry has largely operated on the principle of self-regulation. Europe on the other hand has a long history of state control and regulatory intervention, and Olswang argues that this historic legacy puts European industry at a disadvantage. He believes Europe is struggling to come to terms with the Digital Age and clinging on to regulatory structures that no longer work.

Olswang describes some of the main ongoing work that policy makers and regulators around the world are doing to try and bring regulation in line with the developments in the market. He believes that regulation should be reactive and not attempt to anticipate and regulate future developments. He points out the futility of resisting change, which will happen anyway and urges us to embrace the future. Furthermore he sees a very limited role for content regulation and looks to competition policy to provide the most appropriate framework for communications regulation in the Digital Age.

Brian Kahin, a senior adviser on policy development and GII issues at the US Executive Office of the President, discusses the impact of convergence. The GII is representative of a major process of technology and industry convergence. Traditionally separate industries like telecommunications, broadcasting, publishing and computing are coming together. However, the convergence in the GII market has not been matched by a convergence in policy and regulatory domains. The respective industry sectors are subject to different and often conflicting sets of regulation. Kahin explains the difficulty in developing sound policies in an environment that changes so rapidly and how the restructuring of the policy landscape compounds the problem. He believes that the sense of boundless new opportunity of the GII does not translate well from business into policy development and law which is fundamentally based upon local concerns and national jurisdictions.

Our last and visionary contributor in this section is Peter Cochrane who reminds us of how far-reaching and profound the technology development we are witnessing really is. If you are a GII non-believer, you won't be after listening to him. He defines the GII as a 'global grid of chaos' and argues that no aspect of our society will remain untouched by the speed of IT – soon all we do will be totally dependent on IT. He believes that nations that try to impose regulation and put a framework for society in place first, before learning how to use the GII for wealth creation, are heading for catastrophe. He says that the slow communication and control processes, and the hierarchical management structures of yesterday, do not fit and will not work with the fast-moving IT era. Like Gilhooly, he calls for a radical change to how commerce and business operate within the GII.

The organizations capable of embracing and mastering rapid change will be the winners. The Wired World with its single GII is truly a paradise for gatekeepers, let's hope it will be many of them and that the power will not be limited to a handful of global giants. ∎

Denis Gilhooly

Senior Adviser, World Bank

THE TWILIGHT OF TELECOMMUNICATIONS

Towards the Global Internet Infrastructure

The world of communications has been turned upside down in the late 1990s. In less than a decade, the spread of digital technology, the mass market phenomena of wireless telephony and the Internet, and the liberalization and privatization of telecommunications markets have led to revolutionary economic shifts in the market. We live in an age where the cellular telephone is an icon of contemporary culture, where sales of personal computers outstrip those of televisions, where more electronic than postal mail is delivered and where cross-border traffic over the Internet exceeds that on the telephone network. Next-generation networks centred on low-cost telecommunications and information technologies are modelling the nervous system of the new world economy.

For governments, industry and consumers, the communications revolution is extending far beyond the boundaries of the communications sector, with the widespread availability of powerful but affordable communications having a profound effect on the pattern of worldwide commercial, economic and social development. Electronic networks place established business strategies, market structures, regulatory constructs, even notions of national sovereignty, under enormous strain. Adapting to the stresses and distresses of a global networked economy is the stuff of business survival. Yet, nowhere is the trauma of adjustment being felt more keenly than within the communications industry itself. After more than a century of stable development, the structure of the telecommunications value chain is undergoing total transformation, and it is happening in real time.

As with today's telecommunications value chain, the key to the multimedia value chain of tomorrow will be maintaining control of the customer – the ability to understand customers' requirements and trends, the ability to control the distribution of value along the chain. Where the telecommunications and multimedia value chains differ, however, is that infrastructure owners – in most cases, the incumbent telecommunications operators – will no longer command exclusive channels to customers. Rather, they will be shared among network operators, content providers, systems integrators and multiple market entrants. Even today, digital technology and the arrival of competition have rendered the structure of the existing telecommunications value chain and its pricing methodologies incoherent. Yet those vestiges that remain are increasingly denying the benefits of next-generation networks to individual and corporate consumers alike.

... the structure of the telecommunications value chain is undergoing total transformation, and it is happening in real time.

The central paradox of the convergence era is that, while the telecommunications operators are the investors, owners and gatekeepers of the vast, global fibre optic network that has grown up over the past decade, the content and computing conglomerates are basing their expansion plans on the assumption that bandwidth will be free and access open. This stark clash in cultures is indicative of a huge power play among industrial interests, the outcome of which will set the pace and character of the communications revolution. Already, multimedia applications are emerging that can only profitably be handled by tomorrow's pricing and delivery mechanisms. However, until the relics of the old telecommunications order are swept away – relics of pricing, ownership, regulation and technology – the goal of a truly Global Information Infrastructure (GII) will remain elusive.

Towards the Global Information Infrastructure

The concept of the GII was first presented by the Vice President of the US, Al Gore, in March 1994. In his keynote address at the International Telecommunication Union's (ITU) World Development Conference in Buenos Aires, he proposed the linking of National Information Infrastructures around a common set of principles, and the accelerated introduction of communication and information technologies in both developed and developing countries. Backed by strong growth in the American semiconductor, software, computing and networking industries, he argued that liberalizing telecommunications markets and promoting use of the Internet would bring significant increases in output and productivity, at low incremental cost, and boost worldwide economic development.

This vision has since been spectacularly realized in the US, with the Department of Commerce estimating that computing and communications now generate between 25 and 40 per cent of America's real economic growth. While the US continues to outpace its international trading rivals in the use of IT, dramatic progress has been made at the global level in the shift towards private-sector ownership, with five billion people living in market economies compared to only one billion less than ten years ago. In many cases, privatization of State-owned telephone companies has kick-started local stock markets, reinforcing the trend towards telecommunications competition. The year 1998 was likely to mark a watershed in market liberalization as it was in that year that the World Trade Organization's (WTO) Basic Telecommunication Agreement was implemented, there was the breakthrough in commercial Internet Protocol (IP) telephony services and the launch of the first generation of Global Mobile Personal Communications by Satellite Systems.

As we enter the next millennium, the advent of global communications networks such as the Internet, Global System for Mobile (GSM) and new Low Earth Orbit (LEO) satellite systems will lead to an explosion in the world's wired population. According to the ITU, in 1998 there were some 750 million telephone users in the world, 120 million Internet users and 150 million cellular phone users. By the year 2001, there will be some 110 million host computers connected to the Internet, implying a user base of around 300 million. That would put the number of Internet users only marginally behind the number of cellular telephone users (estimated at around 400 million) and it would imply that the majority of personal computers in that year (estimated to be some 450 million) would also be connected to the Internet. Put another way, at the start of 1997, there were an estimated 8.6 million users for every 100 main telephones. By the year 2000, there will be some 30 Internet users for every 100 telephony users (see Figure 1).

Effectively putting an end to telecommunications scarcity, the significance of this growth goes far beyond the simple number of connections. Fibre optic technology has already transformed the world's long-distance and transoceanic networks by providing superabundant communications capacity (bandwidth), reducing marginal costs to near zero and undermining the basis for today's distance-dependent pricing. Now, wireless and cable television technologies are challenging the scale economics of the existing local exchange network based on wireline technology and buried copper. The old utility model of natural monopoly is rapidly being replaced by the delivery of new, alternative access technologies via competing providers of local telecommunications services. Increasingly, providing as much potential for telecommunications competition as possible will become the focus for structural reform within the sector, as opposed to the simple transfer of the monopoly telecommunications company from the public to the private sector, as is too often the case today.

For its part, the Internet is forcing major changes in the structure of the telecommunications value chain. It is also emerging as a prototype of the new economy – lowering barriers to market entry, stripping out layers in the distribution chain and greatly increasing the tradability of services across frontiers. In this environment, employment, pay, taxation and productivity will all be determined by the new economics of distributed information. By the year 2001, the Internet will have created a

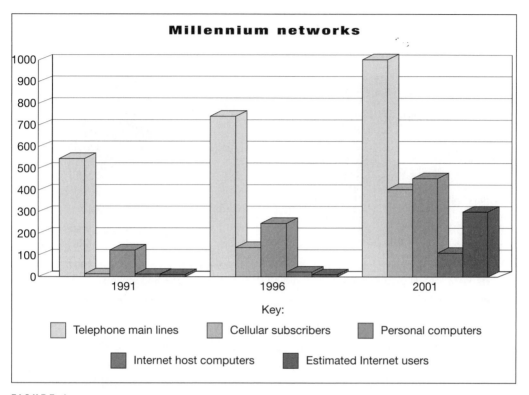

FIGURE 1

Source: ITU

single market of 300 million computer-literate consumers worldwide. Electronic commerce will be an inevitable consequence of the US and Europe's proposed electronic tariff-free zone, transforming traditional business and life patterns as both the size and location of a firm become less relevant. Small and large businesses can benefit from reduced transaction costs, improved customer service and new sales opportunities.

The corollary will be the emergence of new competitors from unexpected directions and inequalities between those countries that are able and willing to exploit new opportunities and those that are not. For developing countries, the stakes could not be higher. The World Bank estimates that emerging economies will need to invest $60–70 billion annually just to catch up with demand – more than twice as much as is being spent today, and that is just for a basic telephone service. The disparities between regions of the world for data communications and Internet access are much greater than for voice service and much greater than for mobile voice service. North America has the same number of telephone lines as all of Asia and it has twice as many cellular telephones, but North America has ten times the number of Internet connections as all of Asia. In the medium term, next-generation networks may at last offer a new development trajectory for emerging economies and help to bridge the huge gap between information-rich and information-poor peoples (see Figure 2).

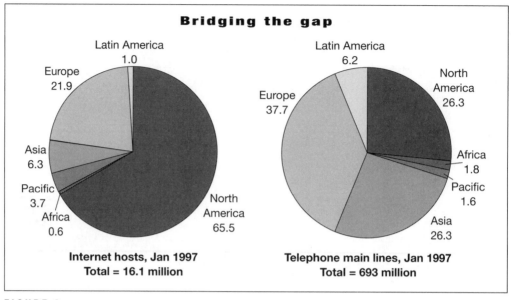

FIGURE 2

Source: ITU

Ultimately, the radical nature of fibre optic, wireless and Internet technologies is set to deliver the unique benefits of universal broadband access. Low-cost access to high-capacity communications wherever and whenever demand arises will be essential in order to meet the needs of the multimedia marketplace. Why universal? Universal coverage is well matched to key development trends in the global economy, national economies and society as geographic location declines as an indicator of wealth and communications requirements. Why broadband? Broadband capability is suited to the virtuous circle of increasing communications functionality and customer expectations for communications functionality. Why access? Access is, and will continue to be, the key bottleneck in telecommunications, even at a time when the local access market is sustaining its financial value, as the long-distance and international market is threatened by the erosion of historical cross-subsidies.

Few dispute the foundations of a successful GII – a ubiquitous, low-cost, reliable, safe, public Internet; predictable, non-stop, self-healing corporate networks (Intranets); and free market telecommunications in local, long-distance and international networks. The problem is how to get from here to there. The massive decline in the cost of communicating, the increase in the power of computing and the shift to digital technology have been immensely positive forces for economic growth and change. At the same time, they have created deep-seated confusion and uncertainty within the traditional telecommunications community. The knock-on effects have been investment paralysis in advanced broadband facilities, defensive strategies aimed more at protecting market share than stimulating consumer demand and delay in the cross-industry acceptance of the Internet as the next-generation telecommunications infrastructure. Without adequate efforts to alter these trends, the GII is set to fall far short of expectations.

The Internet is the GII

The natural inertia of the telecommunications industry can be seen most clearly in its sluggish response to the communications phenomenon of the century – the Internet. Currently, about 120 million users are navigating the Internet, the number of domain name registrations having passed 2 million. Traffic is doubling every 100 days on the Internet, while the growth rate in Internet hosts has been close to 90 per cent per year during the last seven years, reaching a total of 30 million Internet host computers by the beginning of 1998. This unprecedented growth has meant that Internet-related technologies have already achieved critical mass in the marketplace and become the focus of attention of investment for software developers and equipment manufacturers worldwide.

The rate of progress has accelerated dramatically now that it is widely accepted that open Internet standards are the way forward. The Internet protocol is now the preferred protocol for most new corporate networks – Intranets – and the World Wide Web standards have become the preferred tools for most new corporate-wide area applications. Perhaps more important – although the Internet has traditionally been used to provide services that are complementary to those of the telecommunications operators, such as electronic mail or browsing of remote servers – increasingly, the Internet is also being used to provide services that are in direct competition to those of the telecommunications operators, such as voice telephony, fax or data transfer.

> Traffic is doubling every 100 days on the Internet ...

Surprisingly, many telecommunications operators continue to view the Internet as too small in relation to the telephone network – with some 750 million users and $763 billion gained from the provision of public telecommunications services in 1998 – to pose a serious threat to current revenues and investments. Partly this is a result of ingrained chauvinism. As the brain-child of the computing and networking industries, the Internet comes from beyond the sphere of influence and control of the telecommunications industry, and directly challenges the market dominance on which that industry has traditionally based its strength. Partly it is a symptom of congenital myopia. The overwhelming significance of the Internet for telecommunications operators and manufacturers lies not in where it is today, but where it will have evolved to in five to ten years' time.

Fundamentally, the Internet marks the beginning of the great discontinuity of technological convergence between telephone, television and computer. Reversing the relationship between quality, functionality and price, the Internet turns telecommunications orthodoxy on its head (see Figure 3). Today, the Internet is being run on top of the telephone network. Tomorrow, telephony may end up running on top of the Internet. Not only is a completely unregulated network threatening to topple its highly regulated predecessor, but the Internet also embodies many of the key characteristics of the future telecommunications marketplace – the arrival of local-global telephony, sep-

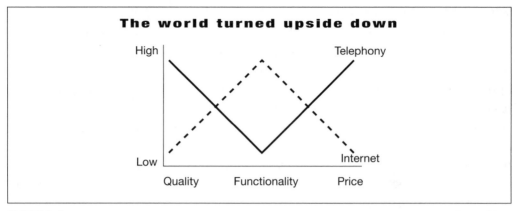

FIGURE 3

Source: Telenor

aration of networks and service provision, availability of affordable mass access and provision of scaleable broadband communications. All of these position the Internet at the vanguard of the communications revolution.

However, if it provides a compelling and attractive model for the future evolution of both the communications sector and the GII, the Internet is also perceived as undermining the very operational and economic foundations of the public telephone network. Growth of the public Internet, for example, largely based on flat-rate charges, challenges the usage-based charging structure of voice telephony, while the proliferation of Intranets is seen as cannibalizing current leased-line revenues from large corporations. Similarly, the 'full-circuit' pricing regime responsible for the spectacular international expansion of the Internet subverts the 'half-circuit' regime of the established international settlement and accounting rate system. The telecommunications giants are justifiably nervous that the Internet will eliminate much of their existing sources of profit and competitive advantage.

This trepidation extends to capital investment. The telecommunications industry is investing billions of dollars in infrastructures and acquisitions to implement strategies for change. However, many of these investments carry high risks – particularly the upgrading of national, narrowband access networks to deliver broadband services – due to the low rate of return and high market risk involved. The problem is further complicated because the existing communications infrastructure based on circuit-switched economics is ill matched to an Internet-dominated future based on packet switching. The stark choice is either to find new ways to use that existing infrastructure or face the prospect of massive write-offs in stranded investments.

Overall, the Internet has become a prime source of uncertainty and instability in the telecommunications world. Lowering barriers to market entry, it offers all the raw materials needed by competitors to create new products and services with guaranteed quality of service. Yet, due to fear and inertia, the telecommunications operators and manufacturers have become trapped in a mind-set of Internet denial –

resisting the dissection of their markets and services, and continuing to sell end-to-end integrated solutions whenever possible; delaying the introduction of innovative pricing schemes to stimulate multimedia demand; stalling investment in broadband capacity and new local access technologies. The irony is that, looking at the threat, the telecommunications industry is apt to miss the opportunity, which is to overhaul its decrepit pricing models and load its networks with killer Internet applications.

Despite its success, the Internet is still 'work in progress' and very much at the start of its growth curve. The high market valuations placed on Internet Service Providers (ISP) contrasts with the lack of a viable business model for the medium and initial areas of weakness, such as quality of service and security, which must be addressed to ensure mainstream commercial acceptance. These problems will find solutions. The major challenge now is making the leap to the next-generation Internet that will deliver the multimedia future of low-cost, universal broadband access. Increasingly, however, it is evident that without a radical breakthrough in the price performance characteristics of today's telecommunications networks, this leap will fail to occur. Where that breakthrough will come is not yet clear, but the concern is that the telecommunications industry will delay rather than hasten its arrival.

Still short of being a wholly mass market phenomenon, the Internet is probably the closest the information industries will come to convergence during this millennium. For all intents and purposes, the Internet is the Global Information Infrastructure. As the precursor to the mainstream communications medium of the next decade, it will continue to blur traditional distinctions between the various communications sectors. All industry players will be forced to rethink their strategies as market structures and value chains are transformed. So, in this period of chaotic transition from today's telecommunications value chain, to tomorrow's multimedia value chain what scenarios can be generated? What strategic and investment choices will be faced by governments, industry and consumers? Specifically, what challenges and opportunities await the incumbent telecommunications operators?

> ... the Internet is probably the closest the information industries will come to convergence during this millennium.

Challenges and opportunities – from Teleway to Netway

A challenge already being faced by telecommunications operators is increased competition in infrastructure provision – from access technologies, such as fixed radio access and Low-Earth-Orbit (LEO) satellites; economies of scale in core transmission, such as increased backbone capacity; and, of course, reduced margins in their core voice telephony business. The opportunity is to act as gatekeeper, effectively 'owning' the customers by means of local access and backbone domination and retaining more value compared to service provision and content packaging. A more nascent challenge is increased competition from non-facilities-based service providers where regulation favours service competition, with network unbundling, service unbundling and service packaging by value-added resellers. The opportunity is in value-added services, offering systems integration for businesses, diversifying into value-added services, bundling value-added services with network services – all expanding the value of the infrastructure.

However, by far the most serious challenge for the telecommunications operators is the threat of dominance by content providers. In the context of computing and communications, this will occur when processing at the edge of the network with generic software results in more value extracted by content packagers, infrastructure becomes a commodity and operators lose control of the customers. The opportunity is to package content with access, extending residential focus or linking infrastructure with content via alliances or buyouts. In the context of mass media and communications, the convergence of telecommunications and digital broadcasting will see the take up of Web TV and interactive television applications, with interconnection between television and telephone networks and concentration of political and media power. Alternatively, the continued separation of telecommunications and digital broadcasting will lead to proprietary set top boxes, few killer applications and political sensitivity to media issues with cultural exceptions on content.

A number of uncertainties from the demand side will affect these outcomes. Foremost will be the mass or niche market take-up of broadband services. Other factors will include mobility, economic growth and Internet usage. Mass market penetration of broadband services will require a sophisticated customer base and a wide range of applications, ranging from electronic commerce to health applications. Niche market uptake is likely to result from poor security perception with viruses and black-outs, delays in new broadband delivery mechanisms, such as Digital Subscriber Loop (xDSL), satellites and fibre optics, and limited use of private business networks. Mobility will be predicated on evolution versus revolution. Evolution via compromise on next-generation mobile standards, sub-optimal spectrum availability, limited demand for fixed–mobile convergence and demand for restricted mobility such as Digital Enhanced Cordless Telecommunication (DECT) and Personal Handyphone System (PHS). Revolution will result from the proof of code Division Multiple Access (xDMA) spectral efficiency, active secondary markets for spectrum and the fast take-up of dual mode satellite services.

In a cycle of sustained economic growth, political stability, an increase in services within economic production, the impact of communications on productivity and 'IT society'-type government programmes will all prevail. Crisis conditions will result from financial uncertainties, growth concentrated in urban areas and failure of infrastructure development programmes. Last, but certainly not least, the Internet. With regard to Internet usage, widespread Internet use will rely on strong multilingual content creation, good perception of quality, with mechanisms for prioritizing traffic and voiceover IP. Niche usage will see the residential Internet remaining a toy, congestion due to lack of regional backbones, usage pricing inhibiting take-up, and strong content regulation.

Given these diverse factors, it is possible to project slow, medium and fast scenarios for the development of the GII – 'Teleway', 'Highway' and 'Netway' (see Figure 4).

Teleway

The Teleway scenario sees success for cellular operators with telecommunications operator alliances focusing on fixed–mobile convergence. Fixed wireless access and Low-Earth-Orbit (LEO) satellites experience slow take-up and Internet security issues remain unresolved, such that broadband networks are limited to business applications. Incumbent telecommunications operators continue to dominate residential markets with only slow upgrades to existing networks. Data rates increase only slowly. Also we see the possible marginalization of developing countries.

Highway

In the Highway scenario global alliances are formed between infrastructure operators, network interconnection replace Internet-peering arrangements and favour network concentration for backbone capacity and Internet applications enjoy widespread take-up with electronic commerce rather than multimedia entertainment becoming dominant. Security is assured by the network owner with metropolitan area networks and corporate networks developed for the business community and xDSL proving successful for residential broadband networks.

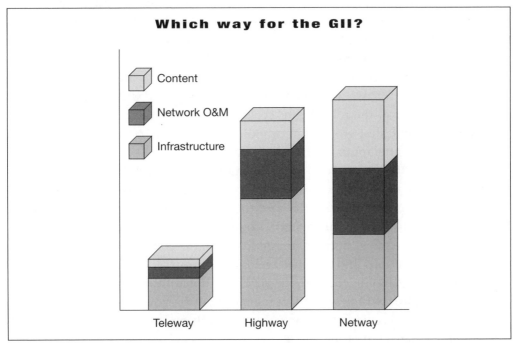

FIGURE 4

Source: Analysys

Netway

The Netway scenario sees intense competition for operators, with many second operators licensed and the success of broadband terrestrial wireless and satellites. Bottlenecks are removed in local access. The Internet is perceived as secure and commercial multimedia applications become widespread. However, network operators lose control of bandwidth that is ceded to the user's side and to the content originator's side. Infrastructure becomes commoditized and users pay for content rather than usage.

Conclusion

The Netway, or next-generation Internet, scenario is likely to be the most desirable outcome in the context of the global economy. The market is already shifting under the feet of the telecommunications giants. As telecommunications traffic moves decisively from the telephone network to the Internet around the turn of the century, the economics of the sector will be transformed. Bandwidth is likely to become a tradable commodity, with 'capacity futures' bought and sold in spot markets. The ownership and control of the infrastructure will decline dramatically in importance. As new, 'virtual' players enter the market with near-zero cost bases, incumbents will struggle to compete with oversized workforces and outdated equipment. In this twilight world, the future of the telecommunications companies looks decidedly bleak.

Alternatively, the Teleway and Highway scenarios will see the collision between the new world of the Internet-based on flat-rate charges and packet-switched technology and the more traditional world of voice telephony based on usage charges and circuit-switched technology becoming a major roadblock to change. Niche players will struggle to take on existing brands or force the break-up of vertically integrated telecommunication businesses. Liberalization and globalization will lead only to a world of super-carrier economies of scale. No breakthrough in the price performance characteristics of today's telecommunications networks will be forthcoming. Incumbents will covet the role of gatekeeper and continue to dictate pricing trends. The Internet – the fastest-growing network in the history of communications – will be frustrated in its attempt to reach its full potential.

For more than 100 years, access to communications networks has largely been dictated by wealth – the wealth of a nation, a corporation or an individual. With the end of telecommunications scarcity and the arrival of the Internet, it has at last become possible to reverse this bias. All countries, even the poorest among them, today face a rising competitiveness threshold due to the communications revolution, yet telecommunications and Internet access offer unprecedented opportunities for developed and developing countries to play in a Global Internet Infrastructure. The stakes are high, for, without watchful management by government, industry and consumers, the gatekeepers will try to ensure that this opportunity remains the privilege not of the many, but of the few. ■

Simon Olswang

Senior Partner, Olswang

REGULATION: PATHWAYS IN THE WIRED WORLD

Traditionally, the Americans and Europeans have approached media regulation from opposite directions. The First Amendment in the US – enshrining freedom of speech in the Constitution – set the direction. American commitment to capitalism – assisted by fierce pro-competition anti-trust legislation originating at the end of the nineteenth century – did the rest. The provision of radio, television and telephone services was exclusively the business of the market.

Throughout Europe, broadcasting was too important to be left to the people. The British Broadcasting Corporation (BBC) was established in 1928; the State broadcasters of other Western European countries were replaced by public service broadcasters, such as the BBC, following the end of World War II. In Italy, and especially in Germany, the constitution of the public broadcasters was an explicit bulwark against the re-emergence of Fascism. Telephone systems were developed under the aegis of the State post offices and, until relatively recently, were known as PTTs (Post, Telephones and Telegraph).

For Americans, the Wired World of digital convergence is merely an extension of an existing and very familiar marketplace. Arguably, even, it is the *product* of that marketplace. For Europeans, to an extent imprisoned by their history, the communications market is unfamiliar and alien territory, very much not of their own making.

The United Kingdom, under Margaret Thatcher, was the first country in Europe to explore this new territory. The catalyst was not so much a sudden falling in love with competition as a political agenda to denationalize – or privatize, as it came to be known – the large parts of the economy hitherto owned by the State. The privatization of British Telecom (BT), at the time a recent creation carved out of The Post

Office, initially had the effect merely of creating a private monopoly in place of a State monopoly. This required the creation of a new kind of regulator – the Office of Telecommunications (Oftel), charged with creating the conditions under which a competitive marketplace with other players could develop, and, until competition emerged, enforcing rules aimed at mimicking that competition. Oftel oversaw the creation of Mercury, a rival telephone operator belonging to Cable & Wireless, another privatized monopoly, which was allowed to undercut BT, skim off profitable business and enjoy very favourable interconnection terms with BT. This 'pro-competitive' regime was extended to the cable television franchises that had been created in 1985 and were permitted to offer telephone connection as well as television pictures to their subscribers (albeit, until 1990, cable had to team up with either BT or Mercury to do so). Oftel was given wide powers to regulate cable's relationship with BT and generally to make and then police new rules designed to stimulate a market and enforce competition where initially there was none.

Continental Europe looked on askance, but, as the UK model was seen to work, the theme was eventually taken up by the European Commission, the Liberalisation of Telecommunications Directive setting the framework for the eventual privatization of European telephony. Most European member states were required to introduce telecommunications competition by 1998.

Changes in television and broadcasting – still directly or indirectly the preserve of the State – went in parallel, but more slowly. The European attachment to the concept of broadcasting as a public service, intended to ensure that what had been scarce spectrum was used to provide Europeans with what was thought by government to be good for them, was and remains strong and has been difficult to reconcile with the competitive marketplace familiar to Americans.

However, the onward rush of technology, fuelled by the forces of the US marketplace, will not wait. European digital TV is no doubt at least as technically advanced as in the US, telephone networks as sophisticated, and the Internet is everywhere. Yet, even as Europeans try to come to terms with the Digital Age, we hold on to our legacy of State control and seem to display a natural tendency to wish to continue to operate within familiar structures, even when confronted by evidence that these are being superseded. In 1998, the old structures are still very strong. Even where telecoms markets have been opened up to competition, the former State-owned telephone companies in their new private liveries remain dominant. The television market is dominated by public service broadcasters and free-to-air licensed commercial broadcasters (or even, in France, a State-licensed monopoly terrestrial Pay-TV broadcaster, Canal Plus). Rival networks and subscription TV services are, with the exception of France, relatively recent creations and, for ordinary consumers, the new services digital broadcasting will make possible are still on the horizon.

Not withstanding the accelerating rate of private investment (including a large proportion of US investment) in European infrastructure, talent and creative output,

Europe's existing industries of film and television production and distribution continue to face the problems (for them) of a fragmented market within Europe and a massive (and increasing) trade deficit with the US. The new services, ranging from multi-channel digital TV to interactive and Internet-based services, while offering new opportunities, will not automatically improve the situation. These services are no more Eurocentric than the established media of cinema and video, which the US-based studios so dominate. If anything, the reverse is true: most of the major suppliers of software protocols and programming content are based in the US and are ahead of Europe in terms of capital investment, entrepreneurialism, management expertise and distribution networks. Europe, therefore, has reason to fear that these new sectors will also be dominated by the US, especially given the continuing appeal of American-badged content and the greater willingness of US-based companies to invest in Europe's audio-visual future than many of their European counterparts.

> **Even where telecoms markets have been opened up to competition, the former State-owned telephone companies in their new private liveries remain dominant.**

European governments and the European Commission continue to seek ways to correct this imbalance. Quotas are no longer workable and, with the cost of direct subsidies large enough to make any impact now far beyond the ability and willingness of the European taxpayer to pay for them, regulation may seem to be the answer.

Martin Bangemann, the Commissioner for Information Technology, Communications and Research and Development at the European Commission, is a leading representative of European politicians who, emulating President Clinton and Vice President Al Gore, have embraced technological convergence as a 'good thing'. In 1997, he introduced the Commission's green paper eloquently entitled, 'On the Convergence of the Telecommunications, Media and Information Sectors and the Implications for Regulation: Towards an Information Society' with the proposition that convergence 'will open the door to the further integration of the world economy'. Heralding the Information Society, the green paper defines its objective as being to create an environment 'which supports rather than holds back the process of change', the alternative being to leave Europe's business and citizens travelling 'in the slow lane of an information revolution which is being embraced by business users and by governments throughout the world.'

Evidently the Commission is playing for high stakes. It is therefore perhaps legitimate to ask the question 'Can regulation do the job?' Undoubtedly the existence of the marketplace and, indeed, the absence of regulation may have provided the conditions, but there is little evidence that the US regulatory structure assisted with commercial Internet development. The benefit for the US of having a single national regulator for broadcasting and telecommunications – the Federal Communications Commission (FCC) – is probably offset by the overlapping jurisdictions of the FCC, the Federal Trade Commission, the Department of Justice and a plethora of different tax authorities when it comes to transactions over the Internet, not to mention the responsibility of Customs or the Pentagon for encryption matters. Nor is there evidence that European regulation has fettered the development of Internet service providers (ISPs) or the use of the Web. Perhaps what really has counted are the advantages to US businesses and citizens of free local telephone calls, competition in long-distance calls, much cheaper equipment, the abundance of US venture capital suited to technological information and above all, perhaps the very size of the US market itself, where, for a given percentage penetration, absolute revenue flows are so much higher.

Yet governments, even the US government, persist in a belief that they can encourage convergence by changing the law. Two years in the making, the 1996 US Telecommunications Act shows how things can go spectacularly wrong. By permitting the adoption of ADSL (Asymmetrical Digital Subscriber Line) technology, which allows television delivery via telephone wires, and by taking the lid off cable rate rises, the legislation was intended to let the telecommunications companies (the 'telcos') compete with cable. However, the result was the opposite. After spending hundreds of millions of dollars, the telcos pulled back. Freed from the spectre of competition, the cable companies were able to increase rates, and hence margins, and slow down the rate of investment required for cable to consolidate its ownership of the home by adding more capacity, greater speed and interactivity. Legislators cannot predict the future – it is too complicated. Almost by definition, the unexpected always happens and, even if it did not, change is too rapid and the legislative process too slow.

What happened with the US telcos after the 1996 Act illustrates another paradox. Just because something can technologically be done, it does not mean it will necessarily happen. Video-On-Demand (VOD) is a classic example. In early 1995, it was thought that VOD was possible and would therefore change the video business. People would want movies at home, the technology would make it possible and so it would happen. In reality, VOD is rather inefficient. If a government were to pay to re-wire the whole country with the broadband structure of tomorrow, it would produce a whole raft of new business. However, no government can afford to do that; indeed, governments are going in the opposite direction. Left to business, new networks will be built only where they can be commercially justified. VOD requires a broadband infrastructure to be built to every home, or else data compression considerably more advanced than is available today. However, looking at video rental habits – the best analogy to VOD – 70 per cent of rentals are of the top 20 films. The top five films account for 30 per cent of totals and half the people who come to the video shop cannot get their first choice of film. So, if the video shops had the films that people really wanted, the top five would account for more than 30 per cent. Thus, although technically possible, for VOD to work you need new infrastructure, technology and

> **Just because something can technologically be done, it does not mean it will necessarily happen.**

capital, and new customers willing to pay more. You also need the incumbents – the owners of the existing business – to support the change rather than do their best to kill it. Thus, VOD, although technically possible, could not justify its costs and has turned out to be the last thing the studios want.

If European governments know that convergence will happen but not how, and cannot in any case legislate fast enough to give the process a hand or affect its shape, an alternative is to look to the future and try to work backwards to the present, helping to identify the gaps and the obstacles in the way of the creation of the new markets and proposing ways to overcome these obstacles. There have been a number of attempts to do this: the April 1998 submission by the British Screen Advisory Council to the European Audio-visual Conference (of which I was an author) is one example. The submission made by Oftel to the UK House of Commons Culture Select Committee around the same time is another. In its submission ('Beyond the PC, the TV and the Telephone, Part II'), Oftel looks forward to an 'open state' in which shortage of distribution capacity will have largely disappeared and content suppliers will be able to choose to supply services to customers on a commercial basis using any or all of the different distribution networks. Assuming a five- to ten-year time horizon for this transformation to take place, Oftel sees interoperability as becoming 'more and more an inescapable public policy issue' and looks forward to the 'open state' in which only five types of rule survive in the long term.

These five types of rule are:

- general competition law
- general consumer protection law
- rules to deal with market failures in the communications sector (such as access control and interoperability)
- rules to ensure delivery of social and consumer policy goals (such as those regarding universal service)
- rules for content providers ('negative' content rules for all, 'positive' content rules only for public service providers, rules to enable viewers to control what they see and rules on media ownership).

The primary importance of a general competition law is significant. We have seen that competition law is at the heart of US regulation. In Europe, Articles 85 and 86 of the Treaty of Rome, outlawing anti-competitive behaviour, closely parallel the US approach. Both the US and the European regimes are, or have the capacity to be, highly active and interventionist. The Microsoft saga, like the AT&T saga or the IBM saga before it, attests to the tenacity of US regulators (increasingly working closely with their counterparts in Brussels). In Europe, five of the nine instances in which the European Commission has blocked a merger are in the media area – including the link-up between Bertelsmann, the Kirch Group and Deutsche Telekom to market and manage digital Pay-TV services in Germany (the Commission also blocked the earlier attempt by the same partners to work together). In France and Spain, the governments are active in promoting competing digital satellite TV platforms to the point of using legal measures to slow down the market leader (Canal Plus in both countries) while conferring advantages on Canal Plus' rivals (TPS and Via Digital, respectively). With the UK about to import the Articles 85 and 86 regime into its domestic legislation, a trend much in evidence across Europe (for example in Italy), the foundations for a truly supranational global regulatory framework are all but there.

Competition law, however, has its limitations, particularly in a marketplace growing as rapidly as that of communications. It regulates concentrations and the abuse of dominant positions. However, before abuse can be regulated, dominant positions have first to be in place. This produces the following conundrum: if dominant positions are not in place – because they are prohibited – progress may not take place and consumers may be denied the benefits. The blocking by the European Commission of the Bertelsmann/Kirch/Telekom joint venture is a substantial contributory factor in the failure of digital TV to become established in Germany. It may also have contributed to the increasingly fragile state of the Kirch Group, its digital TV platform, DF-1, succeeding in attracting less than one quarter of the subscriber levels it needs to be viable; it is generally thought to be losing $1.5 million per day as a result. By contrast, the merger of Sky Television and BSB in the UK in November 1990, not withstanding their complete defiance of the regulations that had come into force the week before with the Broadcasting Act 1990, led to the creation of a substantial market for Pay-TV in the UK (by mid-1998, more than 25 per cent of homes took premium sport and movie channels) alongside well-funded and highly successful terrestrial services, not to mention a flourishing video rental market. BSkyB, as the merged company became known, is undoubtedly dominant – it is the monopoly provider of satellite TV services and the main provider of programming to cable – and it effectively came into existence by using another country's non-regulated satellite (Luxembourg's Astra) in place of the regulated British satellite.

The BSkyB example also illustrates that if a dominant position is established and, as a result, progress is made in building new markets, all the gatekeeper issues of access are raised.

Another problem is the speed with which competition law operates with regard to alleged abuses, and the tendency for the law to become a factor only when the abuse has already taken place. The market may well have changed to such an extent that, by the time a ruling is made, the issues are long since dead. Indeed, proponents of the effectiveness of competition law will tend to attach more importance to the behaviour-modifying force of an ongoing investigation than to the judgment itself; this is a lesson of the Department of Justice's case against IBM, which seems now as if it is being applied to Microsoft.

The model for regulating the 'converging' communications world attempts to address these issues by legislating general competition law principles as the 'law of the land' that all parties are required to observe, plus the creation of powerful, independent specialist regulators with overwhelming powers to apply the rules to specific areas of the marketplace where market failure is likely. Thus, initially, on the privatization of BT, the specialist regulator Oftel moved in to 'rig' the marketplace to bring about competition. Later, in 1996, by the admission of the then Director General of Telecommunications, Don Cruickshank, Oftel stretched its powers to the utmost to capture conditional access systems within its purview and instituted licensing procedures for conditional access, access control and interoperability. Like the policy makers in Brussels, Oftel would like to see competing open platforms in the UK. If, as is more likely, a single, proprietary, closed platform comes to dominate, Oftel wants to be able to ensure that all service providers have access to customers on a fair and transparent basis. Thus, conditional access charges will be regulated, along with the terms on which third parties are granted access to the digital TV network.

The advantages of having an independent, specialist regulator who devises structures and procedures to secure objectives within the overall framework set by the legislature include:

- a stable and predictable regime
- consistency and coherence in the way rules are applied
- transparent and accountable procedures
- detailed rules only where necessary.

The specialist regulator offers flexibility, responsiveness to the actual, as opposed to theoretical, needs of the marketplace and an ability to intervene quickly.

Achieving these advantages requires a high degree of autonomy for, and trust in, the regulator. There must be consumer representation, of which the regulator must be required to take notice. The regulator must foster an environment in which firms are motivated to try and in which they are disincentivized neither by the threat that, if they succeed in getting into a dominant position they will be stomped on, nor by resignation that, if they should encounter a firm in a dominant position, there will be no help or redress. Firms and consumers must have the certainty that the regulator will intervene sufficiently to prevent abuse and in a manner that is transparent and consistent.

It is an approach in which, increasingly, content regulation, so beloved of Europeans, will be reduced to 'negative' content rules for all – generally, the existing law of the land applicable to all publications – and 'positive' content rules only for public service broadcasters, be they publicly funded or granted special privileges by the State, such as monopolies in terrestrial television advertising (of course, the power of the State to confer such privileges will itself

> **The specialist regulator offers flexibility, responsiveness to the actual, as opposed to theoretical, needs of the marketplace and an ability to intervene quickly.**

diminish). In addition, because of the role of the media in a democratic society, there will remain special concentration rules in relation to media ownership.

Even if many in Europe might acknowledge that this is the way to the future, others argue that the digital future is still far away. In practice, for the foreseeable future, things will remain much as they are at present: most consumers will receive their television from analogue, free-to-air terrestrial broadcast or basic, analogue cable. Those with digital boxes will be few. The Internet and the PC world will remain separate, or at least marginal, to the main business of licence fee-funded, advertising-supported television.

This view was loudly expressed when 300 or so of the European audio-visual industries' policy makers and opinion formers gathered at the European Audio-visual Conference, held in Birmingham, UK, in April 1998 under the auspices of the European Commission and the UK Government. This forum was dominated by the powerful lobby of established public service broadcasters, in whose ranks should be counted the licensed commercial broadcasters, such as the ITV companies and Channel 5 in the UK. Standing shoulder-to-shoulder with these broadcasters are the European film and television producers with whom they have a symbiotic relationship: these allies may well, on occasion, be tempted to view regulation as a defence against competition, and subsidy as an alternative to the full rigours of the marketplace. The broadcasters and producers are supported by the bodies in charge of regulating TV, no doubt for the perfectly understandable reason that regulating existing structures is precisely what they exist to do. At Birmingham, delegates were warned by one speaker to learn the language of telecommunications regulation or see the telecommunications regulators – so much more adept at dealing with issues of interconnection, interoperability, network access, tariff-based regulation and competition – take over. To those broadcasters and producers who were paying attention, this would have seemed a dismal prospect. Yet, none the less, the debate that started in telecommunications is gaining ground, not least in the UK, where the experience of having – in Oftel – a pro-competitive communications regulator is widely shared.

This does not mean that there is only one model for Europe – the UK model – that all countries should slavishly follow. The concept in Europe of 'subsidiarity', not unlike the concept in the US of 'States' rights', is a valid response to the need for each member state to find its own way through the maze and take account of local conditions. In the UK, the notion of public service broadcasting is captured by the idea of 'mission' or 'remit'; this idea has a certain resource with the more fluid concepts of English common law. Neither is automatically nor straightforwardly applicable to other countries. Just as we see the shoots of a global system of competition law emerging in the US and Europe, if Europe wishes to embrace the converging world, the European Commission and European governments will need to define and adopt a set of common principles for communications regulation. Even while asserting that 'the future is far away', the Birmingham Conference conceded that gatekeeper issues, conditional access and self-regulation/self-protection for the Internet needed urgently to be addressed.

A failure to take these matters seriously and an insistence on clinging too firmly to the present structure may put Europe's television industries in danger of emulating Europe's motorcycle industry (or shipbuilding industry) and being expelled from the market by newcomers from far away. This danger is evident for the UK's ITV companies. Enjoying the protection afforded by their licences, they have, until very recently, used their position as monopoly exploiters of a captive market (the market for commercial TV air-time in the UK) to largely avoid investing in and developing programming for use in other channels and other delivery systems. Instead, they have driven down their costs and maximized revenues. Thus, when, eventually and inevitably, their historical position erodes, they will find themselves exposed to having no business at all.

Paradoxically, the BBC, although a public service broadcaster, has acted more 'commercially' to embrace the convergence world. Across Europe, incumbent commercial broadcasters are unenthusiastic for the opportunities to develop new services for new markets that compete with their existing incumbencies and it is the most powerful public service broadcasters – the ones with guaranteed revenues by means of a licence fee – that are eager to colonize the territories to which 'their' listeners and viewers are migrating. Thus, no commercial terrestrial broadcaster in Europe is engaged in developing digital services unless – like Carlton, Granada and United News and Media (three owners of ITV licences) in the UK, or TF1 and M6 in France, or Antena 3 in Spain – they have more or less been corralled by their governments or their licensing authorities to do so. No, the push towards digital television comes mainly from the newer entrants, the Pay-TV operators (dominated by BSkyB and Canal Plus) and the telecoms operators.

> ... an insistence on clinging too firmly to the present structure may put Europe's television industries in danger of ... being expelled from the market by newcomers from far away.

As what we are likely to see emerge in the various European national markets (and probably in other non-American markets) is either one infrastructure with competing premium programme providers or multiple-delivery infrastructures with a single, dominant, premium programme provider, you might imagine that today's commercial broadcasters had quite an interest in the outcome of developments and a desire to influence that outcome. Is their seeming indifference perhaps a function of their trust in an effective regulator, able to hold the ring, Oftel-style, that will ensure that, however the market evolves, they will be allowed to participate in it? If so, they should be aware that effective regulation requires strong competitors as much as it enables strong competition to occur.

From these reflections on the differences between US and European experiences of the communications market, and between the kinds of regulation that have historically prevailed across Europe and the ones that will be needed in the future, four principles emerge:

- Regulation cannot be other than reactive. Attempts to foresee the future and legislate to shape it are doomed to fail, not least because, anticipating the shape regulation is taking, the most aggressive players promote strategies to avoid or undermine that regulation.

- Europe must therefore embrace the future. It will happen anyway, even in a country such as Germany where the media regulators have been accustomed to work with a State-dominated cable system and a heavily circumscribed TV services sector. However, the objectives of the Convergence green paper will only be secured by establishing a regulatory framework that is flexible and future-friendly rather than inflexible and future-averse – something that even Germany's media regulators are beginning to recognize.

- There is only a limited role for content regulation. 'Negative' content regulation – outlawing obscene or racist content, for example – will apply to all the media (how it will be enforced is another question). 'Positive' content regulation – mandating the inclusion in services of certain kinds of content – will only remain possible so long as public service broadcasting lasts. In time, it will yield to initiatives around the subsidizing by governments of certain content and regulation to ensure that this subsidised content gains fair access – possibly even privileged access – to the networks.

- Competition policy provides the framework within which the model of communications regulation can best work. However, in the communications market, general competition rules – the 'law of the land' – need to be supplemented by powerful, independent and knowledgeable regulators that are able to act quickly and can apply special rules in particular areas susceptible to market failure. The ability to enact these special rules may diminish, but then so should the need for them: they exist to make the transition to a world of competing communications networks, platforms and services possible – a transition that will tend to involve dominant players or gatekeepers, the existence and behaviour of which may well be anti-competitive. Such regulators, therefore, are the necessary bridge connecting the European communications present to the communications future. ■

Brian Kahin

Senior Policy Analyst
Office of Science and Technology Policy
Executive Office of the President

CONVERGENCE, VALUE AND CHANGE

At the simplest level, the Internet brings together three recurrent themes of the information age:

- convergence
- value
- change.

Let's look at each in turn. Convergence has been talked about for a long time, but it is only with the development of the Internet and the World Wide Web that digital convergence has been fully realized. Although the word convergence suggests a blurring of boundaries, the Web shows it to be a complex and paradoxical phenomenon that generates a variety of new products and services.

Moore's law – the doubling of computing performance relative to cost every 18 months – is the best-known manifestation of the second theme, new value. However, it is only a specific case of what I will describe as a 'cost–value implosion'. This includes not only greater functionality and greater access to information, but new forms of value – such as community and convenience – that are difficult to define and measure.

The third theme – accelerated change – is closely linked to the first two. It may seem self-evident, but it goes beyond the simple notion of cheaper, faster, when it becomes the product of leveraged technological and market changes. It can then produce genuine surprises, challenging established business models and disrupting accustomed balances in laws and policy.

Convergence

Convergence is loosely used to mean many things. In one sense, it is manifest at the lowest levels of infrastructure where it has long made sense to share rights of way, trenches and poles. Thus, the telegraph followed the railroad, and telephone and telegraph wires were strung together. The notion of the technological convergence dates back to the mid-1960s when the Federal Communications Commission (FCC) launched the first Computer Inquiry. It has since assumed many forms. The interactive videodisc, introduced in 1976, married the random access characteristics of the book with video and sound. In the frenzy of cable television franchising in the early 1980s, prospective cable operators promised data communications over cable. The initial excitement about the Information Superhighway in the early 1990s centred on the expectation that cable and telephone companies would compete in offering both telephone service and switched video.

> ... 'cost–value implosion' ... includes not only greater functionality and access to information, but new forms of value ... that are difficult to articulate and measure.

Earlier forms of technological convergence were usually limited to mixing or linking together known media formats or services. For example, the public packet-switched networks that emerged in the late 1970s represented an adaptation of communications to computing, but they served primarily to substitute for long-distance telephone in facilitating remote access to a few large computers. This is how 'electronic publishing' was born, but it was costly and served only a limited business and professional market.

Convergence is also associated with vertical integration. In markets that are underdeveloped or constrained by a scarcity of distribution channels, the impetus to integrate vertically may be strong even if there are no clear economies of scope. For example, in audio-visual markets, vertical integration has assured producers and packagers a distribution outlet for their products and, conversely, has assured outlets a regular source of supply. Thus, the major television networks sought to own and operate stations, or at least control a large number of affiliates. Historically, these strategies invited antitrust scrutiny and regulation because distribution outlets were scarce, so the FCC regulated the economic power of the broadcast networks and sought to encourage additional networks. In contrast to the broadcast industry, the cable industry integrated backwards by developing programme services to supply its expanding channel capacity. However, these services were forced to license to others by the 1992 Cable Act, and this gave much-needed impetus to Direct Broadcast Satellite (DBS) services. (As an aside, this phenomenon is not limited to the electronic media. The major studios in the US controlled which films were shown by owning cinemas until the Justice Department succeeded in breaking up this vertical control in the late 1940s.)

The move from analogue to digital technology enables the convergence of different forms of content – video, sound, image, text, data and computer code – in a common system. They can be integrated in a communications stream, as in ISDN (Integrated Services Digital Network), or in published products, such as CD-ROMs.

The web browser enables the integration of published information with the full evolved functionality of the personal computer. There was once speculation that the browser might replace the personal computer operating system as the primary strategic platform on which computer applications would be built. Microsoft sought to avoid this result by pouring resources into the development of its browser – Internet Explorer – making it available for free, and finally building it into the evolving Windows operating system.

The rise of the browser as a platform for content and new applications *and* as the principal interface for experiencing the Internet places it at the heart of the Global Information Infrastructure. It embodies the three-way convergence of information, communications and computing in a tightly integrated package. It is infrastructure embodied in software: the central command station for the individual user and the platform on which the expanding resources, functionality and bandwidth of the Internet will be implemented.

This level of interdomain convergence around the World Wide Web is qualitatively different from the lesser forms of structural convergence. The Web reveals the inadequacy of the concept of convergence and the blurring it suggests. Yes, old boundaries are blurred, but the landscape at the centre of this new multidimensional infrastructure is a rich, finely articulated, multidimensional space that differs dramatically from the conventional pipeline of product development, manufacture and distribution. Figures 1 and 2 contrast the linear, one-way channel of traditional publishing with the multidimensional environment of an information infrastructure. In this multidimensional strategic space, there are opportunities for adding value in many different directions – a wealth of possibilities for niche products and services with the Internet and the Web driving development and investment from the centre.

> ... the browser as a platform for content and new applications and as the principal interface for experiencing the Internet [is] at the heart of the Global Information Infrastructure.

Figure 2 is limited in that it shows only general-purpose infrastructure; it does not show the opportunities for sector- and market-specific infrastructure development and the transformation not only of publishing, but also of marketing, commerce and

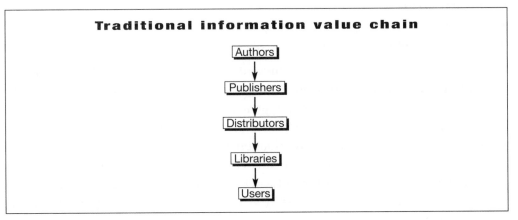

FIGURE 1

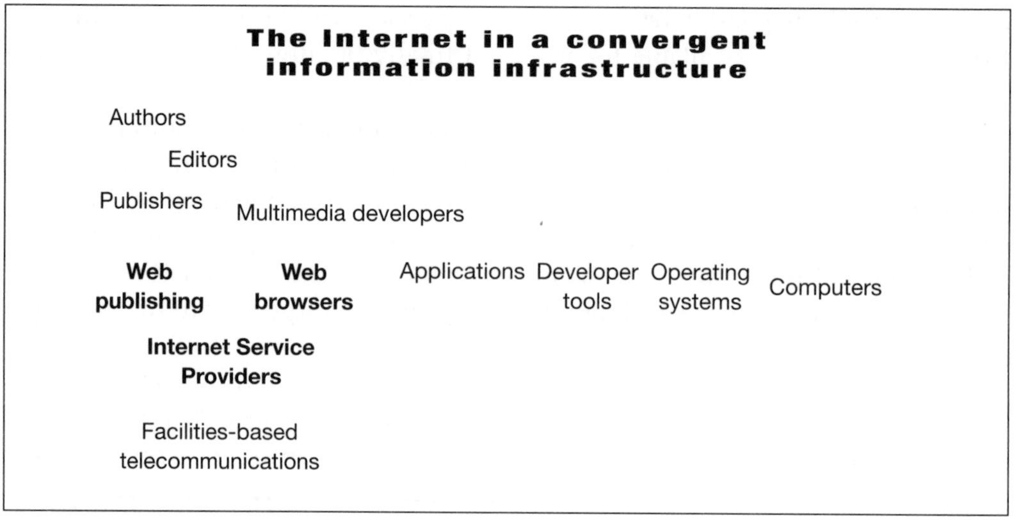

**The Internet in a convergent
information infrastructure**

Authors

    Editors

Publishers

    Multimedia developers

**Web
publishing**   **Web
browsers**   Applications   Developer   Operating   Computers
                                  tools   systems

**Internet Service
Providers**

Facilities-based
telecommunications

FIGURE 2

the business enterprise. The success of Web technology led to the growth of intranets – an information infrastructure based on Internet and Web technology that enables re-engineering of the firm – and extranets – infrastructure for automating and engineering the firm's relationships with its suppliers, partners and customers. Other institutions, industry sectors and even the less adaptable sectors of the economy – health, education and government – are following with new Internet-based infrastructures of their own.

The cost–value implosion

Figure 3 shows more closely how the three principal elements of the Internet – Internet Service Providers, web sites, and web browsers reflect the three aspects of information infrastructure:

- data networking
- publishing
- distributed computing.

The integration of connectivity, content and human interaction on the Web allows networks to be created out of words, images, documents, and the logic that links them. It is not just that text becomes hypertext, internally linked by super-footnotes. Text becomes the intelligent switching that connects the user to all the world's resources – people, organizations, information, services. It provides the context, community and navigational hooks that define cyberspace. The most commonplace and unassuming form of information and the least demanding of bandwidth, text nevertheless takes on such new roles and new value as to invite comparisons to the invention of moveable type and the printing press.

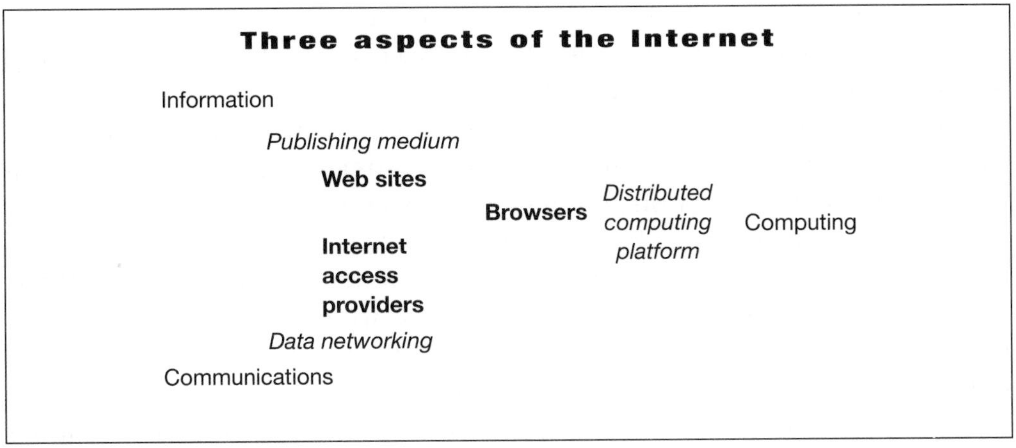

Three aspects of the Internet

Information

　Publishing medium

　　Web sites

　　　　　　Browsers *Distributed computing platform* Computing

　　Internet access providers

　　Data networking

Communications

FIGURE 3

At the same time, the fundamental economics of text have been radically transformed. Digitization enables text to be encoded with extreme efficiency and placed in the same media and distribution channels as voice, video and other kinds of information. Encoded as bits, text is a couple of orders of magnitude more efficient than voice for conveying information, but it can ride on the same underlying infrastructure. Thus, the Internet exploits the efficiencies of digitized text by taking advantage of an existing infrastructure built to serve the bandwidth requirements of voice. Even the ordinary dial-up lines that are commonly viewed as the principal bottleneck in the communications infrastructure can transmit the text equivalent of an entire book in 10–15 minutes using a standard modem.

From the user's perspective, the costs of accessing and retrieving information are reduced, while the information retrieved becomes more valuable because it is readily searchable and editable. From the producers' perspective, the costs associated with manufacturing and delivery nearly disappear, while costs associated with marketing and sales may be significantly reduced. Barriers to entry are lowered, but this means that publishers face increased competition from new publishers, as well as from volunteered information, web-surfing and other new forms of engagement.

In sum, prices come down while perceived value goes up, and the ratio of price to perceived value plummets. This phenomenon was initially obscured by the fact that much of the information initially posted on the Web was volunteered information with low perceived value. However, advertising has facilitated the publishing of quality material, often at no direct cost to the consumer.

The decline of vertical integration?

On-line services, such as AOL, CompuServe and Prodigy, originally followed the cable model of vertical integration by putting content, software and access into an integrated package. The Internet makes the same products and services available unbundled in the form of web sites, browsers and Internet service providers. While two or all three of these elements are often marketed as a package, they can be used separately or combined independently by users.

Like cable operators, on-line services developed their own material or exclusive relationships with outside publishers. Would-be electronic publishers had to negotiate access to audiences via the on-line services and, typically, received a royalty (based on the on-line service's hourly access fee) of 20 per cent or less. Now publishers can set up their own web sites and reach customers directly without having to pay a toll to an intermediary on-line service. For those who cannot afford a dedicated Internet connection over a leased line, there are thousands of commercial servers that will maintain web sites with good, high-speed connections at a very reasonable cost. In fact, the costs of mounting a few pages are so low that many Internet access providers bundle personal web pages into their basic service package or allow larger amounts of personal publishing for an additional $5–10 a month. Advertiser-supported services, such as Geocities and Trident, make web server space for personal pages available free. Anybody can post content, point to content, and aggregate pointers to content with a minimum of effort. Everyone can be their own electronic publisher and their own electronic librarian.

In the US, the standard for unlimited access for its long-distance customers remains around $20 a month for unlimited, or nearly unlimited, access. There are thousands of Internet service providers because barriers to entry are so low. Essentially, all that is needed to go into business is a leased line, a monthly access fee paid to a large provider, a server, a modem pool and some basic knowledge of Internet protocols.

Everyone can be their own electronic publisher and their own electronic librarian.

Despite the low costs for basic Internet access and web browser software, users must still have a computer. For many years, the cost of an entry-level computer was reckoned at $2000, although, thanks to Moore's Law, you got increasingly powerful machines for the same money. Within the last year or two, it has become possible to purchase a very capable computer for $1000 or less. Nevertheless, the investment in end-user equipment required for using the Internet contrasts dramatically with investment in a telephone. An ordinary handset costs $10–20 and requires no expertise to use. Without even considering the investment in learning computer and Internet fundamentals, the computer still costs nearly two orders of magnitude more than the handset.

The situation is reversed when it comes to the user's cost of transactions (see Figures 4 and 5). The information conveyed in 12 minutes of speaking time translates to a few seconds of text throughput on an ordinary dial-up connection. The marginal cost of this transaction over the Internet is minute, even calculated at a metered rate of $1.50 an hour. The same information conveyed by voice in a toll call may be a couple of dollars, or as much as $20 for a prime-time trans-Pacific call.

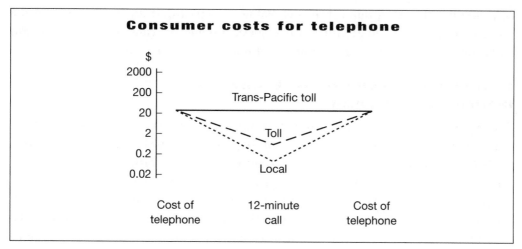

FIGURE 4

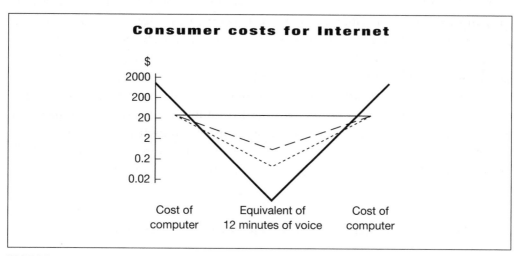

FIGURE 5

Figures 4 and 5 illustrate that an international call of this length can easily cost more than the handset. By contrast, text transactions on the Internet are distance independent, and a fixed monthly fee of $20, roughly equivalent to our 12-minute trans-Pacific call, buys virtually unlimited access to other Internet users anywhere in the world.

This comparison dramatically illustrates the cost–value implosion, as well as the shift from the provider-centred infrastructure of telephone monopolies to a user-centred infrastructure put together from the bottom up with computers and commodity Internet communications. Value is migrating from the network to the premises of the user, where it benefits from economies of scale in mass production and economies of scope in the versatility of microcomputers.

Policy development in a changing information space

The exponential growth of the Internet, measured by the number of hosts, has been remarkably constant, but there have been major discontinuities in its use. Although by 1992 the Internet was well-developed and used a wide variety of ways of transporting information, the appearance and spectacular growth of the Web was unanticipated. By 1994, the Web was gaining widespread attention, but search engines and advertising were all but invisible. Since 1996, there has been less fundamental change; 'push' technology has not proved as transformative as was once expected. Nevertheless, the functionality of the Internet continues to grow rapidly in sophistication and deployment. The Internet is increasingly understood as a broad enabler of business and commerce, not just as a new communications vehicle.

It is difficult to develop sound policy in an environment that changes this radically in so short a time. Historically, the three corners of information infrastructure have represented distinct industries with distinct economic characteristics and policy environments. In fact, each of these arenas was subject to policy values and legal/regulatory regimes that set it apart from other industry sectors (see Figure 6).

Communications industries have historically been subject to the most intense regulation because they have been dependent on public rights of way or spectrum and/or been seen as natural monopolies. By contrast, content industries (at least to the extent they have not been linked to a communications infrastructure) have enjoyed special protection from government intervention. The computing industry

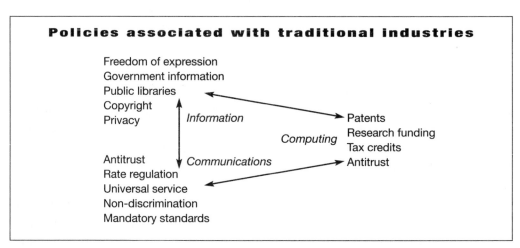

FIGURE 6

has been largely free from regulation, but has benefited from substantial public funding for advancing the technology and knowledge base.

Technological and market convergence brings these different policies and values into contact and conflict with each other (Ithiel de Sola Pool's *Technologies of Freedom*, MIT Press, 1983, is the classic study of policy convergence in this environment, but, given the early state of the computer revolution when the book was published, it naturally focuses on content/communications convergence). This policy convergence is more than a bilateral blurring as it takes place in the same multidimensional space that is shaping the marketplace. Policy makers face this complex, fast-changing environment with more and more information that is less and less complete.

Policy development becomes an increasingly dangerous undertaking that can skew the marketplace and develop a constituency for more bad policy. As the Internet makes markets more efficient, drives prices towards cost and narrows margins, the risks and costs of bad policy grow. Most of those who are adversely affected are entrepreneurs or technologists who cannot readily expend resources on either law suits or efforts to effect policy changes. Life on the Net is too fast and short.

A pervasive difficulty in making good policy is that the Internet offers too many options, and they change too quickly. Take universal service. Instead of a single 3-kilohertz analogue line, the end user can choose from many levels of connection at different prices, from dial-up over voice lines to high-speed access via cable or specially conditioned telephone lines (ADSL – Asynchronous Digital Subscriber Line). The end user can choose from different providers and different physical paths. Another variable is the performance and capacity of the user's computer. Much depends on the user's software, their ability to use the software and skills at navigating the Internet. And all of this is a moving target. A difficult problem for voice telephony becomes virtually intractable for the Internet.

Some traditional communications policy problems seem greatly alleviated on the Internet. Problems of channel scarcity seem to be disappearing. However, the new abundance of 'channels' and communications options, and the breakdown of traditional publisher and carrier categories raise new problems of where different kinds of liability should attach. New technology-enabled infrastructures, such as the Platform for Internet Content Selection (PICS), which enables parents to select trusted third parties to rate web sites and use these ratings to limit access by children, may help re-establish appropriate boundaries, but they raise new problems of definition and default setting as they do so.

At the same time, the expansion of options and lowered barriers to entry are resulting in an enormous outpouring of material, much of it available from remote jurisdictions. Difficulty in developing and enforcing liability standards across jurisdictional boundaries compounds the problems of domestic policy development and implementation.

While the Internet seems to undercut public laws and regulations that operate within jurisdictions, its facility for negotiating and contracting across distances and borders may encourage a new flowering of private law. Private arrangements and communities of interest can be formed at will, independent of geography and supported by web sites, mailing lists and other *ad hoc* networks defined by software and information. However, deluged by information, will anybody have the time, and take the time, to read the terms – especially if they are written by lawyers!

Unfortunately, the sense of boundless new opportunity that characterizes Internet-driven markets does not translate well from business to policy development and law. Instead of eliciting excitement and capital investment, the turmoil may be overwhelming. In place of niche positioning, there are blurred categories and jurisdictional ambiguity. The institutional constraints of legislative and judicial decision-making virtually guarantee that problems will be addressed too narrowly. In the worst cases, the process may be subject to capture by those who can turn policy paralysis and confusion to marketplace advantage. ■

An earlier version of this paper appeared in *The Internet as Paradigm*, the 1997 Annual Review of the Institute for Information Studies (Aspen Institute and Nortel). This article reflects Mr Kahin's personal views and does not necessarily represent the views of the US government.

Peter Cochrane

Head of Research, BT Laboratories

THE GLOBAL GRID OF CHAOS

For millennia we have lived in a world dominated by atoms, where natural physical boundaries have defined the limits of human expedition and development. The majority of our understanding, knowledge and experience has been gained in this bounded, slow-moving and dominantly random environment. Our society, commercial and governmental frameworks have evolved slowly to meet the limited needs of this world, and nothing much changed for hundreds of years.

Today, our world is dominated by bits, with a global grid of on-line information, experience and commerce that has no form, few constraints and virtually no limits. It is a world devoid of control – something new, naturally chaotic and very fast to react and change.

It is hard to imagine any aspect of our lives that is not now dominated by bits traversing global networks. Everything we eat, drink, wear, consume, is organized and delivered by Information Technology (IT) at a rate most people cannot conceive. This technology is allowing the creation of a global information economy that will ultimately see an Information Society. And it will arrive in that order, not the other way around. For those nations seeking to get the framework of society in order first, before creating the wealth-generating mechanisms, there will follow catastrophe. The reason? No one knows or can even imagine how the Information Society will look, be configured or operate. It will evolve, and continue to evolve, in the wake of the technology and an increasingly dominant bit economy.

> Today, our world is dominated by bits ... and virtually no limits. It is ... devoid of control – something new, naturally chaotic and very fast to react and change.

Today, our world is dominated by bits

ANIMATION: IAN MATTHEWS

The raw elements of IT see our ability to transport, process and store bits doubling every one to two years, while the cost per bit plummets by a factor of two to three in the same time period. Nothing in our past history has progressed so fast, and nothing has prepared us for the resulting changes inflicted on all aspects of our lives. Every institution, organization, group and individual has been, or will be, affected by these changes. Conversations between computers every day already eclipse ours over all time. We only number 6 billion while they are over 14 billion, and 10,000 transistors are manufactured for every man, woman and child on the planet every day. Machines 1000-fold more powerful than those of today will be with us in ten years, and 1,000,000 times in fewer than 20 years. At some point they will become intelligent and help us solve the really difficult and important problems that face our species. In the meantime, it will be quite a ride!

Let us consider the main bastions of our society and the likely impact on them of this growing world of networked bits. Specifically, globally available education and training, healthcare, work and commerce, governance and the nation state. Nothing will escape the attention of the change mechanisms brought about by our growing dependence on, and demand for, more IT. For sure, opting out is not viable – there is no hiding place, no escape. To prosper, we have to embrace change in a new and faster way.

Education and training

Education and training have always been a vital ingredient of any civilization, and remain so today. However, the established 'sage on the stage' and book-dominated paradigm is grossly inefficient, and insufficient, to meet the needs of an IT-dominated world. Would you employ someone who could not read and write – I think not. Would you employ someone who was IT illiterate – well, only in a low-margin business of the past. The major wealth-creating businesses are generally high margin, highly automated and controlled by IT. What, though, should we be doing in education?

It would be a great mistake to turn the clock back to concentrate on the three Rs and classics alone. It is necessary to embrace the power of IT to enhance the process of education across the board. There are no longer any educated people anywhere. Lawyers know nothing about medicine, medics know nothing about technology, and a technologist may know a little about optical fibre, radio, computing or software. The true polymath is no more, and yet we all have to become more eclectic and holistic to survive the world of work that will see more change in the next 20 years than in the previous 200.

Multimedia holds out a partial solution, with the simulation and modelling of the complex rendered in graphical formats that we can assimilate faster than lines of mathematics, script or static pictures. To be able to *watch* nuclear fusion, the dissection of a human wrist or experience five different interpretations of some classic play is distinctly more edifying than static characters on paper. Of course, some things cannot be catered for by multimedia, but that proportion is a fast-diminishing minority. Do you suppose a resurrected Newton or Byron would reach out for a quill pen? I think not. He would go with the technology of the day – a PC.

Students at school, college and university should not expect these institutions to provide all the computers all of the time. Increasingly, it will fall to the individual to provide their own. Governments do not feed and clothe us, nor should they get involved with providing everyone with a PC – it is a hopeless task. Many students already have more computing power at home than is available at their place of education. Given an assignment, their search routine is Compact Disk (CD), the Web, book. The reason? IT is fast, efficient and low cost. Books are expensive, unavailable and slow. They can also be a dead medium, lacking any animation or interaction.

The availability of educational material now extends well beyond the school, college and university. Education on CD and on-line is a reality and a threat to the established institutions. Students have a choice of material and, increasingly, institution and teacher. In a multimedia world, there is a real pressure to return to the 'guide at the side', more of a partnership and mentoring regime. So, who is going to win when universities have to compete for students distributed across the globe?

In a world where technology degrees have a half-life of less than five years, and demand is growing for education and training at the desk, home, hotel and place of work, it will be the institutions that move quickest that win. Like logarithm tables in the 1600s, once produced, there is no point repeating the exercise. So, when a good 'Master Class' on optimization, self-organization, economics, statistics or whatever is available on-line or on CD, there will be little room for a second. We might thus expect to see very few really great teachers and an awful lot more coaches.

Further developments are already in evidence. Parents who opt to educate their children at home are on the increase, as are the number of companies choosing to run their own virtual universities. IT will only serve to make this easier and more available across an increasing spectrum of interests.

Healthcare

Everywhere, there are great difficulties in healthcare. No nation can cope with the combination of increasing demand driven by the demographics of age, growing customer expectations driven by technological advances and exponentially rising costs. No amount of taxation money can correct these trends because the operational model is both old and wrong. Like it or not, healthcare is driven by the economics of availability, and doctors, nurses, pharmacists, specialists and so on are in short supply. The only things that appear to be universally available in abundance are administrators and managers. No other business could survive such a skill imbalance, except, perhaps, government.

Some antiquated systems can see the generation of upwards of 60 pieces of paper for a single visit to an outpatients department. At least 25 per cent of all hospital records are lost at any one time, resulting in multiple X-rays, examinations and expensive mistakes. The poor handwriting and errors made during the drug prescription process introduce more waste at the point of dispensing. Extra telephone calls and cross-checks exceed 30 per cent of the pharmacists' time. Nursing staff spend only 25 per cent of their time with patients, while 25 per cent is devoted to filling in forms, 25 per cent looking for records, and 25 per cent physically collecting and transporting information from one location to another. Operating theatres and specialist equipment costing millions are only in use from 08.00 to 17.00 on weekdays.

A radical change in the processes involved in patient care is long overdue. IT can cure much of this by introducing unified electronic record systems, automatic scheduling of appointments and operations, cross-checks on diagnoses, prescriptions and aftercare. There will also have to be prioritization on the basis of patient behaviour. Can any system afford to continually try to repair people who systematically try to kill themselves by misusing tobacco, alcohol and drugs? I think not! In the future, the maxim may well be 'patient, heal thyself'. With insufficient resources, each of us will have to become more responsible. Preventive medicine is far more effective than any curative process. So what can IT do in this arena?

The next big advance will be the datamining of patient records. In these, there is a wealth of information on the symptoms, diagnosis, treatment and outcome of millions of case histories. Once in a database, the possibilities are endless. No doctor can know everything, and getting to a specialist is an opportunity way beyond the average. Personal Computer (PC)-based doctors already equal their human counterparts in some aspects of diagnosis. A marked feature of PC–patient interaction is the level of honesty in response to detailed questions. This often surpasses the equivalent human–human session and can lead to greater accuracy of diagnosis and speed of treatment.

There are specialist web sites for almost every human ailment. These span the basic facts and figures on diagnosis, treatment and survival, through to support groups. Many supply drugs and medicines by post from far-flung places on the planet where the laws and limitations on the use of medicines are markedly different to those of the UK. The advantages and risks to the individual user and the healthcare system are obvious. In the UK, we spend about £40 billion on our National Health Service, and an estimated £40 billion outside the system for alternative treatments and services. So far, no one has dimensioned Internet-based spending, but it is growing fast. Arranging an operation in the US or Europe via this medium is now straightforward, and there are no waiting lists. All you need is a PC, Internet access and money.

The development of head-mounted and hand-held cameras for surgeons and doctors, and remote sensory systems worn by patients coupled into the telecommunications networks have already demonstrated great potential. Specialists can perform, participate, support and guide operations across the planet. They can conduct foetal scanning, X-ray, MRI (Magnetic Resonance Imaging) and other diagnostic processes remotely, not needing to leave their home hospital. Patients with heart, breathing, kidney and other ailments can be remotely examined and advised by a paramedic. A doctor need then only be brought in for the exceptional and dangerous cases. All of this is under test. Might the patients then choose a doctor in the US where this is possible, and where money grants instant access? Again, the advantages and dangers are very clear.

Work

Work is a place to *go* to in the minds of most people. In reality, it is an activity, and something increasing numbers of us *do* rather than go to. For the bit worker, it has spread into the reaches of leisure and home life to become a continuum. The division between work and play can be hard to define. Location is no limiting factor, and neither is travel. The road warrior is increasingly the norm. Many have no permanent office, they just pitch camp wherever they happen to be and get on-line.

Of course, there will always be people who go to work, the place, because that is where the plant, point of trade, transportation of things or human gathering is. However, even here IT is already dominant as it facilitates and controls processes and communication to realize great operational advantage. Think back to the typing pool and the letter. Business communications between several people would take weeks to achieve some outcome that can now be realized in hours or days be e-mail and telephone. Think back to manufacturing and logistics organized by humans. Costly stockholdings, overcapacity, empty containers, late deliveries and shortages were the norm. With Artificial Intelligence control systems, just-in-time production and delivery processes, costs have been drastically reduced, quality improved and customer satisfaction enhanced to levels that were unthinkable just a decade ago.

The next step in the evolution of work will be the multitasking nomad – people who have skills to sell in the electronic market who are not confined to one employer or, indeed, singular employment. Very few companies are in business for 100 years, and only a few last for 40 years. In an IT world, this is likely to drop below ten years. The workforce in this arena will thus become increasingly nomadic, and will turn to multiple parallel employment and a share of the action for long-term security. Already in the UK, some young people are engaged by upwards of 20 employers a year on a contractual basis. This is especially so in the computer science, programming, system analyst and operational research areas. However, there are many others, such as pharmacy, the media, investment banking and IT-related consultancy. In the fastest moving sectors, the average half-life of an individual job is falling into the lower single figures. In this world, individuals only have their skills to sell. They have to keep ahead, maintain a relevant education and training, at the same time earning their keep.

An interesting feature of this on-line job employment market is the resurgence of the barter economy. People can work for money, equipment, time and expertise of a fellow worker, and, of course, education and training. This creates new opportunities for self-support within like-minded groups of people on a global scale. This is where people share knowledge and information because it is necessary to do so to survive, and it is counter to the past where the longevity of information allowed people to be controlists. Of course, none of this is restricted to any one country – it is invisible and so, unfortunately for governments, it completely bypasses the tax system.

Commerce and business

Until very recently, commerce and business have been dominated by slow communication and control processes, with steeply hierarchical management structures. These were most probably derived from early military command structures and have served us well in commerce and government throughout the industrialization process. However, they do not fit, and will not serve, the faster moving IT era. Here, chaos is the natural order, due to rapid communication, decision-making, and correlated human/machine activity instigated by mechanisms that would astonish the Victorians.

Not so long ago, it seemed every parent had to buy their child a Cabbage Patch doll for Christmas, then it was Buzz Lightyear, and no one can guess what it will be next. France winning the 1998 World Cup will see Adidas move into overtime to meet demand for its products. A simple headline in the newspaper, a feature on the evening news and thousands besiege every chemist shop in the land demanding a new contraceptive pill. When the London Stock Market had its electronic Big Bang in October 1986, it suffered an instant buy–sell synchrony that had to be repaired by introducing staggered delays and decision thresholds. Today, over 10 per cent of all trading is conducted by machines acting on the short-term chaos of the market. People cannot compete because the processes are far too fast. In such a world, steep hierarchies of people, electronic networks and equipment do not work. Low and flat is the order of the day, as discovered by Mother Nature over millions of years.

Customers no longer want choice, they want what they want. They want the goods and services they define, on time, of good quality and at a good price. Moreover, they can get generally what they demand because there is now global competition and a global market. If you can get on-line, it is difficult to find anything you cannot buy electronically. Search, find, order, pay and have delivered to your door by FedEx from the US in few days. Everything from books, to wine, power tools, medicines and legal services are now available on-line. No middlemen – distributors, wholesalers and shops – in the loop, and, without their percentages, the customized producer sells more at a higher price, and the customer pays less.

Many people balk at passing their credit card details over the Net because of the security risk, but this is an emotional response invoked by an irrational and uninformed media. There is not a single recorded instance of anyone, anywhere, anytime, being defrauded by having their card number intercepted on the Net. This is more than can be said for garages, restaurants and other establishments where they get a signed copy of your card.

> ... steep hierarchies of people, electronic networks and equipment do not work. Low and flat is the order of the day ...

Companies have traditionally established customer trust and loyalty through brand and country identification. However, increasingly, members of the public dominantly identify with brands as companies become multinational. There are obvious exceptions of course – Sony, Nike, Mercedes, Boeing and Rolls-Royce all have very strong flag value. However, each has become the integrator of components manufactured across the world. The economics of global production make it impossible to be a 'do-it-all' company. Everything that can be outsourced has to be outsourced to specialists who can do it cheaper and faster. However, without IT, this would not be possible or viable. Just-in-time production and delivery is not an empty slogan, it is a necessity in an increasingly competitive world.

People who buy expensive, branded cars, washing machines, hi-fi, TV and PCs might be shocked to visit the assembly plant. Very often, the components – if not the complete box for several brands – come from a single production line, and the badge is often just an illusion. How come? If you are a component supplier to these giant assembly lines, it is essential to address the world market and sell to as many as possible. And the world market may only support around four manufacturers of internal combustion engines, drive chains, turbines, Random Access Memory (RAM) chips and so on – just enough to ensure competition and efficiency.

Many businesses do not approach purchase price, stock control, process optimization, marketing, sales and support in a unified manner. However, each is important to success. Moreover, these artificial divides are generally augmented by other damaging divisions of organizational self-interest. Steep hierarchies tend to create pseudo internal markets, where stovepipe solutions inhibit, or often totally prevent, competition between product lines and revenue streams within the company. This can be fatal. When IT is used effectively, a company can realize a true internal market with trading at all levels in and out of its confines. This leads to lower costs, faster recovery times and greater vitality and revenues.

Governance

Governance should be about creating and sustaining environments in which individuals, groups and organizations can succeed and prosper in the broadest sense. Unfortunately, it seems more often to be about control and inhibiting success. How come? Well, most governments follow a sixteenth- or seventeenth-century model that was fine for a pre-industrial age, but is now hopelessly inadequate. How can people out of touch with technology and modern business practice hope to govern or manage wisely? How can ten or more layers of people communicating by paper and voting by filing through a door to be counted like sheep move fast enough for a world of bits? They cannot! It is fundamentally impossible to manage something you do not understand, especially when it is so grossly different to what has gone before.

In defence of governments, it has to be said that they stand little chance in the face of a world that is moving so very fast. Democracy is a delicate organ that evolved over a long experiential period, and it would be very brave, or foolhardy, to try to change it drastically. However, it may just collapse under its own weight! Unfortunately, electronic democracy will not wait, it is here and accelerating. Perhaps the trick is to get both to coexist, but the opportunities for head-on clashes are legion. What constitutes pornography is different in every country, as are the laws on encryption, databases, security, secrecy and hacking.

Given the lack, and probable impossibility, of policing, government edicts and the law will increasingly be ignored and flouted. Taxable activities will go unseen and monies uncollected, goods will be move undetected. It is a new and grey market.

Nation states

Nation states have been with us for a long time, and will probably survive for an even longer time, provided the glue that binds them is not undone. IT looks likely to sustain virtual communities where business and exchange is undertaken invisibly and unchecked. Any large-scale attempt to interfere with, control or dismantle the Internet and Intranets would have dire consequences, for that is where global companies now work. The impact on the international economy of any such action would likely bring down entire economies. Somehow both systems will have to evolve to coexist. ■

THE MARKET

---

contributors

David Potter is Chairman, Psion Group Plc. Since founding Psion in 1980, he has successfully guided the company through the last eighteen turbulent years of the microcomputer revolution. Psion was listed on the London Stock Exchange in 1988. Over the last five years Psion has seen an average compound growth rate of 42 per cent with the majority of its sales now in export markets.

David Potter plays an active role in a number of companies, organizations and institutions outside Psion. He served on the 1997 National Committee of Inquiry into Higher Education (The Dearing Committee), and now serves as a Board Member of the Higher Education Funding Council for England. In the 1997 New Year's Honours list, David Potter was awarded the CBE for Services to Manufacturing Industry.

Jim Barksdale, President & Chief Executive Officer, Netscape Communications Corporation, joined Netscape in January 1995. He has served on the board of the company since October 1994. Before coming to Netscape, Barksdale served as CEO of AT&T Wireless Services, following the merger of AT&T and McCaw Cellular Communications. From January 1992 until the merger in September 1994, he held the positions of President and Chief Operating Officer of McCaw, a company with revenues that exceeded $2 billion in 1993. Prior to McCaw, Barksdale spent 12 years with Federal Express Corporation where he served as Chief Information Officer from 1979 to 1983, overseeing the development and implementation of the company's world-renowned customer service and package-tracking systems. In 1983 he became Executive Vice President and Chief Operating Officer, overseeing the company's growth from $1 billion to $7.7 billion in revenues and its expansion into 135 countries. Under his leadership, Federal Express became the first service company to receive the Malcolm Baldrige National Quality Award. He holds a BA from the University of Mississippi.

John Patrick is Vice President of Internet technology, IBM Corporation. John's role is to lead the company's effort to create innovative technologies that will Web-enable computer users worldwide, and has created a number of innovative programs including the alphaWorks web site which is IBM's on-line research and development laboratory for advanced Internet technology. In addition, he serves as chairman of the Global Internet Project. As one of the leading Internet visionaries, John shares his observations and insights with people around the world, inspiring new product ideas, new applications and innovative ways to use the Internet to help people meet their goals. With IBM for more than 31 years, John was a pioneer and developer of IBM's leasing business at IBM Credit Corporation, today the largest computer leasing company in the world. He was subsequently the chief financial officer of various business units of IBM and was also Vice President of Operations for IBM's Computer Integrated Manufacturing Business. In 1992, John became Vice President of Marketing for Personal Systems and was responsible for creating the successful ThinkPad brand.

Karel Van Miert has been a Member of the European Commission since 1989. His first mandate was to be in charge of Transport, Credit and Investment and Consumer Policy. Since 1993 he has been in charge of Competition Policy.

Karel Van Miert's professional as well as political career is most impressive. He became Chairman of the Flemish Socialist Party in 1977. He was also the Vice Chairman of the Confederation of Socialist Parties of the European Community in 1978–80. Karel Van Miert was a Member of the European Parliament between 1979–85 and a Member of the Belgian Chamber of Representatives between 1985–88. He was Vice President of the Socialist International between 1986–92.

His academic background includes a degree in Diplomatic Sciences from the University of Ghent in 1966, with a thesis summa cum laude on the supranational character of the European Commission; and a postgraduate degree from the European University Centre of Nancy. Since 1978, Karl Van Miert has been part-time Professor of European Integration at the Vrije Universiteit Brussel (Free University of Brussels). He has written various publications on European integration.

BIG THROUGH SMALL
GETS BEAUTIFUL

Technology and physical infrastructure are only a small part of what's needed to deliver the promises of the Wired World. The challenge really begins with understanding what people and organizations will want to use the GII for. What kind of products and services will add value and will be of interest to the market? Who are the customers and what do they need or want?

The previous section painted a convincing picture of an on-line world where electronic networks span the globe and millions of people and organizations are connected to the Internet. We have at least a multinational, if not global, information infrastructure in place. The question is what impact will this have in the marketplace.

In this section we will be exposed to some of the key players in the market who are busy shaping the new market environment. We will learn of their experience of market success as well as market failures. We will visit a computer industry veteran and successful entrepreneur called David Potter. He founded Psion back in 1980 and has since developed his ideas and start-up business into an international world leader in mobile computing and network communications. We will also look in on the 'good old' Big Blue. John Patrick of IBM will describe how IBM sees the Internet challenge. IBM has gone through massive change and is deeply involved in building the on-line markets of the Wired World. And we will meet Netscape, the new kid on the block, which took the world by storm in 1994 with the release of its Internet Navigator browser. Netscape managed to become a major market player and succeeded in creating an instant global brand almost overnight. Jim Barksdale will give us his views of the market and he will provide some practical examples of what companies do or should be doing. Finally we will have an audience with Europe's Mr Competition. Karel Van Miert, the competition regulator of the EU, will explain the role of competition law and share his perspectives on how the market is developing.

An ongoing theme throughout this book which every contributor is referring to is the astonishing rate of technology development and change which is taking place throughout society. There are numerous references in this book to Moore's Law – the now famous statement from Gordon Moore, founder of Intel in 1965, which says computing power of the micro-processor doubles every year to 18 months while the cost decreases proportionally. David Potter believes this rate of technology development is sustainable for another 20 years. It seems technology will not be the limiting factor in terms of making progress.

Jim Barksdale argues that we need to be more concerned with how to grow the value of networks rather than the processing power of hardware, and to illustrate this he refers to the so-called Metcalfe's law which he says supersedes Moore's law. Both Potter and Barksdale agree that what creates market success is not technology itself or the products, but the knowhow of what to do with technology and exploit new business opportunities that come along.

Potter sums up the key lessons that can be learnt from the Psion story. He points out that entrepreneurship, innovation and change are three words at the heart of what Psion is. His recipe for success is to make sure the management and the company have the ability to change and learn progressively. He describes the continuous struggle pursuing change and innovation in a market that is becoming increasingly global and brutally competitive. Like Simon Olswang in his chapter, Potter also worries about Europe's ability to compete. He warns us that Europe may be wrongly focused on protecting the past, while America is focused on creating the future and therefore getting on with it.

Barksdale demonstrates how new business can be built in the new Net Economy without physical retail space using Internet and virtual space. He points out that a company cannot possibly reach a billion customers in the conventional way, but you can via the Internet. He describes how the virtual marketplace is emerging and the rise of so-called portal sites. He is convinced that there is an enormous market potential in electronic commerce and he quotes estimates from Forrester Research which says by 2002 the value of goods and services being traded over the Internet will amount to US $327 billion.

John Patrick is equally a promoter and believer in the glory of Internet commerce. Think of it – a billion potential customers hooked up to the same network and directly individually reachable for interactive advertising – a marketer's dream come true! However, what all Internet companies and e-commerce enthusiasts know is that it is anything but easy to do.

Patrick is also the Chairman of something called the Global Internet Project which was set up in 1996 by a group of companies from around the world to help overcome common problems and to promote market initiatives in the development of Internet. The project is concerned with issues like access, scalability, security, privacy, governance, electronic transactions and quality of content. The reason why Patrick and IBM are so deeply involved in this project is that they believe that companies, policy makers and regulators have got to work together to ensure a successful development of the Wired World marketplace. This view is echoed in many political camps and indeed by all the government representatives in this book.

Karel Van Miert describes how the globalization of the world economy and the convergence of technologies and industries have boosted the potential for competition. Van Miert is also making the point that innovation often comes from companies, which are at least at the time relatively small and he is concerned with how competition regulation can protect and encourage innovation. To him it seems that larger companies are often trying to catch up with the small. If it is the case that the smaller enterprises are in effect the creative force of our economy, then it seems to me vital that we have a competition policy in place that recognizes this. Van Miert reminds us what the purpose of competition law is and that it is a key instrument to make sure the markets are as free and open as possible, and to protect against the abuse of market power by dominant players.

Do you have to be small to be beautiful? It seems to become more difficult for companies to be creative, innovative and resilient enough to change rapidly as they grow into large global enterprises. Potter argues that historically new business has been created by green-field operations and that business innovation frequently comes from the grass roots. The large successful company giants owe much of their success to smaller enterprises.

Yet in the new competitive environment it will be hard for the smaller enterprise to survive. A growing trend is for companies to achieve the balance of competitive muscle and creative resources by forming strategic partnerships with each other – clusters of alliances between very small and very large enterprises are becoming part of the new market landscape. Perhaps this is the way forward and that through successful partnerships, entrepreneurs and smaller companies can infect the larger giants with their beauty. ■

David Potter

Chairman, Psion Group Plc

BUILDING SUCCESS IN A GLOBAL MARKET

Lessons from Europe

I start this chapter by trying to provide a sense of what it has been like to develop Psion in a European context, and to articulate some of the issues as seen from the 'left field' position of our company. Our industry – the microcomputer industry – feels a little like the motor car industry must have done in the 1910s or 1920s, or like the aircraft industry in the 1930s – a Wild West frontier market of great flux and development, one that many enter and where many get shot.

The Psion story

The Psion Group is capitalized on the London Stock Exchange at over half a billion dollars and is a world leader in mobile digital computing and communication products. The Psion Group is probably best known for its palmtop computers, but the Group's business is broader. Psion Industrial designs, manufactures and supplies hand-held computers for commercial and industrial environments; Psion Dacom is Europe's leading supplier, and one of the world's largest producers, of PC card products; the Group half-owns Therefore Limited, one of London's creative product design companies. The Group is the largest shareholder in Symbian, in partnership with Nokia, Ericsson and Motorola. Symbian's EPOC software is set to become the standard operating system software for the next generation of mobile computing and communication products. The Psion Group employs over 1000 people in nine companies based in the UK, the US, Holland and Germany, complemented by a worldwide distribution network.

Origins

Psion's story has been one of organic development. When I founded Psion in 1980, I had three assets. The first was capital of £60,000, made from stock market investments over the preceding six years. I hurry to add that my timing in this – from November 1974 – was most fortunate. The second was my software expertise, gained while working as an academic in the US. The third was an understanding of the potential of this new industry. Believe it or not, the established mainframe and minicomputer industry of the time saw microcomputers as toys. And therein lies a lesson in itself.

Psion's earliest success came from software publishing. This business involved very little capital and our turnover, profit and experience grew rapidly. With this as a base, I began to recruit development staff. Hence, the next phase in our evolution – software development. As a software product company Psion was rapidly successful and highly profitable with products such as Vu-File and Flight Simulator – the latter selling more than a million units.

The nature of capitalism is such that profit attracts competition like bees to a honey pot. The likes of Robert Maxwell with Mirrorsoft and Richard Branson with Virgin Games made this very clear – together with others, sporting pink hair and earrings. The result was shorter and shorter product lifecycles, with increasing product sophistication. The core question was, 'If it is so easy for *us* to enter and make large profits, what's to stop others?' The answer was clearly 'Very little.' As Andy Grove of Intel has said, 'Only the paranoid survive.' To survive, Psion needed to move into different markets. One answer was applications software; the other was much more radical.

Endless analysis, endless discussion and endless agonizing followed. This process of strategic introspection is, I believe, vital. In the autumn of 1982, I found myself sitting in a Greek restaurant with one of my colleagues, Charles Davies, who had been my brightest doctoral student. We began to sketch out on napkins a hole in the market and a hardware product to fill it. What we identified was a personal, portable hand-held computing device that could store and manipulate information. A radical, though simple idea but one which took two years of development to turn into reality.

The Organiser

In 1984, we launched Psion's first hardware product, the Organiser. This was a virgin product in a virgin market – high risk and high reward territory. Not only was making a physical product very capital-intensive, but we also had to acquire entirely new skills, such as design, engineering, manufacturing, inventory management as well as many others. With this transition we were confronting, for the first time we raised additional equity capital. The year of 1984 was a difficult one, one of which we lost money, but where the foundation for future growth and great opportunity was laid. By the beginning of 1985, the core management team of seven very able executive directors was in place. This team remained as a coherent powerful group for 11 very successful years, which saw the Group grow 25 times over.

Carving out virgin territory in business is fun and creative. Where were the outlets for our products? One answer was to look for parallels, such as Hewlett-Packard's programmable calculators of the time. We tore into their distribution with a much more exciting proposition. I call the first ten years of Psion's history our Che Guevara years. We had a strong team culture, smart people, enormous commitment and a great belief in our ability to move nimbly and rapidly through the jungle of markets and technology.

World competition

Having avoided domestic competition in software markets, the competition now appeared on a global scale. In 1988 – the year Psion was first listed on the London Stock Exchange – Sharp and Casio entered European and American markets with carefully emulated 'Organiser' products. What was interesting was the way that they had studied the functionality, marketing and distribution of our products. Surprisingly, we did not feel under price pressure. Instead Sharp and Casio put us under pressure with *Kaizen* – continuous development.

> I call the first ten years of Psion's history our Che Guevara years.

Psion had two advantages in the face of these Japanese behemoths. First, a clear long-term vision; second, software and a systems approach. While they were pursuing *Kaizen* and 8-bit technology, from 1988 we were pursuing a more radical approach based on 16-bit technology that would harness the capabilities of semiconductors in the 1990s. Always striving to enable or facilitate the user, we also built a Windows software environment. The route we chose was painful but superior. The year 1991 was a second year of loss for Psion. However, it was also one of our most successful years as we introduced our 16-bit technology in the Series 3 palmtop family.

Building on this base and technology lead, we introduced many new models, leading to great success and profitability over the next five years as Psion's turnover grew at an annual compound growth rate of 40 per cent. In the late 1990s, Psion's success and profit are still attracting others. We have seen competition from Apple and the Newton, Sharp, Casio, Motorola, Sony and now we have Microsoft and Windows CE. However, in the last decade, Psion's business has broadened into a diversity of markets. We have a difficult road ahead, but – driven by paranoia – a richness of opportunities.

Generalizing from the Psion experience

What does this story of Psion tell us more generally?

- It tells us in a small way that Europe can compete in new technology markets and in innovation – just as SAP in Germany or Nokia and Ericsson in digital cellular technology have done.

- It tells us that markets are increasingly global and brutally competitive.
- It tells us of the continuous struggle to pursue continuous change and innovation in technology markets. It's fear that drives Bill Gates' Microsoft, not greed.
- It tells us that the companies that succeed and survive in the long run are not based on one product or one idea, but those that do it again and again and again.
- It tells us that through growth, a company, its founder and management have to change and learn progressively as their size evolves.

Entrepreneurship, innovation, change – these three words are at the heart of what Psion is and the commercial environment in which it operates. These words also hold, I believe, important lessons for many other companies throughout the European economies. My core concerns, therefore, are with a world of change, flux and continuous innovation.

Global economic order – a world based on change

Above all, 'change' is the economic condition that now confronts the world. To illustrate, here as just a few ways in which the world has changed during Psion's short life:

- the 'Rust Bowl' phenomenon of the 1980s and the collapse of traditional industries in Europe and America – coal mining, the textile industry or shipbuilding
- unemployment in the UK jumped from 0.5 to over 3 million – in Germany and France unemployment remains stubbornly at 12 or 13 per cent
- the Soviet Empire has gone, to be replaced by a new, open and more integrated world order
- the Telex machine used to be the primary official communication for export business – it was driven out first by the fax, and now by instant digital communications.

Under these conditions, the competitive environment has changed dramatically. Increasingly, we're all playing in the Olympic Games, not the local athletics ground. I doubt that there has ever been such a period of dynamic change in world history as now.

In addition to political and transport drivers, the most critical force in global economic development is the digital revolution. I doubt that I can overstate how fundamentally the digital revolution is changing, and will continue to change, both our personal and economic environments. Historians look for milestones. The end of the Soviet Empire may mark the end of the twentieth century, but the start of the twenty-first century is marked by the digital revolution, and most of that revolution's impact is still to come.

The raw material for the digital revolution is the integrated circuit. The benchmark for progress has been Moore's Law, coined by Gordon Moore, founder of Intel. In 1965, Moore observed that the number of circuits on any given area of silicon chip would double every year to 18 months. His projection suggested that computer power would improve a thousand-fold every ten years. And it gets better. The dynamics of the semiconductor industry dictate that, in the 18 months it takes for processing power or memory to double, the price-performance ratio halves. In effect, the same processing power or memory can be bought at the end of any given 18-month period for half the price that was paid at the beginning of that time. Better yet, this has been going on for the last 30 years. Even better still, this is likely to continue for another 20 years.

By any standard, this is an astonishing rate of development. The impact of the digital revolution is like taking a train from the coast up into the mountains. Watch from the windows for a few minutes and the landscape doesn't seem to change. Fall asleep for two hours and the landscape has changed beyond recognition.

IT has made the commercial environment in which most companies now operate an increasingly global one. The phenomenal improvements in communications make it possible to organize production on a global scale; components can be sourced from just about anywhere in the world. It is just as easy to specify a part, schedule deliveries and receive the part from Khoushong in Taiwan as it is from Watford. And, I tell you, it probably gets to our factory in Greenford faster than round the M25. In the future, this will apply to retailing and service industries as much as finance, making cars or computers.

The future belongs to the small – why capitalism works

This world of change really is at odds with much of the conventional wisdom and the mantras of the day, particularly in Europe. The question most commonly asked of me by interviewers and journalists since 1984 has been, 'When is your company going to die?' The more polite may not ask the question, but it is what is going through their minds. Why? Because of the implicit belief that the world belongs to the big, in spite of the enormous evidence to the contrary.

> **It is just as easy to specify a part, schedule deliveries and receive the part from Khoushong in Taiwan as it is from Watford.**

IBM owned the mainframe computer industry, but the minicomputer business was created by green-field operations – Digital, Wang, Data General and Prime. And where are they now? The microcomputer industry was created by new start-up companies of the likes of Apple, Intel, Microsoft, Cisco, Compaq and Sun. This nearly killed the biggest giant of all, IBM.

In 1951, a small $3m company in Rochester, New York came up with the great concept of electronic photocopying. So, it tried to sell the idea to the big electronic companies of the time – in particular, the biggest, RCA – do you remember it? RCA laughed at the idea of replacing carbon paper and so the Haloid Corporation had to do it by itself. It became the Xerox Corporation. Where is RCA today? Gone.

There's more irony. Xerox built the Palo Alto Research Centre (PARC) to ensure it didn't turn into an RCA. Fifteen years later, PARC invented Windows, the mouse, icons and pull-down menus for microcomputers. Xerox, though, couldn't see the market for these. It was left to Steve Jobs of Apple to see it and later lose it to Bill Gates and Microsoft.

History demonstrates again and again that new business and innovation come from the grass roots. This is why capitalism works and Communism doesn't. In truth, in large companies we are trained to remove business risk. Business, however, turns on risk, so removing business risk can remove business opportunity. This is the paradox that – in Europe particularly – we must confront. Executives, boards, audit committees frequently ask, 'Where are the risks and how can we remove them?' Perhaps they should rephrase their question, 'How can we increase risk?' No, not literally, but my equation is risk = opportunity. We cannot avoid the change, so let us grasp the opportunity.

A business model based on change

This is why Psion's business model is based on change. Our core process is innovation. I believe that accepting and embracing change is an essential facet of business survival as we enter the next century. What, though, does a business model based on change mean in practice?

Companies that operate in the technology sector – and, increasingly, in virtually any other sector – actually have no other choice. Successful companies constantly renew themselves – Hewlett-Packard's business model explicitly sets this out as a company objective. Those companies that stand still are effectively going backwards and will die. Successful companies are actively using the changing business environment to provide a constant source of new business opportunities.

The implications seen from a European perspective

It is already clear that few segments of the economy will be immune to, or protected from, this global, competitive, digital economy. Europe's old traditional heavy industries have moved to lower cost developing economies. Media businesses are multiplying globally, so that the *Financial Times* is competing with *The Wall Street Journal*. The BBC is competing with CNN. Reuters is competing with Bloomberg and the expanding hordes of small information providers that are competing with both of them. Who needs Reed-Elsevier or Pergamon Press in the future? Not the academics who read their scientific journals – they can get them digitally, and they are already the editors.

We have seen many of our investment banks dismembered and slotted into foreign banks, and, equally, fund management appears to be going global. What about retailing. Are Marks & Spencer or Boots or Tesco or Dixons immune? Absolutely not. Dell Computers, Psion, soap makers and manufacturers of underwear and socks will be supplying directly through digital networks. Already, if you want to buy a book, by far the easiest way to do so is by visiting Amazon.com on the Internet. It's already one of the biggest suppliers of books in the world. I could go on, but I have made my point. Very few industries are, or will be, immune to this cyclone of change.

I have often felt in Europe that I am walking backwards into the future. In Europe as a whole, I do not believe that we have yet fully accepted the new world order I have been describing. In France and Germany, there is so much endeavour focused on fruitless protectionism rather than embracing change as the core process.

Over recent years, I have spent much time in Tokyo, Taipei, Boston, San Francisco or Palo Alto. What does Europe feel like from those countries? Like the Greeks to Rome in 50 BC. And how is Britain seen from Palo Alto? As boring and quaint. This is how the conservatism of Europe is seen from these more dynamic economies.

The language used by the new, dynamic, knowledge-based companies in America includes words and phrases such as 'product space', 'crossing the chasm', 'geek', 'displacing the old paradigm', 'virtual operation', 'inside the tornado', 'object-link-embedding', 'mice in free space', 'hyper-competitive marketing'.

From this side of the Atlantic, it may seem weird, but Europe shouldn't sneer. The significance of this 'geek-speak', of this new language, is that it is created to describe a new order and new ideas. It demonstrates the fertility of what is going on. Therefore, a major question for Europe as competition becomes global is, 'Are we trying to protect the past ?' or as in America, 'Are we interested in creating the future?' What is clear is that Europe has adapted less well than America.

The search for high added-value activities

It is not only the Psions of this world that are subject to a globally competitive world. If we are to prosper in Europe, I believe we must all embrace a culture of change, but how do we do that and where are the opportunities?

As traditional industries in the United Kingdom have declined, they have been replaced, at least in part, by new industries. These include pharmaceuticals, IT, biotechnology, international fund management, design houses, information services, communications, new media, semiconductors, and many others. Three features characterize these new industries:

- the employment of highly skilled designers, engineers, scientists, software specialists, economists, marketing and production personnel
- a high rate of technological development
- the capital-intensive nature of the activity.

The core requirement is that the activity creates high added value. It is only by adding high value that sufficient margin can be created to cover the high levels of pay and meet the aspirations of the developed European market. In short, the innovative creation of products and services, rather than the process of manufacturing, becomes the vital competence for the most advanced economies.

Because the process of manufacturing is becoming easier, fewer jobs are required in the manufacturing sector, and so we have seen considerable growth in the service sector. Over the last 15 years, the conventional wisdom has become 'Britain's future lies in services.' However, in this there is a paradox. As we import more, where are the foreign earnings going to come from to pay for all the imported manufactured goods? After all, you can't export many Arthur Andersen audit clerks or Maurice Saatchis. The truth is that employment in so-called manufacturing has declined to 20 per cent of the workforce in Britain, but it still earns 67 per cent of exports and foreign exchange income. Obviously, if we are to maintain our standard of living in Europe in the future, the export of goods will have to generate the great majority of foreign exchange earnings in the future.

> ... the innovative creation of products and services, rather than the process of manufacturing, becomes the vital competence for the most advanced economies.

However, I believe there is a solution. We need to move away from thinking about the process of manufacturing as a source of added value and competitive advantage *per se*. We also need to change the language of how business, policy makers and government talk about the economy. Do you know that the Department of Trade and Industry classifies 'tanning' as one of the ten major business sectors in Britain? This is mad. This is the language of yesterday. Listen in Europe, and you hear a vernacular of 'market share, conglomeration, the merging of tired old brands in a declining spirits trade, services and monopolizations'. Contrast this with the language of Silicon Valley I described earlier.

We need to stop talking about the service sector or the manufacturing sector. Bill Clinton once said 'It's the economy, stupid.' Paraphrasing him 'It's the product, stupid.' The high ground of profit will be given to those who control the products and markets. It does not matter who manufactures them; it matters who creates them and, therefore, who owns them and develops them. Microsoft, Intel, Reuters, Glaxo and Psion are product and Intellectual Property Rights-owning companies.

The manufacturing is easy. It does not provide the core competitive advantage. Innovation, creativity, market development in the general sense, design – these are the activities that count. Competitive advantage in Europe must come from knowledge-based activities. The service sector is not enough.

We must excite the young, the brightest and the best in these knowledge-based creative activities. And it is essential to foster world-class science and technology universities, and imbue them with an entrepreneurial culture.

Standards in the new industries

Standards in the new industries are creating opportunities for European entrepreneurs. The new industries are becoming more sophisticated and require a close interdependence between suppliers. Standards are therefore critical. Nowhere is this more important than in the IT and communications industry.

There's an interesting contrast between the US and Europe in how standards are set. Take IT first. In America, with its Darwinian culture, it's the John Wayne, or gunfight at the OK Corral approach that is used. Whoever is left standing at the end establishes the standard. In IT, where America has been particularly dominant, this has been the mechanic – viz the IBM 360 O/S in the 1960s and 1970s, and Microsoft with Windows in the 1990s.

However, here's a contrary example from Europe. We have a more cooperative culture. And, in digital cellular phones, European companies sat around a table and agreed a standard – GSM. GSM has been so successful that it is now a *de facto* world standard. And it is Nokia, Ericsson, Philips and Siemens that dominate the enormous – and growing – technology markets.

This story demonstrates an opportunity for Europe, but will we grasp it? ■

This chapter has been developed and edited from the author's Stockton Lecture, given at the London Business School in 1998. The previous version of the Lecture first appeared in the spring 1998 issue of *Business Strategy Review*, published for London Business School by Blackwell Publishers.

James L. Barksdale

President and CEO
Netscape Communications Corporation

RAMPING UP FOR THE NET ECONOMY

Technology – particularly networking technology – has increasingly affected the way business is done. Telephones, fax machines and cell phones, for example, have become indispensable, helping us to meet business challenges more quickly and efficiently than was possible in the past. Today, it is Internet technology that is making a difference, causing us to make profound changes to the ways we conduct business.

Way back in 1994, when Netscape first distributed its Netscape Navigator browser over the Internet, we thought of the browser as a marvellous, easy-to-use tool for graphical point-and-click navigation around global networks. Customers could use it to look at product and service information on any company's web site. We soon realized the browser could also give employees easy access to corporate information via Intranets, which are corporate networks built on Internet technology. Next, we recognized the value of extending that corporate information out to customers, partners and suppliers via Extranets. Currently, we're seeing businesses use open standards Internet technology to link their entire supply chains together and create vertical trading communities on-line.

While Intranets help companies to cut costs and improve communication among employees, and Extranets help companies to better communicate one-to-one with customers, partners and suppliers, these new, real-time, on-line vertical trading communities help to tightly connect business to business in a world where all commerce is electronic – the Net Economy. The boundaries between web site, Intranet and Extranet have blurred.

Metcalfe's Law supersedes Moore's Law

For more than 30 years, we've all been excited about Moore's Law, which states that every 18 months or so the speed of microprocessors doubles and the cost decreases proportionally. Today, however, companies such as Citibank or Ford Motor Company or Federal Express, all good customers of Netscape's, are no longer constrained by processor speed. Moore's Law is not going to do a whole lot more for these companies.

The important law to pay attention to now is Metcalfe's Law. This is named after Bob Metcalfe, inventor of Ethernet and founder of 3Com. Metcalfe's Law states that the value of a network grows exponentially. Every endpoint that's added can then be connected to all the other endpoints. In other words, the number of endpoints squared is an indicator of the value of a network. The network that doesn't reach everywhere is of little value. Think about what a tough job the first telephone salesman had. Who was the first customer going to talk to?

Companies today are driven more by the networking truths of Metcalfe's Law than by the hardware truths of Moore's Law. That's one of the features of the Net Economy. And to make sure they can take full advantage of Metcalfe's Law, companies are looking to their Information Technology (IT) departments to build networks that are reliable and interconnect all facets of the business.

IT – a strategic asset

Until very recently, IT departments used to act as cost centres, and their main activities were purchasing, deploying and maintaining hardware and software systems. Today, though, IT departments are increasingly facing line-of-business pressures. They're now expected to produce new products and services to reach customers.

Why has this change come about? It's because, in the Net Economy, business issues and technology issues go hand in hand. In a globally networked business environment, understanding how technology can help your company grow new revenue streams and reduce expenses is a critical part of making your company successful.

Look at E*Trade, for example. It's a new company launched solely as an on-line service for selling mutual funds and stocks. Even though it's a relative newcomer, E*Trade has the second-highest market share of all on-line financial services firms. The company's entire business revolves around its IT infrastructure. E*Trade was able to get on the Internet quicker than anybody else and provide a great service, even though it had never been in the business before. That, of course, drives bigger companies such as Charles Schwab, Merrill Lynch and others to follow suit. They're forced into action by the small, innovative companies that set the trends and try out new ways of doing things.

Companies are becoming much better at leveraging technology to their greatest strategic advantage. They're creating new revenue streams by offering their core businesses as services on the Net, thereby not only reaching millions of customers and partners around the world, but also gaining the ability to forge tighter relationships with them. They're cutting costs by streamlining business processes among their employees, partners and suppliers. They're deploying advanced business applications as services across their entire trading network so that everything from a simple information request to sophisticated commerce can be conducted on-line in real time – just think of the efficiencies.

As a result, no IT department today should be looked at as a cost centre. Instead, everyone should be asking 'How do I do what Michael Dell does?' He sells $5 to $6 million of products a day over the Internet. The IT systems he uses to do this are all automated, and they tie into his back-end legacy systems. The Dell story is now famous: a billion-dollar market created in 18 months. It doesn't matter which industry you're in, people notice that. Businesspeople look at Dell's success and ask either 'How does that affect my business?' or 'How do I take advantage of that opportunity?' All you need are a few of those kinds of successes, and pretty soon everybody wants to jump on the bandwagon.

IT departments have traditionally worried about how to maximize efficiency inside their organizations. The Net Economy has forced them to think about how to build an infrastructure that lets them communicate easily with a network of business partners and customers outside the organization.

For our communications to remain private and our electronic commerce transactions to remain safe, we need to ensure that our public and private infrastructure is secured by means of strong encryption. Encryption is simply a way to scramble (encrypt) and unscramble (decrypt) digital information during transmission or for purposes of storage. A world without encryption for the Internet would be like a world without envelopes for letters. Every communication would be like a postcard.

Virtual space versus bricks and mortar

It used to be that to build your business, you needed to think about bricks and mortar – in other words, physical retail space. In the new world of the Net Economy, however, your showroom can exist solely in virtual space. Amazon.com, a relative newcomer to the book business (and a business that has its 'shop' solely on-line), now has a higher market capitalization than Barnes & Noble, America's largest booksellers. Yet Barnes & Noble has been in the business much longer and has about $1 billion in hard assets in retail outlets. How did this happen, and what does it mean?

A world without encryption for the Internet would be like a world without envelopes for letters.

The secret to many great opportunities on the Internet is that there are things you can do in virtual space that you can't do in real space. Amazon.com can pretend to have 2.5 million volumes on the shelves when you go to its bookshop, even though everybody knows they are not all on one shelf. Amazon.com can give the appearance of something no bookshop in the world can give in real space – it can look like a virtual British Library or the US Library of Congress.

Obviously not everything is going to be disintermediated, but I do think we're going to find more ways to have customers intermediate. We're going to find new values for our assets and our core competences in the Net Economy.

A few years ago, Citibank was going through a major transformation that culminated when John Reed, the Chairman and CEO of Citicorp, announced that the company wanted to reach a billion customers by the year 2010. That is an enormous goal.

A company can't get to a billion customers – or 100 million customers – in the conventional way, using the traditional bricks-and-mortar real estate. Citibank realized that for them to achieve that sort of scale and create such opportunities, they'd have to do things in a different way, a more economical way, and not be dependent on the ways of the past. Citibank has to provide access points to its services that are very, very easy for its customers to get to. It has to develop and retain a relationship with each customer that's broad and deep, yet costs less to maintain then ever before. To accomplish this, the company's IT department is building a high-performance, scalable, centrally managed, open standards-based infrastructure so that Citibank can not only connect easily with new customers, but also interconnect all of its legacy systems with its business partners and *their* legacy systems.

End-to-end commerce

This kind of end-to-end commerce is a critical aspect of the Net Economy. In this interconnected world, companies are running their IT departments as if they were Internet Service Providers (ISPs). They're providing large-scale Internet applications to their customers, partners, and suppliers. At Netscape, we call IT departments that are doing this Enterprise Service Providers (ESPs).

As ESPs, IT departments have a new set of requirements. Their systems have to be up and running 24 hours a day, 7 days a week. To ensure consistency of access and service across the Net – and to cut administration costs – the systems should be centrally managed. They must also be able to scale upwards extremely well. IT groups never know how many customers or partners they're going to have to connect with – it could be 100, 1000, 10,000, or 10 million. They just need to be ready. And they need to be able to easily connect to partners' legacy systems.

According to Peter Drucker, the purpose of any business is to create and keep customers. As IT departments and business line-managers begin to participate in the Net Economy, they have an unprecedented opportunity to make major contributions to the bottom line as they develop new customer-focused applications and services. It's a whole new business role for IT. And it's a new way to use technology to meet business goals.

The rise of portal sites

Lately, we've seen the rise of portal sites as a way to gather information, services and products in one convenient place on the Internet. Portals are more than just gateways or doorways to a collection of content. They also provide directories, search engines and other services to help people locate what they're trying to find. In fact, portals are now providing a lot of services and features, such as free e-mail, stock quotes and personalization, that aim to keep visitors coming back. Netscape has a major portal on the Internet called Netcenter, which reaches 8 to 9 million individuals every day. Other major portal sites are run by Yahoo! and Excite.

In addition to being a convenient place for consumers to find goods and services, portals – with their large amounts of daily traffic – are also good places for businesses to find customers. Companies can significantly lower the costs of acquiring customers and gain an immediate return on investment by setting up shop on a portal site. To top it off, the portal companies themselves are discovering important new revenue opportunities through partnership deals, advertising revenue and transaction fees. All in all, business-to-consumer commerce on portals is not only possible, it's also profitable.

One aspect of business-to-consumer commerce to keep in mind is that any firm doing business on-line must be sure to manage personal data about its customers ethically. Customers fear that their personal information may be collected by web sites and shared with people or businesses they don't know. Customers demand to be informed about data collection practices, and, indeed, many laws in Europe, Canada, Australia and elsewhere require companies to manage data in certain ways. It is in every business' best legal and financial interests to have a privacy policy prominently placed on its web site – to participate in industry self-regulatory efforts, become aware of applicable laws and, most important, listen to customers and their demands for privacy protection. If customers trust you, they will return again – satisfied and loyal.

In addition to the business-to-consumer side of portals, we're starting to see portals organize information, services and products for enterprises. They're creating new business-to-business trading networks that link up the entire supply and distribution chain. According to Forrester Research, by 2001 the Internet will connect more than 1.3 million companies worldwide, and by 2002, the total value of goods and services traded between companies over the Internet will reach $327 billion. These new business-to-business trading networks can provide companies with access to outsourced services and give them a way to conduct business with many more companies than they could have done on their own.

The Internet's power as a tool for commerce and communications is unprecedented. It's important that both consumers and businesses continue to have choice and that no single software company becomes the sole gateway to the digital marketplace the Internet creates. If that happens, it would be as if 90 per cent or more of the real estate in the world were owned by one company. For the global networked economy to remain vital, there must be room for everyone to participate.

Convergence

I spent 14 years of my business career with two networking companies – Federal Express and McCaw Cellular – that were very dependent on having appropriate IT systems and applications to run their businesses. In both cases, I witnessed the convergence of two or more different industries. At Federal Express, for example, it was the convergence of the airline industry, trucking industry and computer industry. You put them all together and you create a whole new product set.

At McCaw Cellular, the largest cellular company in the world, Craig McCaw was one of the first people to see the convergence of radio telephony, which gives you mobility, the conventional telephone system, which gives you ubiquity, and the computer industry, which gives you the high-speed ability to switch from cell to cell, which theretofore had not been possible. That convergence created the cellular telephone industry, which has grown at least a couple, if not more, orders of magnitude larger than people projected just 12 years ago.

The same kind of convergence is happening now in the development of the Net Economy. The enterprise software businesses and the portal businesses are coming together. Convergence is where great opportunities are always created – seemingly disparate businesses come together to create new, as yet undefined opportunities. Previously, I discussed how businesses are using enterprise software to their strategic advantage by becoming ESPs. According to analysts, the ESPs and portal markets combined are estimated to be worth more than $40 billion by 2001. Let's look at how ESPs and portals work together.

The Ford Motor Company offers one example. Ford sees that the total cost of ownership of an automobile is three times as great as the cost of the automobile itself. How does Ford penetrate those other markets? How does Ford get into the insurance market? How does it get into financing? How does it get into giving you better road services or better lease deals? Ford can offer those services as an ESP, and then it can meet new customers via portal sites.

Convergence is where great opportunities are always created – seemingly disparate businesses come together to create new, as yet undefined opportunities.

As another example, Telefonica – the largest supplier of telecommunications services in the Spanish-speaking world – remotely hosts services for small companies that want to conduct business with other companies over the Internet. Telefonica provides these small businesses with the Internet infrastructure and electronic commerce applications they need to do that. This points out another opportunity – telecommunications companies and ISPs can host these systems and become ESPs – as well as business-to-business trading portals – for their customers. Again, we see the convergence of ESPs and portals.

Shortage of IT staff

Companies that want to implement these types of systems have two main problems right now: they don't have the IT staff, and they don't have the IT budget. That's because the Year 2000 problem is draining budgets. And if you live in Europe, you not only have to deal with the Year 2000 problem, but you also have to handle the conversion to the Euro, which is an even bigger cost. On top of all that, there's a shortage of talented people that would exist even if there weren't a shortage of money.

How does a company take advantage of these new Net Economy opportunities if it's facing those restrictions? It has to find a new way of doing things. The old way is that a company buys or builds a system, deploys it, maintains it and lives with it. After the system grew up from being a pretty little baby and wasn't so pretty any more, people would start critiquing it and then the company would upgrade it. And so the cycle would be repeated – buy, build, deploy, maintain, upgrade; buy, build, deploy, maintain, upgrade – in a never-ending process. Couple this never-ending upgrading process with the restrictions that the Year 2000 problem and the conversion to the Euro are placing on IT staffs and you can see the double bind that companies are in now. Yet they see this great new shiny thing out in front of them – the opportunities of the Net Economy.

Internet technology offers an entirely new way of deploying and managing systems centrally so that administration costs can be reduced. In addition, companies have the option of outsourcing these systems, as in the earlier Telefonica hosting example.

Another way companies are dealing with IT shortages is that they are beginning to implement operating systems and software applications that are based on open source code, such as the Linux operating system. 'Open source code' is software code that is freely available on the Internet for all developers to modify and help develop. In the open source code software development model, intellectual property information is shared so that everyone can benefit from it. By working together, the Internet community of developers can create what no one company could ever afford or be able to do on its own – and do it quickly and efficiently. The kind of distributed development that open source code offers lets everyone be more productive. Corporate developers, for example, can implement just the enhancements they need without having to develop the code themselves.

Some people ask, 'Is open source code software reliable?' It can actually be more reliable than commercial software, because it has such a large pool of developers and beta-testers working with it. With enough diverse people examining the code, just about every bug is bound to be uncovered and its fix apparent to at least one developer. Linux, for example, recently won an award for reliability, winning out over commercially available operating systems.

New business models

The ability to understand how this new Net Economy is going to change your business model and everything you do every day is a critical part of making your company successful in the future. The Internet has created a mass-market opportunity that many businesses are very excited about, but it's a new way of meeting and interacting with customers. It's not like running a TV ad, which is the old way of marketing to millions of people. That's because in the new way of marketing to millions, via the Internet, customers can answer back. You have to process the trans-action. The old broadcast model for media doesn't work. The Internet really is a new medium. It creates new kinds of interaction and transaction opportunities.

In addition, a company's time to market is quicker on the Net. Products a company can bring on-line today, it tries out today. No one knows all the products and services that consumers will need in the coming years. One of the key things about the software that companies use is that it must let them innovate much faster so they can quickly test products and services to determine what works and what doesn't.

At Netscape, we have a lot of experience doing business on the Internet. We're the first enterprise software company to be born in the Internet era, and we've built our products to endure the rigours of Internet-scale traffic. We've pioneered many of the industry's frameworks, technologies and models of doing business on the Net. And, yes, even we have had to implement a new business model quickly to remain competitive in the Net Economy.

... time to market is quicker on the Net. Products a company can bring on-line today, it tries out today.

Let me explain. In 1996, browser sales contributed up to 45 per cent of our revenue; by the fourth quarter of 1997, our browser revenue stood at 13 per cent. Because of pricing pressure from one of our competitors, we were forced to give away our browser for free in 1998. To replace this revenue stream, we developed a new business model for Netscape: we now run two related businesses – an enterprise soft-ware and services business and a portal business. We provide enterprise software and services to help companies create an infrastructure for deploying and managing Internet applications; we provide electronic commerce products to help companies do business on the Internet; and we provide access to the digital marketplace via our portal Netcenter.

Adjusting our business model was analogous to running a very fast race and changing our trainers at the same time. Yet, this is a business model we're very excited about, and our customers are sharing that enthusiasm. This model also recog-nizes the important contribution our browser still makes, as the browser serves both the enterprise software business and the portal business. What's more, not only did we rip the revenue out of Netscape Communicator when we made it free, but we also made the intellectual property of the product – the source code – available to every-one who wants to help co-develop it. It's a great opportunity to leverage the power of the Internet and enlist an army of developers to help advance the functionality and features of the browser for all users.

The Internet's popularity skyrocketed after Marc Andreessen and a team of stu-dents created the first graphical browser back in 1993. This new medium – the Internet – has been instrumental in improving communication and business processes and launching the Net Economy. There's certainly no going back. We can only go forward, and we're going forward as fast as we possibly can. ■

John Patrick

Vice President, Internet Technology, IBM, and
Chairman, Global Internet Project

THE OPPORTUNITY AND THE CHALLENGE TO SUSTAIN RAPID INTERNET GROWTH

A policy architecture for the Internet

P eter Drucker, the renowned management consultant, once remarked that 'most businesses suffer from indigestion, not starvation.' Too much success and overly rapid growth can be more dangerous to the health of an organization than failure to attract an audience or find a market.

Nowhere is this more true than on the Internet. The average Internet service provider experiences a 100 to 200 per cent growth in traffic on the Internet per year, and it doesn't take Deep Blue to calculate that, before too long, the Internet risks buckling under the weight of its own success.

The fact that the Internet has been so rapidly and widely adopted has led us to treat it like a natural resource, as fundamental to the Information Age as clean air and fresh water. The more we use it, the more we take it for granted. We just expect the Internet to be there, just as we expect the lights to go on when we flip a switch or the dial tone to greet us when we pick up the telephone. However, we can't take the Internet for granted, any more than we can other resources. As Internet usage begins to reach critical mass, the industry must take steps to ensure that the Internet is 'always on', with open access and participation to all.

As we stand at this crossroads, private industry, educational institutions and government agencies have been working, often on separate planes, to create a policy framework to address the issues fundamental to managing the Internet's growth.

The Global Internet Project has developed an approach to crystallize these efforts. Formed in 1996, this group is a collection of senior executives from more than a dozen companies around the world. The main objective of the Global Internet Project is to collaboratively raise awareness of the challenges to Internet growth and help formulate technology and public policy recommendations to assure that marketplace initiatives, rather than government regulation, will shape the Internet's growth. There is a Global Internet Project web site (http://www.gip.org) and this will be expanded to provide linkages to key policy areas, partner organizations that are focusing in the policy areas, ongoing projects in each area, and relevant protocols and standards.

To meet this objective, the Global Internet Project is using a pyramid model to define a policy architecture composed of the six critical Internet building blocks that are being addressed by the industry (Figure 1).

- *Level 1* Infrastructure – the challenge of meeting the demand for reliable and scaleable access to the Internet.
- *Level 2* Governance – addressing the question of who or what owns or controls the Internet and when such mechanisms are necessary.
- *Level 3* Security – the policies, procedures and protocols necessary to ensure the safety of electronic communications on the Internet.
- *Level 4* Privacy – protecting the confidentiality of information shared digitally.

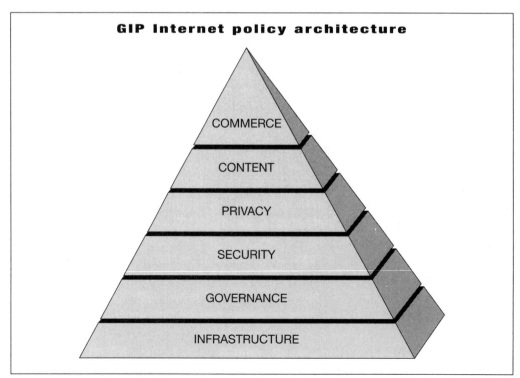

GIP Internet policy architecture

COMMERCE

CONTENT

PRIVACY

SECURITY

GOVERNANCE

INFRASTRUCTURE

FIGURE 1

- *Level 5* Content – empowering users of the Web to maximize their time on-line by viewing only the content they want to see.
- *Level 6* Commerce – ensuring that electronic transactions on the Internet develop in a manner conducive to the emergence of a global economy.

Level 1 Infrastructure – building a true superhighway

While it's become fashionable to speak about the 'Information Superhighway' this roadway is quickly reaching its capacity. That's because we're asking the Internet to do things it was never designed for – high-speed access to millions of people using billions of devices to conduct trillions of transactions 24 hours a day, across borders, languages, cultures and time zones. The road is getting clogged – fast.

One of the top priorities is to build the 'real' Information Superhighway. At its most basic level, the goal is more 'speed', which can be achieved by building a bigger pipeline with more bandwidth capacity. However, adding more lanes to the digital road is only part of the solution. We also need to deal with new challenges, such as quality of service when data, voice and video are all competing for the same bandwidth; reliability and continuous access; interconnectivity between subnetworks; and 'first mile' on ramps from the home, at work or on-the-go.

This is a new way of engineering, which is why the Internet requires a different infrastructure design based on a new generation of tools, protocols and standards. To meet this requirement, a number of important initiatives are already under way. A few examples illustrate the breadth of activity.

- Internet2 (http://www.internet2.edu) is a collaborative effort by more than 120 universities to develop advanced Internet technology and applications vital to the research and education missions of higher education. Internet2 is a project of the University Corporation for Advanced Internet Development (UCAID) with support from industry and government. Another UCAID (http://www.ucaid.edu) initiative, the Abilene Project, is developing an advanced network to serve as the backbone network for the Internet2 project.
- The Internet Engineering Task Force (http://www.itef.org) is concentrating on a wide range of areas, including applications, standards, networking and routing, operations and management, security and transport.
- The Metropolitan Research and Education Network (http://www.mren.org) is one of the world's most advanced high-performance broadband networks. MREN supports a wide range of advanced, high-bandwidth applications, such as deep computing, digital video, medical imaging and high-energy physics.
- The Corporation for National Research Initiatives (CNRI) is also involved in a series of projects relevant to the Internet's emerging infrastructure. More information can be found at http://www.cnri.reston.va.us.

Level 2 Governance — rewriting the rules of the road

As the Internet becomes the primary channel for commerce worldwide, determining how the Internet is to be managed is a vital issue. Our highway needs rules of the road, and a way to enforce them firmly but fairly.

The Global Internet Project believes that the marketplace, not government, is best able to promote open access, provide a level playing field, stimulate innovation, offer security, protect privacy and respect intellectual property with the fewest and least intrusive oversight mechanisms. Accordingly, the industry is identifying the mechanisms that demonstrate its ability to self-govern in critical areas, such as privacy and content selection. In some cases, international non-profit bodies are evolving to address issues such as domain names, and we may see other issues addressed in a similar manner in the future.

The idea that the industry leads was clearly set forth in the Framework for Global Electronic Commerce developed by the US Government with substantial input from the private sector (http://www.ecommerce.gov). This wide-ranging initiative to develop and manage the Global Information Infrastructure (GII) embraces five principles:

- the private sector should lead
- governments should avoid undue restrictions on electronic commerce
- where governmental involvement is needed, its aim should be to support and enforce a predictable, minimalist, consistent and simple legal environment for commerce
- governments should recognize the unique qualities of the Internet
- electronic commerce (e-commerce) over the Internet should be facilitated on a global basis.

The US Government is not the only government to espouse these principles. Both the European Union and the Ministry of International Trade and Industry (MITI) of Japan are also committed to industry leadership and self-regulation (for more information, see 'European Initiative in Electronic Commerce' (http://www.ispo.cec.be/ecommerce) and 'Towards the Age of the Digital Economy – for Rapid Progress in the Japanese Economy and World Economic Growth in the 21st Century' (http://www.miti.go.jp/intro-e/a228100e.html)).

Level 3 Security — driving safely on the information superhighway

Like any other road, the Internet must be safe to travel. In digital terms, this means that all members of the Internet community must have the confidence that information and transactions are secure.

Digital travellers want their data to be protected. While the Secure Sockets Layer (SSL) that is virtually ubiquitous on the Internet provides a basic level of security, it's easy to be lulled into a false sense of confidence. An SSL-secure credit card transaction, for example, does not mean that the recipient of that transaction has been authenticated and verified or that the recipient will keep the information confidential. Similarly, the state of the art for system intrusion advances more quickly than the art of protecting systems. This means that security requires policy, management and constant monitoring and verification.

All parties concerned with security must have a reference point for new trends, tools and techniques for invading and protecting networks, as well as audit procedures to make sure testing is proactive and continuous, and not conducted only after security has been breached. Also, there are legitimate public policy issues surrounding the encryption of data and who should hold the keys that unlock the information. Some government agencies believe that they should have ultimate access, while most in the private sector believe that security should reside in the hands of the information owner.

Level 4 Privacy – protecting personal preferences and consumer rights

Creating an Information Superhighway is not a licence to drive into every aspect of a person's life. Nor does it release governments or businesses from their ethical and legal responsibilities to protect the data they receive and collect electronically. As the Internet becomes central to daily life, the fundamental right to privacy must be protected. People want to be sure that their private lives do not become an open book for casual reading by social predators, economic purveyors or governmental big brothers. Several surveys have indicated that concern about privacy is one of the major inhibitors to e-commerce.

Not surprisingly, Internet privacy is a likely target for government intervention. Fortunately, there are several excellent private-sector initiatives designed to protect personal rights and offer consumers protection, including TRUSTe and BBBOnLine.

- TRUSTe (http://www.truste.org) is an independent, non-profit organization dedicated to establishing a trusting Internet environment. The TRUSTe privacy program is championed by CommerceNet and the Electronic Frontier Foundation (EFF) for its principles of disclosure and informed consent. TRUSTe participants are required to use the organization's branded, on-line 'seal' or trustmark to signify disclosure of a web site's personal information privacy policy. Sites that display the trustmark have formally agreed to adhere to the TRUSTe privacy principles, disclose their information-gathering and dissemination practices, and submit to a comprehensive assurance process.
- The Better Business Bureau Online (BBBOnLine) is dedicated to fostering an ethical on-line marketplace by means of voluntary self-regulation and consumer advocacy (www.bbbonline.org). Companies that meet high BBBOnLine ethical standards may exhibit the BBBOnLine seal on their web site. Consumers are able to click on the BBBOnLine seal and instantly get a BBB company report.

- A coalition of 12 IT associations in the US has developed a 'High-tech Industry Self-regulatory Privacy Plan', which includes enforcement mechanisms. These associations are promoting the adoption of measures and practices by their members. Their plan can be used as a model for other industry sectors.
- The Worldwide Web Consortium (W3C) has introduced the Platform for Privacy Preferences (P3P), a technology that serves as a privacy assistant, giving users the ability to make informed decisions regarding their experience and their ability to control the use of their information. P3P (http://www.w3.org/p3p/) will enable web sites to express their privacy practices and users to exercise preferences over those practices. P3P products will allow users to be informed of site practices and allow users to tailor their relationships to specific sites accordingly. Sites with practices that fall within the range of a user's preference can be accessed 'seamlessly', otherwise users will be notified of a site's practices and have the opportunity to agree to those terms or other terms and continue browsing or not as they wish.

Level 5 Content labelling — 'children at play' and other digital roadsigns

Like any good highway, the Internet needs clear roadsigns to tell us what's ahead and direct us to our destination. As anyone who has travelled the Internet can tell you, the sheer volume of information at your fingertips can make the Internet more confusing than any physical road system.

The key to good Internet signage is easy-to-use, simple-to-understand 'content labelling'. For instance, content labelling is of critical concern to parents and educators who want appropriate filtering for children, as well as for people of all ages and walks of life who want to sort through the 'information glut' of the Internet more effectively.

Content control is ripe for intense government regulation, but the marketplace is moving quickly to provide the tools by which people can make their own choices

> ... the Internet is open for business, and the Internet of the future will require initiatives expressly designed to promote free enterprise in cyberspace.

about where to go and what to do and see on the Internet. For example, the World Wide Web Consortium (W3C) has developed the Platform for Internet Content Selection (PICS). PICS (http://www.w3.org/PICS/) is a technical platform that offers a highly flexible tool for filtering Internet content to provide user-defined, customized access. PICS does not rate the content, but empowers any individual or organization to develop its own rating systems, distribute labels for Internet content and create standard label-reading software and services. Many on-line service providers have easily usable filters built into their systems, and various content selection products are widely available for parents and educators.

Level 6 Commerce – driving a hard bargain on the Internet

Electronic commerce (e-commerce) sits on top of the policy architecture pyramid, and is the critical factor driving the growth of the Internet. As we know, the Internet is open for business, and the Internet of the future will require initiatives expressly designed to promote free enterprise in cyberspace. Three particular initiatives that illustrate a positive, market-driven approach to stimulating e-commerce are CommerceNet, the Information Technology Association of America (ITAA) and RosettaNet.

- CommerceNet (http://www.commerce.net) is a global, non-profit organization comprised of nearly 500 companies and organizations engaged in the research and conduct of e-commerce. CommerceNet's mission is to make e-commerce easy, trusted and ubiquitous in the spirit of market-driven economics. To accomplish this, CommerceNet provides research on emerging business and technology trends, public policy advocacy, the stimulation of new business opportunities, a test bed for new ideas and concepts and interoperability among developing e-commerce standards and applications.
- The Information Technology Association of America (ITAA) is developing, in conjunction with its members, a series of programs focused on the business practices component of e-commerce. These programs explain to those eager, but not ready for e-commerce the business case for e-commerce, implementation processes, best practices, metrics and vendor selection.
- RosettaNet was formed to develop business practices and high-level standards for the IT supply chain. The effort – which includes value-added resellers of IT, leading software, networking and hardware companies as well as the ITAA – is already showing results from successful pilot programmes. By agreeing on common approaches, RosettaNet is a good model of how specific segments of industry need to come together to agree on common approaches to make e-commerce a profitable reality.

The Global Internet Project – the mortar for the policy architecture

Taken together, the six layers of policy architecture described – infrastructure, governance, security, privacy, content and commerce – provide the 'bricks' for building a foundation of Internet public policy. However the structure requires 'mortar' to hold it together.

The Global Internet Project is committed to helping make all the pieces fit. By being committed to education, cooperation and marketplace initiatives, the Global Internet Project is emerging as an effective collaborator and champion for ideas and activities developed throughout the private sector and in cooperation with governmental agencies. On this foundation of information and education, the Global Internet Project leverages the prestige and resources of its constituent members to formulate new and effective policies and procedures to protect individual rights, promote e-commerce and support standards and interoperability.

Wherever appropriate, the Global Internet Project works hand-in-hand with its partners in the private sector, as well as government organizations, to implement change, evaluate its impact and, when successful, apply the benefits of this innovation to businesses and individuals alike.

All of this will only happen, however, if business, consumers, educators and public policy advocates recognize that the success of the Internet means it's time to take action, not time to take the Internet for granted. Positive change should not be left to chance. It is the product of creativity, commitment and common purpose by the entire Internet community. The Global Internet Project stands ready to help coordinate this effort. ■

Karel Van Miert

Member of the European Commission

COMPETITION RULES OK

We live in interesting times. The pace of technological change is difficult to comprehend even for those who are most directly involved. The opportunities made possible by the communications revolution are only beginning to become apparent. The edges are blurring between sectors that a few years ago were clearly distinct. In some cases, the divisions between sectors have disappeared altogether. Other contributors to this book are in a far better position to describe, or at least to speculate about, the implications of this revolution in terms of the products and services that will be offered, and the wider impact of the revolution on society. I therefore treat the revolution and its increasing importance as a fact. The purpose of this chapter, consequently, is to draw out the main implications of the communications revolution for competition law and its enforcement agencies, in terms of both what has changed and what has remained the same.

First, I will look at the two major changes that have brought about tremendous improvements in the potential for competition – globalization and convergence.

Positive aspects of globalization

Technological developments in communications industries have been as much the driving force of globalization as they have been driven by it. The wired world is thus both parent and child of the increasing global integration of economies and cultures. Nations still try to influence flows of information, resources and money across their borders – as the history of the European common market demonstrates. However, modern communications technologies make this more and more difficult, if not impossible. Knowledge and finance can be transferred across the world as electronic blips moving at the speed of light. Globalization has carried with it an increase in the size and importance of corporations. Today, only half of the 100 largest economic units in the world are nations; the other half are transnational corporations, and cross-border trade is increasing every year. Competition benefits as geographical partitioning of markets becomes increasingly difficult. Producers benefit from economies of scale and scope. Consumers benefit from the availability of a wide range of products.

Positive aspects of convergence

The most impressive aspect of the wired world is the manner in which previously different technologies have come together. Telecommunications companies now discover that there are profits from the actual content of signals travelling along their wires as well as the transport of those signals. Software companies have realized the importance of the change from data-based computing to communications. Software companies also need access to telecommunications in order to deliver their products more quickly and efficiently than before. These combinations of technologies can lead to the creation of new products and services at a pace previously unimaginable.

It is probably this whirlwind that more than anything else leads some to argue for a more *laissez-faire* attitude on the part of competition regulators. It is certainly true that the whirlwind begets innovation, and the genuinely impressive innovation has often been carried out by companies that, at the time at least, were relatively small.

Indeed, I sometimes get the impression when dealing with larger companies that they are playing catch-up with smaller ones. When Worldcom and MCI sought, unsuccessfully, to convince me that merging their Internet businesses would pose no competition problem, they maintained that their Internet activities would benefit from no synergies or cost savings as a result of the merger. In retrospect, they may regard this as a rather double-edged admission.

The role of competition law

On the basis of the above, you could legitimately ask what role remains for the competition rules. However, the optimistic world view outlined above only tells half of the story.

Competition law is not an end in itself, but, rather, a means to ensure an end – that of ensuring that markets are as free as possible. Free markets in turn ensure the most efficient production and allocation of resources. However, this is only Pareto optimal and is not necessarily the solution to all of society's ills. Efficiency of production is not necessarily the same as quality of production, and efficiency of allocation is not necessarily the same as equitability of allocation. In the non-wired world, societies often choose to depart from free market principles in the production and allocation of certain resources. The provision of certain services is often subjected to certain minimum quality or coverage requirements and, thus, at least in part, insulated from the vagaries of the free market. Health and education are perhaps the most obvious sectors, but similar considerations may also apply to telecommunications and broadcasting. Such choices may also be made in the wired world – ensuring the availability of the Internet in schools or libraries is one example – and these choices will remain just as legitimate.

Free market economics and competition law are two sides of the same coin. Economics describes the theory of free markets, competition law deals with the practice of ensuring that markets remain free. Some believe, however, that this sector is so dynamic and fast-moving that any regulatory intervention – be it from sector-specific regulation or competition law – is liable to impede the development of the sector. This is naïve. Companies have a legal duty to their shareholders to maximise their profits. This is best achieved by increasing market share at the expense of your competitors. In fact, a company's ultimate goal is to insulate itself from competition, maximizing profits and minimizing consumer welfare. The role of competition authorities is to ensure that competition has an opportunity to develop. Competition law protects competition and not competitors. It aims at ensuring that the market, and not the view of an individual market player, is the ultimate determinant of success.

> Free market economics and competition law are two sides of the same coin.

Increasingly, this important characteristic of the competition rules is recognized by market operators in wired sectors. The frontier mentality of those who believe that 'the Internet is another country' and should not be subject to the existing laws of society is giving way to a recognition that, just as in all other aspects of human society, a law-less society collapses into a lawless society.

Globalization and the competition rules

An increasingly common response to greater global competition is for firms to enter alliances or joint ventures in order to gain access to new markets. In fact, mergers and alliances such as Boeing and McDonnell Douglas or BA and American Airlines, which cross both borders and jurisdictions, are becoming almost commonplace. Although globalization has extremely positive effects on competition by opening markets and increasing product choice for consumers, it can also spur companies into taking action to insulate their traditional markets. Distinguishing in a global context between alliances that aim to serve new markets and those that aim to protect market positions in existing ones can be extremely difficult. Globalization also means that the negative effects of market behaviour in one jurisdiction can have far-reaching effects elsewhere.

However, while trade barriers across the globe have continued to fall, the international laws to cope with anti-trust violations have not kept pace. Cooperation between law enforcers is now an increasingly high priority. The Commission has adopted a dual approach to this.

First, and foremost, we are developing formal bilateral relations with our major trading partners. In particular, I recently signed a positive comity agreement with the

US on competition law matters, extending the 1991 agreement. This is a major step forward in our bilateral relations with the US authorities, providing as it does for competition law authority to leave investigation of a case to the other when the 'centre of gravity' of the case lies within its jurisdiction.

The 1991 agreement already allowed for close collaboration and exchange of non-confidential information in cases falling under both EU and US jurisdiction Despite occasional difficulties, the agreement has had the beneficial effect of developing mutual understanding and respect between the EU and US authorities. It has also paved the way for the recent legislation. However, while bilateral agreements will play an important part in solving problems, we do not expect them to resolve all disputes or be appropriate in all circumstances. We are therefore also pursuing a complementary approach of helping the development of a multilateral framework of competition rules – indeed, it was following an initiative from the EU that the World Trade Organization (WTO) set up its working group to look at what might be included in such a multilateral framework.

While we await the outcome of the group with interest, there is one important point to clarify. These discussions are not about creating an overarching competition authority; rather the discussions are focused much more at the level of ensuring Member Countries have appropriate rules and that they apply them correctly. Based on these rules, competition authorities would have a margin of discretion to reach their own conclusions and act accordingly.

Convergence and the competition rules

Just as globalization entails risks to competition as well as benefits, so convergence is not the free market nirvana that some appear to think. Innovation and competition can only flourish where people continue to compete on the basis of their performance, not on the basis of their position. I have seen two major threats to the present very positive situation.

First, important routes to market are often in the hands of those with market power – those with control over limited or essential resources. In most of Europe, ISPs must deal with the dominant telecoms operator either for infrastructure capacity or for customer local loop access. Where, as is often the case, the telecoms company is also a competitor to the ISP the conflict of interest is clear, as is the risk to competition. The allegations made against Microsoft and Intel would, if proven, similarly demonstrate the risks to competition inherent in the very existence of gatekeepers.

Second are what I regard as defensive alliances. Two or more companies with strong positions in their home markets ally to strengthen their position on future convergent markets. Although not necessarily unlawful, such alliances require extremely careful scrutiny. This is particularly the case where the alliance in question relates to a network industry, given the market power network externalities provide to the owner of the network.

Competition problems in the Information Society

Market power in information industries can therefore arise either via network externalities – operating systems, computing hardware configurations, communications networks – or the limitations of particular resources – local loop infrastructure, radio frequency spectrum, particular forms of content, set top boxes. Market developments, such as alliances, can have the effect of creating or limiting access to a resource or adding to the power of a particular network so as to create difficulties on that or related markets.

It is sometimes argued that the very pace of technological change prevents the concentration of market power. I find that difficult to accept as it ignores two important considerations. First, in times of rapid development, users will tend towards the relative security of the most well-established operators. Second, there is often the possibility that market concentration in one area can be used to influence technological change in other areas. The better view, which also finds support in anti-trust cases in the US, is that rapid technological change increases the risk of market concentration, rather than decreasing it. This position was put to the Commission during the discussions in relation to the Worldcom and MCI case I mentioned earlier, and is my first example.

> **Market developments, such as alliances, can have the effect of creating or limiting access to a resource or adding to the power of a particular network ...**

The merger between Worldcom and MCI was approved by the European Commission in July 1998, only after the parties had agreed to remove all overlap between their Internet-related businesses. The Internet is a network interconnecting users throughout the world. Worldcom and MCI each had a substantial number of users connected to the Internet via their networks. There was a very real risk, had this merger simply been approved, that the Internet, from being a highly competitive network of networks, would have been tipped into the control of a single company with more than half of the Internet's users.

My second example is that of a particularly difficult case in Europe, two German Pay-TV companies sought to merge to form a monopoly on the German Pay-TV market. In addition, together with Deutsche Telekom, they intended to produce a single digital set top box (allowing digital transmission signals to be viewed on analogue television sets). The set top box was proprietary, and other companies wishing to use that box would be dependent on the alliance for access. The evidence in Europe is that consumers will be reluctant to purchase a number of different set top boxes. The case raised particular problems given the proposed monopoly on the Pay-TV market. In addition, however, the combination of a monopoly on the Pay-TV market, leading to the creation of a monopoly set top box and the proprietary nature of that box would have eliminated any possibility for future competition, either in the Pay-TV market or, indeed, any other market that would be dependent on that set top box. Proposals were put to the parties that would have prevented the monopolization of the Pay-TV market, thus preventing the creation of a monopoly box. Two parties accepted them, one refused and the agreements were therefore prohibited.

In one case in the US, a preliminary injunction was awarded against Intel on the basis that it owned an essential facility in x86 processors. The court's preliminary conclusion was that the refusal to supply CPUs and information on the part of Intel could constitute a violation of the Sherman Act, 'because they are not available from alternative sources and cannot be feasibly duplicated, and because competitors cannot effectively compete in the relevant markets without access to them'.

The Federal Trade Commission has commenced a further and similar action against Intel. The benefits of interoperability contributed to the success of a particular company in a particular market, but that very success led to a risk that that company would try and leverage its position in that market into other markets. Even given that Intel may have achieved its success by producing an excellent product, it could use that success to secure a position in other markets, irrespective of the merits of its other products in those markets.

The above three examples – relating to the sectors of communications, broadcasting and computing – show the very real risks to competition that can occur in high-tech industries. The first shows the potential power of networks in themselves, and the risks to competition that would result from any one company controlling the majority of a network, especially one as important as the Internet. The second example shows both the chilling effect on markets and technical development that can be caused by monopolization and the perhaps surprising belief on the part of some companies that they can propose to monopolize a market through a merger. If the companies concerned had been prepared to leave the market open to competition, no prohibition would have been necessary. This third example shows the possible risks of leveraging market power in one field into others. This example raises similar issues to those at the centre of the litigation by the US Department of Justice against Microsoft.

Mythological beasts

The above examples show clearly that this sector is not immune to problems of dominance and monopoly leveraging. They raise a question, however, of how far the competition rules should intervene in the business activities of companies in this sector. The Worldcom and MCI case was perhaps the easiest from this point of view: eliminating an overlapping business where the parties themselves admitted there were no synergies is hardly problematic.

The Kirch and Bertelsmann case was more difficult, provoking comment in some quarters, including the usually sensible *Financial Times*, that in risky high-tech sectors such as digital TV, perhaps monopolies should be allowed in order to seed the market and encourage it to grow. It seems strange to me that essentially the same technical developments that transformed telecommunications and allowed its liberalization should be regarded by some as justifying the creation of new monopolies. Are we saying that some digital services are only financially viable if they bring together all of the potential competitors? In effect, that these services are natural monopolies? The paradox becomes all the more evident when you consider how an end could be put to these monopolies once they had been created. Are we to assume that these new monopolists will voluntarily relinquish their power at some point in the future?

A more sophisticated case against the involvement of the competition rules in these sectors has been put by Microsoft in its defence in the proceedings in the US. Microsoft argues, among other things, that a competition authority should not determine product development. I agree. Neither should a monopolist. That particular privilege should be left to the market.

If interoperability of a particular product or service is particularly important, then open, consensus-driven standardization ensures that the benefits of interoperability are achieved in a pro-competitive way. If, instead, market developments lead to a proprietary product or service becoming the *de facto* standard – which Bill Gates admits Windows is – there are significant risks to competition of that product or service being used to extend dominance into related markets. It is neither realistic nor in the public interest for competition authorities and courts to stand aside and allow a monopolist to determine the development of an entire industry.

Conclusion

In the past, the competition rules have adapted to changes in markets and market structures. In this context, the communications revolution does not require a re-appraisal of the need for the competition rules, but an informed application of those rules to the new circumstances.

Unlike the traditional Chinese curse, I regard it as a privilege to be living in interesting times. However, with privilege comes responsibility and I take that responsibility very seriously. I do not regard this responsibility as being about abstract economics or obscure points of competition law. Rather, it is about ensuring that the benefits of the communications revolution are available to all, not simply concentrated in the hands of the few. ■

I am grateful to Kevin Coates, Jonathan Denness, Olivier Guersent and Linsey McCallum for their contributions to this article.

CONTENT

---

contributors

Will Wyatt is Chief Executive, BBC Broadcast and Deputy Director General of the BBC. Before the BBC's restructuring in June 1996, he was Managing Director, Network Television, a post he took up on 29 April 1991, in succession to Sir Paul Fox. At the same time, he joined the Board of BBC Enterprises (now BBC Worldwide). Wyatt was previously Assistant Managing Director, a job he had held since December 1988.

Wyatt became Head of Presentation Programmes in 1977, Head of Documentary Features in January 1981, then Head of Features and Documentaries Group, Television in 1987, responsible for such programmes as *40 Minutes, Crimewatch, Around The World in 80 Days, Children In Need*, BBC-1 single documentaries, *Rough Justice, Comrades, The Duty Men, Holiday, An Ocean Apart*, and *Out Of The Doll's House*.

He is a Director of the Broadcasting Audience Research Board and BBC Subscription TV, and also a Governor of the London Institute. His book *The Man Who Was B. Traven* was published in 1980.

David Puttnam CBE, Chief Executive, Enigma Productions, is the Oscar-winning producer of *Chariots of Fire, The Killing Fields, Midnight Express, Local Hero*, and *The Mission*. He was Chairman of Columbia Pictures from 1986 to 1988 and now works principally in the field of education, serving as an adviser to a number of UK government departments; as Chancellor of the University of Sunderland; as a governor and a lecturer at the London School of Economics. In 1995 he received a knighthood for his services to the British Film Industry and in August 1997 he was appointed to the House of Lords. His book *The Undeclared War* was published in the UK by HarperCollins in 1997.

Simon Murison-Bowie, Director of Oxford Interactive Learning, Oxford University Press, has been involved in electronic publishing from the very start, responsible for setting up video and software publishing at Oxford University Press. Over a long career in publishing, he has been involved in curriculum development, and in textbook commissioning and writing. He has worked and lectured in Europe, the Middle East, Eastern Africa and North and South America. His current efforts are focused on the opportunities which arise from the convergence of the need for lifelong learning with the emergence of technology which permits the effective delivery of distance learning in new ways.

Roberto Minio, MA M.Sc. (Oxon) is Head of Publishing and New Media Group, Pira International. With a background in computing and publishing, Roberto Minio has been involved in the development of electronic and new media publishing since the early 1980s at Carnegie-Mellon University in the US, at Springer-Verlag and the German National Computing Research Centre (GMD-IPSI) in Germany and at Pira International in the UK.

Roberto Minio has consulted and presented widely on the impact and opportunities of technological developments for the content industries. He has advised the European Commission on the development of the research agendas for the fourth and fifth Framework Programmmes. He heads up the Publishing and New Media Group at Pira International and is Research Manager for the International Electronic Publishing Research Centre. Currently Roberto is also managing the 'Wired World' Project at Templeton College, Oxford.

Hugh Brett is a consultant with the London firm of specialist solicitors Llewelyn Zietman. He was the founder in 1981 and senior partner of the specialist intellectual property practice Dallas Brett in Oxford. He has written extensively on intellectual property issues and has lectured widely in the UK and abroad. In 1977 he founded the *European Intellectual Property Review* which he continues to edit and is a member of the Intellectual Property Section of the British Computer Society. He sits on the Intellectual Property Committee of the Law Society and has been a member of the Copyright Tribunal. In 1977 he was appointed a Professorial Fellow in the Centre for Commercial Law at Queen Mary & Westfield College.

by Anne Leer

HAVE BANDWIDTH, NEED CONTENT

The Global Information Infrastructure (GII) is worthless without people and content – technology alone is dead. Yet so much focus and so much investment have been made in technology itself without enough thought about what we want to use technology for and how. Defenders of the many rather mindless IT investments around the world will claim it is a chicken and egg problem. They will defend their technology-oriented strategy and explain they need the infrastructure in place before they can move on to think about content and GII applications. I fear many organizations are in for a very expensive lesson. Perhaps their investments would have been more successful if more effort had been spent on understanding what is required to make the technology work.

During 1997 there was a growing realization in both political and commercial camps that once the GII was in place we would have a great infrastructure with virtually unlimited bandwidth, but then so what? What would we fill it with? Where would all the wonderful content come from which would make the GII come alive? And suddenly we got an urgent focus on the so-called 'content industries' and the content race was on to secure high-value branded content for the pipes.

The terms 'content' and 'content providers' were invented by the telecommunication industry as labels for all of that stuff and all of those businesses that they really didn't understand but had to embrace. Because it is in 'content' that many of the telcos see future growth and salvation from market saturation of telephony services. The old telcos are sitting on that entire infrastructure, owning all that bandwidth, reading the forecasts of vanishing revenues in voice telephony and equipment. The only way forward is to move up the value curve, to get into value-added services and new kinds of infrastructure traffic. In other words get into 'content' and we see all kinds of mergers and partnerships between telecommunication, software and media companies. I believe this is the beginning of the real process of convergence.

We have devoted this section to discussing content – the lifeblood of the GII. We will meet representatives of some of the best 'content providers' in the world, although they would prefer to be referred to as broadcasters, filmmakers and publishers. We will learn how the BBC is responding to the Digital Age and Will Wyatt will describe how the public service role of the BBC is challenged in the new environment. We will visit Lord Puttnam, the accomplished filmmaker, and share his reflections and perspectives about the evolving Wired World. We will also pay a visit to the world's largest educational and academic publishing house, Oxford University Press, which has grown from humble beginnings in thirteenth-century Oxford to a multinational company with offices in 62 countries. Simon Murison-Bowie will give an insight into the effective use of technology from an educational publisher's point of view. We will then move on to Roberto Minio, a senior expert on publishing and electronic media, who will explain the fundamental shifts taking place in the publishing industry and how new business models are shaping up in the market. Finally, Hugh Brett, an experienced intellectual property lawyer, will discuss critical copyright issues related to content in a digital environment.

The BBC has decided to embrace the Digital Age and be available on all media platforms. Will Wyatt is confident about the future of the BBC and its ability to adapt to new media. He says the main dilemma is that the BBC's creative aspirations outstrip the ability to fund them all.

The BBC has grown from providing two channels to 14 channels over a period of six years. Much of this expansion is made possible through strategic partnerships with commercial players. Wyatt believes it is essential to maintain the division between BBC's public service broadcasting activities funded by the licence fee and the commercial activities carried out by BBC Worldwide. He also believes the licence fee provides the best possible funding model. He argues that all other funding models have the fundamental flaw of taking major benefit away from the public in order to make them pay more to have it returned. The licence fee model has been under much scrutiny and constant debate, and that will continue as long as an organization like the BBC is entitled to collect over £2 billion a year to fund its service.

Lord Puttnam is right when he says the heart of this revolution is not about technology at all, but about the proliferation of information and content. Technology is merely a bridge, not a destination. He points out the most fundamental question is who will create, distribute and own this content? He argues that there are enormous economic, cultural and political stakes at risk. There is plenty of evidence that the intellectual property industries represent a massive and growing share of the economy. However, Puttnam questions how the European economy can grow when there is a $6.8 billion trade imbalance of payments in the filmed entertainment sector alone, between the US and Europe. The US leadership and dominance in the content industries as well as in respect to GII and Internet are beyond dispute. Puttnam warns us that the development of the Information Society and the potential dominance of the US could become one of the cultural time bombs of the twenty-first century. He reminds us that film, television, books, music and images shape attitudes and behaviour and have the power to reinforce or undermine the values of society. What kind of content will the world's people be flooded with once the convergence of media and technolgy is a reality? Will the content be relevant to individual circumstance and cultural context?

Simon Murison-Bowie's concern is to create and deliver meaningful and effective educational content in a networked environment. He quickly dismisses the idea of pumping 'content' into the GII and have people connect to be filled up with all kinds of information that supposedly would make them more employable and knowledgeable. He says the idea of a learner as a receptacle into which information is poured is one that educators have long argued against. The great opportunities with the Internet is the interaction made possible between learners, tutors and resources and the scope for customizing the delivery of learning materials to meet individual needs. Murison-Bowie has found that this creates complex challenges for both publishers and educators. He says what is needed is good models to help us understand and organize both the educational process and the publishing process. In his chapter he describes how Oxford University Press has gone about creating one such model.

Traditional publishers, like the incumbent telecommunication operators, are faced with a massive pressure to change and reinvent the old ways of doing their business. Roberto Minio sums this process up in his chapter in terms of publishers having to learn how to extend their business from Bibles to new Buyables. He means that publishing today is about much more than putting nice tangible objects like books and videos and magazines into the market. It's about managing and packaging assets and digital content stores. It is about understanding and managing new entrants and shifts in the value chain. It's about new and much more complex business models. It is also about a very fast-changing competitive environment in which you may have to learn how to collaborate with your main competitors if you want to survive.

Hugh Brett gives us a crash course on copyright law and he explains how copyright law has evolved since its birth in the UK in 1709. He argues that the notion of copyright is more valid than ever and that copyright law has successfully embraced the new media forms created by digital technology. Brett points out that the latest copyright legislation is a very strong legal basis for copyright protection of content in digital form. He argues that there is a unresolved conflict between governments' desire to have free availability and access to information, and the commitment that the same governments have made to the continued protection of intellectual property rights. He also urges rights owners and publishers to pay close attention to market demands regardless of the legal rights they have and are entitled to exercise.

The rich spectrum of opinion in this section brings some overriding points to the surface: the vital importance of high-quality and engaging content, the need to encourage investment in and creative exploitation of our intellectual capital and cultural resources, the necessity of coming up with policies and regulation which underpin the values and standards we want to have for content in the Wired World. ∎

Will Wyatt

Chief Executive, BBC Broadcast

THE BBC IN A DIGITAL WORLD

The arrival of the Digital Age is not a threat but a challenge to the BBC. It is a rich opportunity that we have quickly seized to show the vitality of the BBC's public purpose. The enthusiastic response to the digital challenge by programme makers, technologists and resource providers has enabled the BBC to continue to be a broadcasting pioneer, as it was with the first television service in 1936 and the first British colour television service in 1967.

The BBC, unshackled by shareholder and market restraints, has been more alert than other broadcasters to the potential of the Digital Age. We were determined to be there at the start in order to ensure all licence payers would have the opportunity to enjoy the full benefits of the new technology. We will be available on all platforms because universality is the central feature of public service broadcasting. In 1998, the BBC launched more new television services than in the previous 75 years of our history. Now we also offer our free-to-air digital service to the licence payer, which includes widescreen BBC1 and BBC2, BBC Choice, News 24 and BBC Parliament. BBC Learning will be launched in 1999 as the UK's first dedicated public service learning channel, while BBC Digital Radio already reaches 60 per cent of the UK population.

The arrival of the Digital Age is not a threat but a challenge to the BBC.

Today's transition from analogue to digital broadcasting means the arrival of a new world for broadcasters. It marks a sea change greater than anything – probably even the advent of television itself – that we have witnessed before. Digital means more channels, more convenience, the promise of personalization as well as more competition, market fragmentation and complex regulatory questions. How many years will it be before analogue-only broadcasters will be seen as anachronistic to audiences as black and white TV channels would look today?

Ten milestones in the BBC's history

18 October 1922	British Broadcasting Company formed (established as the British Broadcasting Corporation 1 January 1927)	20 April 1964	BBC2 began
		30 September 1967	Radio 1 began and the Home Service, Third Programme and Light Programme became Radios 4, 3 and 2
13 August 1927	First BBC Prom from Queen's Hall		
		23 September 1974	Regular CEEFAX service began
2 November 1936	First BBC Television service began	11 November 1997	BBC News 24 launched
2 June 1953	Coronation of Queen Elizabeth II – first State occasion to be televised	23 September 1998	BBC Choice launched on digital terrestrial and digital satellite
24 September 1957	BBC Television for Schools began		

The inevitable question for the BBC is how can public service broadcasting flourish in the digital environment? Perhaps the last time a comparable question was asked was in the 1950s when the end of the BBC's monopoly transformed the broadcasting land-scape. Back in 1955, ITV's arrival soon took 70 per cent of the TV audience from the BBC. Lord Reith assumed that his Cassandra-like warnings about competition had been fulfilled. He had compared the breaking of the BBC's broadcasting monopoly to the arrival of smallpox, the Black Death and, for impenetrable reasons, greyhound racing.

However, Lord Reith's pessimism was unjustified. The BBC swiftly found its own competitive and creative instincts. Today, with spectrum scarcity replaced by spec-trum abundance, the BBC is facing much stiffer competition, but is thriving in the increasingly competitive marketplace. Despite the unparalleled number of rivals, the BBC currently has 45 per cent of the public's viewing and listening with only 30 per cent of the revenues in the British broadcasting market.

Our aim is to ensure that, in the Digital Age, the BBC continues to be the most watched and heard broadcaster in the UK, providing distinctive and inventive pro-grammes that satisfy all licence payers. The BBC's main dilemma is that its creative aspirations outstrip its capacity to fund them all. As it would be wrong to strip any of our core analogue services in order to benefit digital, we are forced to look for effi-ciencies elsewhere and argue persuasively for a licence fee increase.

A properly funded BBC is still the best guarantee of a vibrant and original broadcast-ing sector in the UK. A healthy BBC, providing distinctive channels and services across all platforms, is essential for a creative domestic broadcasting market. So long as the BBC focuses on serving its varied audiences – and provides a haven for creative talent with its unique portfolio of programme-making skills – then I believe public service broadcasting will survive all the challenges thrown at it by any competition in the digital future.

The licence fee guarantees the breadth of quality programming that appeals to the enormously varied interests and enthusiasms of our audiences. I accept that, in many ways, it is an oddity. It has been investigated, scrutinized and dissected on countless occasions, but all the scrutineers have – sometimes to their bitter disappointment – concluded that it remains the best and most efficient way to fund an independent public service broadcasting organization. No doubt there will be more debates about the funding of the BBC in a multi-channel world and there will be yet more convoluted arguments for subscription, encoding, pay-per-view offerings and government subsidies. However, none of these would be able to rival the unique relationship with audiences that the licence fee ensures. All these alternative options share the fundamental flaw of taking a major benefit away from the public in order to make them pay more to have it returned.

The mixed economy of British broadcasting has created a success story that is widely envied. The pace of change in broadcasting makes it impossible to predict the precise shape of the industry in 15 years' time, but I am convinced that there will still be a very strong case for the licence fee and the BBC is as determined as ever to demonstrate its value. If a future generation did manage to un-invent the BBC, no other generation would be able to re-invent it. This successful combination of political will, public policy and a simple funding mechanism would be beyond the reach of any future generation's ability to recreate it.

There is no reason for the values and principles of public service broadcasting not to flourish in the digital era.

Hypothetically, the BBC could be a very successful commercial business, but there would be enormous tradeoffs that would mean neglecting many sections of the population. There is no reason for the values and principles of public service broadcasting not to flourish in the digital era. Indeed, the opposite is true – the technology enables us to deliver new, exciting services to our immensely varied audiences. The digital potential strengthens the value of the licence fee because we will provide appropriate programmes that many of the subscription and commercial channels will be increasingly unwilling to offer.

For example, BBC Learning will support and encourage hands-on learning for children and students. It will also motivate adults to acquire new skills for work and encourage the wider audience to develop their personal interests at times that suit them. BBC Learning will actively encourage audiences to move confidently between TV – the interactivity made available by means of the set top box – and linked material in print and on-line. BBC Choice, launched in September 1998, is a highly innovative channel that imaginatively complements BBC1 and BBC2's schedules.

The BBC's public service remit means that in the future, as today, we must provide value for money for all licence payers. Unlike other broadcasters, the BBC cannot and does not want to pick and choose its viewers and listeners. It is not for us to single out groups of premium customers for special attention or identify market segments to be especially served at the expense of others – we must serve all. That is why we have recently invested great effort and time in undertaking highly sophisticated analyses of the make-up of our different audiences to ensure that we have an accurate picture of the many faces of Britain.

This has been invaluable in seeing clearly how people use broadcasting today, understanding their changing needs and future expectations from the BBC, revealing which groups are served well and which served less well. This bank of data enables us to fill gaps in our programming, position our radio and TV services more clearly and accurately in the new broadcasting world and implement new commissioning and programme strategies to surprise and delight audiences and retain their loyalty. A better understanding of audience needs was essential because the first lesson to be derived from the exponential growth in the number of channels and networks is that there has been a change in the balance of power. The audience, armed with the zapper, the grazer's weapon, is able to wrest power from the traditional duumvirate of the producer and programme supplier.

However, those who believe that the digital revolution will happen overnight need to pepper their optimism with some caution. There will still be a substantial minority of viewers left behind by all this technological excitement. There are models that suggest in ten years' time 25 per cent of the population will still have analogue sets and aerials and they will still be getting four or possibly five channels from the same television receiver they have now. The BBC has to make sure that those who cannot afford, or are disinclined, to become wired up are not neglected.

It is against this background of major change that the BBC's own reorganization should be viewed, from the introduction of Producer Choice to the separation of the Broadcast and Production functions. The two are linked because the BBC needed a new coordinated and focused structure, covering television, radio and multimedia, that would be appropriate for the fast-moving Digital Age. The separation of commissioning in Broadcast from the programme-making area of Production means that the BBC can focus, now and in the future, on a strategy to serve all its audiences via its services and programme genres. This unified scheduling structure for radio and television also enables the BBC to create a succession of pan-BBC projects with a strong national appeal.

Over the last five years, with satellite and cable, the BBC has increased the number of TV channels we supply from two to ten. With the arrival of digital, in 1999, there will be 14 BBC channels. In addition, there is the expanding Internet, the third broadcast medium. BBC Online has proved to be an instant success among the rapidly growing number of people with access to the Internet. It is estimated that BBC Online is the largest media-based web site in the UK and new sites are being developed all the time. A public consultation that has been held about BBC Online will help to determine the strategy for its future growth. We are working hard to ensure that people are not left out of the new information society and committed to preventing the growth of an 'information-poor' class in our society. The BBC will have an important role as a 'trusted guide' to help licence payers with digital media to navigate their way through the confusing world of on-demand services in the future. This will be an extension of the trusted role the BBC has established today in news, documentary and consumer affairs, and BBC Online will have a crucial role in providing this guidance.

The increasing globalization of broadcasting is shrinking the world and eroding frontiers. Today it is impossible to think of the BBC solely in terms of being a UK broadcaster. Thanks to the achievements of the World Service, we have for many decades been the world's most successful international radio broadcaster. The BBC has now emerged as one of the few leading global broadcasters in all media. The international challenge over the next decade for the BBC is to be the world's first choice for authoritative and impartial television news and to offer a showcase for British talent in markets across the world. This will simultaneously benefit the UK and bring revenues to the BBC that will be reinvested in core public services for the benefit of licence payers. It will also strengthen the BBC brand across the world.

The template for the BBC's global strategy is the ambitious new partnership with Discovery Communications. This enables the BBC to exploit its programme-making expertise and rich archive, while Discovery provides the start-up funding to launch various channels across the world. Recent channel launches in Latin America and the US under this arrangement point the way to future developments. The partnership with Flextech to develop subscription channels in the UK has a similar shape, with the BBC holding editorial control of the channels and ploughing profit back into licence fee-funded services, and Flextech financing the development and operating costs. We are ensuring that these pioneering new channels offer the same high standards to audiences as the BBC's core broadcasting services. This shows that our public service values are as relevant in the digital world as they are in the analogue environment.

The division between the BBC as a public service broadcaster funded by the licence fee and its commercial activities brought together within BBC Worldwide will continue to be crucial. The BBC has very tight fair trading rules and protocols because it is essential to demonstrate to our competitors – and to our own Board of Governors – that we do not, and will not, subsidize the BBC's commercial activities from the publicly funded ones. Commercial activities will never be allowed to be a drain on the licence fee. Naturally, we accept that it would be unjustifiable to support commercial enterprises competing with other broadcasters' commercial activities that do not have the benefit of public funding. Our commercial strategy will continue to be based on partnership because the BBC does not have the resources to fund long-term capital investment on its own.

> During its long history, the BBC has pioneered major changes in broadcasting – in technology as much as in creative programming.

During its long history, the BBC has pioneered major changes in broadcasting – in technology as much as in creative programming. We are glad and proud to be pioneers in the digital adventure. Our job is to take the values, purposes and standards of public services broadcasting from the analogue to the digital world – to guarantee there is the range and depth, the independence and innovation, the intensity and delight that broadcasting is capable of.

Conclusion

In the past, the competition rules have adapted to changes in markets and market structures. In this context, the communications revolution does not require a reappraisal of the need for the competition rules, but an informed application of those rules to the new circumstances.

Unlike the traditional Chinese curse, I regard it as a privilege to be living in interesting times. However, with privilege comes responsibility and I take that responsibility very seriously. I do not regard this responsibility as being about abstract economics or obscure points of competition law. Rather, it is about ensuring that the benefits of the communications revolution are available to all, not simply concentrated in the hands of the few. ■

Key facts

- The BBC is a public corporation, set up by Royal Charter to provide broadcasting services at home and abroad.

- The BBC receives £2 billion in income from the licence fee – there are over 21 million TV licences in force in the UK.

- The television licence fee pays for national television networks BBC 1 and BBC 2; national radio stations – Radios 1, 2, 3, 4 and 5 Live; national radio services in Northern Ireland, Scotland and Wales – including services in Welsh and Gaelic languages; and 38 English local radio services.

- BBC Worldwide – the BBC's commercial arm – generates £75 million a year for the BBC, which is ploughed into programmes and services for licence payers.

- BBC News has 42 overseas bureaux and over 200 specialist correspondents worldwide and employs around 2300 people producing output for 12 BBC channels and services.

- Of UK teachers, 88 per cent use BBC television programmes in the classroom, while 64 per cent use the BBC's radio cassettes.

- The BBC launched News 24, a 24-hour news channel for UK digital platforms, in November 1997.

- BBC Choice, the BBC's first new entertainment channel for 34 years, was launched on digital platforms in September 1998.

- The BBC World Service – the international radio service funded by Government Grant-In-Aid – broadcasts to 144 million regular listeners a week in 45 languages, including English.

- BBC Online is the number one UK Internet content site with 21 million page impressions per month.

Lord Puttnam CBE

Chief Executive, Enigma Productions

FILLING UP THE PIPELINES

In 1964, a hitherto obscure professor of English literature, working in Canada, published what will surely come to be seen as one of the most visionary books of the century. The professor's name was Herbert Marshall McLuhan, and the book was *Understanding Media: The Extensions of Man* (Massachusetts Institute of Technology, 1994). It was the book that first introduced phrases such as the 'global village', the 'Age of Information' and, most famously of all, 'The Medium is the Message'.

It's a truly remarkable book. Long before the creation of the Internet, long before the computer had become an essential part of everyday life, McLuhan perceptively sensed where our society was heading, anticipating the advent of the 'Wired World'.

As McLuhan put it in his book: 'Marketing and consumption tend to become one with learning, enlightenment and the intake of information. The electronic age is literally one of illumination.'

Now, 35 years later, McLuhan's vision is finally being fulfilled, and fulfilled in ways that all of us can bear witness to in our daily lives. The convergence of the printed word and the technologies of television, computers and the Internet is now rapidly blurring many of the distinctions we have traditionally taken for granted, such as those between 'printed' and 'electronic' information.

It's not just books and the printed word that are being affected by this extraordinary transformation. The whole process of physical interaction has ceased to be a necessity in order to trade in many, many types of goods and services – from buying the weekly groceries to investing in stocks and shares – and it's clear that an ever-increasing amount of our trade and commerce is, and will be, conducted electronically. By way of an example, the Chief Executive of the Internet unit at the US phone service Worldcom estimates that, in the US, traditional voice calls will represent just 1 per cent of total telecoms traffic by 2003.

And these new technologies are developing at a quite breathtaking pace. For example, the volume of traffic on the Internet doubles every hundred days – equivalent to a ten-fold increase every year (US Department of Commerce, The Emerging Digital Economy, speech by William M. Daley, US Secretary of Commerce, 15 April 1998). It took radio almost 40 years to get to the point where it had 50 million users; it took television only 13 years to acquire that same 50 million audience. However, it took just four years for the Internet to grow from an obscure network used by a few universities to the point at which it had 50 million users.

As a result, a new global economy is emerging that is fundamentally driven by two things – information and images. And these in themselves are increasingly intertwined, as ever-increasing levels of information are conveyed by means of images and, in particular, moving images. As Marshall McLuhan eloquently put it in his book, in the new Age of Information, 'commodities come to possess more and more the character of information'.

It's essential to remember that, at heart, this revolution is not fundamentally a technological revolution at all – technology is simply what makes the revolution possible, and, as such, it's a bridge, not a destination.

The real revolution is in the proliferation of information or, to use that rather ugly term, 'content'. The inescapable question that looms over all these developments – the absolutely fundamental question – is quite simply who will create, distribute and own this content? The economic, cultural and political stakes in all of this are enormous.

A glance at today's film and television industry is surely sufficient confirmation. As a result of Hollywood's dominance of the global film industry and its huge influence over much of the world's television, it's now fairly commonplace to assert that the audiovisual industry is, after aerospace, America's greatest export. In fact, it would probably be more accurate to acknowledge that the number one position is now occupied by the 'intellectual property industry', of which films, television programming and software represent a massive and still-growing share.

> ... technology is simply what makes the revolution possible, and, as such, it's a bridge, not a destination.

The effects of all of this in terms of the filmed entertainment sector alone are all too tangible. The imbalance of payments between Europe and the US is now running at around $6.8 billion a year. At present rates of growth, this will, in very short order, undoubtedly cross the $10 billion mark. From a European point of view, at some point these numbers become simply unsustainable. We cannot grow a European economy, create European jobs and a European future while dealing with these levels of trade imbalance. The whole point of world trade is to create some form of visible equilibrium, or at least to have that as your long-term objective.

It's when the implications of all this are considered in broader terms that it becomes even more alarming. For, in truth, what has become increasingly evident over the last 20 years or so is that movies are no longer just about what's playing at the local multiplex next Saturday night. Their impact is much, much more than that. Today's movies are really 'brand names'. Every single film put out by the Hollywood studios is, in a way, its own brand, which, when successful, becomes a locomotive dragging behind it many, many other sectors of the economy – everything from fashion to fast food chains, books and video games. An entire panoply of products and services latch on to the back of a successful movie, to the extent that with *Titanic* having already generated over a billion dollars around the globe from box office sales outside of North America – never mind video and television – it will probably generate several billion more on the back of the other commercial activities drawn along in its wake.

And now, new, hybrid sectors of the audio-visual industry contain a potential for growth that already makes them more important than the traditional feature film industry. In 1997, spending on interactive entertainment software in Western Europe reached $4.5 billion, for the first time overtaking spending on both the cinema box offices and total spending on purchasing videos (*Screen Digest*, July 1998).

Yet this market remains dominated by games, and more sophisticated forms of narrative entertainment have yet to emerge. For the moment, most of the on-line services that have made money have been business applications – book and record shops, sales of airline tickets. However, the products themselves are still delivered to consumers by old-fashioned mail – we are still some way off from the situation in which moving images, records and books are distributed as bytes in the so-called 'weightless economy'.

Despite vast amounts of hype, some new platforms, such as CD-ROMs and CD-I have failed to live up to expectations, and sales of these products have plummeted. Even if it's something of a truism, the lesson is clear – no matter how sophisticated the technology, unless the software really engages the consumer, there is no chance of the platform developing into a mass-market form.

In the twenty-first century, such intellectual property will increasingly be disseminated by electronic means – whether via a computer, television set or, more likely, a combination of the two. It is probable that our entire conception of what we mean by 'content' and, more broadly, 'culture', will start to change in a world where such convergence is a reality. The history of cinema offers an illuminating parallel. A hundred years ago, who would have dreamed that the 'Kinematograph' – that ghostly medium of moving images, then barely two years old – would become widely acknowledged as one of the most influential cultural forms of the twentieth century? Indeed, when one of the medium's founding fathers Louis Lumière hired Felix Mesguich as his first cameraman, he warned him, 'You know, Mesguich, we're not offering a job with much in the way of prospects, it's more of a fairground job; it may last six months, a year, perhaps more, probably less.' (For a more detailed discussion of the origins of cinema and its rapid growth, see David Puttnam, *The Undeclared War,*

HarperCollins, 1997.) Likewise, many of the self-appointed custodians of traditional culture dismissed cinema as mere novelty for the great unwashed masses – one more craze that would quickly burn itself out amid the gloomy city slums where it had most firmly taken root.

In Europe, the development of film was, for the most part, left in the hands of scientists, inventors and magicians. In those early days, cinema was principally seen either as a scientific tool or a device for producing mind-boggling visual tricks – the forerunner of today's special effects movies. In fact, it took quite a long time for cinema to realize its potential as a wholly distinct form of art and entertainment.

As it turned out, Lumière was fairly accurate about Mesguich's personal job prospects, but spectacularly wrong about cinema itself. It was public appetite that helped show the way forward. They soon grew tired of novelty films, of the seemingly endless stream of dancing bears, boxing kangaroos and exploding policeman that passed for entertainment. They wanted stories – bigger and better stories. They flocked to the first thrillers – most notably *The Great Train Robbery* made by Edwin Porter in 1903. If you look at it today, it comes across as a crude attempt to film a relatively mediocre play in 12 minutes, but had enormous impact at the time it was first screened. Just over 25 years later, the release of *The Jazz Singer* marked the advent of sound in the form of feature-length 'talkies' and film took an enormous leap in a new direction. Then, 50 years after *The Jazz Singer*, came *Close Encounters of the Third Kind*, and cinema again took another huge leap forward. So, there's a 75-year gap between *The Great Train Robbery*, an utterly crude product, to the very sophisticated, *Close Encounters*.

What we're looking at at the moment, in terms of the new technologies, is akin to *The Great Train Robbery*: crude, book-based and relatively predictable. However, once the real potential of a technology has been demonstrated, there is no going back. *The Great Train Robbery* beckoned to the imagination of filmmakers of the likes of D.W. Griffith, who, by a process of creative alchemy, were able to build on Porter's basic ideas and turn them into a very sophisticated way of telling stories using moving images. What we are waiting for are the latter-day equivalents of Griffith who will have the energy, confidence and talent to carry the technology forward.

However, far and away the most significant development of this new 'wired world' is the increasing convergence between entertainment and education. The entertainment industry has established itself as the most effective and efficient means of addressing people, ever created – particularly young people. If the skills involved in creating that entertainment are brought to bear on a new area, such as education, the opportunity exists to be phenomenally effective. Equally, looked at from another perspective, all of us know that education is, in every respect, a fast-growing global business. Together with training, it accounts for about 15 per cent of the EU's total GDP – the figure rising every year. The demand for education in the developing countries is also increasing at an exponential rate. The United Nations Development Agency anticipates that, in the next 30 years, as many people will be seeking formal educational qualifications as have done since the dawn of mankind.

It now seems likely that moving images will assume an increasingly central role in educational systems throughout Europe; and as information technology becomes more and more essential to the functioning of our education system, the need for fresh programming and support materials is going to grow, and at a prodigious rate.

All of this should only serve to remind us that the best infrastructure in the world is pretty well worthless without the most valuable resource of all – well-trained and highly motivated teachers. We must recognize the need to give our teachers the necessary training, not just to understand and use these new tools, but the confidence to see them as exactly that – really valuable tools. This is especially important when the role of the teacher is itself changing so rapidly. For, as the National Council for Educational Technology has put it, our teachers are inevitably moving from being the deliverers of knowledge to the managers of learning. This gives teachers right across the educational system – in schools, universities, furthur education colleges, wherever – new and even more significant responsibilities as guides for the future. They are explorers helping our children feel their way into an untested but potentially information-rich and information-accessible world.

The average teacher comes into contact with about 15,000 young people during the course of a 40-year career. It's virtually impossible to think of any other large group of people with anything like that level of influence. As Henry Adams once put it, 'A teacher affects eternity; he can never tell where his influence stops.' However, to return to the future, if the opportunities created by the explosion in demand for software are huge, so too are the dangers.

> ... teachers are inevitably moving from being the deliverers of knowledge to the managers of learning.

It's some years now since the American Vice President Al Gore's pessimistic warning of a society divided between information 'haves' and 'have nots', but his warning remains just as valid, just as pertinent today – in fact, perhaps more so. We've got to ensure that the gap between the haves and the have nots does not come to simply mirror existing economic and social inequalities. In education, for example, there's already more than sufficient evidence that children with computers at home do rather better when in the classroom than those who do not have such facilities. In the US, there are already signs that a gap is opening up. Only 14 per cent of pupils from poor households have access to computers at home, compared to 82 per cent of students from more affluent backgrounds. (Children's Partnership, *Where We Stand*, May 1996).

It's vital to ensure that all children, everywhere, have an opportunity to share in the advantages of this wired world of the future. We have a fundamental obligation to give them the skills and confidence they need to use the learning tools of today and tomorrow, and use them effectively throughout their entire lives.

There are other dangers, too. Films, television and, increasingly, the images and ideas transmitted across the Internet, shape attitudes, create conventions of style and behaviour; they reinforce or undermine the wider values of society. It is inconceivable that we should pretend that film and television do not have a significant impact on our lives. Stories and images are among the principal means by which human society has always transmitted its values and beliefs, from generation to generation and community to community. The sheer responsibility of making films is awesome – you really are tinkering around in people's minds and imprinting images, messages, thoughts that may well remain for life. To me, unquestionably the best form of regulation is to nurture a far better informed generation of filmmakers – people who really understand what the medium is all about, what its challenge and its potential could be. Unfortunately, all too often, when their power is called into question, filmmakers go into a form of emotional and ethical denial.

The only protection that individuals have against all of this is an instinctive awareness of the degree to which they can be manipulated and a knowledge of the techniques that can be used.

The very real problems that we in the liberal democracies of the West are experiencing in regulating the Internet demonstrate just how difficult it is to control the way in which information is disseminated by these new technologies. However, as we move towards the possibility of a more genuinely plural democracy, increasingly informed by moving images rather than text, we have to ask ourselves how we create a cultivated and sophisticated electorate, one that has the capacity to understand these things.

You can sit almost anywhere in the world with a large or small group of people and arrive quite quickly at a consensus set of values, and yet few of those values are regularly represented in today's mainstream cinema – most especially in much of Hollywood's output. In fact, quite the opposite – they are challenged and questioned, and to a far greater degree than they are in real life. In these circumstances, it should be a matter of concern that America's extraordinary dominance in the field of films, television and the moving image goes on intensifying. This concern is only heightened by the fact that they're already so far ahead of us in terms of Internet-based entertainment and information.

The development of the Information Society and the potential domination of the United States, raises the very real prospect of a fundamental dislocation between the world of the imagination, created and stimulated by the moving image, and the everyday lives of people around the globe. We have no idea what the consequences of such a dislocation might be, for it is genuinely without any form of social precedent. However, it is surely no exaggeration to say that it has the potential to be one of the cultural time-bombs of the twenty-first century. The liberating and democratizing possibilities of new technologies must be realized so that we all have greater access to accurate information, and perhaps a more direct say in the way our communities and countries are run.

In January 1998, at the World Economic Forum in Davos, Hillary Rodham Clinton proclaimed that 'American culture is America's biggest export', citing the examples of fashion, music and movies. Surely that's a challenge the rest of the world – particularly the nations of Western Europe – should be rising to, rather than bowing down before. It would be tragic if that meant building a fortress to protect ourselves from America. We have, in the European Union, the largest market in the developed world, intellectual and technical resources of enormous depth and a cultural inheritance of almost incalculable richness. Surely we should be developing strategies that will encourage the intelligent exploitation of these vast assets, both for our own benefit and for the benefit of the world as a whole. In the UK, there is clearly massive potential in our creative industries – film, music, fashion, publishing and so on – that already have a turnover of around £55 billion a year and are growing at twice the pace of the rest of the economy. This has absolutely nothing to do with the media-inspired myth of 'Cool Britannia' – it's simply a recent fact of economic life. Companies based on knowledge, creativity and services are taking over as engines of national output from the more traditional, product-based economy. So, what we need to do now is invest capital in our workforce, in building up companies seriously capable of challenging the titans of the American entertainment business, as well as companies such as Microsoft and Netscape that currently appear to have such an iron grip on new and on-line media. The task is all the more urgent when you consider that, over the last 18 months, Microsoft has invested the equivalent of the French Canal+'s earnings in TV-related activities.

> **It would be tragic if that meant building a fortress to protect ourselves from America.**

Politicians and businesspeople across Europe seem to have genuinely taken on board the idea of a 'creative economy' and all that flows from it; they have finally woken up to the fact that there will never be a return to the days when the world of work conjured up visions of 10,000 men, and a few women, marching through the factory gates each morning. More and more, it's accepted that our future lies in being a 'brain-based' society, not a 'metal-bashing' one.

There's absolutely no reason we in Europe can't use publishing, film, music and the other creative industries in exactly the same way as the Americans have used their movie industry – both as sources of cultural and economic value in their own right and as so many elements of a powerful locomotive, pulling or promoting exports of all kinds around the world.

We in Europe have to start considering how we use the creative skills we appear to have in such extraordinary abundance to optimize their economic value in such a way as to at last free up their cultural and, in some cases, even spiritual value to allow our creative genius to move from being merely funded and tolerated to a point at which it achieves genuine economic freedom and success. Only then can we project a confident and forward-looking image, an image that is a true reflection of the creative richness of a thoroughly modern group of trading nations.

That is the real challenge facing us as we enter the twenty-first century and the era of a genuinely Creative Economy. ■

Simon Murison-Bowie

Director, Oxford Interactive Learning
Oxford University Press

FORMS AND FUNCTIONS OF DIGITAL CONTENT IN EDUCATION

Assume that the local, national, global grid for learning/knowledge exists, is installed in a variety of effective ways, customized to the learning needs and technological environments of the populations they serve. Imagine managed services in place, every piece of the machinery running smoothly, or at least with an identifiable and proficient fixer who will actually fix rather than suggest an upgrade. Pretend that every learner and – more problematical this – every teacher feels comfortable with this networked world and is a happy citizen anxious to be a good, lifelong learner. What then?

These scenarios all paint pictures of plugging the 'content' into these networks that is going to promote the necessary learning. Pump enough 'content' into the grid and our good citizens can connect and fill themselves with the next bits of information that will increase their employability, self-esteem and the number of training certificates on the walls of their teleworking environment.

But of course it isn't like that.

This chapter sets out to explore why it is necessary to think most carefully beyond the network infrastructure; in fact, if it were not already too late, the infrastructure should follow on from the definitions and analyses of how digital technologies can impact upon the processes of education. The plurals in the previous sentence are not an accident; they are there to emphasize that we are not seeking one solution, one set of technologies, one educational process. The matter is complex and, no matter how 'content' is defined, the term is not going to be a satisfactory portmanteau to contain the number of necessary issues.

It has become commonplace to discuss the impact of technology on education in terms of 'where' and 'when'. The existence of digital networks releases us from the prison of the institution, allowing education to be delivered to the workplace, home, wherever. Similarly, time constraints cease to exist, so education is available whenever you want it. The Open University in Britain has some remarkable evidence from its early use of e-mail by students, showing continuous activity throughout the 24 hours of a day, 7 days of a week. Certainly there were peaks and troughs – early evening being one of the latter (they have to eat), late evening being one of the former – but there was no time when there was no significant incoming traffic to the Open University's Milton Keynes e-mail server.

It is this where and when dimension that is the background to the distance and open learning debate. I shall come on to the issue of tutorial support in the context of distance learning later, but is worth pointing out here that systems premised on a definition of distance learning as just an extension of teaching go a long way to minimizing the where and when freedoms. Video conferencing techniques, for example, can begin to put back in place the constraints of place and time. Sir John Daniel, Vice Chancellor of the Open University, characterizes much US distance learning as being just such an extension of a professor's or lecturer's reach, whereas practice in the UK and Asia is more about extending the possibilities for learning across a broader band of technology-aided interactivity.

The where and when issue has also been presented as part of the solution to problems of access and the cost of higher education. Again, Daniel, in his book *Mega-universities and Knowledge Media* (Kogan Page, 1996), presents compelling statistics to show that the cost of delivery of programmes to schools enrolled in large-scale Open University-type institutions is the only sustainable way of bringing education to large numbers of learners. Glenn Jones has been making the same

> ... systems premised on a definition of distance learning as just an extension of teaching go a long way to minimizing the where and when freedoms.

point since 1991 (see his book *'Cyberschools'*, Jones Digital Century, 1997). Both these thinkers answer the question 'Why technology in education?' with the imperative of cost realities based on the when and where issue.

In considering the impact of digital networks, it is time, however, to move the argument on to 'what' and 'how' questions. How do they impact on *what* people learn and *how* they learn? Forgetting the reality imperative for a moment, if the nature of what learners learn and the methods by which they learn are not materially and beneficially changed, then, despite the convenience of when and where, let us forget about the technology. If the medium does not affect the message, then let's forget about the medium – it would be better to spread the educational spend in other ways. However, it is because technology can and does impact upon what we can learn and how we learn it that we must allow it into the equation. Seymour

Papert of MIT Media Lab is attributed with pointing out that 'an eighteenth-century surgeon visiting a modern operating theatre would have only the dimmest understanding of what was going on. Medicines, methods, machines, anaesthetics and antiseptics would all be unfamiliar. A teacher from the eighteenth century, by contrast, would have no difficulty comprehending the pedagogy, technology or purpose of what she or he observed in the typical 1990s' classroom: lectures, pencils, chalk boards, active teachers, passive students', (Charles W. Bray, *Wingspread Journal*, 17.2, The Johnson Foundation, 1995). How come (as I have questioned at greater length elsewhere – *TESOL Journal*, 3.1, 1993) the teaching profession is the last profession on earth to embrace technology? Is the threat to their humanism so great or have we failed to get across the material effect it would have on the what and the how?

Let me provide a small example of what I mean by 'material effect'. In the early stages of learning English as a second or foreign language, a student will be told by their teacher, a textbook, grammar or dictionary that 'any' is the negative or interrogative form of 'some' – 'I have some apples in my basket', 'Do you have any apples in your basket?', 'No I haven't any apples in my basket' and so on.

Instead of referencing the secondary-source grammars and dictionaries, suppose we use the computer to find for us a number of examples of the word 'any' in context. With access to computer-readable texts and a simple piece of software, we can produce a concordance of the word 'any' – that is, a set of contexts in which the word appears in authentic primary-source material. Study of such a concordance will quickly show that the rule given above concerning the use of 'any' accounts for only a small part of the evidence. The rule must be rewritten. The 'what' to be learnt then becomes different. Such study of linguistic corpus material has become commonplace in the world of dictionary making, which now has access to very large amounts of data. The British National Corpus, for example, begun in the early 1990s, provides lexicographers with access to 100 million words of written and spoken English (see http://info.ox.ac.uk/bnc/ for more on this). Our understanding of language – not just the meanings of single words, but how they fit together, the discovery of fixed word groupings, what constitutes a unit of language and so on – is fundamentally changed by technology – a material effect on the what of learning.

This small example additionally shows how digital resources can affect the 'how' of learning, too. *MicroConcord* (Mike Scott and Tim Johns, OUP, 1993) was an early concordance program developed especially for use by teachers and learners of English as a second or foreign language. In the *Manual*, which accompanies this program, building on work initiated by Tim Johns of the University of Birmingham, I began to sketch a methodology of language learning based on a set of techniques by which learners can work with authentic language to understand how it really works. Learners become researchers, setting up their own hypotheses, testing them against the evidence, modifying them accordingly until they reach a better understanding of language – a material effect on the how of learning, 'data-driven learning' in Tim

Johns' words. There is now the bi-annual conference Teaching and Language Corpora devoted to exploring this area. The one recently held in Oxford attracted more than 30 papers from 21 countries (see http://users.ox.ac.uk/~talc98/).

To understand the full impact of digital technologies on the what and how of learning, we need to widen the discussion from these examples. The idea of the learner as a receptacle into which information is poured is one educators have long argued against. The ubiquitous use of the word 'content', particularly by those who want to get into it as a means of diversifying from some aspect of technology, is, nevertheless, a reminder that the receptacle model survives in the minds of non-educators. Put briefly, there is general acceptance that learning is all about individuals constructing their own reality based on the evidence from, and their experience of, the world about them. This world is, of course, different for each individual and is also changing all the time. One way in which it is changing is the accumulation of information about the world (such as this chapter and this book), our means of getting access to this information (such as via a web site that may develop from this book) and the ways in which it is presented (such as the rich mix provided by multimedia).

In a world where information is accumulating at an unprecedented rate, our learner as receptacle may be expected to overflow rather quickly. How does our learner as constructivist fare, though? How do they manage to convert all this information into knowledge, something that will be a useful part of their humanity? And how does this happen on a continuing basis as knowledge (personal and global) evolves? Neurological evidence provides some clues, in presenting the brain as a learning organism, set to atrophy if it is not engaged in the process of learning – good for life-long learning, but also a reason to exercise great caution over what is done with the young mind. To inhibit the early stages of learning will kill the potential.

Without some thought being given to these fundamental questions, we cannot organize access to the information. Resources may be unprecedentedly copious and rich, but how do we give educational focus to those fashionable but essentially unteleological activities of browsing and surfing?

We need a comprehensive model structure on which we can build answers to these questions, and criteria by which we can judge the success of the various attempts made to address these issues. Most importantly, we need to put in place an integrated and modular framework with which we can begin to deliver educational materials and services to make use of the digital infrastructure. The rest of this chapter will set out the headings for such a model structure and a mirroring set of functionalities of a delivery system.

A useful starting point is the 'Conversational Framework' set out by Diana Laurillard in her book *Rethinking University Teaching* (Routledge, 1993) and elaborated on in a number of talks. In the context of this discussion, it is a particularly helpful framework in that it locates knowledge as part of the *process* of learning. For a proper understanding, I refer you to Laurillard's book, but I give an essence of what she writes here in order to structure this discussion. Figure 1 shows the four elements of the framework:

- the teacher's conceptual knowledge
- the learner's conceptual knowledge
- the teacher's experiential knowledge
- the learner's experiential knowledge.

It is the 'conversation' that teacher and learner have at the two levels of conceptual knowledge and experiential knowledge that brings about learning. The learner is encouraged to construct their own knowledge in the process of the conversation or dialogue – or 'interaction' as we might call it in a post-Socratic world. Arrows 1–4 in Figure 1 indicate the iterative descriptions that are part of this process. The learner constructs a description based on the teacher's framework. By means of comment and consequent modification, the learner is encouraged to get closer to the framework.

Arrows 5–8 in Figure 1 indicate the same kind of iterative, approximating process, but here it is to do with the setting of tasks and achievement of goals – focused experimentation building towards a knowledge of cause and effect or the procedural skills relevant to the topic such as analysis, or observation.

Arrows 9 and 10 show the interaction between the doing and the description, and how each is modified by the other. Arrows 11 and 12 indicate how the teacher also learns, by reflecting on the learner's engagement with the task and adapting the description, and by reflecting on the learner's description and adapting the goal of the task.

Laurillard has extended her use of this framework to look more closely at the 'description' part (1–4) and at the 'doing' part (5–8) of the framework to consider the ways in which the description and doing have been achieved in traditional education

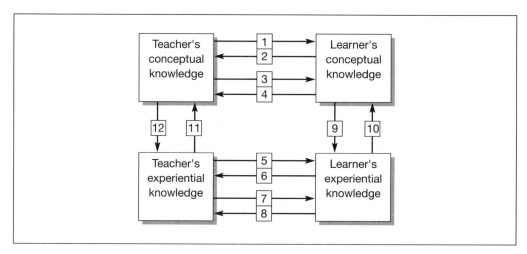

FIGURE 1

Source: After Diana Laurillard

and relate the various technologies to them. Figure 2 lists some of these ways, both traditional and electronic. This serves several purposes. First, it enables us to see the various technologies as component parts of specific teaching and learning processes and not just as bits of available technologies. Second, it enables us to compare the traditional with the electronic and discuss the strengths and weaknesses of each. Third, it gives us a basis on which to develop and extend a given technology in the context of a specific educational application. Let us take two examples of such applications. First, the provision of simple-to-use multimedia tools, which allow learners to describe and develop their understanding of conceptual knowledge with a much greater richness than would be the case with a written essay. A simple Powerpoint presentation might help me to get across the points being made in this article, for example. Second, the development of software that permits easy-to-use 3-D animation will add meaningful reality to scientific simulations – a worthier application for the faster and more powerful chips than yet another violent shoot-'em-up game. We can begin to see now where the technology can make the difference, where it can have a material effect on the what and how.

The Laurillard framework can be extended to help us understand better the place of conceptual knowledge and address the 'functions of content'. The teacher's conceptual knowledge is, of course, but part of all conceptual knowledge, which (as we have seen) is changing all the time – 'Do not confine your children to your own learning for they were born in another time' (Hebrew proverb, quoted in Charles Bray – see above).

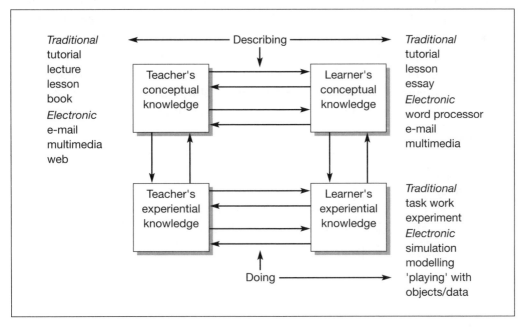

FIGURE 2   Source: After Diana Laurillard

If the top left-hand box of Figure 1 is taken to be not only the *teacher's* conceptual knowledge, but, potentially, *all* conceptual knowledge, then its place in the process of education needs some pretty careful analysis. Dumping it all in some pot labelled 'content' does nothing more than enable us to put a lid on it. How do we bring into focus those parts of 'all conceptual knowledge' that are going to aid the learner to construct their own knowledge? How do we ensure that what is brought into focus is reliable, authentic and relevant? How, in other words, do we turn 'all conceptual knowledge' into resources for learning? See Figure 3 (a) and (b).

Traditionally, representations of 'all conceptual knowledge' have been contained in the great libraries of the world, from Alexandria to Bodley. The teacher's job was to point the learner at certain books within the library. Digital depositories such as the World Wide Web change this paradigm, putting the learner directly in touch with the source material, but without teacher, Dewey or librarian to recommend one book over another or show where to find it. Our learner ends up lost among the virtual stacks, easily distracted by trivia and irrelevancies on the way. So, quality and relevance of resources remain, as ever, the issues. Quantity and availability have to be channelled. A methodology that includes the initial mediation by teachers of this resource – a first task may be set with respect to specific resources (text, web sites and so on), and a second task may be set where the learner must find their own resources. In this way, the learner is given the tools and the motivation to be an effective learner.

Learning to learn is another major topic of central importance, which can only be touched on here. One aspect of it, though, merits attention. It is a truism that every learner is different and will therefore learn and construct their own reality in unique ways. Using what we know about learning styles and multiple intelligences theory (see, for example, Howard Gardner, *Frames of Mind: The Theory of Multiple Intelligences*, Basic Books, 1993), we are able to draw up profiles of learners that will indicate whether or not an individual has a strong linguistic and interpersonal profile or, perhaps, one that emphasizes intrapersonal and musical intelligences. This profile could be used as the starting point for sending or encouraging a learner along certain

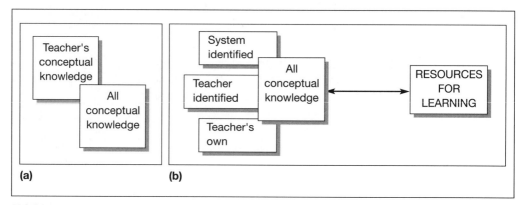

FIGURE 3

Source: After Diana Laurillard

resource pathways that are likely to promote effective learning in that individual. If the profile emphasizes a strength in linguistic intelligence, then textual resources are likely to be beneficial. If spatial intelligence is to the fore, then diagram-rich resources may promote better understanding. This is a crude interpretation and much research needs to be done. If, however, profile/resource matching can be shown to be truly beneficial, then this is a serious challenge to resource builders. To what extent are we able to create, identify and adapt resources so that individuals will be able to track through them in ways that match their intelligences profile? On the other hand, it does provide some hope for creators and publishers of learning materials. If it is possible to use the broad-band capability of CD-ROM, Digital Versatile Disk (DVD) and so on as resource dumps and then use the Internet to provide dynamic, adaptive pathways through these and other, on-line resources, then perhaps we can remove some of the cost barriers of handcrafting the material for one, generalized type of learner.

At Oxford University Press we have begun to address these issues, to define a new role for publishing in the networked world of technology-aided learning. As an academic and educational publishing house of long standing, we have learnt to reinvent ourselves to meet the changing needs of education around the world. Our response to the current challenge has been to set up Oxford Interactive Learning, which is tasked with finding ways of capitalizing on our vast fund of intellectual property and our expertise in creating more. Our work has been premised on the principles that technology must serve pedagogy, not vice versa, and technology must make a difference, particularly to the what and how of learning. The when and where, we believe, follow. In starting out, we analysed those aspects of the learning process that are disadvantaged by distance, permanent or temporary. At one end of the spectrum of distance learning might be placed an MBA programme undertaken remotely by a student or businessperson in, say, Kuala Lumpur, from a business school in, say, London. At the other end of the spectrum might be placed a schoolchild doing their maths homework.

This analysis led us to the identification of a number of key areas of disadvantage traditionally associated with the learner working at a distance:

■ lack of a community of fellow learners
■ no immediate access to tutorial support or, in many cases, none at all
■ absence of a personalized/individualized path of learning
■ remoteness of examination and accreditation.

Each of these can be ameliorated by appropriate technology and, in a number of important ways, the networked learner's situation is an improvement on that which existed in the past. Let's look briefly at each in turn.

A community of learners can be established via digital communication networks. This community may be the virtual class of similar learners progressing through a particular learning programme, working with the same on-line tutor. It can extend to other classes anywhere in the world. As in a real school, discussion will take place on a specific task, about the course in general or larger issues. A 'communication space' organized around these different kinds of discourse, making use of appropriate technologies, taking into account the subject matter of what is being learnt, can create a community of learners of global proportions. Some communication will be asynchronous, using e-mail, discussion forums and so on while other communication will be synchronous, using Web telephony, video conferencing, real-time electronic whiteboard and so on. For the latter, an on-line diary allows learners to make appointments with one another and, of course, with tutors – something that may well be complicated when working across time zones.

The introduction of an on-line tutor removes many of the obstacles to distance learning, but, at the same time, leads to a new set of issues. What constitutes good practice for an on-line tutor? How much contact, synchronous and asynchronous, should be provided for? The learning model discussed above suggests answers to some of these questions. There will be business model issues that will need to be taken into account in answering some of the others. The role of the tutor will be different to that operating in a more traditional set-up, however, not just because of the environment but also because materials and services constructed around an understanding of the potential of on-line learning will place the responsibility for some of the mediation of the learning process traditionally carried out by the teacher on the materials themselves. Here we come to the third of the points above, the individualization of the process of learning.

The earlier discussion concerning learner profiling provides one facet of individualization. If we know what is likely to work in terms of resources for a particular individual, then we can construct a pathway through those resources likely to lead to effective learning for that individual. We can, additionally, monitor the individual's performance and build up a database of the learner's successes and failures. Building on this knowledge, the system can suggest finely tuned guidance or, of course, the tutor can override this guidance, replacing it with their own.

This building up of databases around individual learners can also be used to confront the final point of disadvantage. Learners can be given a realistic view of when they are ready to sit an examination or seek accreditation in other ways. Further, we are already beginning to see the introduction of examinations that can be taken on-line.

... it is paramount that their purpose is clear, the navigation is transparent and it offers insights.

Our work has led us to create the Oxford Interactive Learning Framework, which is a means by which educational resources and services can be delivered in an integrated fashion. The Framework is a flexible, modular concept, adaptable to a wide variety of learning situations and technological environments. It also provides a methodology for creating materials and learning programmes based on an understanding of the pedagogic potential of the technologies. The resources may be off-line, multimedia resources, books or audio or video cassettes, or they may be dynamic data delivered on-line. Materials may be supplements to, or updates of, what may have already been supplied. At all times, however, it is paramount that their purpose is clear, the navigation is transparent and it offers insights. Learners' needs can be assessed and their profiles established. Their performance can be monitored, recorded and used to establish future learning paths. All this is done in a digital community of fellow learners, with support available when it is required.

To conclude, any consideration of the forms and functions of digital content in education will lead to a complex picture. At the present stage of our understanding, it is as important to ask the right questions as it is to suggest answers. ■

Roberto Minio

Head of Publishing and New Media Group,
Pira International

FROM BIBLES TO NEW BUYABLES
Traditional publishers and the digital challenge

Publishing and its role in the Wired World

This chapter is based on my experience of working for, and with, different publishers, often struggling to find their way into (or, some of them, out of) the new media jungle – a big part of which is now a wired jungle. As the quantity of information increases, the quality of what is communicated and the way it is presented becomes even more critical. Publishing activities do, therefore, have a key role to play in all wired walks of life; whether it is undertaken by 'publishers' or not is another question. Publishers are going through a process of reinventing publishing and, in many respects, they run into some of the same strategic issues in reinventing their businesses as companies in other industry sectors that are also driven by the wired imperative. However, there is another side to it too. Because information and content management are critical to all kinds of businesses, publishing is visibly becoming a part of everybody's business and the reinvention of publishing (in which publishers are forced to engage) hopefully offers an opportunity for other businesses to re-examine the place and means of publishing activities within their own organizations.

Whether wired or not, publishers are in the business of mediating communication by encapsulating information, literature, entertainment, persuasion or knowledge in their products. The mediation process also involves identification, quality assurance, enhancement, filtering and effective distribution. The growing amount of content, and increasing means available for its communication (or at least transfer), exacerbates the need for effective mediation.

We could therefore be forgiven for thinking that the Wired World must have been made for publishers which for centuries, have added value to communication processes by commissioning, creating, selecting, verifying, packaging, manufacturing and delivering authors' messages to their audiences. The Wired World does indeed offer new horizons of opportunity for traditional publishers, but it also offers new worlds of publishing opportunity to other organizations that with backgrounds in other domains of communication, learning, business, entertainment, performance, advertising or their supporting infrastructures – also have many of the aspirations and skills needed to add value by publishing in the Wired World.

One thing we can already be sure of is that the increase in available content and communications facilities will not be matched by an increase in the number of hours in the day. Hence, there will, in any case, be increased competition for audience attention. The totality of successful communication will only be increased by the creative invention and evolution of even richer communication media, formats and genres than we have now. This is the basic driver of, and fundamental challenge for, the reinvention of publishing.

No doubt the ultimate success of some genre over others in this evolution will involve serendipity as well as creativity and market forces, but it is already evident – both from the failure of some multimedia efforts and from the successful development of content on the Net – that success will require both depth of specialist skills – in design, expression, programming, distributed resource management – and breadth of strengths – a distribution network, staying power made possible by deep pockets, and innovation. Because this combination of depth and breadth is unlikely to be found in just one kind of organization, partnership is an essential feature of the future landscape.

Publishing is spoken of as one industry sector, but it is by no means homogeneous. Publishers have traditionally been defined by their products – books, magazines, newspapers – with quite diverse subgroups within these sectors, often with quite different core activities and business models. Now that nearly all publishers have ceased to be printers themselves, there is even less that they all have in common.

Books may be fiction, non-fiction, educational, professional or STM (which stands for 'scientific, technical and medical'). Book publishers' traditional strengths are in commissioning authors and building a list, identification of target populations with disposable income, product promotion, product distribution and warehousing, management of price and production costs, copyright and rights trading, and (a modern development) re-use of copyright material in parallel and new media publishing.

> ... success will require both depth of specialist skills ... and breadth of strengths ...

Newspapers can be national, regional or local, and periodicals may be directed at the consumer, professionals or at some specialist group. Periodical publishers' strengths are in editorial direction, brand image exploitation, maintaining distribution networks, protecting advertising revenue, competition with other leisure time products, marketing and pricing, controlling production and materials costs, and commission-based services generated from readership enquiry systems. For both newspapers and periodicals, balancing and maintaining the revenue streams from sales and advertising is a key issue.

If these are the traditional publishers and their core activities, who then will be the new publishers? Who are the competitors for the audiences spare media minutes of attention, and who are the partners with the complementary skills capable of inventing and branding the genres for the Wired World? Producers and broadcasters, music labels and film studios, educational enterprises and advertising agencies are among the organizations that are in the frame; and these are beginning to share in the dubious honour of being categorized as part of the 'content industry'. Individuals, too, can of course more readily become publishers and share in the action as a result of the lowering of the financial barriers to replication and distribution of products.

Corporations deserve special mention. Important roles for publishing in the corporate setting include internal communications, intranet content management, flow of information into the organization, brand-supporting publications, as well as product documentation. The traditional boundaries that determine which of these publishing activities are contracted out (company magazines, for example) and which are considered intrinsic parts of the business' processes are increasingly fluid. Decisions of corporations on how to handle the management of their content can, by their scale alone, have a significant impact on the evolution of successful genres.

The talk of convergence is of convergence of industries – telecommunications, IT and publishing. Are these the complementary partners, along with the traditional publishers' suppliers of design, formatting and delivery services? And what will be the genres of publication themselves?

Convergence of products in the bit world suggests all-integrating 'interactive multimedia', but, as Alan Kay used to say of the DynaBook, that is more akin to 'paper' than 'the book'. Examples of product applications are closer to hand. The management and exploitation of content is needed in many other domains that are less obviously 'publishing', such as direct marketing and teleshopping, point-of-sale, training, clubs and community management, directories and databases, games, and these represent fruitful fields for new genre evolution.

With the ubiquity of information, and the demand for its better management and exploitation, some of the publishing activities and processes – and some of the skills of publishers – have a key role to play in the Wired World, (whether this be in commercial or corporate publishing or in new ways of exploiting information and knowledge).

Reinvention is much underrated

'Don't reinvent the wheel' is a common plea of budget holders to innovators and developers. It is certainly true that the integration – as opposed to invention – of the second, third and particularly the fourth wheel have had a huge impact, but reinvention is much underrated. Often it is the reinvented wheel that works best. Even if it lacks the striking originality of the first, the background knowledge on which the first was built has been better internalized by the inventive society, team or individual. Second, the very process of reinvention can be what generates the value.

Recent studies of the impact of IT on productivity (reported by Erik Brynjolfsson and Lorin M. Hitt in 'Beyond the productivity paradox' in the *Communications of the ACM*, August 1998), underline the importance for all businesses of reinventing themselves to secure benefits from IT. The key risk illustrated by businesses where productivity has not improved appears to be from the adoption of attractive, flexible IT solutions without making allowance in the organization for the additional responsibility taken on by exposing oneself to managing that flexibility. A process of reinvention can avoid this pitfall.

Reinvention has a special status in publishing. Commercial publishers are continually reinventing what they do as they produce new books reacting creatively and proactively to market demands or opportunities. A fascinating experiment carried out in the 1970s involved having a manuscript sent to five US publishers (university presses) and tracked through the process of publication by each of the five. The results were documented in a compendium (imaginatively called '*One Book, Five Ways*, published by William Kauffmann Inc., 1977). In spite of the developments in publishing technologies since then, the book remains, to this day, an insightful introduction to book publishing processes. At least one of the publishers described how they weighed the manuscript in order to estimate the book's eventual list price! In a preface to the book, Robert Maxwell is quoted, making the point that every publication is unique, however similar they look on the surface – each one being a newly (re)invented solution to the problem of how best, within commercial constraints, to help the author succeed in their intended communication with the reading audience.

This kind of reinvention (new market need, new product), has, however, been *within* the product frame of the particular publisher, creating new instances of products, new books, new magazine titles, reacting creatively to market needs and adapting processes to do the job. The reinvention of publishing in a Wired World needs to take us outside the current product frame to support the kind of flexibility that technology enables publishing to offer and users to require.

Change, shifts and invariants

Plus ça change ...

How big is the current change? My favourite example of a comparable technology-enabled paradigm shift occurred in the Middle Ages. The hardware was the abacus (reinvented or re-discovered); Arabic numerals were the software. Alexander Murray's excellent book *Reason and Society in the Middle Ages* (Clarendon Press, 1978) argues how these technologies underpinned and enabled the evolutionary development, out of the Dark Ages, of a numerate culture and society in Western Europe, a society that could now trade with money (superseding the many previously existing mechanisms for property exchange), a society with what is effectively a whole new intellectual capability.

The analogy runs deep – the evolution in that case was wrought with projects (pan-European consortia of monks working on the definitive date for Easter) and false starts as well as the eventual empowerment of a broader populace.

What then are the essential characteristics of change this time? It is wiredness itself – the ability to organize that is even less dependent on time and space, together with the dichotomy, eloquently presented by Nicholas Negroponte in *Being Digital* (1996), between the world of atoms and the world of bits. If new societal intellectual capabilities evolve, they may well be to do with new modes of communication.

The impact on publishing

As publishing has been concerned with mediating communications across time and space, even in the short term this can certainly have a fundamental impact. Most people think of publishers as those who invest in the production replication and delivery of publications, and of these, replication and delivery are now virtually free. However, publishers are at the interface of atoms and bits, and that makes a total change harder. The scale of change is huge, touching practically all aspects of publishers' business, even if the perceived scale is often smaller when quantified in terms of short-term measures, such as the percentage of revenue from sales of electronic products (even for traditional STM publishers heavily involved in electronic publishing, this is only in the order of 15 per cent).

The pace of change is fast, as indicated by the industry's suppliers 'velocity of conversion to digital'. In terms of the total spend on digital versus analogue processes, R. R. Donnelley, the leading US printer, which now describes itself as the 'foremost printing and information management company in the world', went from a 5 per cent spend on digital in 1994 to 50 per cent in 1997. Comparable figures for the North American Graphic Arts Suppliers Association range from 25 per cent in 1994 to 50 per cent in 1997 (Sun Microsystems, 1998).

The direction of change is towards the new needs of the empowered marketplace, including the expectations of different and possibly short-lived niche groups of users as well as different individual users' personalized or situation-specific needs. This requires shift from single-product-for-all thinking towards devising a multiplicity of options that can flexibly meet diverse needs.

This multiplicity can happen in at least three ways:

■ new products
■ new businesses
■ reinvention with a real shift of focus.

New product Traditional publishers have been experimenting with new products and still are. Gradually, the secure picture of publishers meeting and sharing their relief that no one else appears to be making money with electronic products either is eroding. However, as Nigel Stapleton of Reed-Elsevier made clear at the FT Electronic

Publishing Conference in 1997, it is a long haul and can require deep pockets. Some excellent CD-ROM and on-line products have been developed with impressive creative designs, but they have often been isolated rather than part of a 'list-building' strategy.

It would be interesting to compare the amounts spent by publishers on buying each other (at least in the UK in the 1980s without profiting from doing so) with the comparatively small amounts spent on experimenting with new products or processes.

> **Gradually, the secure picture of publishers meeting and sharing their relief that no one else appears to be making money with electronic products either is eroding.**

New businesses New businesses such as Helicon – the successful result of the management buyout of the Hutchinson encyclopaedia database – illustrate how the innovative elements within an established company can take an asset 'from within' and be sufficiently flexible and quick to develop its potential in a way in which the original home of the product was unable to do.

It is not a new phenomenon that 'established players have a vested interest in the existing ways of doing things and tend not to run so fast with the new idea' (in the words of Kathleen Smith, an analyst with Renaissance Capital commenting on the relative strengths of the Internet bookshop Amazon.com versus established booksellers such as Barnes & Noble). In such a climate of radically changed technological possibility, small companies have the edge in that they can invent themselves quicker than established corporations can reinvent their existing structures.

... plus c'est la même chose

In the face of all this change, there are important invariants, too. Most of all, the major functions of communication – informing, educating, entertaining, persuading or performing transactions – are stable and continue to represent the main intended outcomes of successful communication.

The communicative roles of author/creator and user/reader will no doubt be influenced by Multi User Domains (MUDs), chat rooms and multisource broadcasting, and the familiarity of information on demand. This is not to say that the functions do not change at all, but their evolution is on a grander timescale – that of the 'new intellectual capability'.

Publishers need an architecture, reputation or brand, and access to strategic assets. The reputations of publishers are, of course, not invariant, but they are more stable than the pace of technology. So, too, are those strengths of theirs that are rooted in relationships, such as market knowledge and 'author share'. What does change, however, is how the functions are fulfilled – by what kinds of products, produced by what kinds of process, involving what kinds of players, all that can change.

From Bibles to new Buyables

Designer products invented by users – the users' reinvention of publishing

Publishing products are designed to meet communication needs. While we understand the capabilities and impacts of existing products really well, we do not yet have a good understanding of the new genres of commercial products that will be sufficiently desirable to be buyable, which for commercial players will, after all, be the measure of success. The new Buyables will evolve as a result of users reinventing publishing. That – the marketplace accompanied by some serendipity – will determine which genres are the wealth-creating exploitations of content in the future.

The initial benefits of being a wired digital reader include the opportunity to aggregate content yourself, increased choice and speed, and having the option to communicate back to the author or an intermediary. Experiencing these, readers will discover new ways to use the content, context and communication structures available to them. For example, they might develop expectations of being able to capture the right information on demand, learning in a virtual community or finding information associated with their current task.

Sample Buyables

Publishers old and new are developing Buyables to meet the users' evolving needs. In the information and knowledge domain, for example, rich, knowledge-based publications are being built with automatically generated presentation. Exploiting indexing and knowledge-acquisition skills, early products of this kind were built around reference works. Electronic journals (exploiting author share – a critical mass of authors in a particular area) are integrated with niche community management, such as BioMedNet, which also exploits journalistic skills. Peopleware in the form of brokerage services offer seamless access to person-to-person communication to add value to directories of specialists.

An example of news, promotion and entertainment, local newspapers have relied on their community both for advertising and editorial sources. On-line services require community source management, but also need background information to provide an acceptably attractive environment. ZIP2/CitySearch has developed an effectively manageable format and achieved an economy of scale by providing these services to many local newspapers along with content and server hosting.

Rights only?

Whichever new product genres emerge as winners, these new Buyables will involve different components, quite possibly contributed by different players:

- the objects – content, navigation mechanisms and context
- the shapes – appropriate topologies and structures of communication (linear, circular, star, network, moderated, personalized, situated)
- the modes – such as visual, multimedia and interaction.

Associated with the objects are Intellectual Property Rights (IPRs) – the traditional economic basis for publishing – that can be owned, traded and exploited. Buyables with different shapes rely on different kinds of location and communication possibilities that may be supported by channels or service providers. The modes reflect different types of perceptual or interactive experiences that the product can offer, for example when used or played on a particular device.

For conventional publishing, the physical object was the product. Digitally, it is then all too easy to conclude, mistakenly, that all digital content transactions are rights transactions. These three categories provide a means of describing key aspects – the rights, service and platform aspects – of commercial publishing products. Integrating these aspects in fruitful ways technically requires identification mechanisms and rich metadata; integrating them into a success requires alliances and interwoven partnerships.

The challenge for the publisher with a strength in access to strategic assets – whether these be content or relationships with content creators – is to mould the partnerships and prepare those assets for quick production of the desired products.

Designer processes

Publishing processes are designed to meet the needs of producing the Buyables efficiently. Given certain Buyables, the publishers' reinvention involves finding and managing the new processes and partners. Publishers need to play an active role in the change by participating in the redesign. In the past, they have often expected this of their service providers, but they can no longer afford to do so.

Just as new product genres evolve, so too do new process genres in the Wired World, driven by globalization, competition to deliver and technology-enabled flexibility. The multiplicity of product options and the division of processes into smaller, more specialist functions increases the demand for flexibility in the production process, the need for effective project management, as opposed to production controlling, and, on the technical side, that there be open interfaces between tasks, even if they are embedded in different organizational compartments.

The extension of the e-business infrastructure beyond Electronic Data Interchange (EDI) is critical in this regard to making it easy to handle richer message sets and prototype working automated commercial relationships rapidly.

Processes and partnerships

One example of a redesigned process is for print, which will not disappear with the Wired World. The Virtual Warehouse is a print on demand scenario. For educational use, digital printing devices can now produce customized textbooks and course packs at an acceptable unit cost. With this technology and this original aim, McGraw-Hill's PRIMIS system is now a reality, with a communication structure that supports distribute and print. A similar approach has been used to offer a 'never out of print' service, according to which a book will be produced on demand when ordered. In both cases, the key to success is eradicating the overhead in the internal communication and transactions that, while acceptable amortized over a significant print run, make individual on demand printing wholly uneconomic.

A different kind of automated process partnership is exemplified by MediaDNA, a small company in San Diego offering a service to wrap e-newsletters with 'rights envelopes' to enable issues of the newsletters to be forwarded freely between interested potential readers. The security element in the envelope can be specified by the publisher so that, for example, a non-subscriber recipient can be allowed one free access to the issue.

Where has all the value gone?

The conventional product-focused value chain (see Figure 1) is not the right model for publishing in the Wired World.

The subtler chain takes into account the need to manage content in order to support reuse, cross-media trading or hybrid exploitation of rights and 'reaggregation' of product from a neutral content store (see Figure 2).

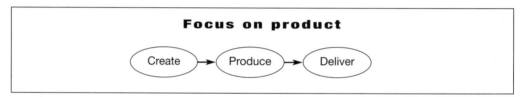

FIGURE 1

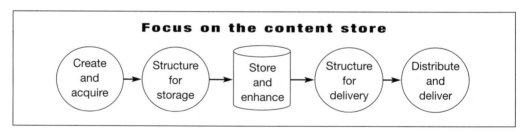

FIGURE 2

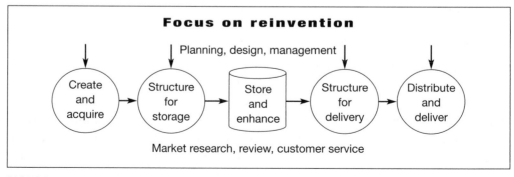

FIGURE 3

However, this still keeps the focus on the value of the content and the content-manipulation processes alone.

In the Wired World, both products and processes can be and need to be designed to meet the end users' needs. The digitization of content enables the separation of function and form, making possible the disaggregation and reaggregation of product. The digitisation of commerce enables the separation of business interface and workflow from organization, and allows for the disaggregation and reaggregation of processes.

As the Buyables and process genres become better understood, the reaggregation can become ever more efficient and perhaps then we shall be so efficient at producing the specifically requested Buyables, that a simpler model will suffice again. Meanwhile, the publisher (new or old) needs to focus on the development of relationships, content, design abilities, market making and market matching (see Figure 3).

Taken together, these need a new approach, a new understanding of what the publisher is doing – integrated media management. In this the focus moves from production to reinvention itself, namely the design of the hybrid, the 'metaproduct'. The publisher's list was just one such metaproduct. With the value in the design, the focus can also move to more project management, less building. The planning (process *and* product), design and management drive the actual production processes, while market research and review, in turn, feed the planning and design.

Conclusion

The functions and forms of publishing are essential for the development of the Wired World. Publishers need to find ways of fulfilling their important role as the means and capabilities evolve from the users' point of view. The growth of knowledge communication, the growth of entertainment, the huge need for education surely make this a growing, not a declining, world. So, while it will require staying power for some existing players and ingenuity for all, there is much communication to be mediated and every reason for publishers to keep on reinventing themselves to meet the challenge of the Wired World. ■

Hugh Brett

Lawyer and Consultant,
Llewelyn Zietman, Solicitors, London

COPYRIGHT IN A DIGITAL AGE

Background

The English are admired for their long-standing institutions, which have survived for centuries by adapting to meet new demands. Parliament and the monarchy are examples. Both institutions originated many years ago and have, over the centuries, altered so that today, with some of their ancient trappings, they fit into our democratic society. Another similar institution some might argue is the UK's long-standing copyright law, but for how long can it survive?

An overriding question for copyright and indeed for industries, such as publishing, that have traditionally survived because of the legal protection copyright offers is whether or not copyright can adapt and remain relevant in the Digital Age.

The first Copyright Act

The UK was the first country to enact a copyright law. It was passed in the reign of Queen Anne, in 1709. The limited purpose of the 1709 Act was to protect the literary works of authors by protecting their copyright.

The scope of copyright expanded over the years and now embraces new formats beyond literary works, which Parliament deemed worthy of protection. Copyright law has been adapted by legislation to meet the requirements of progress, so that in the course of time, designs, dramatic works, films, and broadcasting have all been embraced within the family of copyright. Today, copyright law protects numerous formats that could not have been contemplated by the initiators of the first Copyright Act in 1709.

1998 UK Copyright Act and Digitization

The latest UK copyright law is to be found in the Copyright, Designs and Patents Act 1988. The Act states that copyright will apply to musical and artistic works, films, sound recordings, photographs, broadcasts, and cable programmes. In each category, a physical object – such as a book, picture, audiotape or film – will identify the copyright work. The advent of computers and digitization has changed the traditional way of looking at copyright by removing its obvious connection with a physical product.

Text, music and pictures can now be stored in zeros and ones so that the traditional separation and identification of copyright works by defining them by reference to their physical form is not appropriate. Pictures, written words and music can be held on computer disks so that the physical object is lost. It has led some commentators – among them Nicholas Negroponte, the founder of the MIT media lab – to suggest that 'Copyright law is totally out of date. It is a Gutenberg artefact. Since it is a reactive process, it will probably have to break down completely before it is corrected.'

Digital technology not only challenges the conceptual approaches of copyright, but also the heart of copyright. The essence of copyright is to prevent the copying of copyright works, but works stored in a digital format can easily be copied by simply tapping a computer button, creating a copy that will look as good as the original. Information stored digitally can be transmitted speedily to anyone having a computer and telephone link, no matter where they are in the world. Vast chunks of information can be stored digitally. One CD-ROM holds 300,000 pages of text. Such information can be accessed and simply reproduced. If the information is placed on the Internet, the copyright owner has the severe practical problem of how to control access to their copyright information and control unauthorized copying.

The digitizing of text, pictures and music also challenges the traditional role of copyright to protect the integrity of a copyright work. Before the use of zeros and ones to store information, it was not that easy to alter text or 'improve' a picture, for example. Once copyright text is digitized, it is quite simple to amend, and in the case of a digitized photograph new matter can be added or existing items deleted with no difficulty.

The practical problems faced by copyright owners to control the communication of their copyright work by means of electronic dissemination, storage and manipulation are therefore formidable.

Silicone chips and literary works

Despite the enormous practical stresses placed on copyright control by the digitization of copyright works, the legal basis of copyright remains extraordinarily strong. The fact that a literary work can now subsist in a Random Access Memory (RAM) or Read Only Memory (ROM) does not mean that copyright protection is denied to the literary text when it has been reduced to a series of zeros and ones. The 1998 Copyright Act makes this clear. It states that a 'literary work' must be recorded in writing *'or otherwise'*. The words 'or otherwise' mean that text stored within a computer will attract copyright protection just as if it were recorded on a printed page. The definition of a 'literary work' in the Act specifically includes a computer program, and 'writing' is defined as including 'any form of notation or code ... regardless of the method by which, or medium in or which, it is recorded'. The digitization of copyright works has therefore not destroyed copyright protection of text when recorded within a computer.

Copyright infringement issues

Digitized works are also protected under UK copyright law when issues of infringement arise. The influential computer lobby ensured that their proprietary computer programs were protected as if they were literary works, and the copyright of programs and text will be infringed under the 1998 Act when they are reproduced electronically.

The practical problems faced by copyright owners to control the communication of their copyright work by means of electronic dissemination, storage and manipulation are therefore formidable.

The Act defines 'unlawful copying' very widely, including 'storing the work in any medium by electronic means' and 'making copies which are transient'. Copying text, therefore, into a computer or placing text on a web site will infringe copyright, and so will the 'transient' copying of text on a computer screen.

Fair use

Copyright law does not recognize the right to reproduce electronically copyright text without permission or payment. The fair use copyright exemptions under the 1988 Act were drafted before the implications of the Digital Age were fully appreciated. The 1988 exemptions give fair use privileges to libraries and educational bodies only where *photocopying* takes place.

It is a very curious fact that under present copyright law almost every act that a librarian performs involving electronic reproduction will infringe copyright. The exemptions that apply to the photocopying of journal articles, for example, do not apply if a librarian wishes to store a work electronically or wishes to download text in order to fulfil an interlibrary loan. The legal adviser to the Library Association has given vent to the librarians' frustrations in the following vein:

> UK librarians are carefully toeing the copyright line and becoming more and more frustrated. We have the technology, why can't we use it? It is a constant cry. Why can't we use it to improve services to our users? Why shouldn't we be able to create a database of particular articles? Why shouldn't we be able to fulfil interlibrary document requests electronically? Why shouldn't we be able to send copyright works around a network for students to use?

The fact that libraries and others can only claim the benefit of the fair use provisions when the work is photocopied but not when it is reproduced electronically is a maverick situation, which cannot last forever. The Digital Age will lead to a complete review of the copyright fair use provisions.

Publishers' typographical copyright

In one major respect, the digitization of text has made immediate inroads into the legal rights of copyright owners. UK copyright law uniquely gives protection to the 'typographical layout' of a copyright work. Publishers therefore enjoy their own copyright in the text that they have caused to be printed, and this typographical copyright is infringed when the layout is photocopied.

In the pre-Digital Age, the publishers' typographical copyright was a valuable right, because it gave publishers the right to prevent the photocopying of their works without having to rely on their authors' copyright. In the case of infringement, publishers could generally take legal action on the basis of their typographical copyright, without having to call on the authors' copyright.

The electronic reproduction of copyright text will not infringe the publishers' 'typographical' copyright. Publisher are therefore dependent on the authors' copyright when text is reproduced electronically, for example, on a computer screen or on-line. The publishers' right to the ownership of copyright will be important in the digital environment when electronic copying takes place and legal rights need to be justified.

The Information Age

Only an ostrich with its head in the sand could consider that present-day UK Copyright law, which places such extensive restrictions on the delivery of information electronically, could continue without change. The spirit of the age is for greater access to information. The UK government promises a Freedom of Information Bill, and the proposals for the release of government control over Crown copyright material are indicative that the government envisages the free availability of information as a very necessary right in the Digital Age.

The European Union has released a discussion document entitled a 'Green Paper on Public Sector Information in the Information Society'. It calls for greater access to government information and concludes by saying, 'The Information Society is here, Europe's citizens and industry must be enabled to fully exploit its possibilities.'

The European Union is committed to ensuring that information is freely available. How far this commitment will override intellectual property rights has yet to be determined, however.

Copyright reforms from Brussels

The reforms to copyright law arising from the Digital Age will undoubtedly come from Brussels. The European Commission views copyright as an area where reform is required. Reform is necessary because unharmonized copyright laws within the European Union will create trade distortions within the Community. Copyright must also not be used to restrict the availability of information within the European Union.

To date, the European Commission has issued a number of directives in the copyright field. One of its early directives obliged all members of the Community to protect computer programs as if they were literary works. Another directive has introduced the rental and lending right, giving creators the right to control the lending of their copyright works, and another has extended the term of copyright by a further 20 years, to a life and 70 years.

Of special interest to publishers is the directive protecting databases, which became law in the United Kingdom at the start of 1998. It provides for the legal protection of databases, which are defined as 'a collection of independent works ... arranged in a systematic or methodical way'. It is impossible to state with any assurance which databases will, in fact, be protected by the new law. Will it apply to all information collected by publishers? Will publishers be able to use the database right to restrict the use of all electronically stored information? Such questions remain unanswered at the present.

An important feature of the new law is that the owner of the new database right will not be the author but the investor. In most situations, this is therefore likely to be the publisher. The database right could therefore go a long way in supplementing the loss of the publishers' typographical right, which, as has been noticed, does not protect typographical layout when it is reproduced electronically.

Reform of copyright law and the Digital Age

The burning issue for publishers is how long the present pre-digital copyright laws will remain. The writing is on the wall. At the beginning of 1998, the European Commission published a draft directive entitled the 'Harmonisation of Certain Aspects of Copyright and Related Rights in the Information Society'. This is most important because it seeks to identify the boundaries of copyright in the Information Society.

The burning issue for publishers is how long the present pre-digital copyright laws will remain.

The draft directive provides that authors, performers, record producers, filmmakers and broadcasters should enjoy the exclusive right to prevent copying of their works. Publishers are conspicuous by their absence! Publishers do not have their own copyright in their secondary works, unlike record producers. In other words, if publishers are to have any copyright control over their text, they must obtain the copyright through being employers of the authors or the written assignment of the copyright by the author. The benefits of the typographical copyright or something similar do not exist in the EU proposals.

The draft directive proposes the implementation of a number of legal rights designed to protect copyright owners in the Information Age. They are broad in scope, but they are diluted by important exceptions. The exceptions may prove to be more important than the rights themselves.

The main right is that of 'reproduction' which is as extensive as present-day UK copyright law. It will restrict copying, which is indirect and temporary. The intention is to make it unlawful to make temporary, non-visible copies of a copyright text stored in the working memory of a computer. In addition, the directive proposes a 'communication right', which will restrict the electronic transmission of copyright works to the public.

Copyright exceptions

The burning issues for publishers will be the exceptions. These will prove to be complex and contentious. Certain 'temporary acts of reproduction' will not infringe copyright provided they have no independent economic significance, and/or they are reproduced in 'public' establishments, such as libraries. However, what does 'temporary acts of reproduction' include? Does it embrace browsing on a computer, and what is the meaning of 'public'?

National governments can under the draft Directive make exceptions to the 'communication right' if copying is required for the purposes of illustration for teaching or scientific research. Again the extent of these words will be the subject of debate and controversy.

Certain technical devices to be banned

The draft directive includes some very practical proposals against digital copying and the undermining of copyright by the use of technical devices. The draft directive proposes to ban the use of technological equipment that may assist in the unlawful copying of copyright works, and which thereby circumvent the legitimate owners' copyrights. This proposal could be for more effective in protecting the interests of publishers than general legal reforms that, in practice, may prove impossible to enforce effectively.

In addition, the directive requires that national governments must provide adequate legal protection for 'electronic rights management information' systems so that their removal will be illegal, if the object of this were to defeat or facilitate the infringement of copyright. The Commission foresees the importance of tracking devices in digital publishing.

The introduction of provisions banning the use of electronic devices within traditional copyright laws has been criticized. However, given the practical difficulties of controlling the copying of copyright text on the Internet, these very practical restrictions may be the most significant part of the publishers' armoury in protecting their copyright in electronic works.

Global issues

Another draft directive, the 'Harmonisation of Copyright within the European Union', originates from developments initiated by the World Intellectual Property Organisation (WIPO). WIPO is the guardian of the Berne Convention – The International Copyright Treaty for the protection of copyright worldwide.

In 1996, WIPO reviewed the terms of the Berne Convention in the light of the Digital Age. A World Copyright Treaty was adopted that has inspired the reforms proposed by the European Commission. Members of the Berne Convention – that is, most countries in the world – will be required to implement the WIPO changes into their national laws. At the time of writing, an extensive debate is taking place in the US on the implementation of the WIPO Copyright Treaties into US law.

The educational community and US libraries are lobbying hard. They claim that anti-copying devices will deny access to works that are not the subject of copyright and/or have the benefit of fair use. The publishers' response is that fair dealing does not entitle researchers, teachers and library users to use without permission information that may be in the public domain, but can only be accessed by breaking another law. In other words, the fair dealing does not extend to permitting someone to break into a locked library in order to make copies of a book that may be in the public domain. According to US publishers, the use of technical devices to prevent copying is equally legitimate. At the time of writing, the discussion continues.

The US has now joined the Berne Convention, but the present debate within the US Congress reveals the importance of WIPO in reforming national copyright laws internationally. The issues concerning copyright are now global. The activities of WIPO are increasingly relevant in the global digital world.

Summary

Publishers are looking to expand their delivery systems of information beyond the printed word. Once information is on-line, publishers must look to copyright and technological measures to protect cyberspace information. The challenge for copyright is how to provide control in an environment where the digital computer can flawlessly reproduce and effortlessly distribute copyright text globally. The Internet has been described as one gigantic copying machine, and traditional copyright enforcement procedures are no longer very relevant in monitoring the copying of text by a mass of individuals.

> **The Internet has been described as one gigantic copying machine ...**

The European Commission's Directive seeks to protect copyright works when delivered electronically. The legal base will provide extensive protection, but the effectiveness of the initiative will depend very much on the scope of the exceptions. The restriction on technical devices designed to defeat copyright may also be significant.

A brief review of some of the issues faced by publishers is given below.

Libraries

Libraries are increasingly conscious of the opportunities that the Digital Age gives to them. They would like to be able to store information electronically and supply their readers with text on-line. Libraries, as noted, do not have any fair use exceptions for the electronic reproduction of text under the UK Copyright Act, so that all electronic dealings are, in principle, infringements of copyright. The proposals for the harmonization of copyright law by the European Commission offer libraries an opportunity for library practices to fall within the fair dealing exceptions, and the possibility of the storage, accessing text and delivery on-line without fear of infringing copyright. Librarians will be lobbying hard for the widest exemptions.

The library lobby is calling for a fairer balance between the protection of and access to information. The lobby points to the fact that much of the information published by publishers comes from academic communities, which have been paid for out of public funds. It pours scorn on the idea that copyright encourages creativity when, in reality, 'it is a system for rewarding investors in the creation of others', and, in the absence of fair dealing, the public will be at the mercy of publishers, which will be able to charge monopoly prices.

The libraries are not happy either about the use of technical controls to monitor the movement of works in a digital environment. Librarians consider that technical controls could be used by publishers to demand unfair terms for copyright access.

The library community fears that licensing of information will lead to total control by publishers because librarians will be persuaded to take out licences when not strictly required and on unfair terms. The National Electronic Licensing Site Initiative (NELSI) intends to experiment with publishing contracts for the electronic delivery of journals to the academic community. Whether or not model licensing contracts are the solution for the supply of information electronically may be revealed by this initiative.

Ownership of copyright

The ownership of copyright may turn into a thorny question for publishers if they seek to go down the licensing and contractual route in the supply of information to libraries and the educational community. The government is more than likely to hire sophisticated negotiators, who may place publishers on proof that they are the owners of the copyright they purport to licence.

The publishers' typographical copyright will not be applicable and, accordingly, the publisher will have to rely exclusively on the authors' copyright that will, in the absence of an employment situation, need to be assigned to the publisher in writing if the publisher is to have any rights. This is not always a practical solution for publishers involved in the supply of scientific and technical information.

The absence of any primary copyright is particularly difficult for UK publishers because, unlike Continental legal systems, the UK has no law of unfair competition. An unfair competition claim could be brought into play, though, where text was unfairly expropriated and no publishers' copyright existed. The introduction of an unfair competition law should be at the top UK publishers' legal agenda with the increasing adoption of Continental copyright principles and their emphasis on authors' rights.

Fair dealing and licensing contracts

Fair dealing and the scope of copyright exceptions will be hotly disputed. Libraries and the educational community will wish to store and transmit text electronically. Government information will probably be available without cost and free of copyright restrictions. The scope of the draft directives' copyright exceptions will therefore be of crucial importance to publishers.

It will also be important to establish the extent to which contractual arrangements can override the legal copyright exceptions. Some see the solution for libraries and publishers as being a licensing arrangement, which will settle their relationship and the use of copyright material. However, will contractual terms override the fair use provisions?

Fair dealing and the scope of copyright exceptions will be hotly disputed.

The 1998 Database Regulations stipulate that fair use privileges cannot be overridden by contractual arrangements. If the same principles apply to copyright licensing contracts, then the vexed issue of fair use will not be resolved by model licensing contracts because it will not be lawful to impose a royalty on copying that falls within the fair use privileges.

Technical solutions

The new amendments to the Berne Convention providing for the restriction on technical devices that may be used to defeat publishers' encryption devices or management copyright systems are probably the most revolutionary changes that have taken place to international copyright law since the inception of the Berne Convention at the turn of the last century. Publishers using encryption methods may be able to control access to their electronic information, and outlawing devices that may defeat them could prove an effective means of supporting a publishers' on-line communications.

The monitoring of the use of text – for example, on the Internet – may be a very effective means for publishers of controlling the use made of electronic material on the Internet. In many respects, the Digital Age will mean that copyright will be more like a right of remuneration than an exclusive right of control. Collecting Societies will become more prominent and associations such as the Copyright Licensing Agency and the International Federation of Reproduction Rights Organisations will seek increasingly to enter into licensing arrangements based on copyright use.

Research is being undertaken to investigate methods whereby use of text use on the Internet can be tracked. The European Commission's IMPRIMATEUR initiative and the Digital Object Identifier Foundation (DOI), based in Washington and Geneva, may come up with technical solutions that could have a very significant impact on publishers' ability to track and control the copying and the accessing of copyright material.

The Database Regulations

With effect from 1 January 1998, databases are protected under UK law by The Copyright and Rights in Database Regulations. The database right originates from a European directive and its true significance for publishers has yet to be clarified by the courts. Which databases will be protected by the Regulations? Will journals be categorized as databases? If so, this wide definition could be very significant for publishers, given the absence of any publishers' copyright.

The duration of the database right is 15 years, which may be extended if new material is incorporated within the database. Of significance to publishers is the fact that the ownership of the database right will be the investor, not necessarily the creator. The vulnerability of databases to being accessed on-line is recognized in the Regulations and the database right will be infringed if a substantial part is extracted or re-utilized without the owners' permission.

Foreign nationals outside the Community will not have the benefits of the database right within the Community unless EU nationals enjoy equivalent rights in the country of the foreign national. At the time of writing, the US Congress is debating whether or not specific rights should be given to the creators of databases within the US so that US nationals may have the benefit of reciprocal rights.

Conclusion

The European Commission has estimated that, at the turn of the century, some 15 per cent of all publishing will take place on-line. While this is a sizeable percentage, it nevertheless must be borne in mind that much of traditional publishing will remain untouched by the Digital Age. Text will still be delivered in printed format.

Present UK copyright law and the European Union's Copyright Directive provide for extensive copyright protection to publishers in the electronic environment provided the exceptions are contained. The database right may shore up those situations where publishers may find themselves vulnerable as a result of the absence of any copyright protection. UK publishers should certainly be pressing for an unfair competition law, which exists in Continental legal systems, and protects publishers from unfair business practices when copyright principles are inapplicable. The prohibition of anti-copying devices may prove to be a practical solution in controlling mass unauthorized electronic copying.

Undoubtedly great changes will be made to copyright laws as the full implications of the Digital Age are better understood. Publishers will have to watch the demands of users with care and diplomacy. If publishers are perceived to be making balanced demands for copyright protection, then copyright will be able to adapt and survive. However, if extravagant claims are made, then a backlash could emerge from the Internet community, which 'in the public interest' might challenge the institution of copyright as we know it today. ■

TECHNOLOGY

contributors

David Feeny is Vice President of Templeton College, Oxford University and also Director of the Oxford Institute of Information Management. The Institute has a vigorous programme of research and executive teaching. David's own interests centre on the connections between strategy, organizations and information management. Topics include IT's role in creating strategic advantage, implementation of IT-based projects and the sourcing of IT services. Recent research has focused on creating organizational arrangements which foster strategic exploitation of IT. David Feeny's work has won international recognition and has been published in leading IS and general management journals, including *Harvard Business Review*, *Sloan Management Review* and *McKinsey Quarterly*.

David Feeny holds an MA from Oxford University and an MBA from Harvard Business School. Before returning to Oxford in 1984 he was for many years a senior marketing manager with IBM. In addition to his teaching and research activity, he is a consultant to a number of industrial and commercial organizations.

Robert Winter is Director of European Broadcasting Union (EBU) Education Unit. Robert joined the EBU in October 1996 to set up this new educational television unit, formed through the wishes of the public services broadcasters in Europe. The Unit now represents some 20 of the European-based public service broadcasters and a majority of their educational content. Prior to this post in Geneva, Robert was the Senior Commercial and Business Development Manager for BBC News and Current Affairs in London, with responsiblility for the Marketing Department of this Directorate. Previous to this Robert had been the Commercial and Business Development Manager for BBC LPR Resources (BBC TV London studios and all London-based production facilities). While at BBC News, Robert began the re-purposing and re-versioning of news stories into educational programmes, which were broadcast on a weekly basis, across the UK, on the Learning Zone as 'Newsfile'. Robert's training was in the commercial sector, with such organizations as Saatchi & Saatchi, Aspen Communications Plc, Thames Television, Border Television, and in the late 1970s for VPS Goodtimes (the film distribution arm for Sandy Lieberson and Sir David Puttnam).

Nathaniel Borenstein serves on the faculty of the School of Information at the University of Michigan. His achievements include MIME, the Internet standard format for multimedia data interoperation; metamail, a portable MIME implementation with millions of users; the ATOMICMAIL and Safe-Tcl languages for safe and portable interactive electronic mail messages; the First Virtual Green Commerce Model and its implementation, the first operational Internet payment system; and the Andrew Message System, a pioneering multimedia messaging application. He co-founded First Virtual Holdings in 1994, and served as its Chief Scientist for four years. He is the author of three books, two patents, and numerous articles and Internet RFC documents, and serves on the national boards of Computer Professionals for Social Responsibility and the Institute for Global Communications.

Randall S. Hancock is the Senior Vice President of Mainspring, an Internet advisory services firm based in Cambridge, Massachusetts, where he oversees research programmes and consulting activities on Internet initiatives and their impact on businesses across different industries. Randall Hancock has extensive experience working with clients globally to address a wide variety of strategic issues, with a particular focus on the Internet and electronic commerce. Previously, he was the founder and director of the Gemini Strategic Research Group, a unit of Gemini Consulting which provides strategic research and consulting services to Global 2000 clients in the telecommunications, media, and technology markets.

introduction by Anne Leer

HERE TODAY, GONE TOMORROW

Have you ever bought computer equipment at premium prices only to see it being rendered obsolete and surpassed by new and better models at half the cost? Have you ever invested in new software applications only to find them suddenly incompatible and out of date even before you learnt how to use all them properly? Do you feel pressured to keep up with the frequent releases of new models and software versions? Are you happy with your IT investment or are you perhaps fed up with watching your organization buy into an ever-increasing number of short-lived IT tools? Many of us feel overwhelmed by technology development and wonder how we are supposed to cope with the fast-changing technology environment. Organizations struggle to manage their IT investment and most of them do it rather poorly and suffer the consequent cost penalties.

In this section we will examine the technology environment of the Wired World from some very different perspectives. Don't worry, there are no boring technical chapters which you have to be an engineer to understand. We will visit technology experts, but it may surprise you as it did me, that they are more concerned with organizational and social issues then they are with technology itself.

David Feeny has devoted his career to the understanding of the impact of information technology on business organizations and consequent strategic management issues. In his extensive experience working with a range of different types of organization he has identified their common complaints, mistakes and possible success factors with respect to IT. He says that the emphasis on technology and technology-related skills, guarantees adoption, but not exploitation. Successful IT management depends on attitudes, relationships, organizational arrangements and processes. Feeny explains that executives need to learn how to distinguish between 'IT Hype', 'IT Capability', 'Useful IT' and 'Strategic IT'. There is a lot of technology hype around, seducing us into believing there is nothing technology can't do.

There is also a lot of IT capability that we do not need or cannot use. Nicholas Negroponte is often pointing out the need to have what he calls slim software – technology that does the job and no more. He complains about the obese software syndrome – the tendency to pack in excessive programming and functionality that nobody needs. Think of Microsoft Windows NT and you will know what Feeny and Negroponte are on about. Feeny urges us to think about what we actually need and what would be useful and not be tempted to buy into all those products which are merely products in search of a solution. He points out that the most critical task for executives is to master the strategic management of technology and to make sure that the technology investment makes a substantial, rather than marginal contribution to organizational achievement.

Robert Winter of the European Broadcasting Union is working in the midst of an industry in the process of being turned upside down by the digital revolution. Television will never be the same again. Winter describes the many dilemmas broadcasters face in the midst of all this change. Digital technology has lowered the barriers to entry in the television market and broadcasters are faced with many new entrants and fierce competition. Winter believes that broadcasters have no choice but to go digital if they want to survive. Another challenge for broadcasters is that before digital television, broadcasters were used to a one-way life. No so anymore, with interactive television the audience answer back and they also make up their own TV schedules and decide when and where and what they want to see. Broadcasters have to set up customer service departments and develop staff and new skills to provide new services.

Although Winter welcomes many of the technology advances, he says he doesn't buy the total convergence message – that in the future we can do just about anything on our TV – why on earth would we want to? Winter says he doesn't need all that on one unit in his lounge.

Nathaniel Borenstein, now there is surprise – here we have one of the pioneers of Internet, and we might expect him to give us a technologist's enthusiastic account of Internet development and his positive visions of a technology-based future. But it seems working at the heart of technology development, with a deeper understanding than most of the technological capability and the implications, Borenstein has developed a very critical perspective and social concerns. He doesn't doubt the revolutionary impact of the Internet. However, he says, in the past each technology invented has brought with it a mixture of blessings and curses, rarely foreseen by the futurists who witnessed the birth of the technology.

Borenstein believes that in the future the Internet will continue to expand and become much more stratified and sophisticated. It will be faster, far more powerful, cheaper and easy to use. He believes Internet marketing may rapidly become extremely personalized and focused on the individual, if only because of the feedback mechanism the Internet gives the manufacturers of goods and services, tracking and recording everything the customers do. He is deeply concerned about privacy and security issues, and he may leave you with a feeling that both privacy and security could be lost to us in the future.

Randall Hancock's chapter will give you a practical overview of technology developments and how they interrelate. He will describe what he calls the irreversible forces which drives the emergence of the networked economy: technology advances, Internet connectivity, telecommunication capacity, open standards, deregulation and globalization. He believes that technology is one of the most important catalysts in the networked economy, enabling the development of goods and services.

Hancock describes ground-breaking technology developments that will transform the way today's Internet works. For instance, so-called Dense Wave Division Multiplexing

(DWDM) which will increase the capacity of fibre optic cables from two to eighty billion bits per second. Like Barksdale, Hancock is also referring to Metcalfe's law and the importance of understanding the value creation processes of networks. Hancock's chapter also offers a thorough treatment of so-called 'killer applications' and he successfully demystifies the concept, and offers a refreshing rational explanation for how commerce and technology interact in the quest to create new business.

This section will add to a growing theme throughout this book – the emphasis on our values, needs and aspirations. I wonder, could this be the beginning of a global awakening to the fact that technology is overrated. The real value creation begins when the needs of people and organizations drive the technology development and not the other way around. Earlier in this book, Al Gore urged us to learn how to use the benefits of technology to promote our core values. How can we succeed if technology is allowed to stay in the driving seat? ■

David Feeny

Vice President, Templeton College, Oxford University

LASTING IDEAS WITHIN TURBULENT TECHNOLOGY

In 1984, I became one of the co-founders of the Oxford Institute of Information Management at Templeton College. At the time, both industry and government seemed preoccupied with questions about the adoption of Information Technology (IT). There was much interest in the nation's potential to be major providers of the new technologies. Companies and their IT professionals were concerned with the supply of IT – the availability of analysts and programmers to meet the burgeoning demand for new systems development. The focus was very much on the supply of IT and technology itself. Alongside these concerns, there was a pressing need to look at the impact of technology and understand the consequent management issues. The new Institute wanted to respond to this need and put the emphasis on 'information management' rather than 'information technology'. The mission of this new Institute was stated to be:

> To improve the body of knowledge on how to manage information resources, so that information technology can be fully exploited in business, government and other large organizations to the advantage of the host organization, its members and society at large.

The underlying thesis was that successful exploitation of IT is critically dependent on the actions of business managers and senior levels of IT management.

Some years later, in 1998, both mission and thesis remain in place. The goal for government as well as industry should be IT exploitation, not IT adoption. The emphasis on technology and technology-related skills guarantees adoption but not exploitation. The research carried out at the Oxford Institute of Information Management has consistently confirmed that it is management that makes the difference.

How well positioned are managers to take up the challenge? It is common wisdom that most executives are particularly uncomfortable when addressing IT issues. Their typical concerns include the following.

- How do I assess the 'value for money' of my existing investments in IT? It is difficult enough to keep track of IT costs as expenditure is increasingly incurred by end users of IT beyond the formal IT budget. And when it comes to benefits, I must somehow choose between the sophisticated but dubious arithmetic of investment documentation and the general rhetoric that assures me of better decisions, faster outcomes, lower costs and higher quality. Overall, we seem to have invested a great deal without significantly changing the business.

- Given that we have a limited IT budget and an abundance of bids for it, how do I choose between application opportunities? Should I prioritize bids based on rate of return or payback period or ration the budget between functional areas of the business? Is a new Personnel Information System more or less important than a further refinement of Production Scheduling? Should we just increase the IT budget to allow for all 'viable' investment cases?

- How can we ensure that the investments we commission are achieved within budget and timescale? Our track record is notoriously patchy, even though we build in contingencies to figures that are already too large for comfort. Will usage of the new 'breakthrough' set of IT tools mean that things really are different this time?

- When we finally achieve the roll-out of new systems, why are the users of them so ungrateful? Given that the whole purpose of the system was to improve the business, why, so often, do I end up dealing with a series of complaints about lack of 'user friendliness' or coping with business problems that are reportedly due to systems deficiencies?

The wider question, surely, is why so many organizations and executives still exhibit these concerns after more than three decades of rapid development in IT hardware, software and service components. In organizations that embrace the best CASE (Computer-Assisted Software Engineering) tools or object-oriented programming techniques, are new systems delivered on time and do they delight users? Does the engagement of highly qualified consultants result in identification of an IT strategy that resolves the dilemma of investment priorities? Are all these concerns going to be addressed more successfully if the next head of IT is a proven business manager, plucked from another part of the organization? And/or should we invest in intensive IT education for businesspeople and business education for IT people to achieve a 'hybrid' culture in which everyone is comfortable with the issues? Is the ultimate solution to outsource the IT function to expert external service providers ('strategic partners'?) who will resolve these issues for us on a permanent basis?

I would challenge the likely effectiveness of any such initiatives made in isolation based on the research evidence accumulated at the Oxford Institute of Information Management. The information we have suggests that the fundamentals of successful information management lie in attitudes, relationships, organizational arrangements and processes. Organizations can capitalise on new technologies, tools, consultancy and services to further improve its performance if (and only if) these fundamentals are properly addressed. In other words, there are fundamentals that have lasting relevance despite the turbulence of the IT industry. To understand why, we need to identify some prevailing characteristics of IT – factors that help to explain why the executive concerns described above remain so familiar across the years of 'progress' in IT.

For many years now I have been using Figure 1 to explore with executives why information technology provides them with such a challenge. Figure 1 suggests there are four IT domains. While the content of each may vary over time, that they exist as distinct areas remains an important phenomenon.

The first domain is labelled 'IT hype'. Throughout the history of IT, there has been a rhetoric that goes beyond the actuality – a focus on potential capabilities and outcomes. The most obvious example in the second half of the 1990s has been the 'Information Superhighway' which, we are encouraged to believe, will shortly transform the existence of every individual, organization and nation in the universe. IT hype is not just the creature of optimistic IT providers. Heavyweight newspapers, journals and politicians have found it *de rigeur* to issue visionary statements on the subject.

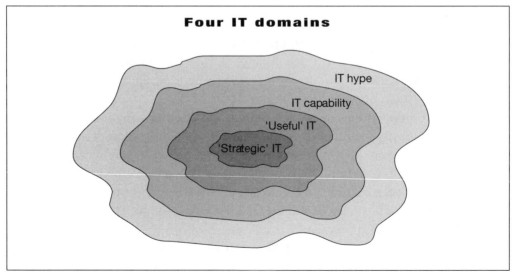

Four IT domains

IT hype

IT capability

'Useful' IT

'Strategic' IT

FIGURE 1

Within the IT hype lies an ever-increasing domain of 'IT capability', comprising the products and services that are available today for organizations to exploit. Here, the counterpart of the information superhighway is the Internet. The Internet, though, truly exists, and has substantial functionality. However, its limitations in performance and security dimensions alone made it a questionable operational tool of real significance for most corporations in 1997/98. Clearly there are many other more mature strands of IT where the current capability is truly quite remarkable, so that the domain as a whole represents a huge toolkit available to organizations, but how much of it is of use?

> ... the fundamentals of successful information management lie in attitudes, relationships, organizational arrangements and processes.

We have probably all experienced some IT products we would characterize as solutions in search of problems. If we define the 'Useful IT' domain as consisting of all the investments that potentially provide at least a minimum acceptable rate of return for the organization, we can reasonably depict this domain as large. While not as large as the IT capability domain, most will feel it is quite large enough to overwhelm any conceivable level of IT budget!

The fourth and smallest domain is labelled 'Strategic IT'. It is probably an unfortunate label to have chosen as some will assume it refers exclusively to grandiose examples, such as the use of airline reservations systems as competitive weapons. However, when I define it as that subset of potential investments that can make a substantial rather than marginal contribution to organizational achievement, I find most managers intuitively recognize its existence – even if they have not directly experienced it.

The diagram, albeit simplistic, now enables us to further examine organizational goals for IT; provide some explanation for historic disappointments and suggest in outline a more convincing and robust way forward.

First, we can define organizational exploitation of IT to be successful navigation through the domains, so that organizational resources become consistently focused on the achievement of 'strategic' rather than 'useful' IT investments. By definition, this will provide significantly better value for money. By illustration (below) we may size the possible significance.

In the early 1990s, Company A was experiencing a series of poor financial results. Others were also suffering within its industry of global giants, but executives of Company A particularly noted the generally excellent performance of Company B – a competitor with comparable scale and product lines. They initiated a series of benchmarking studies that yielded performance data against industry success factors, including the following:

- Company A took 50 per cent longer than Company B to develop a new product.
- Company A's time to deliver against a specific customer order was two to three times that of Company B.

■ Labour productivity in Company B was up to twice that of Company A.

The contribution of IT to this situation? Further studies provided conflicting evidence:

■ Company A's IT activity was assessed by third-party consultants to be world class in its efficiency.
■ Company A was spending more than twice as much on IT as Company B as a percentage of revenue or spend per product shipped.
■ In the specific area of computer-aided engineering – which might contribute to shorter product development times – Company B invested more than Company A

In the language of the diagram, it can be suggested that while Company A had a cadre of excellent IT professionals, they were supporting a portfolio of 'useful IT' investments that contributed far less benefit (at twice the cost) than the more 'strategic' portfolio of Company B.

How had Company A ended up in this position and why have so many of the executives I have worked with positioned their own company's experience as being like that of Company A rather than Company B? Figure 1 provides potential insights into this all too common experience.

Consider three ways of navigating through the domains of Figure 1. The first we can refer to as IT led. Faced with the complexities of IT hype and IT capabilities, senior management look to their Company's IT function to assess these domains profesionally and propose an agenda for IT investment – subject, of course, to executive approval. Most organizations have operated in this way for some part of their history. Company A did so until the mid-1980s. Why have they (and most others) moved away from an IT led process? IT professionals are the obvious people to develop and maintain an authoritative view of IT capability. The difficulty lies in moving from capability to application.

Here we encounter a unique characteristic of IT – its inherent lack of application purpose. If I explain to someone any of a range of traditional technologies – weighing scales, bulldozers or blast furnaces – the applications are obvious. The technology's purpose was defined at the point of manufacture, and its relevance or lack of it to any particular business is easy to discern. However, if I explain what is meant by a multi-media workstation, who knows what relevance it may have within a bank, supermarket chain or government department. Unlike the earlier examples, a workstation's application is defined at the point of use, not the point of manufacture. Its relevance is a function of the imagination of the user, not the product designer, and may take any of a number of forms. For example, in the UK, the Direct Line insurance company moved rapidly from entrant to a mature market to market leader. It used the same core IT products as its entrenched competitors, but it applied them to support a new and superior business model. The technology was embedded in strategic rather than useful initiatives.

This lack of application specificity is the stumbling block within an IT-led process of navigation. Having identified a new area of IT capability, IT professionals are understandably keen to put it to use. They exhibit energy and creativity in identifying how the technology could be used, and in constructing a supporting cost–benefit analysis. Senior management finds itself in the uncomfortable position of adjudicating on a series of strongly argued investment cases. Any negative decision feels like the rejection of an opportunity for improvement. 'Useful IT' is the common result.

In the mid-1980s, Company A abandoned the IT-led approach and adopted what we can call a user-led process. All investment cases for IT would now be developed and argued by the potential beneficiaries – the users of the technology. The role of the IT function was now to efficiently implement the applications that had won users' approval. Many organizations still largely operate such a user-led process. It seems eminently rational, particularly as end users become more sophisticated in their understanding of IT.

Unfortunately, as Company A discovered, the user-led approach tends to parallel the IT-led approach in producing a large portfolio of 'useful IT' investments. There seem to be two reasons for this. First, only a subset of users takes up the challenge, and the members of the subset are those users who have become enthusiasts for IT. They are at least as energetic and creative as the IT community in pursuing opportunities to embrace the exciting technology they have discovered. Second, each is operating within a bounded domain of responsibility, and their proposals therefore represent potential improvements to what may be non-critical aspects of the business. More 'useful IT' results as senior management now finds it even more difficult to deny business-side people the opportunity to improve their performance.

So, how do the Company Bs of this world achieve their focus on 'strategic IT' investments that leverage key dimensions of organizational performance? What is the 'business-led' approach to navigating the four domains that results in an organization understanding what *should* be done – rather than what could be done – with IT? A business-led approach requires one of the three paradigm shifts that characterize successful information management.

The accumulated evidence of our research and experience identifies six characteristics of a business-led approach to IT investment (see Figure 2).

- The trigger point is articulation of a business issue or opportunity that, if successfully addressed, would radically advance the organization's achievement of its vision and strategy. Examples might include a breakthrough in unit costs, reduced time to market or differentiation via new value-added customer services. The starting point is not IT capability, nor an existing business process.

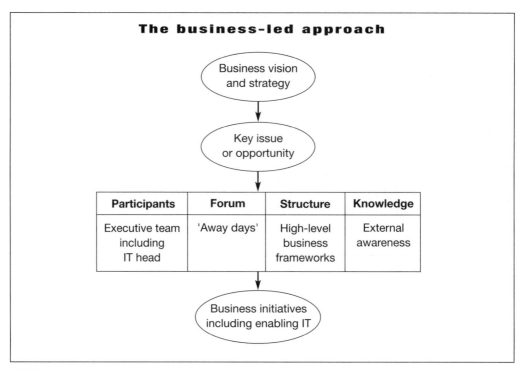

FIGURE 2

- The business issue is owned and addressed by the organization's executive team, including its head of IT. Each brings a functional perspective, but all are focused as a team on how best to address the key issue.
- The team accepts that 'breakthrough' thinking is unlikely to be achieved amid the hurly burly of day-to-day business or routine board meetings. They adopt an 'away day' culture, taking significant time out from operational activity to enable this kind of thinking to occur.
- The team adopts some high-level methodologies – positioning frameworks, value chain concepts and so on – that serve as a common language and structure for debating the issue at hand.
- By means of its own membership or guest members, the team has access to knowledge of how other organizations have addressed this type of issue, including organizations in other sectors and including examples of potential IT contributions.
- The target output is not an IT investment case, but an integrated design for a new business initiative, which spells out requirements for IT as well as for other functional areas.

We can describe this as a paradigm shift because the traditional process of navigation through the domains of Figure 1 is reversed – from outside in to inside out. The business-led process works on the assumption that anything is possible, envisions the ideal business initiative, then checks to see if the necessary IT is available to support it.

If the first paradigm shift has been made, the second is relatively straightforward. It involves evaluating IT investment in a way that flows naturally from a business-led navigation process (see Figure 3). Most organizations still operate investment appraisal processes that demand cost–benefit analyses of proposed IT expenditure. The second paradigm shift involves recognizing that IT *expenditure* does not lead to business benefits. Only the adoption of new business *ideas* can lead to business benefits. If there is no new business idea associated with IT investment, the most that can be expected is that some existing business idea will operate a little more efficiently as old existing technology is replaced by new. On the other hand, as Figure 3 depicts, if a new business idea *is* associated with IT investment, it will not be delivered by IT activity alone – a wider set of changes to business processes, skills,

> **The business-led process works on the assumption that anything is possible, envisions the ideal business initiative, then checks to see if the necessary IT is available to support it.**

structures, measurements must be implied. All of these must be identified, costed, planned for, and championed by relevant line management if the investment is to succeed. Analysis of IT investment in isolation does not make sense. A holistic picture delineates all the elements required to deliver a new business idea and articulates how we shall measure that the new idea has been put in place. It then invites management to judge the value of that idea in profit impact terms and decide whether or not the likely value justifies all (or none) of the necessary investment.

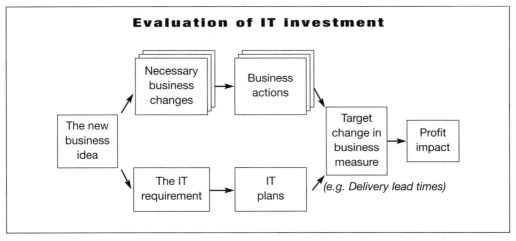

FIGURE 3

There is a third paradigm shift to be made if we are to transform the track record of systems development. The traditional approach to systems development is based on a rational/engineering perspective that leads to a well-structured sequential process, driven by IT professionals but with regular involvement from the business side to confirm satisfaction at checkpoints along the way. The process begins with a statement of requirements and proceeds through external design, internal design, coding and testing. If the application in question is essentially a new technology platform for an existing business idea, this is all well and good. However, if the application is a 'strategic' component of a new business initiative, this traditional process is a route to disaster.

The basic problem comes in the initial phase – the specification of requirements. In a radically new business initiative, the fact is that the business has only a general understanding of its need at the outset. Confronted by a process that presses for a full specification ('Tell me what you need and promise not to change your mind'), users resort to specifying everything they *might* need, in order to be 'safe'. As the specification grows, timescales extend and risks escalate. We are confronted with the all too familiar phenomenon of the two-year development in which few have confidence. Then, a succession of poor experiences generates an environment in which the business feels unable to base its strategy on untimely and uncertain IT developments.

The paradigm shift establishes a new culture, based on the following elements.

- A single project team is set up, comprising all the required resources from both the business and the IT function. Ideally, all team members are committed to the project full time and co-located in order to build good relationships and successful communication.

- The team is made responsible not for creating a system but for delivering clearly specified benefits to the business. Indeed, there are no other success criteria. Hence, if it becomes clear during the project that specifications and plans should change, all team members are motivated to show the necessary flexibility.

- Executive management *mandates,* at the outset, the timescale within which the project must deliver the target benefits. Managers deliberately specify (and stick to) a challenging timescale even though expert opinion may say it is impossible. Nine months is the maximum timescale and it may well be significantly shorter.

- This 'time boxing' forces the team to make decisions about what is really required, to target the adequate rather than the gold-plated system. It drives adherence to the Pareto Principle, – 20 per cent of the effort achieves 80 per cent of the available result.

- Time boxing also encourages the use of prototyping. Instead of creating a full requirements specification, the team iterates through a series of prototypes and achieves the target learning about what is really required.

- The project may be planned as a series of phases within an overall architecture if the team remains convinced that it cannot be achieved within a single nine-month time box. This is still a major step forward. A series of six-month steps that each deliver business benefits is a far better route than a two-year monolith.

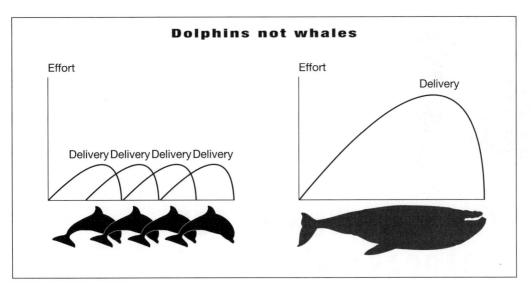

FIGURE 4

Figure 4 – Dolphins not whales – is not a product of my imagination. It was produced by one major corporation seeking to implement the findings of our research, and proved particularly effective in winning hearts and minds. This is surely what paradigm shifts are all about, leading people to a different but better approach that depends on changes in attitudes, understanding and relationships. ■

This chapter has been developed and based upon an introduction I wrote for another book *Managing IT as a Strategic Resource* by Feeny and Islei, McGraw-Hill Publishing Company, 1997, with the kind permission of the publisher.

Robert Winter

Director, European Broadcasting Union (EBU)
Education Unit

DIGITAL DILEMMAS FOR BROADCASTERS

If you check into any reasonable hotel room in Europe, you will usually find a TV that has a package of programmes from the local cable or satellite supplier. Depending on which country you are in, this package may also include a selection of films you can watch on demand, plus a video games handset – for those quiet moments between films. You may also find a fax, a PC modem point and a daily personalized newspaper service, over the fax line. You can programme your TV for an early morning call, order room services, check your statement and pay the bill – all on the same screen.

When I was invited by the Technical Department of the European Broadcasting Union to review a presentation of a new test digital bouquet channel off the satellite from RAI in Italy, I was really very keen to attend – given that this was, apparently, the future. You can imagine my dissatisfaction when I discovered that it was not yet as clever as the hotel room I had just checked out of, and had on offer slightly less than the hotel. The screen in the presentation was, I admit very wide, but when was the last time you heard a member of the public say that television would be OK, if only it was in wide screen?

I've heard that the makers of popular TV soap dramas in the UK are crying over the costs of having to remake their stage sets in order to adapt to this new wide screen format. Most TV sets are slightly smaller than life size because of the current format of the present-day squarer TV screen. I am all for progress, but I wonder if this wide screen aspect really is progress or technology trying to find a use?

To receive these new digital channels or services, we are being asked to either invest in a new, expensive TV – probably with this wide screen format – or in a new set top box. With this new box, we can view the new digital services via our existing TV set, but with the usual 'squarer' TV pictures.

Most new set top boxes will have sophisticated handsets that we can use to access the Web, play games, order goods and so on, from the comfort of your own living room. Mostly, these channels will resemble the services that I was getting in my hotel room. Why we suddenly need all of this in one unit, in our living rooms, I am not sure. Apparently, the future will be that you can do *anything* on your TV and, indeed, that you will want to do *everything*.

This development includes the first stages in the convergence of the narrow band internet with the broadband video or film on demand options. However, have you ever seen the Internet over the TV? It looks terrible, and I am not convinced this will improve. Some things are simply meant to be viewed at one distance and some at another. Go to an art gallery and you can see what I mean.

Much research has been done already into the ideal screen-viewing distance for different programme contents and activities. Those activities we do within a close distance to the screen and those we wish to do further away are well documented. Having the ability to do everything using the one screen may seem an advantage, but, possibly, not for anything other than for very short periods of time.

The clever part about new technology is not the screen size or it being called a PC/TV or TV/PC, but the fat data and clever bits that come into your home and allow you to choose what you do, when you want to do it and using whichever device you wish. In short, I don't buy this total convergence message. I only buy that technology will allow me to do anything, anytime, anywhere, but at my own very selected moments and places.

In this latter area, we probably have another crucial matter, and central dilemma for the broadcasters. The control and choice of programmes has hitherto been in the hands of the television controllers, and those men in dark designer suits we read about in the Sunday papers' colour magazines. However, via digital television and the possibilities now opened up to us, we get to make up our own schedules. Take Mrs A. in Carrington Crescent in England. She can now programme her own TV schedule to suit her particular time constraints. She can order the weekly food and grocery items she needs, and then have them delivered. She can review the car prices across all of the local garage centres and ensure she gets the best price for her new car model. Probably more importantly, though, she can download her latest business economics course from the University of Industry. The video modules she will keep on her TV for viewing at a later date. The economics course notes she will download and transfer to her PC. This will allow her to work at her PC in a convenient way, and enter into two-way course discussions or form meetings with other students and her personal tutor.

The dilemma for the broadcasters is that their technology has delivered a new power into the hands of the many, not just the few. Not only can Mrs A. decide her own viewing and working schedule, but the low cost of entry and ease with which the technology can be used has encouraged many new sectors to be involved in the whole broadcasting industry.

In this case scenario, there will no longer be people who are broadcasters alone. The most successful will also be publishers and distributors. The most successful publishers will also be broadcasters and distributors, and across all media.

One man and his dog anywhere in the world can publish and have a presence on the Internet with as high a profile as a major corporation. Meanwhile, the Internet, when it appears on TV as well, will encourage us to stop viewing scheduled programmes and instead build our own lives, thus developing our own interests and hobbies, or careers, instead of passively watching the TV perhaps!

Many remember that schools television (or, before that, schools radio) was a formidable force and very influential in its time. This has now been severely depleted. Without this educational remit, the undermining of the public service licence fee is following hand in hand. Many European public service broadcasters are being pressured by both the cost of retooling, from analogue to digital production, and the diversity of services that are now offered by the commercial consortia.

Arguably, perhaps, education for us all, will be the greatest winner of this new digital technology age. Teaching and learning can only benefit from the addition of interactive communication. Interactivity can be used for course work and on-line tutor support. The digital distribution age will allow us to complete studying at school, college or at the workplace and at home. Our tutor will be able to be on-line wherever we are, alongside the video modules, the course notes and interactive assessment papers.

In education across Europe, there has been a dramatic increase in lifelong learning and distance learning. This has encouraged many teenagers and adults to start using the vast new array of digital information. From archives available to us, we can all study for new qualifications and receive vocational training. The explosion in digital channels available through the cheaper satellite transponder time allows this information to be carried directly to the home, as never before.

This has allowed universities, colleges and publishers to become true broadcasters of education, across all ages and all subject matter. The traditional educators in the media, the broadcasters, have found themselves sidelined. A university or college can offer accreditation, on-line tutor support and massive advances in on-line learning techniques. The broadcasters, hitherto, have been slow to develop in this new educational market sector. They have launched web sites that have mostly mirrored news and sport or entertainment and magazine programmes, extending their reach and brand loyalty only in these areas. Most have made very expensive mistakes in CD-ROM production or publishing and are very reluctant to expand this area due to the technology changes. Just around the corner, the Internet and the offer of digital television to the home could make the CD-ROM redundant.

Arguably, perhaps, education for us all, will be the greatest winner of this new digital technology age.

The combination of the PC and the TV and being able to review material on either medium, or file the materials from the PC to the TV, or vice versa, gives us a huge flexibility previously only dreamt of.

These developments, to reach us all, will probably at the best take another five to ten years, although substantial trials and a real commercial growth are taking place in this area already.

Those public service broadcasters entering this field, and off the back of the licence fee, are struggling with the other dilemma of all public services. Should they find commercial partners for both content funding and technology help, and can they partner with just one academic institution, or should it be with several?

How can they mix the commercial aspects of education with the 'free access for all' public service remit? Can they, in fact, enter into commercial partnerships or does this mean that they erode their freedom and individuality, granted to them by the unique licence fee system? There is pressure to build partnerships because they have to be able to offer accreditation for their educational content offerings if they are to be of any value or if they wish to stay competitive.

Until such time as we have the University of Channel 4 or similar, the broadcasters have to develop partnerships with private and public concerns in order to develop and provide what the people the want. If they don't, education is lost forever as a core remit and service, probably along with the licence fee. The BBC's Open University programmes have developed along these lines to meet this remit, but the BBC still finds itself hampered by the tags and restraints of its public service origin.

Many of the commercial consortia have entered the European and global markets very easily, grabbing a lead on the public service providers without any restrictions on their own sources of funding or partnerships. These new dynamic commercial parties are actively involved because it is a very profitable area of business. The broadcasters, though, are seeing this lucrative adult market being taken away from them. The commercial consortia are also developing into the pre-school and schools markets, often giving this content away for free, off the back of the paying adult learners. This traditional area for broadcasters, is being packaged and whipped away without a second thought and before they can adjust to this new world. I just wonder, if all media-supported education, when resting in the hands of these new commercial consortia, will remain truly free at school level? How long it will be before the commercial consortia persuade governments to provide financial support, to the tune of the probably scrapped licence fee? They will, after all, be delivering education to 'the masses'.

For public service broadcasters, it is true that technology does have its many benefits in education, but also many more political nightmares and pitfalls. Take, for example, the BBC Online educational pages. They are quite superb and the forerunners of what many of our children will use throughout their time at school and into their adult years. However, the Internet, as it is structured now, is open and global.

Thus, the BBC Education site can be accessed by anyone anywhere in the world. However, the site is funded by the TV licence fee, paid by the residents of the UK. An army of BBC staff is needed to make sure that all on-line enquiries, from pre-school teachers to teenagers and so on, are responded to within 48 hours of their e-mail to the BBC. Therefore, the licence fee in this instance may be supporting global educational on-line developments and supporting the required staff salaries, but for work that is not UK based. There is nothing wrong in this and, of course, in broad terms, it makes a whole lot of sense. However, if you examine the BBC's charter and the complex political issues at stake, any commercial consortia offering the same services and support could cry foul.

This rather rash BBC promise to answer all enquiries within 48 hours also highlights the other very fundamental cultural change broadcasters have had to face. They have only recently learnt that this is a two-way thing. The audience is answering back. Until now, broadcasters have had a one-way life, choosing to produce the programmes they want, broadcasting them at the times they want, based on the audience 'average'. Going back to Mrs A., she does not need this scheduled service any more. The service she wants is an on demand one. She knows she can access the content she wants to see at any time, whenever she wants. There will be very little brand loyalty in this brave new world.

For public service broadcasters, it is true that technology does have its many benefits in education, but also many more political nightmares and pitfalls.

The audience can choose to delete advertising breaks and, perhaps more importantly, use the TV for a whole variety of other subjects and interests rather than watching scheduled programmes.

For commercial broadcasters this is also a real nightmare. It's very true that they can use this technology to define exactly who is watching what – via Pay-TV or other forms of conditional access – but they can also tell that you are at home studying, not just simply viewing, and so not watching a programme that you have just invested a fortune in producing. The audience is likely to start working from home, learning languages and so on using TV courses, delivered by publishers.

In offering these two-way services, broadcasters will have to employ new staff with new customer service and customer care handling skills. The audience will be able to interact for heavens sake, they won't just write a letter to you, for a snippet to be broadcast on *Points of View* or *Radio Postbag*. Broadcasters will need to employ and train staff in new areas and in new ways, previously only required by high street shops, not the 'ivory media towers'. And when we are in the high street, so to speak, who will ensure that *all* members of the public are being supported and cared for?

At a recent major meeting of public service broadcasters, I simply asked if anyone in the room had used the Internet in black and white only or run a CD-ROM without sound or colour? Who had handled a TV remote control or PC mouse with both hands bandaged? Needless to say not many responses. Yet, if we are making technology accessible to all – and, in particular, education available to all via the PC or the PC/TV – how do we expect those with limited sight, hearing or other handicaps, to actually use all of this clever stuff that we are developing, and thereby receive 'equal' educational opportunities?

I'd like to see all of the educational on-line sites judged on their simplicity and ease of use for the challenged, not just the able-bodied among us. How many of the educational web sites can actually be properly and clearly navigated, if, for example, you have a colour vision impairment or a hearing impairment? Not many is the answer. Who will support this area of our new digital business? Well, surely this is an area that the public service broadcasters could excel in and help the rest of us to develop new exemplars. How well broadcasters presently understand the power of images, colours, graphics and sound. Surely this expertise can be put to better use than simply very good opening and closing title graphics for programmes or station identity packages?

The motors of change in digital television can be separated into their technological, legal and economic parts, but, as we have seen above, all of these can interact. New technology makes competition possible from areas never before seen as being historically involved. This greater competition forces developments in technology, thus reducing further the entry level for new participants and increasing the competition once again. The lower barriers bring new partners and new developers into content creation and distribution, sometimes destabilizing traditional broadcasters by diluting their competitive edge.

The new digital channels in education will be able to bring in considerable additional income, but thereby creates many new commercial competitors. The broadcasters, facing this transformation in their own markets, are diversifying or have plans to diversify into all of these new areas – new thematic channels, Pay TV, on-line services, and often at a cost to their traditional programme output. Many of these new areas are, at best and for the moment, marginal in terms of general public accessability, but they require huge resources and man hours to develop and support. How can the public service broadcasters justify this diversification away from their traditional areas for what is a still a marginal activity? Well, if they don't get involved now, these markets will not be accessible as the commercial parties swallow up the competitive lead and edge. The universal versus limited access issue is only going to increase, not decrease as the issues over public funding increase with the spread of access. With the expansion of capacity on cable and satellite channels, the 'must carry' issue for all broadcasters can only become more important.

The issues surrounding gatekeepers, brands, diversification and so on will require most broadcasters to examine their content and service policies and those concerning commercial partnerships. The trend to create new regulatory bodies across all forms of technology is forcing the deregulation of media and is posing probably the most serious threat to public broadcasting. The commercial operators are finding it easier and easier to undermine the financial basis of the public service licence fee by focusing on the wave of new digital developments, using the issues of accessibility, commercial market competition and the redeployment of resources paid for and supported by the licence fee. These are the dilemmas for public service broadcasters in this new digital world.

Finally, if I have one vision, it is that each educational content producer, within the Europeanwide public television service, becomes a national resource knowledge centre. These knowledge centres, existing on servers at each of the main national broadcasters, would be linked via a broadband Intranet, sharing, exchanging and developing new educational content for all media across each of the broadcasters. These centres would then be made available on the Internet to all schools, after school clubs, colleges, universities and adult training centres, plus, of course, to you and me at home, delivering pre-packaged family learning courses. They would be sold to you when appropriate or provided free to schools by a commercial partner or publishing partner and delivered with on-line support provided by the broadcaster and partner.

> **The universal versus limited access issue is only going to increase, not decrease as the issues over public funding increase with the spread of access.**

There has to be a way to do this that does not imply that the licence fee or public service remit comes under threat or needs to be scrapped. Many broadcasters, as most commercial parties know, have the most fantastic archives, resources and expertise. To simply transfer this to new commercial consortia could literally be selling the nation's audio-visual assets to all and any for the highest bid, and not always remaining accessible by the nation that has paid for its origination and creation.

Such a knowledge centre network could deliver any material, in any language, at any time, day or night, and to any location. This is one true benefit of digital television. Allowing the public-service broadcasters and their archives to be opened up to each and every one of us would be the other real benefit. ■

Nathaniel Borenstein

Author and scientist, University of Michigan

THE FUTURE OF THE INTERNET AND THE INTERNET OF THE FUTURE

Ann Arbor, 23 September 2057 (AD) – Recent breakthroughs in translating ancient petro-glyphs from Mediterranean caves have yielded the following tentative translation, into modern colloquial English, of what are believed to be the earliest source documents regarding the history and social impact of technology.

THE FUTURE OF THE WHEEL: The invention of the wheel promises to usher in a new era of change, potentially rivalling the discovery of fire itself. Already, promising experiments have linked two or even more wheels together to facilitate the movement of objects lacking sufficient balance to use a solitary wheel. Researchers predict the development of highly stable multiwheel platforms, permitting wheeled transport of objects that are several orders of magnitude larger or heavier than anything we can transport today. This, in turn, raises hopes for a quantum improvement in agricultural methods. Looking further ahead, futurists envision hitching wheels to animals and perhaps even finding artificial mechanisms to trigger wheeled motion. Thinker Org, commonly acknowledged as the inventor of the wheel, has conclusively demonstrated that, by attaching vines to wheels of differing sizes, he can raise or lower the speed with which a wheel's shaft rotates. While this particular phenomenon appears to be without practical value, it underscores the possible existence of numerous unanticipated applications of wheel technology. Additionally, social thinkers have suggested that, by vastly increasing our agricultural production capabilities, it may be that the wheel will help usher in a new era of peace and prosperity, with our shared wheel-based productivity making fighting over food, and hence most violence between human beings, completely obsolete. Ultimately, the wheel should help to reduce or eliminate most forms of human suffering and facilitate a fundamental change in the way that people relate to each other and to the world as a whole.

The limits on our vision

The future of the wheel, back when the wheel had nothing but a future, undoubtedly looked very rosy and the people who witnessed its birth were undoubtedly optimistic about what it would bring to the world. The wheel of the future, on the other hand, when it came into being in historical times, brought a considerably more mixed legacy. In addition to its undeniable positive effects, the wheel rolled under the chariots that slaughtered the enemies of the Romans, powered the moving tracks of Hitler's tanks as they rolled across Europe and enabled the take-off and landing of Enola Gay on its way to Hiroshima.

The future of the Internet, seen from the edge of a new millennium, is exciting indeed, but what will the Internet of the future actually bring? At the turn of the millennium, a thoughtful, creative, and well-informed technologist might plausibly hope to see up to five or ten years into the future of technology. Those few people who have managed to do so with any measure of consistency are commonly described as forward-thinking, or visionaries, but in the current pace of technological evolution, ten years is nearly the event horizon. Douglas Englebart is widely recognized as having been fantastically ahead of his time for having invented the mouse roughly 15 years before it was popularized by Apple Macintosh. This level of prescience may approximate a current upper bound on our ability to predict the future of technology.

Still, everyone wants to know what the future of the Internet holds. Where our technical vision begins to run out, our social and political agendas quickly step in to take up the slack. Since the beginning of recorded history – though not quite as far back as the fanciful petroglyphs that open this chapter – every new technological breakthrough has been envisioned as leading humanity towards either a utopia or its opposite. In actual practice, of course, each technology has brought with it a mixture of blessings and curses – relatively few of which were foreseen by the futurists who witnessed the technology's birth. If history is to be our guide, any attempt to detail the future of the Internet is likely to prove naive in its assumptions and far off the mark in its conclusions.

It is therefore with significant trepidation that any technologist should approach the task of writing a chapter entitled 'The future of the Internet.' However, non-technical audiences – notably policy makers, social scientists, and business leaders – are always seeking such predictions in the hope of planning more rationally for the future. Also, human nature being what it is, the lack of a true oracle is not accompanied by any shortage of people willing to step up and offer their own answers. Thus, technologists are not let off the hook very easily, and rightly so. If we don't do our best to explain what can (and cannot) be foreseen, the future will inevitably be predicted by those with even less understanding, and the consequences, probably, will be even worse than might otherwise be expected.

As it happens, a great deal of the Internet's technological future seems relatively clear. While discontinuous innovations are impossible to anticipate, much of the Internet's evolution will follow a continuous evolutionary trend that is relatively easy to chart. Predictions based on such evolutionary extrapolation will inevitably overlook some major innovations, but will, none the less, serve to reveal some of the most important social, political and economic changes that the technologies will trigger. Early wheel scientists might well have predicted better technology for rounder, smoother wheels and for more wheel-friendly roads, but they would have been unlikely to predict gears, aeroplanes or on-board computers. So, too, we can predict, with relative confidence, some of the features that the Internet of the future will include, but not the technologies that will make the Internet itself seem quaint and old fashioned – or at least as commonplace as, for example, electric power. A few such predictions, however incomplete, may help inform the decisions of a whole range of institutions that are, at this very moment, being overtaken by the Internet juggernaut.

> A few things are easy to predict. The Internet of the future will be easier to use and overwhelmingly faster and more powerful than it is today.

A few things are easy to predict. The Internet of the future will be easier to use and overwhelmingly faster and more powerful than it is today. Many older communications media – including telephony and broadcast audio and video – will gradually be integrated under the Internet umbrella. Most computer software – and, importantly, high-end cryptographic software – will continue to be made easier for non-experts to use. The cost of connecting machines to the Internet will become vanishingly low, so that nearly every new electrical device – from toasters to toys – will sport an Internet connection if the marketers can come up with even a remotely plausible reason to do so. Inevitably, many such devices will connect to the Internet but gain no more utility from this connection than the cars of the 1950s gained from their chrome ornamentation. Many devices will connect to the Internet for the sole purpose of giving their manufacturers feedback on how they are being used. Given wireless communication and an appropriate pricing model (such as toll-free 800 telephone numbers, where the caller pays nothing), there is no reason to assume that consumers will necessarily even know that such a connection is being made. With this kind of feedback mechanism, Internet-based marketing may rapidly become so extremely personalized and individual focused that each human being will, in a very real sense, encounter their own personal Internet and will feel lost if they try to use a colleague's machine to surf the Net.

It is also reasonably safe to predict that a profusion of technical alternatives and socio-political mechanisms will create multiple tiers of Internet services – some faster, some cheaper, some more or less robust and reliable, and some asymmetrical in their capabilities (such as cable modems that can download data far faster than they upload it). This, in turn, will further stratify society, not just between those who do and do not have Internet access, but between those whose access is more or less enriched and of higher or lower functionality. Old economic inequalities in the ability to obtain and use knowledge will be magnified by technological stratification, so that information will increasingly serve as a form of power, allowing the further amassing of resources. Conversely, a lack of information access – and illiteracy in general – will increasingly doom a subset of the population to marginalization and powerlessness.

Meanwhile, the tendency of information to flow freely – which seems to be a direct consequence of digital technology – is unlikely to be reversed by the wishes and desires of those in authority. Accordingly, governments and other institutions that attempt to staunch this flow will continue to experience extreme difficulties, which will ultimately be understood to be sheer futility. Eventually, fighting against the free flow of information will be understood to be a losing battle, winnable only in very narrow contexts for very limited periods of time. As a consequence of this and the ongoing improvements in software usability, universal access to cryptography will become a *de facto* reality, with *de jure* recognition of this access likely in the longer term. Following close on the heels of this development, however, will be widespread overconfidence in cryptography, which has been portrayed for years, by both its supporters and opponents, as nearly unbreakable. Due to inevitable implementation bugs, user carelessness, advances in processing power and 'end run' attacks, such as Trojan Horses and keyboard sniffers, users of cryptography will inevitably be far less secure than they think they are. The world's governments and other large institutions, once they finally understand this fact, will be able to eavesdrop on most citizens with relative impunity, regardless of whatever cryptographic software happens to be in use.

The free flow of information will also permanently undermine current notions of copyright and intellectual property, though with what consequences is somewhat harder to predict. Mechanisms will emerge that will make it easy for honest citizens to pay what they consider to be a fair price for intellectual property, but tools will also emerge that empower a permanent class of infobandits. It will require no special technical knowledge, merely an antisocial attitude, for these infobandits to refuse, with relative impunity, to pay for nearly anything society puts a monetary value on. The future of industries dependent on intellectual property, in particular, will therefore depend less on enforcement mechanisms than on their ability to convince their customers that the prices they charge are fair, appropriate and worth paying. Good men and women will probably continue to differ on whether or not this is a good thing.

Finally, researchers will continue to predict (as they have since the 1950s with just as little evidence) that truly 'intelligent' machines are just around the corner. Meanwhile, slowly emerging from the world's computer research laboratories, we will see the introduction of massively parallel computers, possibly based on biological structures. Such computers might or might not make the predictions of 'intelligence' come true, but undoubtedly they will have sufficiently revolutionary potential that they might be responsible for the next (post-information-revolution) wave of intrinsically unpredictable change.

As with all technologies, the Internet can be used for good or ill. Money, however, it has been claimed, is the root of all evil, and money is the lens that is currently focusing the most attention on the Internet. It seems painfully likely that the exponential growth in commercial uses of the Internet will cause the Internet to do more harm than good in the short term. In the longer term, non-commercial innovations will slowly produce social benefits that help to mitigate, and perhaps even outweigh, the negative effects. However, their intrinsic lack of commercial relevance will mean that these beneficial effects are slower in coming than the harmful ones. In the short term, we're probably in for a rough ride.

> ... slowly emerging from the world's computer research laboratories, we will see the introduction of massively parallel computers, possibly based on biological structures.

As one example of this more general phenomenon, consider the growing concern for personal privacy.

The privacy and security industry

Perhaps the most cynical Internet business opportunity that I have ever personally contemplated is the (so-far imaginary) Internet Privacy Corporation, or IPC. Imagine, if you will, a for-profit business the sole focus of which is the enhancement of your privacy. The operation of such a business would be a marvellously tricky slope: the less ethically it behaves, the more money it can make.

To begin with, IPC can offer consumers a very simple service: give us your name, e-mail address and all the other information we can persuade you to divulge about yourself and we will, on your behalf, work to get your information removed from every database we can   influence. Where government laws mandate privacy protection, we will automatically invoke that protection on your behalf. By telling us all about yourself, you'll be allowing us to make it much harder for anyone else to find out all about you, for whatever purpose.

However, of course, to be effective, IPC will have to do this on your behalf at regular intervals. To be a sustainable business, therefore, it will need a recurrent revenue stream, most likely based on an annual membership fee. For a regular fee, IPC will protect your privacy to the fullest extent it can manage.

Inevitably, however, IPC will face one of the hardest problems for any organization that has as its revenue model a recurring fee, which it needs to maintain its customers' loyalty. When the annual renewal comes due, IPC will want you to have plenty of warm feelings about the service it is performing for you. At the very least, then, it will probably want to send you a monthly newsletter, telling you all the things it has done for you recently.

So far, the IPC is probably performing a good service and delivering real value. This could go on for some time, but eventually some clever manager, with more economic than moral sense, will begin to imagine how much more this technology can be used for. He might branch out into some of the most egregious forms of junk mail (spam), to stimulate more people to join IPC. Alternatively, he might choose to use his finely honed knowledge of individuals to place selected advertisements ever more strategically in the path of the most sophisticated and privacy sensitive of consumers. Perhaps most simply, he could start telling you about all the databases he has removed your name from lately, even when no such databases exist. In an unchecked, competitive market for personal privacy, a company with few scruples, but excellent execution, is reasonably likely to dominate its more ethical competitors.

Eventually, some kind of abuses by 'pro-privacy' corporations are probably inevitable. If the abuses are alarming enough, we will probably see reactions in the form of government regulations and more effective non-profit privacy watchdog groups, which could, over time, cause us to end up with stronger privacy protection than ever before. However, the powerful commercial focus of today's Internet makes it almost certain that the abuses and harmful effects will come first, with the more salutary effects coming as belated reactions to these abuses. Yet, some things – such as protecting consumer privacy – would really be better handled by non-commercial forces to begin with.

Although privacy is a good example, it is only one of a host of issues raised by the Internet. The ever more commercial Internet will lend itself to a host of abuses that will only be corrected after they are well understood, which means after they have caused significant visible harm.

Security is another good example. The fundamental insecurity of Internet-based communication will not be going away any time soon, and the more people come to understand that fact, the more vulnerable they will feel. Already we can see an entire industry rising up around Internet security, as businesspeople and investors try to protect their assets and advantages while competing on the Internet. Their combination of deep concerns about security, lack of deep technical knowledge and access to commercial-scale budgetary resources creates an irresistible opportunity for unscrupulous entrepreneurs to offer security services of dubious – or even negative – value. Again, the surest path to really big money might be to play both sides of the fence, quietly promoting general fearfulness, or even break-ins, in order to increase the market for security services. As with the privacy industry, the security industry might eventually be brought under control by means of a combination of government regulation and non-profit activism, but this is likely only after the public becomes aware of a pattern of serious abuses.

In all such cases, bewildered and fearful consumers of Internet services – notably including any non-technical individuals and corporations seeking to conduct business on the Net – will seek out what they perceive to be the 'safest' sources of privacy, security and other important services. This kind of emotional safety – as opposed to technical security – is most easily provided by name recognition, which is why 'building brand identity' has become such a mantra for Internet service companies. Ultimately, however, this means that the advantage large companies have over small ones will only increase. Paying a little more for security services will seem well worth while if it means those services are coming from a name you know – perhaps the name of a multinational corporation – rather than a small, local business or entrepreneur. In short, the Internet will only accelerate the trend towards ever-larger corporate players, and will only increase the barriers faced by small-scale entrepreneurs. As the large corporations have fewer local or personal ties and commitments, they are less likely than entrepreneurs to temper their commercialism with respect for the needs of the larger community, which means, in turn, that the trend towards viewing the Internet primarily as a commercial medium will only be encouraged.

Ultimately, however, the Internet is not merely, or even primarily, a commercial medium. It is, first and foremost, a communication medium. However, it is a communication medium with fundamentally new characteristics, for which our civic discourse is deeply unprepared. A single individual can use it to make their voice widely heard more easily than ever before. However, to be widely heard, a voice must attract attention, and we already have an excellent model of the simplest way for someone with nothing significant to say to attract attention in the media – the supermarket tabloids. Novelty and titillation are the fast track to visibility, and the Internet makes it easier than ever for the purveyors of infotrash to be widely heard. This is why we are already seeing, in organizations that try to conduct serious discussions on the Net, that the medium seems to lend disproportionate influence to eccentrics, crackpots and plain old crazy folk. Meanwhile, in reaction to this, there is a growing consumer tendency to place an extremely large amount of trust in a few, large news-gathering institutions with established brand names. The space for open and constructive public dialogue is thus being squeezed out from both ends, and with it the opportunity for the Internet to serve as a significant new venue for civic discourse. It is very difficult to see what, if anything, might ever reverse this trend.

Power and influence on the Internet

Historically, the Internet was built and governed by a technical meritocracy, a sort of old boy network that, by and large, sought to build the Net by consensus and persuasion rather than governance and coercion. A modified form of this meritocracy still exists, in the form of the Internet Engineering Task Force (IETF), which continues to deal reasonably effectively with technical issues. However, the 'meritocratic consensus' approach has been far less successful where the issues are not primarily technical, such as the regulation of free speech or the administration of the global name space (the Domain Name System, or DNS).

By 1996, or thereabouts, it was common for Internet old-timers to observe that the sudden commercial interest in the Net had created a stunning power vacuum that the IETF and other such institutions seemed to be filling, at the most, incompletely. Idealists and dreamers talked, for a few years, about a self-organizing, self-governing Internet in which traditional social structures for power and control were simply absent. Into that void, smiling, stepped a few large multinational corporations that although relatively new to the Internet, well understood the nature of power. A few years on, the power vacuum has largely disappeared, replaced by the interests of a few companies that see the Internet in commercial terms to the exclusion of nearly anything else. (Consider, for example, the way that the IETF, with no formal membership and meetings open to anyone interested, has been displaced in many contexts by the World Wide Web Consortium, membership of which is restricted to corporations willing to pay a minimum of $5000 in annual membership fees.)

Idealists and dreamers talked, for a few years, about a self-organizing, self-governing Internet in which traditional social structures for power and control were simply absent.

If the Internet were simply a commercial medium, none of this would be anything to be all that worried about. Unfortunately, the Internet is far more than that. It is a fundamental technology that will transform human institutions for generations to come. It would be prudent to at least consider informing its administration with considerations beyond the unchecked pursuit of profit.

One planet, one Net

Given these tendencies for short-term abuse of the Internet, the long-term role of the Internet in society may depend on the growth of a consensus around some basic principles. It is in the spirit of promoting such a development that an organization with which I am privileged to be associated – Computer Professionals for Social Responsibility (CPSR) – has put forward a set of principles that we propose should inform the social and political processes that will set policy on the Internet for generations to come. These principles – promulgated under the banner, 'One planet, one Net,' – are described in great detail elsewhere (see http://www.cpsr.org), so I will only summarize them here. It should be stressed that CPSR does not present these principles as revealed divine wisdom, nor does it consider them unchangeable, set in stone. Rather, it has offered them to the Internet community as a starting point from which to construct a vision of an Internet that works, as broadly as possible, on behalf of humanity as a whole.

The seven 'One planet, one Net' principles are deceptively simple.

1 The Net links us all together.
2 The Net must be open and available to all.
3 Net users have the right to communicate.
4 Net users have the right to privacy.
5 People are the Net's stewards, not its owners.
6 Administration of the Net should be open and inclusive.
7 The Net should reflect human diversity, not homogenize it.

Each of these principles warrants a certain amount of consideration and discussion. Together, they provide at least a starting point for thinking about how to work towards an Internet that serves humanity as broadly as possible, in both commercial and non-commercial contexts.

1 The Net links us all together

As a statement of fact, this principle is hard to argue with. Some might call it obvious or even vacuous, but it provides the underpinning for a crucial understanding of the social role of the interconnected set of computer networks we know as the Internet. There is a fundamental dynamic that makes people want to link their networks together, because the utility of such networks seems to rise exponentially with the number of interconnected users. The simple phrase 'The Net links us all together' is really a powerful statement of inclusion. The Net doesn't just link together all of the world's computer geeks or all of the upper-class citizens of the developed world or all of the people who share certain values and beliefs – the Net links us all together. Ultimately, the Net is no more divisible into nations and property than the air we breathe. It is nearly impossible to think clearly about the social policies regarding the Internet without the basic understanding that there is only a single Net that links together all humanity.

2 The Net must be open and available to all

This second principle might seem obvious, too, but there are those who might disagree. Certainly authoritarian governments have already displayed an eagerness to deny Net access to those citizens who might wish to criticize them. More subtly, even democratic governments are likely to be far too eager to deny Net access to prisoners, although many of us would argue that, in most cases, this is no more reasonable than denying them access to reading magazines and maintaining correspondence with the outside world. Subtler still, those whose sole focus is the commercialization of the Net may be working, albeit inadvertently, to deny Net access to the economically underprivileged.

The implications of the second principle are many and important. This principle provides the basis for important arguments in favour of universal equal access to the Net, restraints on governmental controls on citizens and a global Internet largely beyond the reach of national and regional governments. The principle appears simple on the surface, but it has profound long-range implications for the need to limit both governments and commercial forces.

3 Net users have the right to communicate

While certain forms of communication – notably the right to free speech – have been recognized as worthy of protection in many contexts, the Internet forces us to recognize communication more generally as a fundamental human right. Clearly there will be a motivation to deny or severely limit this principle on the part of authoritarian governments, religious fundamentalists and anyone else who would sacrifice freedom of expression for some other ideals.

Such limitations are inherently threatening to human liberty. This third principle provides a foundation from which to defend the use of the Internet for free speech, unpopular minority expression and political dissent. The unique aspects of the Internet as a publication medium require a fundamental strengthening of such guarantees. The Internet offers – for the first time in human history – the prospect that any individual can express their ideas in a form that will be accessible to anyone else with virtually no regard to cost or geography. This third principle is the underlying value that must be maintained to make this prospect a reality.

4 Net users have the right to privacy

Human beings once had a great deal of privacy by default. In small communities, privacy from strangers was less of an issue, and some degree of privacy within the community was a tacit social norm. Technology and population growth have, however, steadily whittled away our privacy, making it an increasingly prized commodity, though not everyone agrees about its value. Police and governments are sometimes far too eager to sacrifice privacy in the name of law and order, and commercial interests are sometimes quick to sacrifice privacy in their quest to make another sale.

This fourth principle provides a clear basis on which to place limits on the uses of the Net by law enforcement officials and spammers alike. More important, it provides the philosophical rationale for universal access to cryptographic privacy and anonymous communication. This deceptively simple but categorical statement directly undermines the efforts of many governments, including those of the United States, to limit popular access to privacy-enhancing technologies.

5 People are the Net's stewards, not its owners

People who have invested millions of dollars in Internet infrastructure – notably the telecommunications giants of the world – would undoubtedly like to see themselves as at least partial owners of the Internet. This, I believe, is a perspective that must be resisted. Such players clearly deserve the chance to obtain substantial economic returns on their investment, but ownership is, fundamentally, an incomplete model for a unique, shared resource like the Net. A power company that builds and owns a hydroelectric dam can still be held responsible for the dam's effect on fish and wildlife.

What the fifth principle implies, therefore, is that society has an interest in the Net that goes beyond the economic interests of those who build and maintain it. While their need to earn a profit must be respected, they must be expected, in return, to respect the fact that the larger needs of society may place limits on their own economic interests. More importantly, each of us as an individual has a responsibility to make our voice heard on behalf of the larger values that may not be adequately championed by commercial interests.

6 Administration of the Net should be open and inclusive

In the early days of the Net, policy-making was essentially open to anyone sophisticated enough to understand the issues. Those days will never return, but the replacement process must be carefully considered. In the absence of formal mechanisms for ensuring a fair hearing for the voices of individuals and social advocacy groups, it is far too likely that powerful corporate interests will dominate the administrative and governance structure of the Net.

If this implies a governance structure that borders on anarchy, so be it. The Internet is inherently an amplification technology, pushing any tendency more towards an extreme, and I, for one, find anarchy far less threatening than monopolistic dominance by powerful corporations.

7 The Net should reflect human diversity, not homogenize it

The world is full of people who, for religious, philosophical or other reasons, believe that they have a handle on ultimate truths. I respect their right to such beliefs, but I deeply fear any attempts to impose such absolutes on others. If God reveals the truth to me, I will no doubt accept it, but if you tell me that God has revealed the truth to you, I will reserve the right to a certain scepticism.

Unless we are willing to globally enshrine one set of beliefs, we must embrace human diversity as part of what makes our lives interesting and worth living. For the Internet, this implies an ongoing commitment to multilingualism, multiculturalism and equal access for all people. Despite all the hype and enthusiasm, this is almost certainly an area where the Net has already done more harm than good, by further promoting English as a universal language and American culture as a universal context for discourse. This seventh principle implies that we should be working to remove the linguistic and cultural limitations that currently make the net a force for uniformity in the world.

Looking forwards, looking backwards

The near future of the Internet is filled with exciting technological improvements, a rapidly expanding commercial sector and mostly negative social consequences. Although the latter are disturbing, little will be achieved by railing against them. Instead, as we move forwards into the great adventure of the future Internet, we should do so with open eyes, well aware of the likelihood of both commercial abuses and genuine harm to the basic social fabric. To the extent that we can anticipate such problems or notice them early, we can limit and mitigate the damage that they do. Ultimately, we face questions asked of every generation in human history, but most acutely of those who live in times of extreme technological change – 'What should we keep from the rich heritage of our past and what should we discard as obsolete?

These questions can only be answered on a case-by-case basis, but it will be far easier to reach wise decisions if we have a clear understanding of the fundamental values that have allowed our ancestors to build the society we have inherited. By looking backwards to the social and ethical structures of our past, and applying them as rigorously as possible to the dilemmas of the present – as attempted in CPSR's principles, for example – we may hope to do a better job at looking forwards towards the kind of society we will leave to our descendants. ■

Earlier versions of this chapter were greatly improved by the helpful comments of Michael Cohen, Harry Hochheiser, Andy Oram, and Henry Walker. Responsibility for all errors – and particularly for all mistaken prognostications – remains completely my own.

Randall S. Hancock

Senior Vice President, Mainspring

THE QUEST FOR KILLER APPLICATIONS

It seems that just about everyone is searching for the next 'killer application'. The end game for entrepreneurs, jackpot for venture capitalists and coveted source of growth for corporate executives, the elusive killer app. has become the mythical Holy Grail pursued by all – the next big thing, the ticket to commercial success in the wired world. Yet, while many embark on the journey to identify and market the next killer app., few actually succeed.

Part of the challenge is that the search for killer apps sometimes diverts attention from the very real steps companies can take to exploit significant developments in the wired world. I shall start by reviewing the forces fuelling the emergence of the networked economy, with particular attention to their impact on potential killer apps. I shall then examine some of the popular thinking about killer apps, suggest some ways to rethink the role killer apps play in creating growth and provide recommendations to companies seeking to develop successful offerings that exploit killer apps in the Wired World.

> ... the elusive killer app. has become the mythical Holy Grail pursued by all ...

The context

The growth of the Internet and emergence of the networked economy has accelerated the quest for killer apps. While previous breakthrough inventions – such as the telephone, radio, television and word processor – were all developed in a non-Wired World, the emerging networked economy has created an environment in which so-called killer apps appear with much greater frequency.

A number of irreversible forces are driving the emergence of this networked economy: technological advances are expanding the realm of what is possible; telecommunications capacity is increasing exponentially; deregulation and open standards are fuelling more competitive markets; globalization is spreading change across continents, and the Internet is connecting us all. Each of these forces contributes to the growth of others – advances in technology enable better, more functional computers, set top boxes and other devices, which in turn increases demand for network bandwidth and so on. The result is a virtuous cycle in which the overall impact of these forces is greater than the sum of them individually (see Figure 1).

Technology is one of the most important catalysts in this environment. The evolution of technology is enabling the development of goods and services that were unimaginable, much less possible, only a few years ago. Gordon Moore, the co-founder of the Intel Corporation, once observed that the number of transistors that could be placed on a single semiconductor doubled roughly every 18 months. This observation, commonly known today as Moore's Law, predicts that computer processing power doubles roughly every year and a half without increasing the cost to the user, which means that almost any product or service based on digital technologies tends to decrease in price dramatically over time.

Similarly, as telecommunications markets deregulate and carriers migrate from analogue to digital networks, Moore's Law is beginning to apply to the global network, too. For example, telecommunications companies are exploiting technologies such as Dense Wave Division Multiplexing (DWDM) to increase the capacity of individual

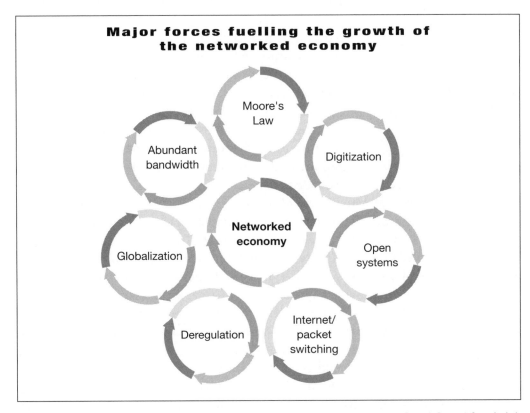

Major forces fuelling the growth of the networked economy

- Moore's Law
- Digitization
- Abundant bandwidth
- Networked economy
- Open systems
- Globalization
- Deregulation
- Internet/packet switching

FIGURE 1

Source: Gemini Strategic Research Group Analysis

fibre optic cables from an already fast 2 billion bits per second to 80 billion bits or more. Network equipment providers, such as Lucent Technologies and Ciena Systems, are preparing DWDM products that will enable speeds in the hundreds of billions of bits per second over the next couple of years, and perhaps in the trillions of bits per second in the not-too-distant future. Incumbent telecommunications providers as well as new carriers such as Qwest Communications and Level 3 Communications are building state-of-the-art networks that promise dramatically more capacity at significantly lower costs. Also, a wide variety of companies, including existing telephone, cable television, electric utility and satellite companies, are racing to provide faster 'last mile' connectivity to the Internet to both consumers and businesses using xDSL (Digital Subscriber Loop), cable modems, wireless and other access technologies. These and other developments virtually guarantee that the supply of network band width will increase over the next several years in ways comparable to the ways computer processing power has increased in the past. For consumers and businesses, this greater band width translates into the ability to use the network to access people, content and services, regardless of their location, at very affordable prices.

As more people join the networked economy, the value realized by everyone increases significantly. This observation is often described as Metcalfe's Law – named after the inventor of the Ethernet networking protocol and founder of 3Com Corporation – which holds that the utility of a network is equal to the square of the number of its users. In other words, while one fax machine connected to a network is useless and two connected have limited value, a million connected fax machines provide tremendous value to users. Similarly, as global Internet penetration increases, both businesses and consumers have more incentive to use and contribute to the Internet's content, thus increasing the overall value of the Internet and convincing more businesses and consumers to join.

> **'viral marketing' – the notion that each delighted user convinces several of their friends to adopt the product, who in turn do the same with their friends.**

The ease and speed at which great ideas can spread via the Internet are allowing some companies to launch products and services that reach market penetration in record time. For example, Israel-based Mirabilis grew its ICQ ('I Seek You') instant messaging user base from nothing to nearly 15 million users within two years by giving away, via the Internet, a software client that allowed Internet users to communicate in real time with their friends and acquaintances. To grow its user base so quickly, ICQ leveraged 'viral marketing' – the notion that each delighted user convinces several of their friends to adopt the product, who in turn do the same with their friends. An example of Metcalfe's Law in action, the ICQ service became more valuable as more people joined the service, further fuelling its dramatic growth. The strategy was so successful that America Online (AOL) purchased Mirabilis in the spring of 1998 for $287 million. Other companies that have pursued a successful viral marketing strategy include Netscape Communications (distributes web browsers via the Internet),

Hotmail (provides web-based e-mail to users where every e-mail sent advertises its services) and Geocities (hosts more than 2 million free personal web sites that in turn attract millions of additional visitors). The 'viral effect' of Metcalfe's Law explains why achieving critical mass in any network is so important, and helps to explain why killer apps are appearing at a much higher rate than in the non-wired past.

The emerging Wired World is changing the very nature of traditional industry structure and reconfiguring how consumers, businesses and governments interconnect with each other. As the global Internet becomes more functional and pervasive, existing market and industry categories are blurred and traditional value chains and customer segmentations are no longer effective. The networked economy becomes a 'value web' of individuals and organizations that connect to each other via a common (that is, the Internet) network (see Figure 2). Individuals are, in effect, at the centre of their own value webs and therefore capable of satisfying many of their needs, exploiting the power of the network to connect to each other as well as the organizations that provide them with the goods and services they desire.

This shift in the competitive landscape is creating incredible change for organizations seeking to serve wired consumers. Markets are becoming more efficient as the availability of information increases and search costs decrease. Individual buying power is increasing due to the end user's vantage point of the centre of the value web, which allows them to identify and compare offerings from a wider selection of providers than ever before. As a result, they are becoming more discriminating consumers. Some companies are leveraging the network to build direct relationships with consumers, thus disintermediating their traditional physical distributors, while others are reintermediating by discovering ways to add significant new value to the distribution channel. Geographical boundaries are eroding as the flow of information and commerce travel unimpeded over the Internet. Viral effects allow a few selected companies to rise from obscurity to become household names overnight. And the rate of change within organizations, industries and even societies continues to increase. Within this context, companies seek out the next magic bullet, those mythical killer apps, that will allow them to survive and prosper in rapidly changing and uncertain markets.

Rethinking killer apps

Ask a dozen executives to define the term 'killer app.' and you'll get as many definitions. The term was originally coined to describe a software application that was so compelling, it convinced users to buy the system the application ran on. Both VisiCalc and Lotus 1-2-3, for example, were popular spreadsheet programs that helped drive demand for personal computers in businesses. Over time, the term has evolved to include nearly any new product or service that is so attractive in terms of functionality and price that a large number of people adopt it. According to some definitions, killer apps have the ability to redefine marketplaces, cannibalize existing goods and services, and create tremendous wealth for the companies that best exploit them.

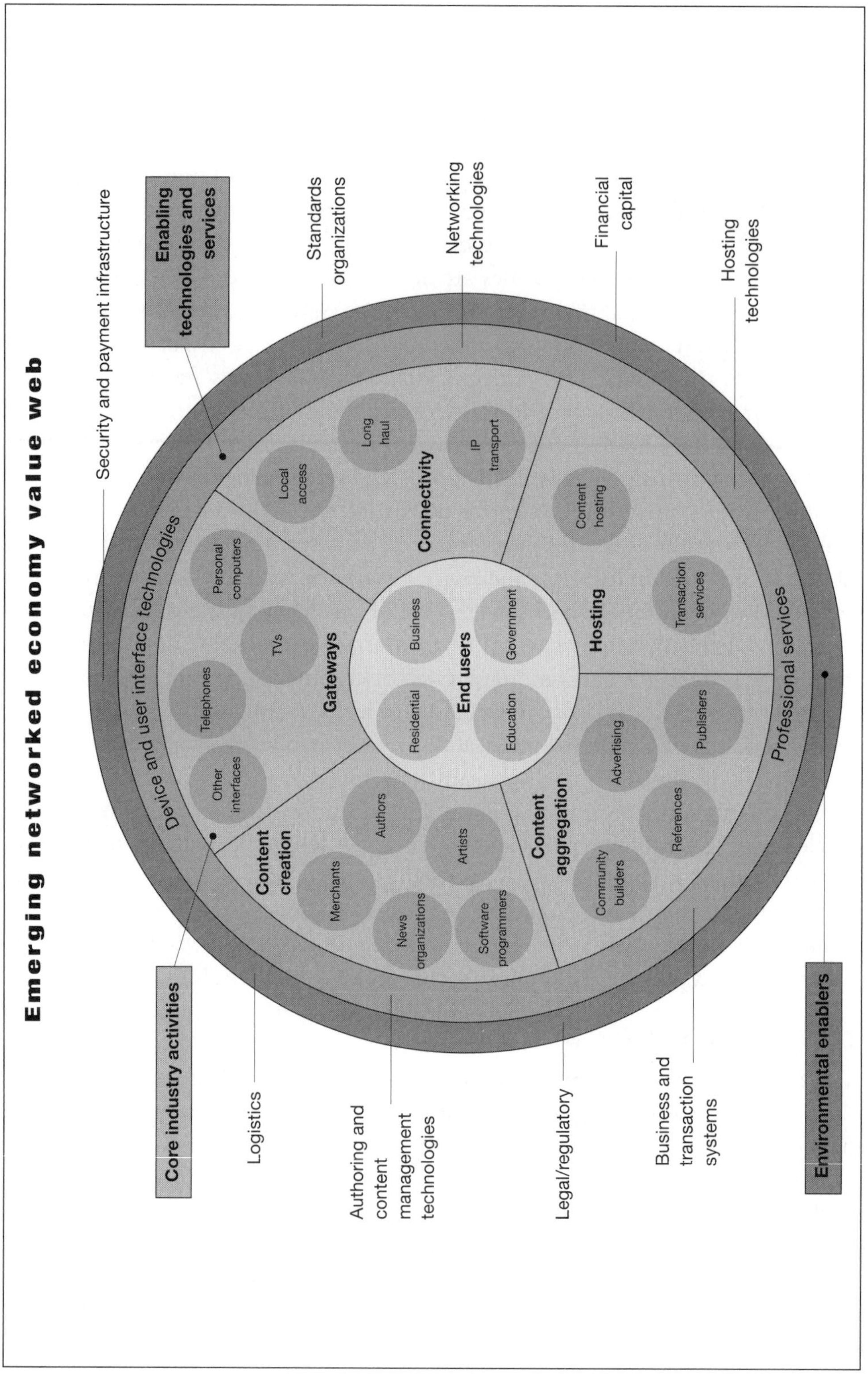

Emerging networked economy value web

Security and payment infrastructure

Enabling technologies and services

Standards organizations

Networking technologies

Financial capital

Hosting technologies

Device and user interface technologies

Core industry activities

Logistics

Authoring and content management technologies

Legal/regulatory

Business and transaction systems

Environmental enablers

Content creation
Merchants
Authors
News organizations
Artists
Software programmers

Gateways
Other interfaces
Telephones
TVs
Personal computers

Connectivity
Local access
Long haul
IP transport

Content aggregation
Community builders
References
Advertising
Publishers

Hosting
Content hosting
Transaction services

End users
Business
Residential
Government
Education

Professional services

Source: Gemini Strategic Research Group Analysis

FIGURE 2

Not surprisingly, the term killer app. has lately been used to describe everything from the World Wide Web to Microsoft's Windows 98 operating system to Internet-based instant messaging and on-line securities trading. Indeed, a quick review of the business press uncovers a long laundry list of products touted as being killer apps. The mere possibility of a killer app. drives business plans, determines investments, instigates mergers and creates billion-dollar market capitalizations for companies with negative earnings. The hype surrounding killer apps has grown exponentially with the evolution of the Wired World, but there is more to the story than most people understand.

The term 'killer app.', in fact, has become misleading. Most people think of killer apps in terms of specific products or services, such as the word processor, spreadsheet, e-mail or Web browser, and therefore focus their energies on creating particular goods or services that they can take to market. All too often, entrepreneurs and engineers make the mistake of concentrating on the technologies they can provide instead of satisfying the underlying needs of end users. As a result, companies create offerings that may be 'cool' from a technology perspective, but aren't necessarily commercially successful. Early attempts with videotext systems (proprietary systems with too much emphasis on information rather than communication), pen-based computing (expensive without enough functionality) and Video-On-Demand (price/performance didn't beat video rentals) are examples of offerings that aimed to become killer apps, but just didn't meet consumer expectations.

Instead of defining killer apps as individual products or services, it is much more useful to think of killer apps as bundles of functionalities or capabilities, delivered at an attractive price, which meet specific underlying needs better than anything else available. For example, using this definition, we can see that the television by itself was not a killer app. Rather, the ability to provide a variety of free (in most markets), advertiser-supported, informative and entertaining video programming into consumer homes was the true killer application. As is true with most killer apps, the success of television relied on the availability of a number of offerings, including television sets, video programming, an infrastructure for broadcasting the television signals and standards connecting everything together. The combination and availability of these 'killer offerings' is what created the killer app. we call television. Similarly, while the steam locomotive was an important invention, it took common rail widths, a network of track connecting cities, passenger cards, and standardized time schedules to make it a killer app. The aeroplane did not become a killer app. until people found a way to hang bombs under the wings (literally a 'killer' app.) or created an infrastructure to carry commercial passenger traffic. Even the wildly successful Palm Pilot personal organizer, with its scheduling and contact management capabilities, would arguably not have been successful without its ability to synchronize data with existing personal computers. Redefining past killer apps around the particular benefits that each provided to end users reveals important lessons (as shown in Table 1).

> ... it is much more useful to think of killer apps as bundles of functionalities or capabilities, delivered at an attractive price, which meet specific underlying needs better than anything else ...

213

Table 1 Selected killer apps redefined

Original killer app.	Redefined around end users' benefits
Radio	Free audio programming in home, business, automobile, and elsewhere.
Telephony	Talk to anyone else in the world who has access to another telephone.
Cellular telephony	Telephone functionality that is person based and mobile, rather than tied to fixed infrastructure.
Television	Free (in most markets) advertising-supported video programming to homes.
Pay-TV	Wider variety of video programming, which is potentially better quality and advertising free.
Typewriter	Can quickly and inexpensively create typeset-like text without need for printing press.
Word processor	Can easily create text that can be edited, saved, copied, printed and manipulated in other ways.
Fax machine	Can send and receive printed materials instantly to and from others without delay of postal system.
Spreadsheet	Can create and perform 'What if ...?' analyses on complex business, financial and other mathematical issues.
Automated teller machine (ATM)	Conduct personal financial transactions 24 hours per day, 7 days per week.
Palm-sized computer	Functionality of an address book, calendar, memo taker and other applications in a small and mobile form factor that can be easily synchronized with a personal computer.
E-mail	Can instantly send and receive informal written communications and electronic attachments inexpensively with other e-mail users.
World Wide Web	Can interactively access a wide range of content and services globally at very low incremental cost.

Successful killer apps are rarely composed of an individual offering. Nearly all require multiple, interconnected components in order to address underlying needs effectively and convince end users to adopt the new solution. The spreadsheet required the personal computer; automated teller networks relied on the existing financial services infrastructure, and the World Wide Web needed a complex system of open standards, telecommunications networks, Internet service providers, equipment and software providers and interactive content in order to take off.

Just as new killer apps can relegate, or even replace, existing offerings, they too can be replaced as new solutions are created that even better meet end users' needs. While television did not replace either radio or motion pictures, its ability to provide video programming directly into consumer homes reduced the impact that both had had on consumers in the past. Cable and satellite-based Pay-TV – which provides significantly greater functionality by providing consumers with a wider variety of high-quality programming targeted to specific interests – is similarly eroding the market share of traditional broadcast-based television networks. The ability of next-generation digital television, Video-On-Demand and Internet-based video to become killer apps will depend on their ability to meet needs and expectations even better than the existing alternatives, at an attractive cost to consumers.

While technology and innovation allow the rapid development of new killer apps, many underlying consumer needs change very slowly. For example, the newspaper, motion picture, radio, television, and World Wide Web all arguably meet personal needs relating to becoming informed and being entertained. Similarly, the postal system, telephone, fax and e-mail all cater to people's desire for communication. Basic human needs – such as for food, protection and safety – as well as social needs – for community, recognition and status – change very little over time. Even more advanced needs – say, the ability to access information, be entertained, communicate with distant others – and conduct transactions effectively, evolve steadily rather than discontinuously. The most successful killer apps are frequently those that target needs that are well understood, providing a solution significantly better than other alternatives.

Although underlying needs are steadily evolving, this does not mean that consumer expectations are not increasing. In fact, the emergence of the Wired World is helping to drive consumer expectations to all-time highs. Increasingly sophisticated consumers, armed with information about what is available at any given cost, are expecting companies to provide them with significantly better offerings, often at lower costs than in the past. For example, while I have always sought to buy consumer electronics products from sources that provided a wide selection, convenience, warranty and good price, the emergence of Internet commerce allows me to choose from a greater number of alternatives, many of which might be located quite far from where I live. Many innovative retailers are developing new business models that allow them to better meet customer needs by understanding individual customers' preferences, distributing products more efficiently by leveraging the Internet, reducing costly physical infrastructure and outsourcing distribution to best-in-class companies, such as Federal Express. As a result, I really can expect to get more product and service for less money. Indeed, providing more value to the consumer at significantly lower costs is what killer apps are all about.

It is commonly thought that those who are first to discover a killer app. are able – by means of first-mover advantage – to establish the new category and dominate it, reaping incredible financial returns. While being first in the market provides a window of opportunity for creating killer offerings, it does not provide any guarantees for long-term success. How many people remember who invented the radio or television? Today's consumer electronics markets are dominated by global powerhouses such as Sony, Hitachi, Mitsubishi, Philips and others. VisiCalc and Lotus 1-2-3 were the first in the spreadsheet category, yet Microsoft's Excel product controls the market today. Similarly, while Netscape invented the web browser, Microsoft has imbedded the functionality into its operating system and continues to take Netscape's market share away. The original personal computer pioneers – companies such as Altair, Apple and IBM – gave way to new companies of the likes of Compaq and Dell. Even AOL's discussion groups, chat rooms and instant messaging capabilities borrowed heavily from earlier on-line providers and Internet-based technologies such as Internet relay chat. Companies that fail to improve and refine their offerings continuously are eventually replaced by those who do.

From this perspective, then, there emerges a framework for thinking about and exploiting killer apps (see Figure 3). Underlying needs drive demand for any application, killer or not. Also, as we have discussed, killer apps are typically made up of a network of killer offerings, usually consisting of multiple goods and services that

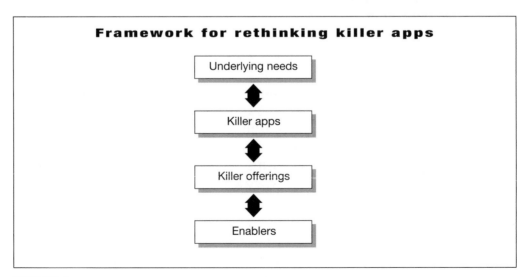

Framework for rethinking killer apps

Underlying needs

Killer apps

Killer offerings

Enablers

FIGURE 3

combine in ways that users find beneficial. These offerings are usually made up of still more components or enablers. The magic that entrepreneurs, investors and corporate executives alike seek is results, when the application of innovation and technology allows companies to provide an offering that meets underlying needs better than ever before.

This framework suggests that while the quest for killer apps is important, the ability of companies to develop competitive offerings and enablers may, in fact, sometimes provide the best opportunities for success. The Intel Corporation, for example, has derived the majority of its shareholder value from enabling a significant portion of the emerging networked economy with its famous computer processors. While certainly not killer apps themselves, processors are key enablers of almost anything that happens in the Wired World. Moreover, demand for processors is linked to the speed at which people require greater processing power in order to use killer apps that arise. Recognizing this, Intel has created a billion-dollar venture capital fund to invest in killer apps that require processing-intensive devices in order to further demand for Intel's core business. This shows that it is important to think beyond applications themselves and understand the very real potential that specific offerings and enablers may play in their successful development.

Exploiting killer apps

Given the rapidly changing and unpredictable nature of the emerging Wired World, there are no guarantees that any company's quest for killer apps will be successful. However, this discussion points to seven specific steps companies can take to improve their chances of not only creating, but, more importantly, exploiting killer apps.

1 *Start with underlying needs* Technology advances quickly and sometimes unpredictably, while end users' needs change in a much more evolutionary fashion. Remember that basic human needs – for food, shelter, clothing, companionship – hardly change at all, and that more advanced needs – for information, communications, entertainment, education, shopping – have remained relatively similar for most of the past decade. Few killer apps cater to previously unknown needs. Most just do a better job of meeting those already understood to exist. Identify your target customer group, determine their needs and preferences, and seek to develop offerings that meet their expectations better than any existing alternatives.

2 *Learn from the past for insights about the future* Past experience offers numerous clues about what might be successful in the future. For example, the extraordinary success of broadcast, cable and satellite television suggests tremendous opportunities in providing consumers with higher quality, digital and on demand video programming. However, the failure of various interactive television and Video-On-Demand efforts suggests that these early offerings do not yet provide users with a better value proposition than the alternative killer app. of the video cassette player coupled with video

rentals. Study past efforts within your relevant market to determine the key drivers of success and failure, and use those results to guide your offering's development strategy.

3 *Understand how Wired World trends make new things possible* Moore's Law, abundant bandwidth, deregulation, open standards and other Wired World trends extend the realm of the possible by allowing companies to provide greater functionality at lower costs than in the past. Something that is not possible with today's technologies may very well be feasible in the near future. Electronic books, Video-On-Demand, wireless data and videoconferencing may all be future killer apps once the right intersection is found between underlying needs and what the technology can provide at a given price. Learn to apply new technologies and capabilities to old problems, creating new solutions valued by your customers.

4 *Take advantage of existing killer apps* Being first is not the only way to play the killer apps game. Whenever possible, identify and exploit the killer apps created by others. Today's emerging killer app. categories – interactive communities, electronic shopping, real-time collaboration and communication, and many others – all provide significant space for innovation. A fast follower strategy can sometimes be effective – learn from the successes and failures of those who have come before you, and build killer offerings that meet end users' needs even better. Alternatively, pursue an Intel strategy and seek to provide enabling components to other companies pursuing the killer app. gambit. Then if you are first in the market with what looks like a killer app., watch out for those who come behind you.

5 *Leverage the network to your advantage* Like gossip among a group of friends, great ideas spread rapidly throughout the Wired World. In particular, electronic offerings have the ability to be distributed via the network at extremely low costs, enabling the creation of a user base in weeks or months, rather than years. Learn from successful viral marketers, such as Mirabilis, Netscape, Hotmail, and Geocities. Whenever possible, harness the viral nature of the network to diffuse your offerings quickly to target customers wherever they are and find ways to convince each delighted customer to convince several additional customers to adopt your offering.

6 *Seek business opportunities as well as consumer ones* While consumer markets often get much of our attention, the size of the business-to-business market is likely to be just as lucrative. Fax machines, word processors, spreadsheets and e-mail all owe much of their existence to initial success in the business environment. Networked commerce provides opportunities for companies to connect with their customers, suppliers and employees, creating opportunities for new offerings and, potentially, killer apps. When evaluating markets, include business organizations and end users in your plans.

7 *If at first you don't succeed, learn and try again* It might sound like a cliché, but the idea that successful companies in the Wired World are those that learn from their mistakes is a sound one. For example, Netscape is seeking to reposition itself, moving away from being a web browser company to become a provider of enter-

prise servers and Internet services. Microsoft has created and closed several on-line content businesses, but continues to invest in the interactive content space. The hallmark of successful Wired World offerings is that they evolve and improve over time. Be willing to take risks, experiment with new offerings, learn from both your successes and mistakes, and refine your offerings to better match what is possible with what people really need.

The quest for killer apps is far from an easy one – by far the majority of those setting out on the journey will either fail entirely or be disappointed with the outcome. This is not meant to discourage the would-be entrepreneur or corporate hero, but to serve as a gentle reminder that the process for discovering and exploiting killer apps is a bit less serendipitous and magical than the pundits might have you believe. Because the Wired World is extending the realm of the possible much faster than ever before, the race for killer apps is in full gear. As you set off on your journey, it is good to have an ambitious destination in mind, but don't forget to make progress continuously along the way. ■

ELECTRONIC COMMERCE

contributors

Donald J. Johnston became Secretary-General of the OECD in 1996, after a career that included serving as Minister in several senior portfolios during ten years in the Canadian Parliament, as well as many years as a practising lawyer with Heenan Blaikie, a prominent legal practice in Canada, which he co-founded in 1972.

Donald Johnston was an elected Member of the Canadian Parliament from 1978–88. He served in the Cabinet as President of the Treasury Board. During his political career in Canada he also served as Minister of Economic and Regional Development, Minister of Science and Technology, Minister of Justice and Attorney General of Canada. In 1990, he became President of the Liberal Party of Canada, and served a second term from 1992.

Donald Johnston taught fiscal law at McGill University in Montreal from 1963–76 and has written many articles on taxation, law and public affairs, as well as several books, including a bestselling political memoir. He studied Art and Law at McGill University, graduating in Law as Gold Medallist in 1958, and then at the University of Grenoble.

Lee Stein is Chairman of Stein & Stein Inc., formed in 1980, which facilitates venture financing and provides advisory and management services to high net worth individuals principally in the entertainment industry. It also serves as General Partner of The Stein Company Ltd, an investment partnership. During the period of the Partnership's involvement in private companies, Lee Stein also assumed various operating roles: Chairman of the Board, CEO, and President of First Virtual Holdings Inc. at the time of the Company's initial public offering on the NASDAQ Stock Market (FVHI), and today serves as a Director; Director and President of Seaport Village on the waterfront in San Diego, CA; Director and Controller of WestAir Airlines (DBA) United Express; and Officer/Director in various private entities.

Lee Stein is an attorney and a member of the Bar of the State of California and the Commonwealth of Pennsylvania. He received his Juris Doctorate from Villanova University School of Law, where he was a member of the Law Review, and received his BS degree in accounting from Syracuse University. After Law School, he served as a tax specialist with the accounting firm of Coopers & Lybrand.

Lee Stein is a Director of the Scripps Foundation for Medicine and Science. He is a member of Young Presidents' Organization (YPO), and former Chairman of Jack Murphy Stadium Authority for the City of San Diego and of the Greater San Diego Chamber of Commerce. His prior civic involvement includes participation with the America's Cup Task Force, All-Star Game Task Force, Super Bowl Task Force, and the City of San Diego Soviet Arts Festival (Marketing Chairman). The County of San Diego issued a proclamation declaring 13 September 1996 as 'Lee Stein Day' as a result of certain civic activities. He is also a frequent speaker and has addressed audiences of the World Bank, the United Nations International Telephone Union, Oxford University, The Wharton School and Columbia University as well as numerous Wall Street conferences.

Deborah Hurley is the Director of the Harvard Information Infrastructure Project at Harvard University http://www.ksg.harvard.edu/iip. She was an official (1988–96) of the Organisation for Economic Co-operation and Development (OECD) in Paris, France, where she had responsibility for identifying emerging issues related to protection of personal data and privacy, security of information systems, cryptography technology and policy, and protection of intellectual property. Deborah Hurley is a member of the Advisory Committee to the US State Department on International Communications and Information Policy and Co-Chair of its Working Group on Privacy, Security and Export Controls. She is also a member of the Advisory Board of the Electronic Privacy Information Center (EPIC).

Michael R. Nelson is Program Director for Internet Technology at IBM. Before joining IBM, he was Director for Technology Policy in the Office of Plans and Policy at the Federal Communications Commission. In this position, he worked on a number of issues, including how to foster electronic commerce, how computing and communications are converging, how FCC policies can spur development and deployment of new technologies, and how to improve the reliability and security of the nation's telecommunications networks. In Spring 1998, Michael Nelson organized and served as the first chairman of the FCC's Working Group on the Year 2000 Problem.

Before joining the FCC in January 1997, Michael Nelson was Special Assistant for Information Technology at the White House Office of Science and Technology Policy (OSTP) where he worked with the President's Science Advisor, Jack Gibbons, and with Vice President Gore on a range of issues relating to the Global Information Infrastructure, including telecommunications policy, information technology, encryption, electronic commerce and information policy.

Before joining OSTP in January 1993, Michael Nelson served for five years as a professional staff member for the Senate's Subcommittee on Science, Technology, and Space, chaired by then Senator Gore. He was the lead Senate staffer for the High-Performance Computing Act. He has a BS in geology from Caltech, and a Ph.D. in geophysics from MIT.

by Anne Leer

FROM MONEY TO INFORMATION TRANSACTIONS

The financial service industry including banks, credit card companies, clearing agencies, stock brokers and others, have for decades perfected the business of electronic financial transactions. However, shifting money around in computer networks is easy compared with the business of dealing with electronic information transactions. The trading of intangible goods and services over global networks raises a number of critical issues such as intellectual property protection, security, privacy, consumer rights, and liabilities. Many of these issues are unresolved and therefore constitute potential barriers to the growth of electronic commerce.

Information is very different to other commodities traded in the electronic market place. Information is intangible and more vulnerable. It's much harder to protect information assets, especially in an Internet environment. Digital technology has created massive opportunities to copy, store, manipulate, change and re-transmit information. If the information is expressed in tangible form, it is often subject to exclusive protection through intellectual property law. Information is also considered to be a public good and an essential instrument of democracy. Many will advocate the free flow of information as a fundamental pre-condition for a healthy society. Time and again the notion of free access to information collides head on with the notion of copyright and the fact that most of the information assets on the Internet are subject to copyright or database protection. Another tug-of-war that is set to intensify as electronic commerce grows is the conflicting rules of competition law that demand non-exclusive behaviour and intellectual property that is fundamentally based on exclusive rights.

This section is focusing on electronic commerce, which is fast becoming a substantial part of economies around the world. In his chapter, the Secretary General of OECD, Donald Johnston quotes some staggering figures that estimate the value of electronic commerce to have been $26 billion in 1997 and it is expected to rise to $1 trillion in 2003-2005. It is hard to make any sense of such big numbers, except it is meant to be evidence of substantial growth and it signifies shifts in the economy. Johnston is a firm believer in the revolutionary nature of the Wired World and says no human enterprise will be spared. Electronic commerce according to him will affect all aspects of the economy from business and markets, to governments, health, education and household activities.

Johnston has a very broad definition of electronic commerce, which encompasses all commercial transactions based on electronic transmission of data over networks. In a computerized society one could argue that his definition would mean most commercial transactions. Precisely what is meant by electronic commerce is often vague. I believe there is a need to debate whether or not electronic commerce needs to be treated as a separate kind of commerce different to traditional commerce.

Lee Stein, a pioneer of electronic commerce with extensive experience of both shifting money and information over networks in a transactional fashion, may surprise you with his rather conservative approach. He says the physical analogue world needs to exist for electronic business to prosper. He argues that electronic commerce does not exist as a separate type of commerce. It is simply an additional channel of distribution, which co-exists with other channels that a business has at its disposal. He points out that although there are customers that will complete on-line transactions and there are products which are electronic only, most of the products and services which are sold successfully over the Internet are those that closely mirror very traditional real world retail activities. He lists the most popular product categories and explains why some businesses are successful and why some are not. He also emphasizes that the hottest Internet stocks are not technology companies, but companies that use technology to give their customers a better experience.

Deborah Hurley's chapter deals in detail with two of the most difficult issues with regard to electronic commerce and the Global Information Society, namely security and privacy. She provides an excellent overview of what the policy issues are and she also describes the regulatory regimes and the various guidelines, which have been developed to address the issues. She warns us that the security of global communication systems that our society has become completely dependent on, is generally in a deplorable state as far as security is concerned. She compares it to a large porous sponge leaking with water. She echoes much of Nathaniel Borenstein's deep concerns about the false sense of security we have and the real vulnerability of the world's networks. Alvin Toffler has also warned us about this. Hurley says the security threat to our information networks is similar to the enemy in a military context. She goes on to propose ways of dealing with the various security problems. The second big nut to crack is privacy. Hurley points out that the US Secretary of Commerce identified privacy as 'the make or break issue' for the success of the digital economy. Hurley insists that personal data belongs to the individual. She believes the control and ownership of personal data is crucial because such data is about our sense of self, individual integrity and autonomy.

Michael Nelson has been at the cutting edge of the policy development for the GII, Internet and elecronic commerce since the beginning. In his chapter he reflects back upon the ideas and perceptions of those early days and he remembers how hard it was to get people to grasp what Al Gore meant when he was talking about building 'Information Superhighways' – that was 1988. Nelson describes how he has witnessed a radical turnaround with respect to the process of making policy. He says many policy makers have come to realize that the old top-down approach to telecommunications and information policy is not only obsolete, it could harm the economic health of their countries. He describes how many governments take a completely new approach to policy-making. He refers to the fact that the US government, the European Union, and other governments have all stated that the private sector, not governments, must take the lead in writing the rules of the road for the Information Highway. Nelson goes on to discuss four areas where governments will be expected to be involved and have policies in place: affordable Internet access, privacy, offensive content, and consumer protection.

Like Stein, Nelson points out that the electronic market is not so different to the traditional market and that many of the policy problems we face in the electronic marketplace are new manifestations of old problems, for example consumer fraud, universal service, security, privacy and so on. Perhaps electronic commerce needs to be redefined as an integrated part of overall commerce, simply extending business into a more complex environment. ∎

Donald J. Johnston

Secretary General, Organisation for Economic
Co-operation and Development

GLOBAL ELECTRONIC COMMERCE – REALIZING THE POTENTIAL

The electronic world: who's in charge here?

Our generation may stand on the very cusp of the greatest technological revolution that human beings have ever faced. Some compare this age of electronic communication with the arrival of the Gutenberg press or with the Industrial Revolution. Yet this revolution, when it has run its course, may have a greater impact on the planet than anything that has preceded it.

The applications of electronic transmissions are just beginning to be felt and the breadth and depth of what lies ahead is only beginning to be fathomed. How and where we are educated, where and how we work and live, our healthcare systems, shops, our commerce, our reading and leisure – no part of human enterprise will be spared. Even our notions of sovereignty and governance could be profoundly affected.

The emergence of electronic commerce – commercial transactions based on the electronic transmission of data over communications networks such as the Internet – heralds a major structural change in the economies of the Organisation for Economic Co-operation and Development (OECD) countries. It will affect all aspects of the economic environment, the organization of firms, consumer behaviour, the workings of government and most spheres of household activity.

Market driven, it holds out the prospect of economic growth, productivity and job creation in enterprises, as well as wider consumer choice and more purchasing power. Electronic transactions, and perhaps electronic flows of money and cash, will become a commonplace of the 'Information Society'.

A few statistics can demonstrate the significance and global nature of electronic commerce. Starting from almost zero in 1995, the total for electronic commerce has been estimated at some $26 billion for 1997; it is predicted to reach $330 billion in 2001–02 and $1 trillion in 2003–05 (these estimates are very speculative and rank among the highest of the dozen estimates generated by various management consultancy or market research firms). To put these estimates into a broader context, the value of US electronic commerce in 1995–97 is the equivalent of 37 per cent of US mail order catalogue shopping, 3 per cent of US purchases using credit/debit cards and 0.5 per cent of the retail sales of a basket of seven OECD economies (OECD estimates – the seven countries are Canada, France, Finland, Germany, Japan, the United Kingdom and the United States). The estimate for 2001–02 suggests that electronic commerce will quickly overwhelm US catalogue shopping. If the optimistic forecast for 2003–05 is realized, OECD-wide electronic commerce will be the equivalent of 15 per cent of the total retail sales of the basket of seven OECD countries. While significant, this level of activity is less than current sales generated by direct marketing in the United States via mail, telephone and newspapers (Direct Marketing Association, 1998).

However, a projected impact even approaching this magnitude raises many important questions. Will trade over the Internet (or whatever it evolves into) be as reliable as commerce in the markets we are familiar with today? Will nation states and supranational bodies be able to regulate electronic commerce? Can consumer privacy be guaranteed? Will telecommunications infrastructures be able to adapt and expand with sufficient speed? How can governments safeguard their tax revenues if cyber-markets move economic activity beyond their jurisdiction? What will the implications for home working be, and for new forms of access to such vital services as healthcare and education? Also, as trade in virtual markets transforms individual sectors, even seemingly unlikely ones, such as agriculture, will governments prove flexible enough to accommodate changes that cannot even be imagined today? It is not surprising that these questions have now reached the agendas of decision makers in boardrooms and government offices all over the world.

In the paragraphs that follow, a number of the most important questions are addressed. However, when looking at 'stewardship of electronic commerce', we must bear in mind that the communications revolution was not inspired by governments. It is a grass-roots phenomenon. The Internet, World Wide Web and electronic commerce have been allowed to develop unfettered, blossoming like flowers pollinated by the random passage of a bumble bee. (The Internet was based on a US government military then research/academic network dating back to the 1960s. The World Wide Web (WWW) was technically created in 1991, but it was the runaway success of the 'Mosaic' browser in 1993 that brought the full graphical potential of the WWW to the fore. Without government or business coordination web sites sprang up everywhere,

> The Internet, World Wide Web and electronic commerce have been allowed to develop unfettered, blossoming like flowers pollinated by the random passage of a bumble bee.

the number of people 'on-line' climbed sharply, business saw the potential of the new audio-visual environment and Internet electronic commerce was born.) The bee metaphor is particularly apt. The emergence of the World Wide Web and Internet electronic commerce is a striking example of an often-ignored reality – planning, coordination and regulation are not always necessary for an idea to germinate. Perhaps, such management virtues can even be counterproductive for visionary and quantum developments at their earliest stages. Serendipity is at the origin of some of our greatest achievements.

Now electronic commerce has moved beyond gestation, past its earliest stages and is most certainly now global. History will undoubtedly record electronic communication as the locomotive that brought the wonders of globalization to the world. The Internet appears to be dismantling national borders in some important respects, changing the face of electronic commerce at a rapid-fire pace, and irreversibly. So, despite the Internet's unmanaged, almost chaos-theory birth, the time has come to consider global stewardship issues.

The global stewardship issues arise for simple reasons:

- electronic commerce is a global phenomenon
- electronic commerce is anticipated to have a significant role in commercial dealings and should stimulate economic growth
- lack of adequate safeguards will inhibit the use of electronic commerce, and could disrupt the level playing field for business competitors and even for governments
- activity that is not globally coordinated will be an obstacle to the free flow of information and trade.

However, the global issues must be defined narrowly and with restraint. Careless responses could threaten to be a straightjacket for the innovation, speed and flexibility that has typified electronic commerce in its developmental stage.

The growth of electronic commerce presents an implicit challenge: how to fashion a sensible, restrained and coordinated approach that will permit electronic commerce to attain its full potential. This means that we must instil public confidence in the legal, economic and financial aspects of this remarkable technology. Otherwise, tomorrow's leaders will not be able to take full advantage of the extraordinary benefits that could be brought to almost every aspect of human existence and to every corner of the globe. Our generation's leadership will be judged by our success or failure in meeting this challenge.

Key issues

Education

The use of the Internet technologies for educational purposes offers amazing and unparalleled opportunities. There is a strong convergence between what these technologies make possible and the sort of education countries around the world are seeking for all. Thus, the emphasis in education today is on teaching how to learn rather than teaching facts, on creativity – including teamwork and individual initiative – on the skills of problem-solving and knowing how to learn as a life-long objective. Above all, education must be grounded in and relate closely to everyday life and experience.

The use of the Internet technologies facilitates all these aims, allowing programmes matched to individual needs, encouraging communication in unrivalled ways, opening up a wealth of resources. Moreover, its intelligent and responsible use in school both mirrors the adult world outside and prepares the young people for full participation within that world in later life.

Partnerships must be established between the worlds of education and commerce, between suppliers and consumers, so that each may come to a fuller realization of the underlying concerns of the other and the constraints within which they operate. Otherwise problems would remain for the suppliers – lacking awareness of the key criteria for development – and the users – unwilling to be committed when uncertain of the quality and appropriateness. Without effective dialogue of this nature, the full educational potential of the Internet and related technologies will not be realized; nor will it be as effective in correcting, as soon as possible, the mismatch between education, on the one hand, and labour market needs on the other.

It is essential to create a successful educational market that is able to take advantage of the new opportunities for delivering effective education over distributed networks. Educational content needs special consideration in the development of electronic commerce in order for quality assurance of learning materials to be firmly in place, common standards encouraged and recognition given to educational achievements outside the traditional institutional environment.

A paramount educational concern in every country is for its young people to become effective and critical users of the Internet technologies, which will ensure the socially coherent Information Society we all want to see.

Consumer protection

Although business-to-business electronic commerce represents about 80 per cent of all electronic commerce, most attention and speculation about electronic commerce has focused on the business-to-consumer segment. With household transactions typically accounting for over half of all domestic final demand (OECD indicators show that domestic final demand is the same as total final demand except that imports have not been included) this focus is not surprising. Moreover, as business PCs and networks are saturated, it is natural for the focus of attention to turn to the household.

As more and more consumers turn to the Internet, concerns are being voiced regarding whether or not there are adequate safeguards to protect the consumers' interests. For instance, consumers may have privacy concerns, as discussed below. Consumers might be exposed to unfair marketing practices. Consumers need adequate systems for redress – that is, there needs to be recourse for customers if the merchandise is defective, unsuitable or never arrives. The mechanisms for redress are very likely to require some international attention – even to determine which court has jurisdiction. And even before getting to court, consumers want to know there are effective mechanisms to lodge complaints and address grievances.

Some of the possible technological solutions that have been mentioned are:

- a labelling system to indicate whether or not a particular on-line vendor has met consumer protection standards
- a notification system to inform consumers about the possible uses of data they submit
- a notification of the types of mechanisms for redress, perhaps including information on legal jurisdiction.

The private sector should take the lead in these innovations. In fact, there are continuous improvements in consumer notices and cautions for on-line shopping. The global response may be simply to coordinate and support the solutions that work.

Privacy

Consumers have reason to be concerned about privacy in the electronic commerce environment. Customers must be confident, secure and certain about what use will be made of information about them and their activities. A number of actions can be taken to respond to customers' concerns.

First, consumers can be educated about the privacy issues. Some of the concerns may be founded on fear of the unknown, about what exactly is happening when a consumer browses a web site, inspects a virtual product or completes an on-line transaction. Education can help to allay these concerns. Where there are real threats to individual privacy, education may well equip consumers to eliminate the threat or reduce it to a level that they find personally acceptable. Merchants should aid in the education process by clearly indicating their privacy practices and the rights and obligations applicable to both the merchant and consumer.

> Merchants should aid in the education process by clearly indicating their privacy practices and the rights and obligations applicable ...

Second, codes of conduct, guidelines, contractual models and legislation can be used to deliver privacy protection. There are questions about whether or not any of these responses, by and of themselves, will be sufficient. Codes of conduct are typically industry-specific and electronic commerce cuts across industry sectors. Guidelines may not be binding and can be flaunted. Contractual models run into conflicts of jurisdiction and enforceability problems as may legislative solutions. Globally coordinated arrangements, involving both business and governments and with viable redress mechanisms, will be required to protect personal privacy fully.

Third, technology itself, so often seen as a tool that can threaten privacy, is also a tool that can be used to protect privacy. Technologies that allow individuals to act anonymously on-line and encryption techniques that can protect the confidentiality of messages are two examples. However, the use of these technologies can be problematical where they are used to hide criminal activities or inappropriate on-line behaviour. A balance needs to be achieved so that users can use technology to protect their privacy without blocking the ability of law enforcement authorities to do their job.

Commercial security issues

Commercial security issues are a vital concern of business-to-business electronic commerce. Business-to-business electronic commerce dominates the total value of electronic commerce activity, accounting for about 80 per cent at present as noted above. This share is probably conservative.

A key reason for electronic commerce – especially the business-to-business segment – growing so quickly is its significant impact on costs associated with inventories, sales execution, procurement, intangibles such as banking and distribution costs. Achieving these gains is contingent on a number of factors, including access to electronic commerce systems and the needed skills. However, what is unique about electronic commerce over the Internet and the efficiency gains it promises is the premium placed on openness. To reap the potential cost savings fully, firms must be willing to open up their internal systems to suppliers and customers. This aspect raises policy issues concerning security and potential anti-competitive effects as firms integrate their operations more closely. Also, a balance must be achieved between openness and confidentiality.

Commercial security is an important part of industry agendas for electronic commerce. In 1997, the OECD commissioned a group of private-sector experts in electronic commerce under the responsibility of John Sacher, Executive Director of Marks & Spencer. The Sacher Report recognized the importance of 'an institutional framework' to support the protection of information systems and data. The institutional framework would address three areas:

- authentication/non-repudiation/data integrity
- certification
- data protection.

Commercial security is also critical to prevent piracy or unauthorized use of copyright material. Of course, the framework has been in the process of development for some time. Industry has developed the 'Secure Electronic Transactions' (SET) initiative and is working on the 'Open Trading Protocol' (OTP) and other initiatives. There are also the OECD's *Guidelines on the Security of Information Systems* (1992) and *Guidelines on Cryptography Policy* (1997).

Commercial security issues also link to questions about law enforcement. For instance, cryptography needs to consider information security and privacy from all its perspectives. It will be an enormous challenge to meet the equally important objectives of confidentiality and law enforcement. Indeed during 1996 the OECD sponsored a series of workshops on the Economics of the Information Society. In the fifth of the series, leading experts from industry and academia came together with government officials to discuss a wide range of issues with regard to the communications revolution. The summary of the proceedings notes the difficulty and importance of bringing together these objectives, with international coordination being seen as vital.

Intellectual property issues

A globally coordinated intellectual property framework will be essential to developing and promoting electronic commerce, particularly in digitized goods such as audio and video material and computer software (for a discussion of this issue see 'Risk Management and the World Wide Web', to be found at http://infoserv2.ita.doc.gov/ocbe/).

An important aspect of law enforcement in international trade in information is the enforcement of copyright of works in digital form. Without adequate protection for intellectual property rights, firms will be reluctant to invest in product innovation and businesses dealing in digitized goods frequently cite intellectual property protection as one of their major concerns in relation to electronic commerce over the Internet (SPA Testimony on the Online Copyright Liability Limitation Act 16 September, 1997).

There are a number of existing mechanisms that provide a degree of intellectual property protection. Copyright law protects most the literal code, signature or form of words or music. However, in the area of software, 'look and feel' copyright is being used to protect features such the user interface, icons and other presentation features. Patent law is used to protect inventive concepts and processes (see David C. Mowery, p. 275, in Merger ed., 1996) and may be used in the field of software, but might have less relevance for audio and video material. However, still, the digitization of information is challenging the current intellectual property laws. The ease with which digital information products can be replicated, transmitted onward, reproduced perfectly and widely and instantly distributed without the knowledge of rights holders is a major focus of current efforts to update the laws protecting intellectual property rights.

The World Trade Organisation Agreement on Trade-related Aspects of Intellectual Property Protection (TRIPS) sets minimum international standards for intellectual property protection (signed in January 1995, the Agreement protects computer programs – both source and object code – as literary works; databases are protected as compilations; the Agreement is due to be reviewed in 2000). Further, the World Intellectual Property Organisation (WIPO) has negotiated two international treaties to extend the basic rights of copyright holders to information, images, music and software residing on the Internet (the WIPO Copyright Treaty and the WIPO Performances and Phonograms Treaty, both adopted on 20 December, 1996).

However, differences in the implementation of the TRIPS Agreement, as well as differences in national intellectual property policy, can affect the actual protection afforded in a particular jurisdiction.

Any rules for monitoring infringement by, for example on-line information service providers or systems operators (sysops) need to be balanced. If the monitoring rules are too stringent, there could be a chilling effect on the legitimate transmission of information.

Tax issues

Business has been very concerned about how taxation will be administered to electronic commerce. For instance, during the OECD Conference on electronic commerce held in Turku, Finland, in November 1997, Madame Cattaui, Secretary-General of the International Chamber of Commerce, estimated that 'business has no more than one and a half years to demonstrate that it can control commercial misuse of the Internet before governments step in to over-regulate, over-tax and over-censor.'

A wide range of speculative proposals has been heard. At one extreme there is a view that electronic commerce should be completely tax free. However, even though tax-free electronic commerce may assist the sector to grow more rapidly, it would also create an uneven playing field that would discriminate against conventional commerce. Apart from creating an unfair uneven playing field such a regime could carry negative economic consequences for growth and job creation.

The other extreme is to introduce special new taxes for electronic commerce. 'Bit' taxes are perhaps the most infamous example. 'Bit' taxes are widely regarded as crude, blunt instruments that do not stand up well to the tax policy principles of equity or fairness. However, the concept persists, creating uncertainty for everyone.

So, neither extreme seems viable. The solution is in between – the neutral application of existing taxes to the electronic commerce environment. However, the practical implications of this position may not be intuitively obvious. Uncertainty is a great hindrance to the growth of electronic commerce, and uncertainty in taxation would be very bad indeed. So, the bottom line is to provide global certainty in the area of taxation and electronic commerce.

Certainty can be obtained by affirming that electronic commerce is already subject to existing international tax law. The OECD does not have proposals for tax-free electronic commerce, nor for 'bit' taxes or any other special taxes, just an assurance that the existing tax principles will be applied. This response avoids economic distortions, allows decades of carefully crafted tax policy and tax law to be applied to the electronic commerce environment too and means that businesses don't have to learn a new set of rules or adjust their business strategies to try to avoid unfavourable tax treatment of either electronic or conventional commerce.

> **Uncertainty is a great hindrance to the growth of electronic commerce, and uncertainty in taxation would be very bad indeed.**

Equally important, the application of existing tax principles to electronic commerce will be carried out in a manner that is neutral, fair and as simple as possible.

International process

Governments, international organizations and the business community have already begun an extensive process to consider global issues in electronic commerce. The OECD has been working on various aspects of the global Information Society for over two decades, but it was in 1996 that electronic commerce became the object of a broad range of activities. These activities have included an unprecedented and intensive dialogue with the international business community, non-member countries and, of course, the OECD members themselves. In addition, the OECD commissioned the Sacher Report and has been holding major international conferences – one at Ministerial level – on electronic commerce.

The process for finding a global stewardship plan must build on all the earlier work. The OECD is working towards a broad, concerted approach by governments and the private sector in order to foster a stable and predictable environment that facilitates growth and maximizes the social and economic potential of electronic commerce. Governments and business must continue to meet and brainstorm – certainly in global conferences of the type mentioned above, but perhaps also in small, focused working groups where technical experts and policy makers can educate one another and develop responsive and moderate solutions. This work is multidisciplinary and will require horizontal cooperation across specialties. In undertaking these sessions with a view to moving towards global stewardship, four goals should be paramount:

- building trust for users and consumers
- establishing ground rules for the electronic commerce marketplace
- enhancing the information infrastructure for electronic commerce
- maximizing the benefits of a Global Information Society.

Conclusion

As electronic commerce enters adolescence, the requirements for stewardship and certainty in electronic commerce appear to be coming together. These tasks will naturally be led by those organizations that have a truly global reach.

At this time, it appears that the OECD must play a key role, providing leadership in the areas of taxation, consumer protection and privacy, working closely with the WIPO and WTO on intellectual property rights and other trade policy issues, with the United Nations on commercial security and with organizations such as the World Customs Organisation, European Union, Council of Europe and Asia-Pacific Economic Co-operation Forum, and others, on a host of other Internet-related matters. Care must be taken that resources are not wasted on overlapping work and that gaps are not left unattended to.

Further, each of these bodies will need to work with private-sector groups such as the Business and Industry Advisory Committee, International Chamber of Commerce, Global Information Infrastructure Commission, international consumer groups and others to build an environment of public- and private-sector trust to truly remove the uncertainty currently surrounding so much of the electronic commerce environment.

This chapter has compared the growth of the Internet to that of flowers. The flowers still need room to grow, still need flexibility to determine the directions in which they will spread, but they also need some attention to ensure they do not become entangled and choked by regulatory weeds. With proper global stewardship, these early flowers will bloom around the world and become one spectacular garden. ∎

Lee Stein

Chairman Stein and Stein Inc.

THE ANALOGUE ANALOGY

The key to electronic commerce

The Internet was born, and the world changed. Actually, the world changed at least twice. First, a wondrous new thing called 'electronic commerce' began to emerge, and with it came predictions of a brave new world order. There were predictions of mass dislocation, that new digital currencies would emerge, governments would fall and retail outlets would disappear.

The second change occurred when reality set in and people began to realize that a physical world analogue needed to exist in order for an electronic business to be successful.

In this chapter, I will argue that the second change – which call 'the analogue analogy – is a fundamental requirement for the success of any player in the electronic commerce game. The first four years of electronic commerce have led us to formulate three requirements for business models that are likely to find success on the Internet. After discussing these three determinants of Internet business success, I will project forward from these determinants to identify two industry categories that I expect will prosper on the Internet, and two industry categories that I believe will do badly.

The nature of electronic commerce

First, we must be clear about what is meant by 'electronic commerce'. In 1994, the phrase was commonly used to describe basic enabling technologies – most particularly the safe movement of credit card numbers over the Internet. Four years later, multiple definitions of the phrase still abound – perhaps as many definitions as there are players.

My belief is that electronic commerce does not exist as a separate type of commerce. Rather, it is simply an additional channel of distribution that overlaps and coincides with all the other channels that a business has at its disposal – in short, new technology in the service of 'business as usual.' Therefore, I define electronic commerce as 'the use of personal computers by businesses or consumers in support of the purchase or sale of information, goods or services'.

There are those who will shop, enter payment and fulfilment information and complete a transaction on-line. There are others who will shop, but not enter any additional information on-line. Instead, they will use a telephone to seek additional information or complete a purchase via a free phone number. Others will shop on-line then go to a shop to purchase the product there so as to have a full tactile experience and a familiar, comfortable way to return the merchandise if necessary. The on-line environment is merely a transactional medium – a channel of information, marketing and fulfilment processes – augmenting normal business, not a standalone industry.

There is, however, a great deal of money to be made (or lost) (see Figures 1 and 2) as buying patterns shift to utilize this new channel. The modalities of interaction are the frontiers for the world change. The components of success include logistics, customer service, order taking, inventory access, delivery, reliability, new product introduction, back-office systems and delivery systems – all at least partially electronic, and all leading to trust and branding. There is nothing fundamentally new here – there is just efficient business using powerful new tools. However, in essence, it is selling the same thing as before – a quality customer experience.

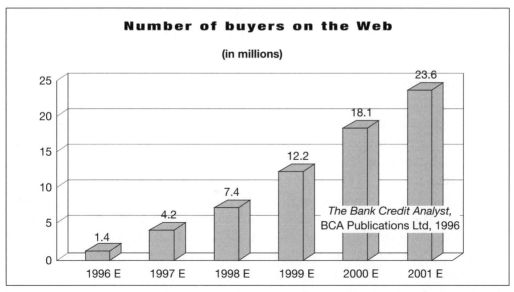

FIGURE 1   Source: John Levinson, Westway Capital

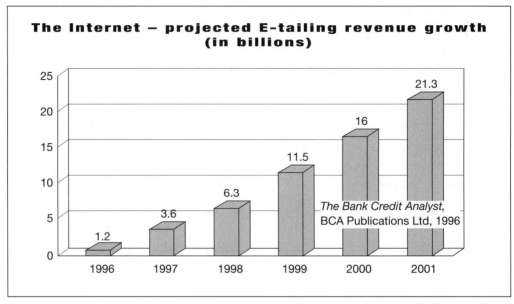

The Internet – projected E-tailing revenue growth (in billions)

The Bank Credit Analyst, BCA Publications Ltd, 1996

FIGURE 2   Source: John Levinson, Westway Capital

The analogue analogy: predicting success or failure in electronic commerce

The basic idea of the analogue analogy is that, in the absence of a genuinely new product, there must be a non-digital and non-Internet analogy in the real world for there to be practical success in the world of electronic commerce. The analogue analogy predicts that three requirements be met in order to achieve success: real-world mirroring, invisible interfaces, and repeatability and loyalty. I shall discuss each of these requirements in turn. All three requirements must be met for practical success in electronic commerce.

Real-world mirroring

The first and most important requirement for an electronic commerce success story is a product or service that mirrors a real-world activity with which people are already familiar. The earliest Internet success stories reflect this reality – an on-line bookshop, auction, music shop, or car dealership are straightforward analogies that consumers can understand.

The importance of mirroring helps explain the failure, to date, of the most ambitious plans to use the Internet to change the market for recorded music. Many people expected that the Internet would prove to be a fundamentally new medium for music, one where individuals would buy songs 'bit-by-bit' instead of in physical form. In an apparent irony, the greatest success in selling music on the Net has been the sale of compact disks, delivered by truck to a physical address.

Conventional wisdom blames bandwidth, disk storage or inadequate copy prevention as the reasons for the failure of bit-by-bit music sales. I am sceptical of this explanation, however, and note that the real world's market for personalized recordings is only a small fraction of the market for pre-selected recording 'packages'. If the physical world market ever demonstrates a stronger demand for personalized recording – for example, if such uses of the minidisk prove to be a runaway success – market forces will inevitably accelerate solutions to such other problems as bandwidth limitations. However, it appears that the majority of consumers simply prefer not to be bothered with the details of constructing highly personalized musical packages, just as a busy driver will often prefer the musical selections of a radio station over a more personal selection of tapes or CDs.

> The first and most important requirement for an electronic commerce success story is a product or service that mirrors a real-world activity with which people are already familiar.

A look at the items sold on the Internet over the past 12 months reinforces the need to mirror the real world (see Table 1).

In short, while the Internet is a medium so filled with possibilities that it invites rich invention and speculation, it is unlikely to change fundamental human preferences and behaviours. Therefore, the business models most likely to succeed will be the ones that are most closely analogous to pre-Internet business models.

Table 1 Top ten of items purchased on-line in 1997/98

Item	Buyers (millions)	Percentage
Software	26.0	38.8
Books	13.0	19.4
Computers	10.1	15.1
Travel	7.5	11.2
Music	6.8	10.2
Food/gifts	6.5	9.7
Clothing	6.2	9.2
Investments	4.2	6.3
Consumer electronics	3.0	4.5
Auto/accessories	2.3	3.5

Source: June 1998 ICONOCAST consensus estimate of seven research studies conducted in 1997/98.

Invisible interfaces

In order to approach ubiquity, electronic commerce needs to become ever more invisible in its mechanisms. The second requirement for success in electronic commerce is that the customer interface fades into the background, becoming essentially invisible to the end user. The interface must permit customers to get what they want, where they want it, the way they want it, and when they want it. Ultimately, the customer interface should become as automatic as steering a car, requiring almost no conscious attention. Such interfaces are, for all practical purposes, invisible.

As user interface designers have known for many years, if you want to make a program's user interface seem less complicated – that is, more invisible in its mechanisms – you generally have to make the program itself more complex. In the case of electronic commerce applications, such invisibility can conceal an impressively complex system, including industrial-strength, scaleable back-office and fulfilment systems. The illusion that the Internet can allow a business to be built 'on the cheap' has been dissolved by, in particular, the encounter with real-world logistics and customer service.

Repeatability and loyalty

The third determinant of success in electronic commerce is that your commercial interactions need be to a sufficiently meaningful positive experience to produce repeatable behaviour that creates recurring revenue and customer loyalty. In the physical world, when a new shopping centre opens people tend to 'surf' the centre. They check out each shop – its products, its location – and walk through the entire centre. After a few visits, habits develop, and people pick their preferred stores, no longer looking at everything. Surfing the centre stops once you find the stores of preference. That is the real-world analogy.

Your first few visits to a new shopping centre in the real world have a straightforward electronic analogy, which is 'surfing' the Net. Surfing the Net is primarily a starting behaviour for new users. After a few surfing visits to Internet locations, habits develop and people pick their preferred sites. This strongly parallels the behaviour in a shopping centre. We stroll, we look around, but we soon pick our favourite shops, the places we prefer to park and the places we like to linger in to just 'hang out'. Habits develop and we minimize our surfing behaviour. Of course, just as in a local shopping centre if a new shop opens and is successful in getting our attention, we will surf over and check it out, and this, too, is an important analogy. Initially, surfing the Net is really like 'training wheels', typical learning behaviour until preferred locations and habits set in. Getting our attention to visit a new location is an art that still requires good old-fashioned brand marketing.

Winners and losers in electronic commerce

As the majority of things that are bought and sold on-line are items that existed long before the Internet, the key question that emerges is, 'Who wins and who loses in the Wired World?' Here we will identify two categories each of winners and losers, but our list is not intended to be exhaustive.

Some winners: logistics and interface providers

One of the most basic industries relevant to electronic commerce is the delivery of physical merchandise. DHL, FedEx and their competitors have a major role in the value chain. The total amount of disposable money for the items in most categories will not change as a result of the Internet. GNP growth, for example, will be determined by many factors, and the Internet is unlikely to play a major role in stimulating supply or demand for physical products or in creating more disposable money for consumers. (Here I am deliberately ignoring the obvious exception of the wealth created by the dramatic run-up in the price of Internet stocks, which is really a product of the financial markets rather than of the Internet itself.) However, although the Internet will not cause more money to be spent, it will cause a reallocation of where and how this money will be spent. If the Wired World is going to shift behaviour so that we no longer need go in person to make a purchase, someone else needs to pick up our merchandise and deliver it to us – the delivery companies, which are increasingly positioning themselves as general providers of outsourced logistics.

Another category of winners will be the interface companies. An interface company is one that develops tools and links to interact with customers and satisfy their needs. Note that by 'customers' we do not restrict our discussion only to consumers, but consider business-to-business applications as well. Although many will focus on consumer interfaces, the winners will be those that solve and master customer interface problems wherever they occur. Some will do this in broad, consumer-oriented ways, but other winners will emerge solving niche business-to-business interface issues. Customer interfaces and the back-office engines to which they connect are the playing field from which a new breed of winner will emerge.

Some losers: legacy technologies and laggards in outsourcing

The biggest losers in electronic commerce are likely to be those companies that are overly tied to legacy technologies. 'Legacy' is defined here as being pre-existing computer systems that were designed to be closed systems rather than to work with open, extendable networks. The five sites that generate the largest volume of on-line purchases – Schwab, Auto-By-Tel, AOL, Dell and Amazon.com – share an interesting common characteristic, which is that each of these companies either had no legacy issues to deal with or was able to develop systems that were not tied to their legacy systems.

Notably missing from the lists of successful on-line transaction processors are the credit card-issuing institutions. These companies might otherwise seem to be naturally well-positioned for electronic commerce. They have excellent branding, contacting masses of consumers daily. Consumers use their credit cards and therefore physically touch the brands of these companies almost daily. These companies also send a written document – their monthly statement – to virtually every consumer in the world, which these consumers must also touch. However, these institutions also have extensive legacy networks that don't talk to each other. Massive technological restructuring would be necessary to solve legacy problems that have been complained about for years. These companies have not shown up on the Internet, other than to market variants on their existing products, such as new credit cards. Their legacy systems can't talk to each other, let alone Internet customers. In the case of Amazon.com I watched with amusement as the analysts predicted the demise of the upstart electronic bookseller when the big superstores arrived. Amazon.com has continued to prosper, however, and its more likely competition is probably CDNow, which has also developed a wired ordering, distribution, customer service and order fulfilment system without any legacy overhang. The recent move by Amazon.com into the CD business shows that the company understands where its real competition is. It moved one vertical market segment away from its core business, rather than attempting to be all things at once. It developed an electronic methodology to sell a product – really any product – that was already sold in the real world. It mirrored an analogue analogy, developed a good customer interface and made the experience sufficiently easy and price sensitive to make it repeatable. All three requirements were met. The logical next step was to use its non-legacy wired systems to enter another vertical market in which the established players are laden with legacy problems.

A second group of losers will be those who fail to grasp the importance of outsourcing and the value-added opportunities offered by the Wired World. It is not a certainty that those who provide added value will win, but it is a virtual certainty that those who fail to provide added value will lose. The companies adding the most value are defining themselves, doing what they do best and outsourcing the rest. Amazon.com for example, doesn't have its own search engine, but uses the AltaVista engine, outsourced from Digital.

Electronic customer service is difficult, and the necessary technologies have barely begun to evolve. Most companies do not really need to conceive, design, build, maintain and enhance their own customer service technologies. If a company cannot buy electronic customer service, it will, of course, have to build it itself. But they will almost always prefer outsourcing where it is an option, as it allows them to allocate scarce internal capital and time resources to their core business. Call centres and outbound bulk postal mail centres were originally operated internally, but today it is far more effective to outsource those functions.

The ability of a company to adapt to today's rate of change is now a fundamental competitive advantage. The more that can be outsourced, the more a company will be able to respond quickly and efficiently to a changing business environment. Such rapid response to change is much harder for companies tied to legacy systems or internal support of non-core technologies.

The hottest Internet stocks are not technology companies, but rather, companies using technology to give their customers better experience. They are using technology to make analogue business succeed – in essence, they are non-Internet, non-digital businesses using scaleable Internet technology to increase value. Many of the component technologies can be bought off the shelf and linked together. The analogue companies that win will be those that outsource critical, cutting-edge technologies. The technology companies that win will be those that build components that can easily be utilized by the analogue companies to permit the rapid addition of value.

Things to watch for

The analogue analogy suggests that the sales cycle in electronic commerce will be an interesting area to watch. In particular, an important question will be how to introduce new products. In the old world, companies used shops, trade shows, public relations and advertising. In the Wired World, without a shop how will people learn about new products? A science will eventually emerge, just as it has emerged in the direct marketing of bulk mail or of outbound telephone calls. No company will have the expertise to do all of this itself – to design, implement and innovate; to know all the discussion groups and chat rooms where a new product should be introduced; and to know how to handle the unique customer service demands of a product early in its life-cycle. Electronic introduction of new products will thus be another important function for outsourcers.

> The hottest Internet stocks are ... non-Internet, non-digital business using scalable Internet technology to increase value.

Mistakes are certainly being made. Netscape begat Yahoo! In its need to generate short-term revenue for Wall Street, Netscape sold the search button on its browser, not recognizing that this button was a key to the largest initial market for on-line advertising. In retrospect, the $5 million dollars that Netscape thus earned seems insignificant given the multi-billion-dollar valuations of Yahoo!, Excite, Infoseek and Lycos.

Then Yahoo! begat Amazon.com by initially avoiding the area of actual sales transactions. Yahoo! saw its analogue analogy as advertising, but followed the model of television advertising too closely. It failed to recognize that some advertising is tied directly to purchasing, such as reply cards in magazines or outdoor signs promoting roadside businesses. Now Amazon.com is apparently trying to avoid begatting an on-line superstore by positioning itself as a general facilitator of on-line purchase transactions, pursuing other vertical market segments rather than pigeonholing itself as a bookseller. As Amazon.com builds brand and trust in the Wired World, consumers will buy much more than books from Amazon.com.

Consumers trust that they can continue to buy from merchants such as Amazon.com because they bought from them in the past with success. It did not matter what they bought, just that it worked and was a good experience. They are training consumers in their methodology so that they will feel no need to become familiar with any others. The next step is that these methodologies will develop into marketplace protocols. Technologies will be built to mimic the most successful methodologies, so that other companies can buy these mechanisms off the shelf. Success in the Wired World requires that an analogue analogy exist, but identifying the *right* analogue analogy remains a challenging task.

Technology is important in making an analogue business more efficient, competitive and successful, but marketing and product development will inevitably carry the day. Marketers will be far more likely than technologists to correctly identify an analogue analogy to exploit.

While good technology is a requirement of successful implementation, building a new electronic commerce business should start with the identification of a new analogue analogy – an area where the electronic analogy to an existing real-world business category has not previously been pursued. I believe that, with electronic commerce still in its infancy, there are still myriad such opportunities awaiting the savvy and stout-hearted entrepreneur. ■

Special thanks to Dr Nathaniel Borenstein for his advice and editing. Additional thanks to Dr Marshall Rose, Karen Chapman, Brad Feld of Softbank, Kawaika Daguio of American Banking Association, Gabe Batista of Network Solutions, and Pierre Wolff of Impulse Network for their intellectual contribution, and credit for putting the Analogue Analogy model into the investment matrix to Jerry Colona of Flatiron Partners.

Deborah Hurley

Director, Harvard Information Infrastructure Project,
Harvard University

SECURITY AND PRIVACY LAWS

The showstoppers of the Global Information Society

A t a conference on the Global Information Infrastructure (GII) at the Organization for Economic Cooperation and Development (OECD) in December 1994, the head of the Delegation of the United States identified privacy and security, along with cryptography and intellectual property, as the showstopper issues of the GII, which, if unresolved, would impede its development and mean it could not be used to its fullest potential. This assertion remains true today. Polls of Internet users consistently cite concerns about security and privacy, which may hamper their participation in the Global Information Society (GIS) and electronic commerce.

Security and privacy for the GIS and electronic commerce are often treated like brand new issues. Rather, the development of measures for the security of information systems and the protection of personal data and privacy are well over two decades old. A lot of work has already been done at international and national levels to establish common principles and rules, with broad acceptance by many countries. The groundwork has been laid. Now, due to the burgeoning growth of the GII and the promise of the GIS and electronic commerce, there is pressure and urgency about providing security and privacy, which, in the view of those in the field, are welcome and long overdue. The current challenges are dissemination and implementation of the international and national frameworks that already exist and, as necessary, the development of new measures and practices to meet current and foreseeable security and privacy needs.

In this chapter, some of the important factors and trends that will influence the security and privacy of the GIS and electronic commerce and the growth of user trust and consumer confidence will be delineated.

The information infrastructure includes computers and communication networks as well as the data and information on them. It also includes all the individuals who interact with the computers, networks, data and information. Moving beyond these obvious elements of the information infrastructure, other components are or will be Intelligent Transport Systems (ITS), locational technologies, such as global positioning technologies, monitoring and surveillance technologies, including sensors, biometric identifiers, and wearable computing.

The information infrastructure is becoming ubiquitous. Worldwide computing and communication capacity will grow explosively, fuelled by dramatic increases in computing power and networks, steep reductions in costs, and advances in miniaturisation. This enabling capacity will be embedded everywhere. There will be more personal computing, and I mean really personal. Computers will evolve from boxes on a desk, which someone uses perhaps several hours each day, to near-constant tools. They will be like watches and glasses, but with intelligence and interactivity with the wearer and the surrounding world. They will be used for a great variety of purposes, not just for business, as is the case for many people today, as well as more consistently over time, collecting information and providing it to others.

In addition to the greater uses of information and communication technologies described above, the convergence of these technologies with biotechnology and nano-technology will continue. For example, the Global Information Infrastructure will include biological information. DNA, after all, is just another data tape, when viewed from an information policy perspective.

Driven in part by the growth of the Global Information Infrastructure, the rights, responsibilities, roles and relationships – the 4Rs – of governments, business, citizens, individuals and various non-State players are shifting. The underlying question is the relative distribution of voice, power and decision-making authority among these parties in the GIS.

Although the new arrangements that will arise from increasing use of information and communication technologies will probably not be wholly outside previous experience, they may call for some examination and recalibration of the boundaries between the various players. These adjustments have occurred throughout history – the Magna Carta and the Bill of Rights are just such exercises in line-drawing and there are many other, less famous examples represented in statute, case law, business practice and social norms.

Information and communication technologies enable the massive collection of data and information to a degree formerly entirely unknown. In addition, in a manner also unprecedented, the data and information may potentially be processed, matched, manipulated and accessed by a wide variety and number of individuals and entities. Once again, therefore, there is a shift or blurring in the boundaries between these various parties, brought about by growing use of information and communication technologies. It will probably be necessary to survey the new GIS terrain and to adjust the markers.

Driven to communicate

There is a deep human need to communicate. It is a profound characteristic of our species. We will go to great efforts to do so from making clay tablets and digging cuneiform into them, repeatedly dipping a quill into ink and scratching it on parchment, and so on, to the era of computer and communication technologies and beyond. An enormous amount of human energy and ingenuity has gone into devising ways to communicate.

For most of mankind's existence, communication was, of necessity, evanescent. Now and into the future, as more and more interactions take place over various information media, a greater proportion of communications are, and will be, recorded and recordable. They will be more durable and much easier to duplicate and distribute that ever before.

The GII is a tool for our communication with one another. It is important to bear this in mind and develop human-centred systems and policies for the Global Information Society. Too often, we are dazzled by the technological innovations and lose sight of their purpose. Time and again – as in the case of France's Minitel – the success of an information system is based on its use for conversation rather than for the data and information that are in it – such as train timetables, telephone directories and weather forecasts. Furthermore, it is axiomatic that, like all tools, the GII will be used in unanticipated ways with unanticipated results.

Coupled with our zeal to communicate is the equally strong desire, at times, to limit the audience for the communication. There are many examples of communications that an individual may wish to make, but that they do not want the whole world to be able to hear. Conversations with a husband or wife, with a boss about a new company strategy, with a co-worker about the boss or with children at bedtime are all fine communications, with nothing inherently wrong or embarrassing about them. At the same time, we do not want everyone to be able to hear them. If everyone *were* able to hear or read our communications, it would very much change the nature of the interactions. Our ability to express ourselves, especially about matters closest to us, such as tenderness or competition, would be hampered.

> Too often, we are dazzled by the technological innovations and lose sight of their purpose.

While information and communication technologies provide many potential benefits, it is important also to ensure that communication systems are not made too transparent and to preserve zones that permit individuals to engage in all the great variety of human discourse. The current, vivid debates about privacy and personal data protection and cryptography are based on this problem.

Locus of control

The question of the locus of control of information and communication is central. Most people, for example, have identity or credit cards with chips or magnetic strips that they carry with them and freely give out. Yet, they do not know, or have any influence over, the information that is encoded on them. Increasingly, intelligence is being added to the end points of information systems, which gives the end user the possibility of more control, due both to the availability of more information and the possibility to create, manipulate and use the information. In the section on privacy below, I advocate a principle for privacy protection that would claim for, and return to, the individual control of their personal information, rather than the third-party model of governmental or industry control that now prevails.

Proportionality

The recollection of the simple but powerful principle of maintaining a sense of proportionality by policy makers and industry would be of great benefit to the development of the GIS and electronic commerce. The solution should be in proportion to the perceived harm or risk. The cure should not be worse than the disease. Some proposals, such as key escrow systems, widespread use of biometric identifiers and DNA collection for trivial transactions, may actually create security and privacy risks rather than reduce them. Similarly, an organization, by oversecuring information assets, may produce new and unanticipated vulnerabilities.

Security of information systems

While there is a lot of good news with regard to information and communication technologies – general improvements in terms of speed, cost and other factors, and their potential economic and social benefits – there is also some bad news. Intrinsic security is growing worse. There are more computers, more networks, more data and information, and, most significantly, more fallible human beings connected to and using the systems.

The security of worldwide information systems is in a generally deplorable state. Imagine a large sponge, extremely porous, laden with water. We rely today on the goodwill of many people, around the world, including young people, not to use their technological knowledge in deleterious ways. At the same time, we are more dependent than ever on the continued functioning of critical information systems, such as those used by hospitals, air traffic control systems, power grids – and communication infrastructures. The threats to the functioning of systems, moreover, come more often not from the hacker or disgruntled employee, but from the insufficiently trained, fatigued or negligent but well-intentioned employee. There is significant potential for major system degradation or failure. In addition, as the GII expands, adding nodes, there are concerns about quality of service. The greater challenges, in the end, may not be technical, as much as those of managing very large and complex organizational structures.

More than ever, there is a need for robust systems that will foster individual trust in the GIS and consumer confidence in the promise of e-commerce. The tenuous situation in which we presently exist is very largely avoidable. The objective of security of information systems is protection from harm resulting from failures of availability, confidentiality, integrity and authentication. Security is only as good as the weakest link in the chain. Traditional risk analysis and management can provide us with a great deal that could be applied to this issue. Moreover, security of information systems must be dynamic – it cannot be static because the information infrastructure itself is always changing. The goal should not be maximum security. Security measures must be in proportion to the risk of harm, so as not to create additional security vulnerabilities. An important feature of information system security that differs from risk in more traditional fields, such as civil engineering, is the learning adversary. This security threat is similar to the enemy in a military context.

> The security of worldwide information systems is in a generally deplorable state. Imagine a large sponge, extremely porous, laden with water.

For well over a decade, it has been widely recognized that there is a need in both the public and private sectors for better information about security threats and breaches. At the same time, organizations are reluctant to make security problems known, for fear of bad publicity and loss of public confidence. However, there is increasing recognition of the interdependence of information systems and their key roles in national and economic security. Moreover, many of these so-called 'critical infrastructures' are in the private sector. There must be better governmental and private-sector cooperation with regard to gathering and dissemination of information about security threats and breaches. The private sector, however, is often opposed to mandated disclosure requirements and uneasy about sharing information with the public sector and potential competitors. The goal of greater cooperation about security threats and breaches is clear, but the road that industry and government will walk to get there is, so far, largely uncharted.

Better security practices may lead to leaner information organizations

Organizations are holding more and more information, which increases their burdens regarding maintaining it properly. Instead of the prevailing concept that many now have, of organizations eager to vacuum up all available information, there may evolve, instead, a much more judicious gathering and use of information, so as to avoid the costs, management responsibilities and potential liabilities of keeping large pools of data and information, especially personal and proprietary information. There may be a move towards a leaner information organization, with greater precision about the information that is collected and retained.

Adopt 'bread and butter' security measures

There tends to be a focus on questions such as cryptography, which is described briefly below. I would maintain that a very high proportion of security is what I call 'bread and butter' security. Such measures include proper password choice and man-

1992 OECD guidelines for the security of information systems

PRINCIPLES

1 Accountability principle
The responsibilities and accountability of owners, providers and users of information systems and other parties concerned with the security of information systems should be explicit.

2 Awareness principle
In order to foster confidence in information systems, owners, providers and users of information systems and other parties should readily be able, consistent with maintaining security, to gain appropriate knowledge of, and be informed about, the existence and general extent of measures, practices and procedures for the security of information systems.

3 Ethics principle
Information systems and the security of information systems should be provided and used in such a manner that the rights and legitimate interests of others are respected.

4 Multidisciplinary principle
Measures, practices and procedures for the security of information systems should take account of, and address, all relevant considerations and viewpoints, including technical, administrative, organizational, operational, commercial, educational and legal.

5 Proportionality principle
Security levels, costs, measures, practices and procedures should be appropriate and proportionate to the value of and degree of reliance on the information systems and to the severity, probability and extent of potential harm, as the requirements for security vary depending on the particular information systems.

6 Integration principle
Measures, practices and procedures for the security of information systems should be co-ordinated and integrated with each other and with other measures, practices and procedures of the organization so as to create a coherent system of security.

7 Timeliness principle
Public and private parties, at both national and international levels, should act in a timely, coordinated manner to prevent and to respond to breaches of information systems.

8 Reassessment principle
The security of information systems should be reassessed periodically, as information systems and the requirements for their security vary over time.

9 Democracy principle
The security of information systems should be compatible with the legitimate use and flow of data and information in a democratic society.

Source: 'Guidelines for the security of information systems', Organisation for Economic Co-operation and Development, Paris, 1992, ASIN: 9264145699 agement, physical security measures, management and organizational practices and procedures. None of them is very glamorous, yet their wider adoption would improve the security of information networks.

Closely related are education and awareness campaigns about security of information systems. Just as rules of the road had to evolve with the growing use of the car, so there is a need to teach the rules of the Information Superhighway. Instruction in good computer security practices should begin at the same time that someone begins to use computers. As many children in developed countries now have computers in their early school years, the related computer security training should also start at that time. In addition, as wider use of bread and butter security measures throughout the civilian population begins to improve the overall civilian security structure, it may create a better base upon which the military may harden its and the nation's information systems.

While enhancing security, preserve the delicate balance of civil liberties

It is imperative that the security of the GII be improved. It is equally important, while measures are taken to provide security, that the delicate balance of civil liberties in a democratic society be preserved. Some have argued that it is inevitable that civil liberties will be diminished in the face of the threat of information warfare. Others assert, equally vociferously, that the battle of security may be won while the war of preserving the democratic construct may be lost, if we sacrifice the civil liberties of a free society in the name of information security. I side with the latter view. The fear is that a failure event will occur that will create a backlash in which people are willing to forgo some of their rights. It is essential to improve the security of the GII to improve trust and confidence in the system and attempt to forestall and diminish the effects of security failures.

Cryptography is, at the moment, an almost unique tool for providing security and privacy

Cryptography provides a powerful solution to the problem that inherent security is worsening. It is thought that the development and use of cryptography are as old as writing itself. Wherever man has sought to express himself, the communications have often been intended for limited audiences, rather than the whole world.

In response to the growth of the Global Information Infrastructure and the clamour of industry and individuals for secure, private communications, national governments are scrambling to formulate policies on cryptography – a powerful, crucial and, at the moment, almost unique tool for assuring the robust operation of the information infrastructure and the security and privacy of communications on worldwide networks. Governments face the additional challenge, in a networked world, that their positions on cryptography must also take account of, and coordinate with, the policies of other nations. Government positions run the gamut from very restrictive requirements on use of cryptography by individuals within national borders, such as in France, to limits on the export of cryptography, as in the US, and on to support for use of encryption for the protection of privacy and electronic commerce, as in Germany.

Good cryptography is inexpensive, with low or no marginal costs. It costs approximately the same as bad or no cryptography. Cryptography should be, and needs to be, designed in at the beginning of a project, not tacked on at the end. A 1998 study reported that 90 bits are sufficient for secret keys over the next 20 years, but that this is the bare minimum, assuming that advances such as DNA computing and quantum computing are not realized within that time.

Due to the growth of the Internet and electronic communications, the wider availability of cryptography technologies, greater public awareness of cryptography and more actual potential need on the part of the general public for cryptography, governments are grappling with the question of whether or not and, if so, when it might be necessary or desirable for governmental authorities and others to be able to gain access to the keys used to encrypt communications or stored data. Consideration of this issue has led some governments to propose systems for so-called key escrow, key recovery or trusted third parties, in order to provide a mechanism for access to keys. The most important question is, 'is key escrow ever necessary?' However, this, among the many matters related to key escrow that are hotly and widely debated, is the query that seems to be least often raised and less often answered. If key escrow is necessary, why and for what?

It is still early days in the development of national cryptography policies. Many national governments began from a standing start in 1995 to develop policies.

Privacy and data protection: the state of play and the trends

In his speech, 'The emerging digital economy', on 15 April 1998, the US Secretary of Commerce, William M. Daley, identified privacy as 'the make or break issue' for the success of the digital economy. A current perception of privacy and protection of personal data is that these notions are extremely vague and highly culturally dependent. This view is unfounded. On the contrary, there already exists a well-established framework – accepted at international level and by many nations – that provides a clear set of common denominators on which global consensus with regard to privacy and data protection may be built. There are two international accords on privacy and data protection, dating from 1980 and 1981, to which many nations are signatories. There is more than 20 years of experience, not only with formulating the principles of privacy and personal data protection, but also with implementing these principles in legislation, standards, business codes of conduct and technological constructs. In the meeting of massive amounts of personal data with computing and communications in the GIS and e-commerce lies a set of important privacy issues that is ripe for resolution.

Current privacy and data protection rules

Currently, there is a variety of measures used to attempt to protect personal data and privacy around the globe, which includes legislation, standards, technological means, industry codes of conduct and business practices and procedures. The particular measures employed differ significantly, depending on geographical location and level of technological development. This degree of variation is generally incompatible with a global network in which information – including personal, identifiable information about individuals, may travel anywhere in the network. The level of protection, for the same personal information, may be different, not due to any intent, but as a result of the norms – whether these be legal, economic, technological, social or ethical – that govern that part of the network.

In the mid-1970s in Europe, as computers began to come into wider use by governments and industry, concern began to grow about the collection, use and automatic processing of data about, and identifiable to, individuals. The abuses of civil liberties and human rights during World War II made many Europeans especially sensitive to the potential harms of large-scale collection, manipulation and retention of records about individuals. European countries, such as Germany, France and Sweden, began to pass data protection legislation.

The trend towards more privacy and personal data protection

This trend towards adopting privacy and data protection legislation has continued consistently to the present. Most Western and Central European countries, as well as other jurisdictions, such as Australia, New Zealand and Hong Kong, now have so-called 'omnibus' data protection legislation. This broadly covers the personal data and privacy of individuals, applies to the public and private sectors, establishes an independent overseeing authority – usually called a data protection commission – incorporates rules governing the collection, use and retention of personal data, and offers recourse and redress for violations. The United States, however, has not adopted omnibus data protection legislation. During the past two decades, legislation to protect certain discrete types of personal data, such as credit records and videotape rental records, has been adopted, creating a so-called 'patchwork' of data protection laws.

The current culmination of the two decades of European policy development is reflected in the European Union Directive 95/46/EC on the protection of individuals with regard to the processing of personal data and on the free movement of such data. The EU Directive was adopted in 1995 and should have been fully implemented by October 1998. The EU Directive contains a significant extraterritorial provision that the flow of personal data from any EU member country may be halted if the jurisdiction to which it is being transferred is deemed not to have an adequate level of protection for personal data. The United States is generally viewed as lacking an adequate level of protection for personal data, due to the absence in the US of omnibus legislation. The issues of US adequacy and the adequacy of data protection policies of US companies, the intentions of the EU and its member countries to enforce the extraterritorial provision after the Directive went fully into force in October 1998, and possible recourse to various international bodies by the EU and the US or other non-EU countries that might also be affected by the Directive are all matters of current, intense debate and governmental consultation.

American companies doing business in Europe have had to adhere to the data protection laws of each of the jurisdictions in which they operate. Many American companies know how to comply, and have been complying, with omnibus data protection legislation in the countries that require it for decades. The irony is that the same companies may not be providing the same level of protection of personal data for Americans or for people in other parts of the world where there is no statutory requirement.

Underpinning the current apparent schism between the EU and US are several relevant international accords. The two international documents drafted and adopted expressly to address questions of privacy and protection of personal data are the 1980 OECD Guidelines on the Protection of Privacy and Transborder Flows of Personal Data and the 1981 Council of Europe Recommendation No. 108 for the Protection of Individuals with Regard to Automatic Processing of Personal Data. Obviously, the documents significantly pre-date the rise of the Internet and the current and foresee-

---

1980 OECD Guidelines for the protection of privacy and transborder flows of personal data

BASIC PRINCIPLES OF NATIONAL APPLICATION

- **Collection limitation principle**
  There should be limits to the collection of personal data and any such data should be obtained by lawful and fair means and, where appropriate, with the knowledge or consent of the data subject.

- **Data quality principle**
  Personal data should be relevant to the purposes for which they are to be used, and, to the extent necessary for those purposes, should be accurate, complete and kept up to date.

- **Purpose specification principle**
  The purposes for which personal data are collected should be specified not later than at the time of data collection and the subsequent use limited to the fulfilment of those purposes or such others as are not incompatible with those purposes and as are specified on each occasion of change of purpose.

- **Use limitation principle**
  Personal data should not be disclosed, made available or otherwise used for purposes other than those specified in accordance with Paragraph 9 [please refer to full OECD Guidelines – see source credit line opposite], except with the consent of the data subject or by the authority of law.

- **Security safeguards principle**
  Personal data should be protected by reasonable security safeguards against such risks as loss or unauthorized access, destruction, use, modification or disclosure of data.

- **Openness principle**
  There should be a general policy of openness about developments, practices and policies with respect to personal data. Means should be readily available of establishing the existence and nature of personal data, and the main purposes of their use, as well as the identity and usual residence of the data controller.

- **Individual participation principle**
  An individual should have the right to obtain from a data controller, or otherwise, confirmation of whether or not the data controller has data relating to them; to have communicated to them, data relating to them within a reasonable time, at a charge, if any, that is not excessive, in a reasonable manner and in a form that is readily intelligible to them; to be given reasons if a request made under the first two rights is denied, and to be able to challenge such denial; and to challenge data relating to them and, if the challenge is successful, to have the data erased, rectified, completed or amended.

- **Accountability principle**
  A data controller should be accountable for complying with measures which give effect to the principles stated above.

BASIC PRINCIPLES OF INTERNATIONAL APPLICATION: FREE FLOW AND LEGITIMATE RESTRICTIONS

[OECD] Member countries should take into consideration the implications for other member countries of domestic processing and re-exportation of personal data.

Member countries should take all reasonable and appropriate steps to ensure that transborder flows of personal data – including transit through a member country – are uninterrupted and secure.

A member country should refrain from restricting transborder flows of personal data between itself and another member country, except where the latter does not yet substantially observe these guidelines or where the re-exportation of such data would circumvent its domestic privacy legislation. A member country may also impose restrictions in respect of certain categories of personal data for which its domestic privacy legislation includes specific regulations in view of the nature of those data and for which the other member country provides no equivalent protection.

Member countries should avoid developing laws, policies and practices in the name of the protection of privacy and individual liberties that would create obstacles to transborder flows of personal data exceeding requirements for such protection.

Source: 'Guidelines for the protection of privacy and transborder flows of personal data', Organisation for Economic Co-operation and Development, Paris, 1981, ASIN: 9264121552 able growth in computing power and networking. None the less, they are viewed as having continued validity and providing a fundamental framework for privacy and personal data protection.

In addition to these two international accords, which address directly and explicitly the protection of personal data and privacy, arguments are made that the provisions of the principal human rights conventions, the Universal Declaration of Human Rights and the European Convention for the Protection of Human Rights and Fundamental Freedoms, also apply to the protection of personal data. Furthermore, it is asserted, the rights of freedom of movement and freedom of association in the two conventions apply to the GII, where an increasing number of transactions are identifiable and traceable as more and more human interactions go on-line, in visits to web sites and common communication zones, such as chat rooms.

Two diverging trends: personal information as property versus privacy and personal data protection as human right

Two equally strong, diverging trends may be discerned in the present debate. They are increasing treatment of personal data as property and growing consideration of protection of privacy and personal data as a fundamental human right. Under the property analysis, the personal data becomes commoditized. The individual claims the value of their personal data and bargains for remuneration in return for its use or disclosure.

In treating privacy and personal data protection as fundamental human rights, they are categorized as inalienable, in the same manner that the right to vote may not be traded or that organs may not be sold. The operative notion is that personal information is so intimately bound up with individual integrity and autonomy that it should not be permissible to bargain it away. Underlying this type of analysis is the strong social norm or public policy determination, usually buttressed by force of law, that, in order to preserve important values, such as the preservation of democracy, social fabric, civic order, and civil society, there are certain elements of the human being that are deemed inviolate and indivisible.

Neither of these trends has prevailed. In fact, the debate is still heating up. I favour the human rights view of privacy and personal data protection for the GIS.

Privacy and personal data protection rules for the GIS

I propose the adoption of three very simple rules as the foundation for protection of privacy and personal data in the twenty-first century.

- *Privacy must be the default*
  Computer and network systems and transactions on them have generally been designed to be identifiable. The history and rationales behind this condition should be examined. Henceforth, the GII should be designed with privacy as the default, which may provide important insights and recommendations for system design and implementation, adoption of legal norms and the social construct.

In this regard, there is a very rich and largely unexplored space between complete identity and full anonymity. It would include, for example, 'authorized user' and 'member of the group'. Many transactions in the physical world are not identifiable. Active efforts should be undertaken to make more interactions on the GII non-identifiable.

- *Claim for, and return to, the individual control and/or ownership of their personal data and information*

  The individual should control and own their personal data. Currently, there is generally a third-party model, with the third party being either the government or the private sector. These entities have personal information about you, that they, by legal requirement or self-regulation, agree to hold and use in certain ways.

  The key question is: 'Who owns the personal data?' Today, people sometimes speak of consumers trading information for some benefit. In my view, it looks like a wholesale giveaway, with the information-gathering entity reaping a windfall and the information provider receiving very little in return. Scams and fishing expeditions abound, such as, in the United States, so-called 'warranty cards', that are entirely unnecessary to invoke the consumer's rights of warranty and ask questions wholly irrelevant to the provision of the warranty, such as the income of the purchaser.

- *Build a global solution*

  In the GIS and in a market of worldwide electronic commerce, the rules for privacy and personal data protection must be harmonious and work as a global solution.

Conclusions

The underlying issue for privacy and security is: 'Who gets to speak and decide on these issues?'

Individuals need to communicate. They need, at times, to limit the audience for their communications. Individuals and organizations need to be able to preserve certain thoughts and activities from the wider community. The locus of control of personal information and communications should be weighted towards the individual.

We already know a lot about security and privacy, but are not implementing it sufficiently. This chapter is a call on business and government leaders to implement the OECD Privacy and Security Guidelines. We need to work towards a global consensus with regard to business practices, law, norms and regimes for security of information systems, privacy and personal data protection.

There is an urgent requirement for more education and awareness of security of information systems and good security practices. There have already been some successful efforts in this regard, which might serve as models. A global campaign should be launched to render more robust the infrastruc-

> We need to work towards a global consensus with regard to business practices, law, norms and regimes for security of information systems, privacy and personal data protection.

ture on which we are all, especially the developed countries, so increasingly dependent. The campaign would be an inexpensive initiative, well worth the many returns that would come from it, both immediately and subsequently.

The United States should move higher up the curve and assume a role as a leader of the trend towards more privacy and data protection. This step would resonate well with the American goals of enabling democratic institutions and market economies.

There should be more efforts to devise technological means to enhance privacy and personal data protection.

Privacy rules must cover both the public and private sectors. Business is already meeting and can meet the privacy challenge, as is the case for US companies in Europe that have been complying with European data protection laws for many years.

Privacy and protection of personal data matter deeply because they go profoundly to our sense of self, individual integrity and autonomy and our ability to express ourselves and communicate with others – both deep human needs. Intensive debate and effort with regard to the principles and implementation of privacy and personal data protection in relation to information and communication technologies is well worth it, not only for itself, but also as a template. Other new technological areas, such as biotechnology and nanotechnology, will present similar and identical challenges. ■

Michael R. Nelson

Program Director, Internet Technology, IBM

POLITICS AND POLICY-MAKING IN THE ELECTRONIC MARKETPLACE

efore joining IBM in July 1998, for ten years I had a once-in-a-lifetime opportunity to be part of the US government's efforts to promote the development of the Internet and electronic commerce. In the Senate, I worked with then Senator Al Gore to pass the High-Performance Computing and Communications Act in 1991, which accelerated the development of Internet and supercomputing technologies. Later, at the White House Office of Science and Technology Policy, I worked with Vice President Gore and other key members of the Clinton Administration to develop and implement its strategies for facilitating the creation of the National Information Infrastructure (NII) and the Global Information Infrastructure (GII). For the last year and a half, at the Federal Communications Commission (FCC), I worked closely with Ira Magaziner and other members of his working group to develop a strategy for promoting global electronic commerce and ensuring the continued explosive growth of the Internet.

I have had an insider's view of a fundamental shift that has occurred in the way telecommunications and information policy are made in Washington and around the world. In ten years, due in part to the extraordinary growth of the Internet and the 'digital economy', many policy makers have come to realize that the old top-down approach to telecommunications and information policy is not only obsolete, it could harm the economic health of their countries.

The result has been a completely new approach to policy-making – a decentralized, bottom-up approach that provides an excellent illustration of Jefferson's maxim that, 'The best government is the one that governs least.' The United States' government, European Union and other governments have all stated that the private sector – not governments – must take the lead in writing the rules of the road for the Information Superhighway.

This is new, unexplored territory. On a number of important 'cyber issues', governments are trying to avoid making policy or exercising their power. The 'Framework for global electronic commerce', which the White House released in mid-1997, outlined the Clinton Administration's strategy for promoting electronic commerce. It was a most unusual report because, on almost every page, it stated what the US government was *not* going to do. The European Union in its electronic commerce report made clear that it did not want 'regulation for regulation's sake', and would rely on the private sector to solve policy problems that in the past national governments would have tried to resolve.

One of the primary reasons for my leaving government was that I wanted to contribute to private-sector efforts to help define the policies that will shape the electronic marketplace. I chose to work for IBM, both because it is leading in the development of many of the key technologies and services needed for electronic commerce and because it has a commitment to work with governments and other companies to find ways to foster the growth of the Internet economy.

A new private sector-led approach to policy-making has been necessitated by:

■ the rapid pace of technology development, which is outpacing the government policy-making process

■ the unprecedented, exponential growth of the number of Internet users, which has created whole new industries in just a few years

■ the fact that the Internet and electronic commerce is global, which makes it very resistant to national efforts to control or regulate it.

In the summer of 1988, when I staffed the first Senate hearing on the Internet and advanced computing technologies, few people in the audience understood what Senator Gore (who chaired the hearing) was talking about when he referred to the 'information superhighway.' And most of those who did listen to him describe his vision of a national fibre optic network – that would 'connect a schoolgirl in Carthage, Tennessee, to an electronic Library of Congress' – assumed that the federal government would plan, build, and pay for it, just as the federal government paid for and oversaw the construction of the interstate highway system.

It is indicative of the shift in perception and politics that in the US today no one would dream of putting the US government in charge of the Information Superhighway. Instead, private companies have competed to see who could develop and deploy the best new Internet technologies and applications most quickly and most economically. When I worked at the White House, I frequently met with foreign delegations and many of them wanted to see the US government's 'master plan' for the growth of the Internet. Most of these delegations could not believe that there was no master plan and that the US government was willing to let the marketplace determine how and how quickly the Internet grew. The explosive growth of the Internet has proven the wisdom of that approach.

It has also validated US government policies designed to foster private-sector investments in the development of the Internet. By funding research, training technical talent and adopting policies to foster competition in the development of the Internet, government created an environment that made possible the unprecedented growth of the Internet and the World Wide Web. In the US, the Next Generation Internet initiative and the Internet2 project are the latest demonstrations of how a relatively small federal government investment in research can leverage major investments and innovation by companies such as IBM and others. While government-funded development of technology has been an essential catalyst, it is the private sector that has made the investment needed to deploy the Internet and find practical, profitable applications for it.

Policy challenges

As the digital economy continues to grow, there will be problems and there will be those both in the US and overseas who will call on governments to take action to control, shape and regulate the development of the Internet and electronic commerce. In this chapter, I would like to explore four policy areas where there has been, and will continue to be, strong political pressure on governments to 'do something':

- affordable Internet access
- privacy
- offensive material
- consumer protection.

During my years at the White House and FCC, I spent more of my time working on these four problems than on all the other serious Internet-related issues – including unsolicited e-mail (spamming), intellectual property protection, Internet taxation, and hacking and information warfare – combined.

Affordable Internet access

Clearly, affordable access to the Internet is a prerequisite if electronic commerce is to become ubiquitous and commonplace. For more than 50 years, universal service – ensuring that all citizens have access to affordable, basic telephone services – has been one of the fundamental goals of traditional telecommunications policy in the US and elsewhere in the developed world. Likewise, in the digital economy, it will be essential that everyone can afford to connect to the Internet, for e-commerce, education, on-line government services, entertainment and much more. Under the old model of universal service, telephone companies were granted monopolies by governments in return for providing telephone services at a regulated price to certain classes of customers (such as those in rural areas) who otherwise might not be able to afford to pay the full cost of these telephones service.

With the Internet, the US government has taken a very different approach. It has focused on fostering competition in the Internet Service Provider (ISP) market, in the belief that that is the best way to provide affordable services to the most people. In order to minimize barriers to entry, the US government does not require anyone to obtain a licence to offer Internet services, nor does it impose special taxes on these services. As a result, there are over 4000 ISPs operating in the US today. Furthermore, the government has adopted policies to promote competition in the market for the leased lines used by ISPs and, as a result, leased line prices in the US are, typically, twice to ten times cheaper than those in Europe (according to a study by the Telecommunications Managers Association) and among the lowest in the world (according to the OECD).

... in the digital economy, it will be essential that everyone can afford to connect to the Internet, for e-commerce, education, on-line government services, entertainment and much more.

However, low prices for Internet services do not automatically mean that all citizens have access to the Internet and, as a result, in the US there has been growing concern about information 'haves' and 'have nots.' In the 1996 Telecommunications Act, Congress took steps to ensure that all American schools and libraries were able to afford to connect to the Internet, so that families unable to afford a computer and an Internet connection at home would still have a way to get on-line. However, rather than take a top-down approach and regulate the price of Internet services, policy makers chose to create a programme that would reimburse a percentage of the costs of wiring classrooms and the costs of Internet services, with the poorest schools receiving the largest discounts. This approach, similar to a voucher system, gives schools and libraries the ability to choose the vendors and services that best meet their needs. At the same time, it fosters competition – and, thus, lower prices – in the Internet services market.

Under the old universal service approach, the government decides who gets to compete in the marketplace and how much they can charge. Under this new approach, the government has a more limited role – ensuring a competitive marketplace where anyone can compete and providing disadvantaged consumers the funds to buy the services they need.

Privacy

One of the most controversial, emotional Internet-related policy issues is on-line privacy. Here, too, there have been two approaches. The old one traces its roots back more than 20 years to European computer privacy laws and regulations that regulate who can compile electronic databases, what kind of personal data they can collect and what can be done with that data. While such an approach may have been effective and practical in the 1970s when only a few major corporations and government agencies had the million-dollar mainframe computers needed to maintain and use electronic databases, it becomes difficult to enforce in a world where over 100 million PCs are connected to the Internet, each capable of storing, processing and transmitting personal data. Nor can such privacy regulations keep pace with all the new technologies and techniques for collecting and using personal information.

Fortunately, new technologies can help provide new solutions. US and European companies are forming coalitions to develop the standards and technologies needed to give web users ways to decide for themselves how to protect their privacy. TrustE (www.truste.org) and the Platform for Privacy Preferences (P3P) developed by the World Wide Web Consortium (www.w3c.org) are just two examples. The US government has supported the On-line Privacy Alliance, a consortium of companies spearheaded by IBM that formed to protect the privacy of individuals on-line. Various groups are developing different techniques, so that consumers will be able to decide which ones best meet their needs.

The Clinton Administration has encouraged the development of such private-sector initiatives. While, in the US, federal and State governments have taken a regulatory approach to protect certain types of particularly sensitive personal data – such as medical records, credit records, government data and personal data about children – in most cases, governments have adopted a very different, bottom-up approach that encourages self-regulation by the private sector. In the case of the Internet, the goal has been to enable Internet users to choose for themselves what level of privacy protection they want. The government's role is to encourage, and in some cases require, web site owners to reveal what information they are collecting about the surfers who visit their site and how they intend to use it. Then people can decide for themselves whether or not they want to use specific sites. Rather than deciding on a single level of privacy protection for all users and all web sites, the government's role is limited to promoting disclosure and enforcing truth in advertising and fraud laws to ensure that web site owners accurately disclose their privacy policies. This approach puts much more faith in the marketplace than the old European approach and assumes that in a competitive environment like the on-line marketplace, consumers will be able to choose between different sites with different levels of privacy protection. It also assumes that on-line companies will be strongly motivated to address their customers' privacy concerns.

In the next year or two, it will be very interesting to see how well new technologies and industry self-regulation work. Also, we will see how both US and European privacy policy evolve in response to private-sector privacy initiatives.

Offensive material

In the US, another hot button cyber issue has been on-line pornography – and, more broadly, offensive and adult material, such as violent or racist literature and videos, on-line gambling and information on bomb-building, drugs and other illegal activities.

The US Congress, in response to public concerns about children using the Internet to access pornographic and indecent material, passed the Communications Decency Act (CDA) as part of the 1996 Telecommunications Act. This legislation took a top-down, government-led approach and would have imposed fines on individuals who made available 'indecent' material over the Internet. It was clear to most people familiar with the Internet that such an approach would not be very effective as, even if the threat of penalties succeeded in discouraging US citizens from posting indecent material, it would not affect pornographic web sites overseas.

In the end, the US courts ruled key provisions of the CDA to be unconstitutional. However, in the years since the passage of the CDA, concerns about protecting children who use the Internet have continued to grow. Fortunately, the private sector is stepping up to this challenge and developing filtering software, rating schemes and special 'family-friendly' Internet services in order to make the Internet safe for children. In the UK and elsewhere, the private sector has led efforts to set up hotlines (see www.internetwatch.org.uk) that parents can call to complain about offensive or illegal material on the Internet. In December 1997, in Washington, DC, the White House helped organize the Internet On-line Summit to highlight and throw its support behind such private-sector efforts.

In the end, these market-based, private-sector approaches are the only effective approach to helping parents and others avoid offensive material on-line. The Internet is extremely resistant to censorship, because 'the Net tends to route around it.' As there is no single body 'in charge' of the Internet, there is no way to set a uniform standard for what is and is not allowed on the Web. Further, because it is global, it is difficult or impossible to impose one nation's or one group's idea of decency on it.

> ... concerns about protecting children who use the Internet have continued to grow. Fortunately, the private sector is stepping up to this challenge ...

Rather than having national governments struggle in vain to restrict what their citizens see on-line, governments must be content to have industry give individual Internet users the tools they need to make their own choices about what does and does not come into their home.

Consumer protection

Consumer protection in cyberspace is another challenge for governments. As the number of Internet users has grown, the number of cases of on-line fraud has grown even faster. The low cost of creating a web site has made the Web a very attractive means for purveyors of get-rich-quick schemes, pyramid schemes and other frauds to reach a global audience of millions of Internet users. Unfortunately, to quote a famous *The New Yorker Magazine* cartoon, 'On the Internet, no one knows you're a dog,' which means that con artists can conceal their true identity and manufacture (or borrow) a legitimate one.

State and national governments have tried to prosecute on-line fraud, with some success, but the difficulty of applying one nation's or State's consumer protection laws to individuals in another jurisdiction means that many on-line crimes will go unpunished.

Fortunately, the private sector is developing solutions to this problem that can work across national boundaries. They are finding ways to authenticate vendors and build trust in cyberspace. Digital signatures are being developed so Internet users can ensure that someone is actually who they say they are. The Better Business Bureau's BBB On-line (www.bbb.org) is providing ratings and posting complaints about unscrupulous on-line merchants.

One of the most interesting examples of 'do-it-yourself' consumer protection can be found at Ebay (www.ebay.com), an on-line flea market that allows individuals and companies in the US to sell all sorts of goods – ranging from camera equipment to financial advice to Beanie Babies – using the Internet. Ebay makes its money by providing a safe, effective environment in which vendors can find customers and vice versa. The most important service it provides is a rating of vendors. If you are thinking of buying from a merchant advertising on Ebay, you can look up that merchant's track record and find out how many other Ebay customers have purchased items from them and how many have filed complaints with Ebay. Ebay vendors will strive to maintain their reputation or else find that they have very few customers. It seems to be working. In the first three years of its operation, Ebay facilitated over 18 million transactions.

Conclusions

In all four of the cases discussed above, Internet users and the policy makers who govern them are faced with serious, vexing problems. In all four cases, governments, in response to public pressure, have tried to use their power to impose solutions, but have found that the traditional top-down regulatory approach, in which governments write and enforce the rules, doesn't work very well in cyberspace. The fact is that no one nation can extend its jurisdiction over a global medium. As a result, either no national laws will apply or we will end up with hundreds of different, often conflicting sets of national rules and regulations applying to a single web site or Internet service. Neither outcome will meet the needs of Internet users.

The pace of Internet development further complicates efforts by national governments to find legislative solutions to Internet policy problems. The policy-making process just cannot keep pace with technological developments, in part because the regulatory process is a slow one and in part because if government tries to write rules and requirements, enterprising engineers and entrepreneurs will find ways around them.

The good news is that governments in the US, Europe and elsewhere are starting to realize the limits of their jurisdiction and power and are instead turning to the private sector for solutions to policy problems, such as pornography, privacy and consumer protection. They are coming to realize that global, private-sector coalitions

– such as the International Chamber of Commerce (www.iccwbo.org), the Global Internet Project (www.gip.org), the World Wide Web Consortium – are better equipped than national governments and intergovernmental bodies to govern the Internet. Most importantly, governments are realizing that they share a common interest with the private sector in meeting the concerns of Internet users by providing them with the tools and information they need to address their concerns themselves.

The fact is that no one nation can extend its jurisdiction over a global medium.

That means encouraging a free, open, competitive marketplace for Internet services and on-line content, so that companies lose sales if they fail to meet their customers' needs – whether these be for less expensive, faster and more reliable Internet connections, better protection of private information, 'family-friendly' Web sites or consumer protection. In the last couple of years, the member governments of the World Trade Organization, by approving the Agreement on Basic Telecommunications and the Information Technology Agreement, have taken a giant step towards making the telecommunications services and computer markets more open and competitive. They must build on this progress by continuing to remove legislative and regulatory barriers that would limit the market for Internet services. In addition, they must avoid imposing rules and regulations on the Internet content industry that would inhibit the development of a vibrant, competitive market for on-line services.

Of course, competition and the free market are not a cure-all, and governments will only rely on the private sector to solve important Internet policy issues if the private sector shows that it will commit the resources necessary to do so. That means companies must look beyond the next quarter's results and consider not only their own bottom line, but also what is good for the long-term vitality of the Internet. We must learn to cooperate with our most fierce competitors on privacy standards, codes of conduct for on-line vendors and other ways to ensure that customers feel that the Internet is a safe, secure place to do business. IBM, SUN, Netscape, AT&T, British Telecom and an increasing number of other companies are joining forces to find ways to ensure that the Internet lives up to its full potential as a ubiquitous platform for electronic commerce, education and other applications.

However, we in the private sector have to act fast. We need to develop global, market-driven solutions before governments lose patience and feel compelled, in response to public pressure, to adopt national, regulatory solutions that attempt, albeit ineffectively, to dictate what users can and cannot do on the Internet. Only if the key Internet-related companies find a way to work together effectively to define rules of the road for the information superhighway will we avoid having a patchwork of conflicting national rules and regulations that could create uncertainty, inhibit investment and slow innovation.

Many of the policy problems we face in the electronic marketplace are new manifestations of old problems (such as consumer fraud, universal service, privacy). Let us hope that governments have enough foresight, wisdom, flexibility and patience to allow the private sector to continue to explore new approaches to these old policy problems. Let us hope, too, that enough companies devote sufficient talent, creativity and vision to the cooperative effort needed to meet the challenges that governments have handed them. ∎

THE NETWORKED ECONOMY

contributors

Dr Charles J. Jonscher is President, Central Europe Trust Company. He studied electrical sciences at Cambridge University before moving to the US to take a doctorate in economics. He joined the teaching faculty at Harvard University and then at Massachusetts Institute of Technology (MIT), as Co-Director of the Research Program on Communications and published works on the productivity impact of IT. In addition to his corporate role, he is currently a Research Affiliate at Harvard University's Program on Information Resources Policy. His forthcoming book *Wired Life* is to be published by Bantam Press in 1999.

Jeffrey Owens, Head of Fiscal Affairs, Organisation for Economic Co-operation and Development (OECD), is a public finance expert, who completed his doctoral work at Cambridge University in the UK in 1973. In addition to his economic degrees, he is a qualified accountant. As professor (Cambridge and American University of Paris) and international civil servant at the OECD in Paris, he has focused his attention on questions of tax policy and tax administration, with particular emphasis on international taxation. He also established a major taxation programme at the OECD and extensively developed the OECD contacts with non-member countries. His earlier work dealt with the development of international currency markets and the implications for monetary policies. He has made numerous contributions to professional journals, has published a number of books and has been the author of many OECD publications on taxation. Dr Owens's position as Head of Fiscal Affairs at the OECD and his frequent participation in international conferences have provided him with a unique international perspective on tax policy. Dr Owens is also a member of the Scientific Committee of the International Institute of Public Finance.

Michael Finley is best known for his thoughtful commentary on the future, and writes a syndicated column 'On the edge' about the human element in the ongoing technological revolution, appearing weekly in the St Paul *Pioneer Press*. He is author of *Techno-Crazed* (Peterson's, 1996), and co-author with Harvey Robbins of *Transcompetition* (McGraw-Hill, 1998) and *Why Teams Don't Work* and *Why Change Doesn't Work*, (Peterson's, 1995 and 1996). *Why Teams Don't Work* was named Best Management Book of 1995, The Americas, by the Booz-Allen & Hamilton/Financial Times Global Business Book Awards. Michael is a member of The Masters Forum, a Minnesota-based executive education group offering the latest insights from the business world's top consultants on issues such as IT, strategy, organizational transformation and personal development. For more information, visit his website at www.skypoint.com/~mfinley

Mark Radcliffe received a Bachelor of Science in Chemistry, magna cum laude, from the University of Michigan and later attended Harvard Law School. He is a partner with Gray Cary Ware & Freidenrich in the Intellectual Property and Technology Practice Group. In April 1997 he was named one of the 100 Most Influential Lawyers in the United States by *The National Law Journal*. He is the co-Editor in Chief of the *Journal of Internet Law*, serves on the Board of Directors of the Computer Law Association, as well as on the editorial board of the *Computer Lawyer*, *Cyberspace Lawyer*. His practice is focused on representing high technology and new media clients both in their licensing and financing transactions. He is the co-author of the *Multimedia Law and Business Handbook (1996)* and *Internet Legal Forms for Business* from Ladera Press (see www.laderapress.com).

by Anne Leer

THE CHANGING WORLD OF ASSET TRADING

The world's economy is changing rapidly. Markets are becoming increasingly global and the economic power can no longer be confined to national territories and traditional trading blocks. Nations around the world have seen their economies grow and change from an agricultural to an industrial economy, and from an industrial economy to an information and knowledge-based economy. In Alvin Toffler's terminology nations have moved through the stages of first, second and third wave economies. I wish economists and politicians would speak more of the complexities of a world economy, which consists of so many different and often conflicting levels and parts. Toffler's economic thinking is refreshing in that respect. In his writings he describes how the different types of economies struggle to coexist in the same world, and the kind of clashes and conflicts this creates. We would like to have an equal global economy for all to participate in, but the fact is that the economic imbalance and discrepancies between the underdeveloped and the developed nations make that impossible.

The optimists among us will hope that the emergence of a global economy would remove trade imbalances. And that the agricultural first wave economies of poor nations could use technology and the benefits of the Wired World to leapfrog past the industrial stage into a knowledge-based economy. But that will not happen without collective international effort from both political and commercial forces. Internet connectivity is not enough to secure economic prosperity, but it is a start.

The fundamental economic shift to a knowledge-based economy means the nature of the core assets and the way they are being traded in the market are changing. Core assets are no longer limited to tangible physical goods and services. Information, intellectual property and knowledge move centre stage in the new economy and account for an increasing percentage of nations' GDP. The previous section described the impact of electronic commerce and how the trading of all kinds of assets tangible or intangible has migrated over to global networks.

This section will look at the overall economy and how it is developing to form the basis for existence in the Wired World. We will hear from Charles Jonscher, a creative economist who has been studying the emerging networked economy. We will go to Paris and visit one of the world's leading tax experts, Jeffrey Owens of the OECD. And we will also pay a visit to one of business America's inspiring thinkers, Michael Finley, who will tell us what happens when the brutes can no longer terrorize us and we'll find pleasure in cooperating with our competitors. Finally we will move on to sunny California and call in on Mark Radcliffe, a highly accomplished lawyer in the multimedia and entertainment industry. If you don't believe the protection of intellectual properties is important, he will probably convince you.

Charles Jonscher describes how the economic characteristics have changed and how we are gradually finding new economic rules to help us manage economic progress in a Wired World. Many of the traditional economic concepts and theories no longer work in a digital environment. For instance, it makes little sense to talk of 'scarce resources' when technology is advancing at an exponential rate. What is scarce about an economic good which does not have size or weight, and which can be reproduced so easily, he asks. Jonscher also points out what he refers to as the 'productivity paradox' – the fact that there is no proven correlation between investments in IT and improved productivity. Like David Feeny in his chapter, Jonscher also confirms that the productivity gain of the Information Age is a myth. He describes the new economy as moving along two different tracks, on the one side behaving like an information economy obsessed with the processing and transmission of vast quantities of data, and the other side operating like a knowledge-intensive economy concerned with the production and use of knowledge by people.

If you are among those people who had hoped that the Internet and the GII would be a tax-free zone, Jeffrey Owens will disappoint you, but with a very convincing argument. He says, even in the Wired World death and taxes should remain unavoidable. Why, you may ask? Is there no escape from the taxman? No, is the answer, in fact I think you will have more luck escaping in the real world than in cyberspace. But of course you are a responsible citizen and would not want to evade your tax duties. Owens will remind us of the legitimate reasons for tax collection and the need to generate income from taxes to fund public services. He argues that the economic activities within electronic networks does not warrant tax exemption and that taxation rules should apply equally and fairly regardless of whether transactions happen on- or off-line. Just imagine, what would happen to our economy if the GII was declared a tax-free zone and some time in the future the most transactions migrate to the GII, there would be nothing left for governments to tax, where would we get the revenues needed for our national budgets? Owens recognizes there are major obstacles to overcome for the virtual taxman in a borderless world. For a start, how would the taxpayer be identified, who would collect the taxes and to which country would the taxes be paid? Owens seems to be on top of it and don't kid yourself – the world's tax authorities are preparing themselves well.

You'll enjoy the next part of our journey to see Michael Finley. You may think at first that he is about to tell you a fairy tale, but far from it. What transpires through his chapter is a vivid and colourful description of how major players, small and large organizations and people, behave in our economy. How the Internet and the Information Age has profoundly changed what he calls brute behaviour in the market. He describes a new economic alternative, which he calls transcompetitive. He explains the reasons why we see increasingly major competitors entering into collaborations. In a world where no orga- nization can monopolize essential information, competitors occasionally cooperate. Successful companies today are increasingly seen to compete with one hand and coop- erate with the other.

Mark Radcliffe will give you an eye-opener or two if you thought that intellectual prop- erty law is irrelevant in the Wired World. On the contrary, he will tell you that the importance of intellectual property is rising dramatically with the growth of the GII. He gives us some staggering examples of just how important it can be for individual compa- nies, for example, the trademark value of Coca Cola is estimated at $39 billion and Texas Instruments received over $770,000,000 in a single year from licensing its patents. Radcliffe provides an excellent list of definitions if you are not quite sure about the differ- ences between trademarks and copyright and patents and other intellectual properties. It should be mandatory knowledge for anybody who wants to be successful in the net- worked economy. He goes on to describe the many challenges to the existing structure of intellectual property law and how it desperately needs to be harmonized across national borders. Intellectual property law has been developed on the basis of national and local jurisdictions and many of the laws will vary from one country to the next. This inevitably leads to confusion and conflict in an economy where transactions are increasingly hap- pening across national borders and where those borders are becoming less meaningful. ■

Dr Charles Jonscher

President, Central Europe Trust Company

THE ECONOMICS OF CYBERSPACE

In 1958, Robert Noyce, a physicist at Fairchild Laboratories, announced the invention of the chip – more correctly called the integrated or microelectronic circuit. He took a piece of highly purified silicon and etched into it carefully controlled quantities of different elements, creating tiny paths along which electric currents could flow. The junctions between these paths became gates, which allowed or disallowed the current flow depending on the voltages applied to metal legs protruding from the silicon chip. The silent opening and shutting of the gates simulated logical operations such as addition and subtraction.

The digital revolution is without precedent in its economic characteristics. The invention of the chip set in train the extraordinary cycle of falling costs and increasing performance that has been the hallmark of the data processing industry. A widely cited economic law of the new era is the one promulgated in 1965 by Gordon Moore, founder of the Intel Corporation. He predicted that the information handling capability of microelectronic circuits (measured by the number of logic components that can be accommodated on each chip) would double each 18 months. Moore's Law, as it has come to be called, has governed with remarkable precision the rate of development of electronic devices. The Intel 8080 chip, dating from 1974, had fewer than 5000 transistors. Two decades later, the Pentium II had more than 5 million. Memory devices have grown in capacity at the same geometric rate: since the first hard drive was sold by IBM in 1956 – with disks 60 cm in diameter, each holding just 100,000 bytes – data density has increased by a factor of two every two years.

Economics – as textbooks explain in their opening paragraphs – is the science of the allocation of scarce resources, of how markets determine the patterns of production and distribution in a world in which tradeoffs must be made – more guns mean less butter. Should we still talk of scarce resources, when the technology of production is advancing at an exponential rate, when this year's shortage is next year's abundance? More fundamentally, the very idea of scarcity is difficult to accept when the underlying resource is not a tangible item but an intangible good called knowledge – that curious resource without either size or weight, but certainly having cost and value.

Since the invention of the chip in that seminal year of 1958, the industry of information processing has developed beyond the wildest expectations of its inventors. The business community at large has responded to the offerings of the new technology industry by purchasing its products in great quantities. The ratio of information to production equipment spending – of expenditure on office technology to that on all the traditional capital equipment used for the physical processes of production and distribution (in factories, in the transportation industry, in the production of chemicals, energy and power, on farms), can be tracked in the United States' economy in successive issues of the *Survey of Current Business*. While only about 1 to 5 in 1970, the ratio reached the symbolically important threshold of 1 to 1 by 1990. The level of business investment in information processing equipment was by then running at over $100 billion per year.

Today, there is nowhere quite like Silicon Valley. The United States is riding a high-tech-driven boom, centred on dynamic hardware and software industries that support thousands of enterprises developing and deploying user applications. Equity markets put exceptionally high valuations on companies that are seen to be set to take advantage of the demands of an information-hungry society. For example, the two Stanford University engineering students who founded the Web directory company Yahoo! received financial backing of $1 million in 1995; the firm is now valued at $2.4 *billion*. Internet Service Provider AOL has a market capitalization of $25 billion against shareholder capitalization in the accounts of $125 *million*. The Microsoft Corporation – producer of intangible zeros and ones on disks – is worth more on the Stock Exchange than the nation's car industry, producer of the tangible product most coveted by the twentieth-century consumer. The mysterious realm of bits in silicon appears able to produce miracles on the stock market to match those in the laboratory.

Two information revolutions: data and knowledge

However, even as computer productivity – and expenditures – race ahead, it is becoming clear that improvements in performance at the data processing level are not being matched by comparable improvements in the performance of an increasingly knowledge-based economy. From 1950 until 1970, average productivity growth in the world's five largest industrial economies reached unprecedented levels of 5 per cent annually. Then, just as computers entered the workplace in significant numbers, it slowed down, to languish at around 2 per cent for most of the next 25 years.

This 'productivity paradox', as it came to be called, has generated a great deal of controversy and soul-searching among scholars, business executives and government bodies. Many excuses are given. Some write of measurement difficulty: the benefits of the new technology are mainly to be seen, we are told, in service sectors such as finance where productivity is difficult to quantify. Some ask us to wait a little longer – the computers and networks have been bedding in and the really big benefits are just around the corner. However, the inescapable fact remains that the very large expenditures being made on computer technology are not affecting economic output in the massive and obvious way that the purchase of production technology did in the preceding several decades. Stephen Roach, Chief Economist at Morgan Stanley, specializes in the IT sector and has studied and surveyed this field for many years. His summary is unambiguous: 'The productivity gains of the Information Age are just a myth. There is not a shred of evidence to show that people are putting out more because of investments in technology.' Paul Strassmann, formerly Vice President at Xerox Corporation, and author of several books on computers and productivity, concludes that there is 'no correlation whatsover between information technology expenditures and any known measure of profitability'. Robert Solow of MIT, Nobel Laureate economist, is equally blunt in his assessment: 'We see computers everywhere except in the productivity statistics.'

The productivity gains of the Information Age are just a myth. There is not a shred of evidence to show that people are putting out more because of investments in technology.

A cloud has loomed over the otherwise remarkable story of the computer industry. While the new technologies are undoubtedly driving a boom in the industries that *produce* them, and produce *for* them, we do not have evidence of a decisive, demonstrable impact on the performance of industries that *use* them.

The clue to the paradox lies in the fact that there have been two information revolutions (see Figure 1). One is in the processing and transmission of data by machines, the other in the creation and use of knowledge by people. The emergence of a knowledge-intensive economy – of what the sociologist Daniel Bell described in 1974 in his book *The Coming of Post-industrial Society* (Heinemann Educational) as one in which 'what matters is not raw muscle power, or capital, but information' – has been followed, not driven, by computers. The computer revolution is a sub-plot in a bigger revolution: the explosion of human knowledge in all its forms – innovation in business and the professions, new forms in arts and entertainment, progress in science and technology. It is part of a much broader transformation of the economy and society centred around ideas and creativity that has been accelerating throughout this century. It is the pre-eminence of human capital over physical resources that is transforming the economy.

From the twin towers of the World Trade Center in downtown New York City, a workforce the size of a small city makes electronic contact with the world outside. The towers epitomize the Information Age, but not because of the technology packed into them. They were built before the days of computers in offices, their purpose to

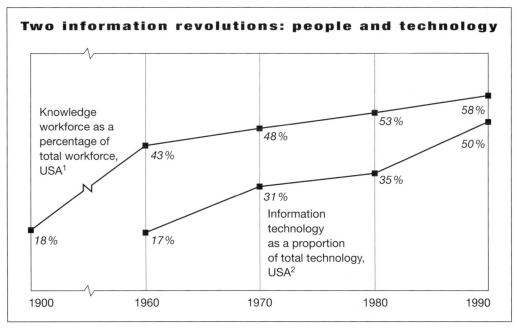

Two information revolutions: people and technology

Knowledge workforce as a percentage of total workforce, USA[1]

18% — 43% — 48% — 53% — 58%

Information technology as a proportion of total technology, USA[2]

17% — 31% — 35% — 50%

1900   1960   1970   1980   1990

FIGURE 1   [1]Source: US Bureau of the Census. [2]Source: US Survey of Current Business

house the burgeoning knowledge workforce. The signboards in the entrance lobbies read like roll-calls of the post-industrial society – publishing firms, law practices, advertising agencies, travel bureaux, insurance companies, stockbrokers, art dealers, designers, media companies.

In the post-industrial era, business leaders have found that the key source of value has shifted from the *production* of goods and services to success in their design and commercialization, marketing and distribution, interaction with customers. Coca-Cola survives by keeping its recipe private and continually rethinking how to sell the taste as lifestyle. It is an ideas company that has long subcontracted out the mixing and bottling of its drink.

As the world becomes comprehensively wired, we will need to keep in mind, carefully, the difference between data, information and knowledge – that raw data is a mass of symbols, information is something more useful distilled from the data and knowledge is a still higher level of meaning – information entering the human thinking process. That latter process is one of unfathomable complexity, a far cry from the rationality of the logic gates in silicon chips. The wiring and the computers that now surround us are the servants, not the masters. The masters are the ideas creators – people who, like the overwhelming majority of readers of this book, work full time in the knowledge economy, not on a farm or a factory floor. The transition to a knowledge economy has given rise to the opportunity to sell huge quantities of information-processing equipment, but the basic dynamic within and between organizations is still that which takes place among people.

A trillion-dollar trial

At one level – the technical – the economics of cyberspace are indeed following previously unseen exponential cost–performance trends. At the level of content, of the knowledge economy, there are unchanging fundamentals. The Labour Theory of Value is a concept in classical economics thinking that originated in 1662 in a treatise written by the English economist Sir William Petty. He observed that the main determinant of the exchange value of a commodity is the amount of labour that goes into its production. This concept, much refined over the centuries, can still serve as our guide to where value will lie in the Information Age.

In a research study by John Gould, a human factors expert at IBM, office professionals from within IBM's research organization were given eight letters to compose. Four were written with the help of word processors and four using pen and paper with a secretary typing a clean copy. The purpose was to see whether or not the use of computers either increased the quality of the written output (as assessed by judges) or reduced the overall cost. The results were negative on both counts. Cognitive scientist Professor Thomas Lindauer also found this result to be the norm when reviewing this and many other studies of office technology productivity for his book *The Trouble with Computers* (MIT Press, 1995). The text of a letter or business memorandum is readily digitized. However, that does not make the letter or the memorandum the product of a digital operation. Rather, it is the product of a human mind, and that is where the cost and quality are primarily determined. There is a yawning gap between data shuffling and thinking.

The new technology has done to data processing what the old technology had done to fabrication. It has introduced – at the level of data and information, not knowledge – mass production. Electronics has brought the cost of digitally processed data down to the cost of the use of the hardware and software doing the processing, which at the margin is practically zero. Operations capable of being done by a computer – be they solving a tax computation or the creation of a digital film character – become replicable, marketable. Processed information has become a commodity. Floppy disks and CD-ROMs collect dust on our desks – piled up high thanks to the economics of duplication; computer-generated bytes lose value as they become available to all. The source of unique advantage, of value, is elsewhere. It is in the minds of the millions who are the idea creators of the post-industrial age.

> The source of unique advantage, of value, is elsewhere. It is in the minds of the millions who are the idea creators of the post-industrial age.

The financial services industry has been the leader in computerization for three decades. Banking requires many numbers to be processed, but, at bottom, it is still about borrowing and lending – in the latter case against safe underlying assets. Yamaichi Securities, the brokerage firm that in November 1997 became Japan's biggest corporate bankruptcy, was at the cutting edge of technology. However, it exposed itself to the wrong sorts of risks, and then engaged in the unwise – and illegal – practice of covering up trading losses. The systems tracked the trades with great sophistication, but were powerless to understand the timeless human instincts of greed and fear which were at play.

In the realm of production of consumer entertainment, analogously, the content is greatly more important than the conduit, and here digital technology has much less to offer. Information channels into the home – up until now using different technologies for voice telephony, television and modem-based computer access – will converge into a uniform digital format delivered by competing operators in what used to be the separate industries of telecommunications, broadcasting and computing. However, the quality of creative output is not primarily dependent on the quality of the available technical formats. Video software began to be created 100 years ago and was already developed to the artistic and creative standards we enjoy today 50 or more years back; some modern films equal in their impact but surely do not surpass a production like *Gone With the Wind*, released in 1939. The real investment in making a programme or film that billions of viewers will watch is in the talent of the scriptwriter and director, and the vast fees commanded by the stars of the moment. The fascination with an actor, rock star or sports idol will not diminish.

The modest impact of new technology on economic performance reflects the fact that, while technology is improving spectacularly in speed and capacity, the most fundamental bottlenecks in information production and consumption are in the minds of the knowledge producers and consumers. The failure of information technology to produce a decisive uplift in economic productivity or in the quality of consumer entertainment has taught us a striking lesson that it would do well to bear in mind in this next round of technological deployment. It is confirmation, by way of a worldwide, trillion-dollar trial that it will be much more difficult to automate what we do with our minds than it was to automate what we do with our hands. We should see it not as a failure of technology, but as a tribute to human skills.

The challenge ahead

The growth of the Internet has re-energized the idea that a technology-based transformation of the economy and society is imminent. Lou Gerstner, Chairman of IBM, made the following statement in his 1997 commencement speech at Wake Forest University:

> We're now riding the next great technology wave: the rise of powerful global networks like the Internet. Something very important is happening here. Networks are collapsing the physical barriers between nations, markets, cultures and people. This connectivity will change everything: the way we access entertainment … and interact with one another.

The initial reaction of business managers to this latest round of technological development has been to invest more heavily. The amount spent on information technology support for the US economy in 1997 was an extraordinary $225 billion. The ratio of expenditure by US businesses on technical support for the office as opposed to industrial processes, which had reached 1 to 1 by the end of the 1980s, has shot up to 2 to 1 in favour of the white-collar sector. In large measure, this is happening on hunch. Reviewing the techniques used by major companies to justify IT investments, Professor Brynjolfsson of MIT points out that 'they reveal surprisingly little formal analysis'.

To some extent, businesses have no choice. First, however disappointing the net efficiency improvements, they are there. In a competitive market, every percentage of cost disadvantage is a nail in the coffin; 5 per cent seals it shut. Even the more churlish commentators on information technology productivity are not suggesting it has failed to yield 5 per cent of cumulative gain in a couple of decades. Second, it is now impossible to maintain the respect of customers, suppliers and, most especially staff without being demonstrably up-to-date on computing. Every 'information worker' must be equipped with a personal computer, digital mobile device and Internet access. Whatever the Morgan Stanley productivity analysis may say, the perception that you have the latest tools on the desktop is vital and, to a degree, perceptions are reality. For that reason alone, corporations would be ill advised to ease up on technology investment, and are not about to do so.

However, at this level – the level of basic processing and communications capability – an end is coming into sight. The human brain can take in some 20,000 hertz (cycles per second) of bandwidth (information-carrying capacity) by means of the auditory nerve from the ear and, perhaps, a million hertz of visual data via the optic nerve. In North America, Japan and Western Europe, most homes, and a large proportion of offices, are already linked by coaxial or fibre optic cables. Unlike copper telephone wires, their predecessors of the last 100 years, such cables have a bandwidth of hundreds of millions of hertz; and once equipped with suitable electronics, they can deliver data to an individual at rates vastly in excess of those that the biological sense organs can absorb.

As for processing power, in the 1990s, microprocessor clock speeds have began to reach multiples of hundreds of millions of operations per second. For the first time, personal computer users have become aware that, when they are engaged in word processing, diary management or the like, the reaction of their machines to commands (provided there are external access to networks or slow memory devices are not involved) is essentially instantaneous – as fast as a human interlocutor can, physiologically, have need for. Nicholas Negroponte of MIT's Media Laboratory has pointed out that the advertisements for computers that our children will read will not describe their processing power – it will simply be adequate.

Digital technology makes uniform the encoding of previously heterogeneous information sources. Information processed in business enterprises that was previously in analogue formats – from the handwritten memo to the photograph-based slide show – will be encoded digitally, making it capable of being stored, transmitted and processed within and outside the firm. Once the process of conversion to digital is done – you can't make a sound, image or document 'more digital' – the emphasis will inevitably revert to content, to the production of knowledge products that has been gaining in economic significance throughout this century.

The new technology is like a digitally formatted stage on which people who work with knowledge will continue to play the parts they, variously, play. The engineers will engineer, marketing executives market, bankers bank, teachers teach. For the technology industry, the task is to continue to develop this stage – this infrastructure of machines and networks – in a form that anyone of reasonable ability can use. For individuals and organisations in any field or endeavour, the challenge ahead is to continue, by means of investment in human capital, to develop the ability to play out those roles – roles in a drama that will be played out between people, not machines.

Employees must be persuaded to give of their best, and customers persuaded to part with their money. Long before the Internet, post-industrial nations had financed the creation of powerful media and techniques for getting through to the hearts and minds of consumers – and thence to their wallets. These techniques – advertising, product positioning, brand-building – will be no less applicable in the networked marketplace. Communications technology does not change the rules of play where human behaviour is concerned – like the fact that brands backed with heavy promotion win over the unsupported ones in the fight for consumer attention.

> **What will retain value, is what computers cannot produce: that most intangible and elusive of economic goods – the creative output of the human mind.**

While microelectronics technology, following Moore's Law, has succeeded in reducing the computer from the size of a car or larger to the size of a notebook, the silicon devices within it still contain nothing more than an array of gates manipulating binary logical propositions. The computer is commoditizing the processing of digital data, not of human knowledge. If it is not bringing the expected gains in economic value, it is because what goes down in cost also goes down in price. When the technology of industrial production spread across the world in the twentieth century, clothing, food and appliances most susceptible to quantity manufacture became cheap; what retained the greatest value was what could not come off a mass production line. As we enter the twenty-first century – a century in which machines will conjure up and process information in essentially limitless quantities – what will retain value, both personally and professionally, is what computers *cannot* produce: that most intangible and elusive of economic goods, but actually the one with the most enduring value – the creative output of the human mind. This is still – in the economist's terminology as well as in common parlance – a scarce resource. ■

Jeffrey Owens

Head of Fiscal Affairs, Organisation for Economic
Co-operation and Development

ELECTRONIC COMMERCE:
TAXING TIMES

In 1998, electronic commerce accounts for approximately $26 billion of world trade. Worldwide, there are only between 80 and 100 million users of the Net. Electronic payment systems are in their infancy. Business-to-consumer transactions that are completely 'on-line' are very much the exception rather than the rule. Traditional mail order business continues to be economically more significant than pure electronic commerce, yet electronic commerce is now near the top of the global political agenda. How can we explain this apparent contradiction?

Perhaps the analogy of the car can help. In 1999, the car will be 100 years old. The inventors at the time intuitively knew that there would be a vast market for this new form of transportation. However, they also knew that few people had the skills to drive, highways were rare and service points few and far between. The pioneers who 'surfed the highways' also recognized that governments and business would need to work together to build the infrastructure, both physical and regulatory, to exploit the vast potential of the car. They were confident that people and businesses would quickly adapt to this new form of transportation. However, even these pioneers would not have predicted that the car could lead to new living patterns (the rise of suburban man), the development of global enterprises and the geo-political importance of the Middle East – or that Gazprom may have become the single largest taxpayer in Russia in 1998.

So it is with electronic commerce today. It is clear that industries producing computers, networking equipment and the software necessary for electronic commerce will grow. It is also clear that certain traditional forms of commerce will suffer, such as retail travel agencies, retailers of shrink-wrapped software and bricks and mortar music stores. However, just as with the car 100 years ago, it is still difficult to predict how the 'wired world' and the technology underlying electronic commerce will change the way we work and play.

The potential for electronic commerce is vast and its ability to promote a truly global village is unparalleled. Other chapters in this book testify to this potential. The challenge to government, business and the social partners is, can they work together to realize the full potential of this new way of doing business?

There are many facets to this challenge and many areas where cooperative action will be required. I want to examine one of these areas – taxation.

The role of the tax authorities

Tax authorities have a role to play in realizing the full potential of electronic commerce. They must provide a fiscal environment within which electronic commerce can flourish. However, they must also ensure that electronic commerce does not undermine the ability of governments to raise the revenues required to finance the public services voted for by the country's citizens.

In striving to achieve these objectives, governments recognise that there are broadly two forms of electronic commerce:

- business-to-business
- business-to-consumers.

While the political debate has tended to focus on the business-to-consumer activities (issues of privacy, consumer rights, for example), it is the business-to-business activities that are, and are likely to remain for the foreseeable future, the dominant part of electronic commerce. Excluding government transactions, approximately 80 per cent of electronic commerce is conducted between businesses. And even within the business segment, there is a wide diversity. Multi-National Enterprises (MNEs), for example, have used the Internet technologies to develop global networks between their subsidiaries. Small- to Medium-sized Enterprises (SMEs) are rapidly exploiting the ways in which the Internet can be used to give them access to overseas markets. Professional service companies in fields as different as architecture and finance are already using the Internet to develop their services to other businesses.

Tax authorities must take account of these different patterns in designing tax systems for the twenty-first century. The needs and problems posed by business-to-consumer transactions should not dictate the treatment of business-to-business transactions. The difficulties of dealing with an increasing number of cross-border transactions by SMEs should not necessarily determine the ways of taxing MNEs.

There has been considerable speculation as to what overall response governments will adopt towards the taxation of electronic commerce in this new, complex environment. At one extreme, there is the view that electronic commerce should in some sense be allowed to take place in a tax-free environment. At the other extreme, there has been speculation on the introduction of new taxes specifically designed to tax electronic commerce (for example, the BYTE tax). Neither of these views is likely to prove acceptable to governments. The first would lead to governments being unable to meet the legitimate demands of their citizens for public services. It would also induce tax distortions in trade patterns. The second approach could hinder the development of electronic commerce and lead to the technology becoming 'tax driven'.

Certainly, electronic commerce is a new and exciting development. However, there is nothing to suggest that the nature of electronic commerce, nor the desire to see it develop, should exclude it from the normal remit of taxation. Even in the 'Wired World', death and taxes should remain unavoidable. To conclude, the transactions undertaken in the world of cyberspace are, in general, not so different from traditional forms of commerce as to require a whole new system of taxation.

The OECD has concluded that, at the present time, the most appropriate way to achieve the twin objectives referred to above is to reach an international consensus on how to apply the existing domestic and international arrangements to electronic commerce.

The broad taxation principles that should govern electronic commerce

The challenge facing tax policy makers is to adapt existing legislation, procedures and practices to overcome any deficiencies that emerge as a result of new means of communication and product delivery. It is with this approach in mind that the OECD has

> **Even in the Wired World, death and taxes should remain unavoidable.**

set about the task of developing framework conditions for the taxation of electronic commerce (the OECD issued a major policy statement in November 1997 entitled 'The Communication Revolution and Global Commerce: Implications for tax policy and administration', and, on 8 October 1998, it issued a set of framework conditions to govern the taxation of electronic commerce). These conditions, which have been drawn up in close cooperation with the European Union, the World Customs Organisation and the business community, will be guided by the following principles.

- *Neutrality* Taxation should seek to be neutral between different forms of electronic commerce and between conventional and electronic forms of commerce. Economically, similar transactions should be treated equally and business decisions should be motivated by economic rather than tax considerations.
- *Effectiveness and fairness* Taxation should produce the right amount of tax at the right time from taxpayers engaged in electronic commerce. The potential for tax evasion and avoidance should be minimized and counteracting measures should be proportional to the risks involved.

- *Certainty and simplicity* The tax rules should be clear and simple to understand so that taxpayers can anticipate the tax consequences in advance of an electronic transaction, including knowing when, where and how the tax is to be accounted for.
- *Efficiency* Compliance costs for taxpayers and administrative costs for the tax authorities should be minimized.
- *Flexibility* The systems for the taxation of electronic commerce should be flexible and dynamic to ensure that they keep pace with technological and commercial developments.

These principles are similar to the widely accepted general tax principles that govern the taxation of traditional business activities. Also, just as there are tradeoffs between the taxation principles as applied to conventional commerce, so there will be tradeoffs between the principles that will apply to electronic commerce.

The implementation challenges facing the 'virtual' inspector

An internationally consistent application of these principles to electronic commerce will help to maintain the fiscal sovereignty of countries, achieve a fair share of the tax base from electronic commerce among countries and should minimize the risk of double taxation and non-taxation.

However, the implementation of these principles in the electronic commerce environment will raise new challenges for tax authorities. Current implementation strategies have been developed in response to the conventional commercial environment, but the electronic commercial environment is different. The four main areas where these challenges arise are:

- tax administration
- consumption taxes
- tax treaties
- transfer pricing.

Tax administration

In the conventional commercial environment, tax administrations rely on being able to identify the taxpayers, obtain access to verifiable information about the taxation affairs of the taxpayers and have efficient mechanisms to collect the tax due.

A business engaged in electronic commerce on the Internet may be identifiable only by its domain name, yet the correspondence between a domain name and the location where the activity is undertaken is tenuous. The point is amusingly illustrated by a cartoon that first appeared in *The New Yorker* magazine where two dogs are seen sitting in front of a computer terminal with the caption 'On the Internet, nobody knows you're a dog.' As SMEs engage more

'On the Internet, nobody knows you're a dog.'

activities in international electronic commerce, this lack of identifiability may become more problematical, and not just for tax authorities. Even with well-known international businesses, the domain name on the Internet may not necessarily indicate whether or not you are dealing with the London, Cayman Islands or New York office of the business. Furthermore, there are cases where the Internet domain name can imply a relationship to a well-known business without any such relationship existing, giving rise to trademark-type disputes.

Without accurate identification of taxpayers, it is difficult to levy taxes. Even if you can identify the taxpayers, but not their physical location in the world, this will give rise to jurisdictional disputes between tax authorities, with all the attendant risks of double taxation.

Responsible businesses engaged in electronic commerce recognize that there are sound commercial reasons for them to work with government to ensure adequate identification. Measures such as the registration of business names, mailing addresses and telephone and fax numbers on their Internet sites will foster consumer confidence. Such measures will also address some of the challenges faced by tax authorities in identifying taxpayers.

In addition to issues of identification, electronic commerce raises questions about the ability of tax authorities to collect information. In the conventional commercial environment, taxpayers keep books and records and provide information to tax authorities to support the assessment of tax. Where tax authorities have the need to verify information provided by taxpayers, they can rely on third-party information, from financial institutions or other intermediaries. In the electronic environment, electronic books and records may be easily stored in a foreign jurisdiction. Encryption, used quite legitimately to protect commercial secrets, may also be used to deny tax authorities access to records. Traditional third-party sources of information may be curtailed as the Internet encourages the process of disintermediation. All of these developments may make it more difficult for tax authorities to obtain the information necessary for the fair administration of the tax rules.

Professional accounting bodies are also facing similar challenges in carrying out commercial audits. Tax administrations can perhaps learn from the ways in which accounting firms are dealing with encryption and other issues.

The problem of encryption can also be alleviated by following commercial practices such as the voluntary use of key recovery or trusted third parties.

A very large part of tax revenue is collected by intermediaries. Employers are responsible for the collection of wage tax; businesses for consumption taxes; financial institutions for taxes on interest and royalties. In some cases, electronic commerce may remove these intermediaries (when, for example, a producer deals directly with the consumer rather than via a retailer), so that tax authorities will be required to collect small amounts from a large number of taxpayers. This may place an unacceptably high compliance cost on taxpayers and high administrative costs on tax authorities.

The technologies that underlie electronic commerce may, however, open up new collection avenues (many countries are already accepting electronic filing of tax returns and payment of taxes). Businesses are already experimenting with building the tax collection function into their commercial operations.

One of the most notable experiments is the e-Christmas initiative of Microsoft, United Parcels Services UPS and others for Christmas 1997. Under this initiative, Christmas gifts could be ordered and paid for on-line, with the payment covering all taxes and duties, which were forwarded to the appropriate jurisdiction, while the gift was delivered to the door of the recipient. This initiative shows that the on-line collection of tax is technically feasible, although practical problems remain.

Tax havens and offshore banking facilities may be used more readily in the 'Wired World'. The average taxpayer may find it increasingly easy to use offshore financial centres. Internet banking will offer simple access, low transaction costs, a degree of anonymity and an immediacy of transferability of funds – all attributes that are not widely available today. If these attributes can be combined with well-run offshore institutions within a secure environment, it is likely that a much wider clientele would be attracted to these services than those using them today. It can also be expected that governments will not stand back in the face of this development.

Consumption taxes

The concept of the place of supply is important in Value Added Tax (VAT) systems. In broad terms, the basis for supply rules falls into two categories:

- those that depend on identification of a relevant establishment (the supplier in some cases and the customer in others
- those that are based on the place of performance or enjoyment.

As electronic commerce makes much more opaque the links between the place of supply, the place where the enterprise is located and where the service is used or consumed, the Internet raises new compliance issues for VAT authorities.

How can VAT authorities respond to these challenges? A three-fold approach is being explored at the OECD:

- to agree that cross-border transactions should be liable to tax in the country where the consumption takes place
- to work towards a common definition of the place of consumption
- to examine whether or not the supply of digitized products should be treated as services for consumption tax purposes.

A successful and internationally coordinated introduction of these principles should go some way to ensuring that VAT does not hinder the development of electronic commerce and, at the same time, that electronic commerce does not undermine the VAT tax base.

As regards customs duties, governments will need to ensure that custom procedures do not hinder the development of on-line ordering and off-line delivery of goods across borders. This can best be achieved by developing simplified customs procedures and reviewing the minimum relief for duties and taxation.

Redefining tax treaties

The Net will cause tricky problems of interpretation for the negotiators of tax treaties. Can existing concepts, such as that of permanent establishment and royalties, be adapted to cover activities on the Internet or should tax authorities be undertaking a more fundamental review?

> As electronic commerce makes much more opaque the links between the place of supply, the place where the enterprise is located and where the service is used or consumed, the Internet raises new compliance issues for VAT authorities.

A central element in determining taxation rights in tax treaties is that of business presence, employed to establish whether or not a permanent establishment exists. Whether or not the operation of an establishment in a country rises to the volume that makes it a permanent establishment is primarily a question of fact. The OECD's Model Tax Convention (which is the basis for bilateral treaties) gives a definition and some guidelines – a permanent establishment is a fixed place of business where the business of an enterprise is wholly or partly carried out. Certain activities are insufficient to draw an enterprise within the taxing jurisdiction of a country. For instance, a 'permanent establishment' does not include 'the use of facilities solely for the purpose of storage, display or delivery of goods or merchandise belonging to the enterprise'.

Does the existence of a web site or a server in a jurisdiction create a permanent establishment and therefore give that jurisdiction the right to tax the income attributed to that enterprise? Treaty negotiators will have to examine this and other questions and, more generally, see how treaty concepts can be applied to new ways of doing business. A group of tax experts meeting at the OECD is expected to provide clarification on these issues during 1999.

Implications for transfer pricing

In principle, electronic commerce offers no new problems, no fundamentally or categorically different dimensions, for transfer pricing (the prices charged for transactions that take place between the different parts of a multinational enterprise). It may, however, increase the complexity of transfer pricing analysis. The development of private Intranets within multinational enterprises puts pressure on the traditional application of the arm's length principle (that is, the principle that transactions between the related enterprises of an MNE should be treated as though they were undertaken between independent enterprises) by stimulating the fuller integration of multinational operations, particularly in the provision of services. This makes it even more difficult than at present for tax authorities to determine what a given transaction actually is and to find a transaction between independent enterprises about which enough is known to conclude that it may be considered a comparable transaction to that undertaken between related enterprises. The OECD's 'Guidelines on Transfer Pricing' specifies that a functional analysis may be required to establish comparability, but with electronic commerce and the use of private Intranets it may be difficult to know who is doing what.

The deeper integration may also bring benefits of synergies over and above the directly measured contributions of the participants. This raises the difficult question of how such benefits should be divided up between the related enterprises. Clearly the issue of transfer pricing can only increase in complexity.

New taxpayers' service opportunities

Electronic commerce technologies open up new ways for tax authorities to undertake the business of administering tax laws and collecting tax revenues and new ways to interact with a wider community. For example:

- Communications between tax authorities and taxpayers can be revolutionized and access to information can be enhanced to help taxpayers comply with their tax obligations.
- Tax registration and filing requirements can be simplified.
- Electronic assessment and collection of tax can become the norm rather than the exception.
- Easier, quicker, more secure ways of paying taxes and of obtaining tax refunds will be facilitated.

Governments must seize the opportunities offered by the new communication technologies to improve the service they provide to taxpayers, reduce the cost of complying with tax rules and use the resources devoted to the collection of taxes more effectively.

The need for an international coordinated approach

Governments jealously guard their fiscal sovereignty. Even in regional groupings such as the European Union, they are reluctant to cede control over the design of their tax systems. The challenge facing tax authorities in this new global environment is how to reconcile national fiscal boundaries with the borderless world of electronic commerce?

First, governments should look critically at the international taxation arrangements that are intended to minimize friction between domestic tax systems. Tax treaties are the main instrument for achieving this international coordination. Although such treaties are primarily bilateral, in practice they operate very much like multilateral treaties as, for the most part, they are based on the OECD model tax convention. Because there are now more than 1500 tax treaties in place around the world, they provide a powerful instrument to ensure that the profits generated from electronic commerce are not subject to double taxation and that all countries receive a fair share of these profits, commensurate with their contribution to the economic activity. At the same time, the non-discrimination provisions found in most tax treaties encourage governments to treat foreign and domestic enterprises in exactly the same way. Similarly the mutual agreement provisions in such treaties provide well-tried mechanisms for resolving disputes between tax authorities. The exchange of information articles that exist in all modern tax treaties discourage taxpayers from taking advantage of the new opportunities opened up by these new communication technologies for tax minimization. Thus, in this new global environment, tax treaties are taking on an increased importance.

The challenge facing tax authorities in this new global environment is how to reconcile national fiscal boundaries with the borderless world of electronic commerce?

Second, government should address the spread of intracompany, cross-border transactions by agreeing on a set of rules for the taxation of multinational enterprises. The OECD took a major step forward in this area in 1995, when a consensus was reached on its *Transfer Pricing Guidelines for Multinational Enterprises and Tax Administrations*. These guidelines provide a common set of rules for the determination of the profits of multinational enterprises, including profits realized from electronic commerce.

Third, governments should work together to design measures to counter 'tax poaching' for electronic commerce. Some commentators have referred to this phenomon as 'the race to the bottom', with countries trying to outbid other countries in terms of the fiscal incentives they provide to those engaged in electronic commerce. You only have to look at the experience of the United States to see what distortion such harmful tax competition can create, with business location decisions becoming tax rather than profit driven. Again, the OECD has addressed this issue by developing a set of guidelines that distinguishes between fair and unfair tax competition and sets out the measures that the international community can take to counter unfair tax competition (*Harmful Tax Competition: An Emerging Global Issue*, OECD, 1998).

To summarize, the institutional arrangements to achieve a coordinated approach to the taxation of electronic commerce are in place, but much remains to be done. OECD countries must engage in a dialogue with countries outside of the OECD to associate them with the instruments referred to above and see how far they meet the special needs of developing countries. The specific provisions in these international instruments must be reviewed to see whether or not they need to be adapted to the electronic age. Business must be prepared to play a more active role in these developments.

To address these issues, the OECD organized, in cooperation with the Canadian Government, a Ministerial Conference in Ottawa on 8 and 9 October 1998. While the conference addressed a wide range of issues (privacy, consumer rights and obligations, encryption, the economic and social implications of electronic commerce), taxation was one of the major themes. The conference brought together more than 700 government officials, senior business executives and representatives of the social partners for a series of round-table discussions. In the tax area, ministers will be asked to welcome a set of framework conditions to govern the taxation of electronic commerce and endorse an ambitious programme of work. Issues were identified where OECD member countries, non-member countries and business need to work together to achieve the stable tax environment that will enable electronic commerce to develop to its full potential and in a manner that protects the revenue base of governments. ■

I would like to thank my colleague Micheal Hardy for his input into the article. The views expressed are my own and do not commit those of the OECD or its member countries.

Michael Finley

Author and consultant

BEYOND COMPETITION IN A WIRED WORLD

Technology, human nature and business in the 2000s

Not so long ago, businesses enjoyed a very narrow scope of ambitions. All they had to do to succeed was establish a first or second place in market share of the product or service they provided, and they were set for years, milking a bountiful cash cow. Products and services did not obsolesce rapidly, and new competitors did not spring out of nowhere. That's the lucky fate that seemed to be in store for some of our most powerful companies a short time ago – IBM, Xerox, Kodak, PanAm, Montgomery Ward. These companies were all huge, and all owed their existence to the 'big iron' – the heavy duty mainframe computing that allowed them to be big and still keep track of things.

Measured by their own success, these technology-driven companies were efficient in their way. They had lots of highly paid specialists working for them, who spoke only the language of their speciality. They had lawyers to give their competitiveness teeth. Their attitude towards the industries they dominated their customers and even their own people was lordly and brutal.

Things have changed. Today it's still a good thing to have a lot of market share, but in every other way the business world is a different place. Product cycles have narrowed to a few months, competitors are everywhere and a cash cow is a rarity. Successful companies today are more likely to be small or medium sized than large. They are more likely to be young than old. They are likely to have a fanatical attachment to their customers and their knowledge workers. Their attitude within their industries is likely to be an interesting combination of competitive and cooperative. The brutal days of the lordly corporation are winding down, done in by the same technology, though at a different stage in its evolution, that made them lordly in the first place.

The brute cycle

Throughout history, brutal organizations – countries, religions, corporations – have ruled their domains by terror. Historically, so long as the brute remained brutal, there was little chance of overthrowing it. Change tended to wait until the brute died or became infirm. Cut off from one another and unable to organize, people hoped its successor was less brutal. The only other 'hope', and it was a faint one, was that the brute would so overstep its bounds that the enemies it made would form an alliance and together overthrow it. This comeuppance, in which the bully is thrashed by its own competitive excess, is called the brute cycle.

As history has evolved, and as communications between groups and the information technology that enabled communication have improved, the hope of overthrowing the brute became less faint. World War II can be seen as a rescue effort of Europe by the Allies that was waged as much in the mass media as on the battlefield. Newspapers, radio, television, telephones and computers all allowed people greater leverage to step up to the brute and overthrow it. It is the same story in industry:

- Coca-Cola and Pepsi are notorious brutes in the soft drink industry, enforcing take-it-or-leave-it contracts limiting shelfspace in shops for competing brands.
- The arrival of a supermarket in a small town spells the inevitable doom of that town's main street businesses.
- Nike, the shoe company, cheerfully brutalizes its competitors, suppliers and employees, and chalks it up to 'competitive fire' – Nike paid the artist who designed their world-famous 'swoosh' $35 – and went on to make hundreds of millions with it.

The brute cycle is not something that 'happens' to bullies. It is what people the bully has bullied do back to the bully. It is the only defence people have against aggression and exploitation. It involves three steps that organizations and individuals have followed unconsciously since the days of Phyrrus and his costly victories.

- *Exchange* This is the information stage, in which victims make contact with one another and with potential allies and exchange information. They decide on a strategy for dealing with the bully. If possible, they extend a peace offering to the bully if they stop what they're doing.

- *Encircle* This is the stage in which victims and allies move together to surround the bully. They link arms and focus attention on the predator and keep it focused on them until their behaviour changes.
- *Exact* This is the action stage, in which victims and allies compel the bully to negotiate or concede. If the bully refuses, they stay encircled forever.

The '3Es' worked sporadically in ancient times as the information flow was usually inadequate to really encircle a predator. In modern times, IT has ratcheted up the power of the 'peasant'. Boycotts – in which a group not only stops buying a product but urges others not to buy it either – use the 3Es. Whistleblowing – the act of exchanging information about the misdeeds occurring on one's own side – never succeeded in other centuries, but works in ours.

Fittingly, the 3Es have enjoyed greatest success in the era of high technology. Commodore and Leading Edge were major computer companies in the 1980s, and they sold millions of computers by hard-balling everyone – suppliers distributors and customers alike. Everyone was afraid of these companies because of their ruthlessness, their unwillingness to take prisoners.

Eventually, both companies came crashing down, due at least in part to the ferocity of their own competitiveness. In the case of Leading Edge, shops frustrated with Leading Edge's indifference to customer complaints refused to stock their computers any more. In the case of Commodore, suppliers rose up in revolt against the company's savage style of supplier relations.

Our power is the knowledge in our heads, and in the connections we form with one another.

What changed? IT itself. In the age of information, individuals and nations for the first time have the key to toppling the most despicable bully – we tell each other what we know. There is no more powerful dynamic of connectedness than this kind of exchange. It transforms us from isolated victims, wondering if our experience is representative, to a networked swarm with a common purpose and understanding. Our power is the knowledge in our heads, and in the connections we form with one another. In business, we hope the number of mass murderers is minimal, but we have bullies, tyrants and supercompeters at every level, from work teams to the executive teams of multinational corporations, who go too far in their quest for market domination. When they cheat, they do so in secret, confident that the story they tell is the story the world will accept. The classic case of overthrow in our time was the crisis surrounding Intel's Pentium chip in 1995. Within a few months of its issue, a mathematician working alone determined that the chip failed to make correct computations involving very long numbers, an aspect of chip intelligence called 'floating point'.

Twenty years ago, the matter would have ended there, with an isolated critic unable to stir interest. However, the controversy took on a life of its own on the

Internet, particularly in techie usenet newsgroups. People who wondered why their PC wasn't making precise calculations were able to compare notes. While Intel denied a problem existed and characterized complaints as isolated incidents, it was too late – too much information had been exchanged, and a Web-based consumer movement arose that would rattle the boardrooms of every company that ever tried to bully its own customer base.

The Net changes everything. Medieval kings controlled information in their realms by owning all the books. Modern political and corporate tyrants control information by owning the mass media, and relegating dissent to the margins. However, in the post-modern connected world we live in, information is much harder to control. People have the means to exchange information – as at Tiananmen Square – even when exchange is forbidden.

By banding together and exchanging information, constituent groups – citizens, consumers, employees, suppliers, subsidiaries and shareholders – acquire leverage against the lies. Intel, the company so embarrassed by such exchange, matured into a company very wise about collaboration. Today, it has exceptional communications with its customer base, and defines its customers as nearly everyone. Indeed, it has created a kind of American *keiretsu*, in which it is a kind of godfather to scores of other companies in many industries, providing them with technology, leadership and direct investment.

The transcompetitive alternative

A world in which no organization has a deathgrip on essential information is a world in which competitors must occasionally cooperate. The history of collaboration in high-tech developments begins in 1992, with a surprising collaboration between nemesis companies Apple and IBM. Apple and IBM were given very little hope of success when they entered into a joint venture with Hewlett-Packard in 1992 to create a common operating system codenamed 'Pink' and, sure enough, the project failed, even after spinning off the new technology to jointly owned Taligent Corp. The venture cost the three companies $100 million, and ended with squabbling over who got what (Linda Picarille, 'Investors may pull Taligent plug', *Computerworld*, 2 October 1995).

However, despite predictions of many industry observers, the reason for the failure ultimately had little to do with the clash of corporate cultures. Apple had always defined itself as the opposite of whatever IBM was. If IBM was East Coast, suit and tie, middle aged and business savvy, Apple took pains to be West Coast, jeans and T-shirt, twentysomething and more interested in technology than business.

Taligent went belly up – and no one ever made any money from 'Pink', but the collaboration proved a powerful point to the two former competitors and was the genesis of a new kind of relationship between them. First, the two companies found out they are *both* global and *both* middle aged. The cultural differences were not so important as people thought they would be. Second, the two staunch competitors had a reason to come together – to join forces to hold off an even more fearsome competitor – Microsoft, which had stolen IBM's dinner right off its plate and treated the Macintosh standard with condescension and contempt.

The operating system joint venture went nowhere, but it laid the groundwork for a more profound alliance involving microprocessors. Eventually, Motorola, IBM and Apple would join together to create the PowerPC chip, which came the closest of any chip in the mid-1990s to competing against Intel's Pentium chip. Also, IBM and Apple would find common cause with a large number of other companies that were alarmed at the Microsoft/Intel relationship – Novell, Netscape, Adobe, Sun Microsystems, Symantec and ADM.

Why collaborate?

The answer to the question 'Why should competitors collaborate?' is that you do it out of self-interest. Nemesis wars are wars of mutually assured destruction. Unless the fix is in (you hit us, then we hit you, but we take pains not to actually do one another any damage), head-to-head competitors exact a terrible toll on one another in terms of resources, resilience and rationality. It becomes a habit, and not a happy one, and from that point on it is simply a game in which two dummies slug one another.

When enmity is high, rationality is low. You must rein in these extremes or risk going over the deep end.

Even in the din of battle, nemesis competitors need one another. Apple and IBM, even as they struggled to outdo one another, profited greatly from one another's existence. Apple inspired IBM to participate in the small systems market, and IBM legitimized Apple's participation in it.

If there is not a battle, consumers may never know about your product. The Apple/IBM war was a spectator sport, and millions of people around the world looked on to see how it was going – more than would have tuned in to an informational commercial about the Apple II.

Microsoft memory

Information exchange gives people memories they used not to have. Hardly an American over the age of seven is unaware of Chairman Bill Gates – the $54-billion man – or of Microsoft's conflictual status as developer of both operating systems (DOS and the many flavours of Windows) and the applications that run on these operating systems. The company's promotion of Windows 95 was the biggest single-product promotion in the history of the world. Microsoft, unlike AT&T, has momentum and ready cash. People see it not as it is today, but as what it is likely to become in ten years – a bigger monopoly than AT&T ever was.

So the company is perpetually encircled. At any moment, there are many hundreds of law suits pending against the company. It is the punching bag of every pundit with two pennies and a newsletter column to rub together. Regulators have nothing to lose by maintaining constant anti-trust vigilance. When Microsoft sought to acquire Intuit in 1996, the deal was quashed because it gave Microsoft access to a bank. People fast-forwarded to a future in which all our cheques said 'Microsoft' in the lower left-hand corner, and shuddered.

Encircled and exposed, Microsoft feels the heat of the world and so pads softly through it, like a cat with a bell around its neck. Not neutered by a long shot, it is apparent to everyone as a potential danger, one that must be watched. John D. Rockefeller of Standard Oil – the company that defined monopoly in the last century – was never hemmed in as Bill Gates is. How has Microsoft responded to this encircling? In the summer of 1997, when Apple was in trouble and its CEO, Gil Amelio, turned out not to be the saviour everyone had hoped, Apple looked in every direction for a white knight company to come along and sweep it up. There were so many companies that 'made sense' as partners – Motorola, Sun, Oracle and even IBM were discussed in the press.

However, the company that actually put up money to keep Apple afloat was Microsoft, in one of the most stunning acts of corporate partnership ever. By all the known rules of competition, Microsoft would have been better off with the disappearance of the number two maker of operating systems, and how easy it would have been for Microsoft to stand by and let Apple choke on its own problems.

> However, the company that actually put up money to keep Apple afloat was Microsoft.

Many were cynical of the partnership, and it is true that the $150 million that passed hands was chicken feed in the larger scale of things. However, even if Microsoft was playing a clever game of killing with kindness, it was a sign that the company is aware that people are watching, in part because of the technologies the two companies have helped create – and, as big as Microsoft is, it can no longer be insensitive to the eyes of the world.

The wisdom we see at work in the Microsoft and Apple collaboration we also see in South Africa, where whites and blacks – no longer prevented from sharing their experiences – are working together to fight racial hatred, street crime and a legacy of cruelty. We see it at United Airlines, where workers are owners and entrepreneurial spirits are flying high. We see it at the NUMMI plant in Fresno, California, where management and workers are setting aside ancient misgivings to make the best cars in North America. We see it in the city of Hong Kong, where an extraordinary amalgam of IT, competitive capitalism and collaborative socialism is fashioning a world city for a new millennium. Bless them, we even see it at Nike Inc., the poster child of American competitive fervour, which is moving forward on, of all things, collaborative sports sponsorship ventures with Japan and Brazil, and which recently agreed to pay that 'swoosh' designer for the value of her contribution 30 years earlier – in the form of stock in the company. That Nike came to this change of heart may be related to the existence of an around-the-clock Net-based Nike Watch, that monitors every corporate exhalation and inhalation, everywhere in the world. Exchange, encircle, exact.

In the transcompetitive age, people are overcoming brute 'human nature' by putting human nature more fully into play.

The lesson? People and companies can still be brutal, but they can also be compelled to do the right thing, when information circulates and acquires its own power. For years, we worried about how computer technology was going to robotize humankind and bring on 1984's dire scenario. However, the actual year 1984 came and went, and the world was not carted off into slavery. Computer networks, and the flood of information they distribute, regardless of its accuracy, have had the diametrically opposite effect. The Iron Curtain, which sought to control information, came down. We're still trying to cope with the freedom we have seized for ourselves. ■

Mark Radcliffe

Partner, Gray Cary Ware & Freidenrich

INTELLECTUAL PROPERTY AND THE GLOBAL INFORMATION INFRASTRUCTURE

The Global Information Infrastructure (GII) promises the ability to work across time zones and country boundaries. It can provide access to hundreds of channels of television programming, thousands of musical recordings and millions of magazines and books. The GII will revolutionize educational systems by linking students and educators in remote locations around the world. It will also dramatically alter healthcare as a result of increasing public awareness of health issues and allowing patients to use the services of physicians located on the other side of the world. Not so long ago a government report estimated that more than half of the US workforce is in 'information-based' jobs.

The importance of intellectual property to many companies is rising dramatically. Texas Instruments received over $770,000,000 in a single year simply by licensing its patents. The value of the Coca-Cola trademark has been estimated to be $39 billion. Thomas Stewart, in his book *Intellectual Capital* (Nicholas Brealey, 1997), stated that four out of the five dollars that Levi Strauss Corporation spends on making jeans go to 'information technology' not to manufacturing. The ownership and exploitation of intellectual property will be particularly critical to the success of companies in the business environment being created by the GII.

Yet the same GII that offers these opportunities also poses fundamental challenges to the current structure of intellectual property law. All intellectual property is based on national law. For example, Turner Broadcasting Corporation does *not* own a 'copyright' in the film *Gone With the Wind:* it owns a US copyright, a French copyright, a German copyright, and copyright in each separate country throughout the world. Similarly, Cadbury Limited does not own the 'Cadbury's' trademark. It owns a French trademark, a US trademark, and UK trademark and trademarks in other countries for chocolate and other food items.

Despite the national nature of these laws, international treaties in the patent, trademark and copyright area produce a minimum level of protection in the laws of most major commercial countries. None the less, the laws can differ in dramatic ways. For example, under US law, many collections of data (such as the white pages of a telephone book) are not protectable under copyright law because they do not have sufficient 'creativity' to qualify for copyright protection; however, the same collection of data would be protectable under the copyright law in all of the European Union countries. Such problems also arise between countries within the European Union. For example, until the implementation of the 1991 Software Directive, most software programs were not protected under German copyright law. In fact, the European Union has adopted five directives to harmonize copyright law and is now considering a sixth.

> The ownership and exploitation of intellectual property will be particularly critical to the success of companies in the business environment being created by the GII.

The four major forms of intellectual property – patents, copyright, Trademarks and Trade Secrets – are described below.

Patents

Patent law protects inventions and processes ('utility patents') that are novel, useful and non-obvious (a less well-known form of patent protection is the design patent, which protects the 'ornamental' parts of a product). A patent owner can prevent others from making, using, selling and importing any goods or providing services incorporating the protected invention. Patents are obtained by going through an application process in which the government reviews the scope of the application and whether or not it meets the standards for patent protection in that country. An example of products protected by utility patents include the microwave oven, genetically engineered bacteria for cleaning up oil spills, Internet search engine technology, a computerized method of running cash management accounts, and computer software for controlling networks.

Copyrights

Copyright laws protect works of authorship. Unlike patents, copyrights do not protect ideas – they only protect the 'expression' of the ideas. Copyrights are protected automatically without application to the government in most commercial countries (the US provides additional rights by means of registration of the copyright).

Typical products protected by copyright law are books, films, music, web sites, television broadcasts, magazines and software. The copyright owner in most countries has the exclusive right to reproduce, translate, make available to the public, adapt and publicly perform (including via broadcast and related transmissions) the copyrighted work.

The rights described above are the 'minimum' rights required under the Berne Convention, but some countries provide different rights. For example, the copyright law in the US grants the copyright owner the exclusive right to reproduce, distribute, modify, publicly perform and publicly display the work.

Trademarks

Trademarks and service marks are words, names, symbols or devices used by manufacturers of goods and providers of services to identify their goods and services. In most countries, Trademark rights are obtained through only by registration with the government (the US, the UK and many members of the British Commonwealth also permit rights to be obtained through use without registration). Trademark law prevents the use of Trademarks or service marks by other parties that are 'confusingly similar'. Examples of Trademarks are 'Mercedes' for automobiles, 'Coca-Cola' for soft drinks, 'Lindt' for chocolates and 'Yamaha' for guitars. Many different companies can use the same word or symbol as a Trademark so long as they use it for different goods. For example, 20 different companies have registered the word 'Apple' as a Trademark in the US. They range from the well-known Apple Computers Inc., which has registered the mark for computers and a variety of computer goods and services, to USTOV, which has registered the word 'Apple' as a Trademark for rice.

Trade Secrets

A Trade Secret is information of any type that is valuable to its owner because it is not generally known and has been kept secret by its owner. Trade Secrets are only protected to the extent that they are not generally known or 'readily ascertainable'. Trade Secret protection is obtained automatically without the need to apply to the government. However, Trade Secrets are only protected against 'misappropriation', which means wrongful taking. Consequently, reverse engineering a product – if it does not violate a contractual or other obligation – is not prevented by Trade Secret law. Trade Secrets can include customer lists, recipes, manufacturing processes and algorithms for software.

GII effects on intellectual property

The laws most dramatically affected by the GII are copyright and Trademark law.

The GII's effects on copyright

Most industrialized countries have signed up to the Berne Convention, which imposes a 'minimum' level of protection for works under the national copyright laws of members of the Convention. Yet copyright laws are based on two very different approaches:

- The Anglo-American tradition emphasizes the economic nature of copyright, which means that copyrights are readily transferable and of limited scope.
- The Continental tradition emphasizes the role of the author and broader protection, which leads to 'moral' rights preventing changes to a work without the original author's permission) that are not transferable and subject to longer terms of protection.

The global nature of the GII highlights the differences between the copyright laws of different countries. For example, the term of copyright protection for many works by individual authors in the European Union countries is now the life of the author plus 70 years – a period based on the prior German law. The equivalent term in the US (and, until recently, the Netherlands and many other countries) is the life of the author plus 50 years. Consequently, a work that would be in 'the public domain' (and no longer protected by copyright) in the US might still be protected under the laws of European Union countries.

The global nature of the GII highlights the differences between the copyright laws of different countries.

This inconsistency already raises problems for companies with global distribution. For example, the Walt Disney Corporation is involved in litigation in the US with the estate of Igor Stravinski relating to the distribution of video cassettes of the movie *Fantasia,* which includes the 'Rite of Spring.' However, the 'Rite of Spring' is in the public domain in the US (the 'Rite of Spring' entered the public domain for reasons other than expiration of the term), but is still under copyright protection in many other countries. In the physical world, Disney could avoid liability for copyright infringement by distributing video cassettes of *Fantasia* only in the US. Yet Disney wishes to distribute the video cassettes worldwide, hence, the litigation. The Internet makes this problem more immediate. If Disney were to make *Fantasia* available on the Internet, it would be liable for copyright infringement if the film was 'broadcast' or distributed into a country where the copyright was still in effect.

In fact, the very operation of the Internet poses difficult questions under copyright law. Internet usenet groups send the submissions by individual subscribers for posting to hundreds, if not thousands, of servers. Under traditional copyright theory, if the person posting the work to the usenet group does not own the copyright or have the right to post it, the operator of each one of these servers would be liable for copyright infringement. This problem was addressed by a San José District Court in the US in a law suit brought by the Church of Scientology. The Church brought a copyright and Trade Secret law suit alleging the unauthorized posting of its private documents against Mr Erlich (the individual who posted it), Mr Klemrud (the bulletin board operator who provided access for Mr Erlich to the usenet group for the posting) and NetCom (the Internet service provider that provided access to the Internet for the bulletin board). The court noted that the application of traditional copyright law liability principles would potentially make each usenet server liable for infringement because it 'reproduced' the document without authorization from the copyright owner. The court recognized that such a result would be absurd and sidestepped traditional copyright law analysis. Instead, the court stated that NetCom would be liable only if it knew of the infringement and took no action.

A similar problem arises from 'caching'. Caching (sometimes referred to as 'mirroring') means the storage of an entire 'copy' of a web site in another location to make the World Wide Web more efficient. For example, an Australian Internet service provider might establish a 'mirror' site in Australia for Australian users of a popular American web site because it is more time consuming to access the American web site through trans-Pacific cables. Yet, such unauthorized 'reproductions' violate copyright law. In addition, such caching results in other problems:

- out-of-date information to the user
- loss of control by the web site owner of the version of the web site seen by the user
- inaccurate visitor counts at the original web site.

The digital nature of the Internet, which permits the easy transmission of 'perfect' copies, also poses serious problems for copyright owners. The scope of copyright law has always been intimately linked with the technology of reproduction. New technologies made new uses of works possible or copying easier. Copyright law has then been extended to encompass such uses or strike a new balance between the scope of legal protection and the availability of more effective reproduction technology. In the twentieth century, copyright law has evolved to deal with the introduction of motion pictures, broadcast television, photocopiers and digital audiotape. Copyright law has frequently been amended to deal with these new technologies. For example, the multiple reproductions required by cable distribution of television programmes produced special amendments to many copyright laws. In fact, the European Union has adopted five directives to harmonize its members' copyright laws on issues from terms to protection of software.

The problems posed by the ability to make perfect digital copies through the use of the GII was so troubling that the World Intellectual Property Organization, a UN organization, convened a Diplomatic Conference in 1996 to propose new treaties to supplement the Berne Convention on these issues. The speed with which this conference was organized was remarkable given the generally slow-moving nature of international treaty negotiations. The attendees at the Conference agreed to add protection to copyright law for new forms of 'technological protection': it will now be a copyright infringement to distribute or use technology, methods and processes that permit 'circumvention' of technological means of protecting copyrighted works. One example of such technological means of protection is the digital envelope technology proposed by IBM in its Crytolope product. Thus, the balance between technological and legal protection available under copyright law has shifted once again due to the new uses of works permitted by the GII.

However, the attendees at the Diplomatic Conference were not able to agree on a major issue – whether or not a 'temporary' copy (such as one stored temporarily on a server transmitting a message) was an infringing copy. If such a temporary copy is an 'infringing copy', then thousands of companies could be unwitting infringers as messages passed briefly through their servers. The scope of such third-party liability is of great concern to Internet service providers, telecommunication companies and web site owners who allow users to post materials. Yet, the scope of such liability is very uncertain. As mentioned previously, one US District Court declined to find Netcom, an Internet service provider, liable for a third party's posting unless it was aware of it. In deciding a similar issue, a French court took a different approach. It ruled that an Internet service provider as well as a web site operator would be liable for a privacy violation caused by the posting of semi-nude photos of a performer on the Internet. Although based on a privacy claim, the court noted that such liability would probably also apply to intellectual property. A new, proposed European Union directive proposes a uniform approach to this issue of liability for third-party infringements.

> By means of technology, 'super distribution' permits the author to control the terms under which a work is used by publishers, aggregators and end users.

The international nature of these problems makes their resolution difficult. Many countries have very different views about potential solutions, and resolution of these issues can be held hostage to other international copyright issues. In addition, many copyright users, such as libraries and educators, are concerned that this new protection goes too far and will upset the carefully 'limited' nature of copyright. They are concerned that the protection of the technical means of protection as well as the works themselves under copyright law could render statutory exemptions for private use and fair dealing (frequently referred to as 'fair use' in the US) a dead letter.

The GII also upsets traditional industry distribution structures. For example, in the book and record companies, it is very common to grant exclusive distribution rights in countries. However, what does such 'exclusivity' mean in the borderless world of the GII? Does it mean that a book publisher will not be able to sell its book from an Internet site in the UK (which is accessible worldwide) because it granted exclusive rights to its distributor to sell the book in France? At the same time, the new technology provides the promise of new methods of exploiting rights – 'super distribution' of works from articles to books in which the author controls (and economically participates) in the distribution of their work via multiple levels of distribution. By means of technology, 'super distribution' permits the author to control the terms under which a work is used by publishers, aggregators and end users. In addition, new technologies could permit the automation of tasks such as rights clearance and fee payment to permit uses previously impossible due to transaction costs.

The effects of GII on Trademarks

The traditional structure of Trademark law is also undermined by the GII. Trademarks are granted for a particular type of goods or services within a particular country. Most countries also require that a Trademark be 'used' within the country within a certain period of time or the registration will become void.

Similar to copyright law, Trademark rights arise on a country-by-country basis. Trademark rights can only be enforced against the unauthorized 'use' within a country in which the Trademark or service mark is protected (generally by registration). In the physical world, such use is relatively easy to establish – the unauthorized sale of goods with a Trademark on them or offering of services in a local area using the infringing service mark. However, in the GII, the question of use becomes much more difficult to determine. For example, does a web site offering to sell products in one country constitute 'use' in another country?

This question was posed in a law suit between Playboy Enterprises, Inc., and Tattilo Editrice, S.p.A ('Tattilo'). Tattilo had adopted the Trademark 'Playmen' in 1967 for its gentlemen's sophisticated magazine published in Italy. The magazine has similar content to *Playboy* magazine. In 1979, Tattilo announced its intention to publish an English-language version and Playboy obtained an injunction prohibiting the use of the 'Playmen' Trademark for Tattilo's magazine in the US, France, UK and Germany. However, the Italian courts ruled that 'Playboy' was a weak mark and not entitled to protection. In 1996, Tattilo put up a web site offering subscriptions to the 'Playmen' web site worldwide. This web site was located on a server in Italy. Playboy brought a suit in New York claiming that this web site was a violation of the injunction issued by the court against the print version of the magazine in 1982. After expressing some concerns about the authority of a US court to order changes to a web site in Italy, the court decided that this use of 'Playmen' was a violation of the injunction. The New York court ordered Tattilo to screen each potential user of its Italian web site to avoid accepting potential subscribers from the US.

Many companies use a Trademark in a limited number of countries and may co-exist with a competitor using a similar Trademark in other countries. Such co-existence may become more difficult in the future as the GII becomes more important. In addition to collisions between companies owning Trademarks in different countries, the GII is also causing a 'convergence' between companies in the area of electronic commerce. Companies that formerly co-existed peacefully using the same Trademark for different goods and services will now come into conflict. For example, FTD in the US has long provided the service of sending orders for flowers electronically. They use a winged Mercury figure as a service mark for these services. The *San José Mercury News* is a newspaper in San José, California, and serves the Silicon Valley. When the *San José Mercury News* put up its web site, Mercury Center, it received a cease and desist letter from FTD claiming infringement of FTD's winged 'Mercury figure' by the paper's use of the service mark 'Mercury Center'. Their prior peaceful co-existence was shattered by the advent of the GII.

As electronic commerce and other GII-enabled services become more important, companies will wish to protect their traditional Trademarks and service marks in this new area. However, only one (or a few) of the Trademark owners will be able to register their marks for the new services. In the US, over 20 companies have the registered the name 'Apple' as a Trademark. Which of them will obtain the rights to use it for electronic commerce?

Domain names – such as apple.com – pose another problem for Trademark law. These domain names are the 'humanly comprehensible' form of the actual Internet Protocol address (which consists entirely of numbers). The Internet Protocol addresses designate the computer to which a message should be sent or on which a web site is hosted. Unfortunately, the domain name system was developed when the Internet was primarily a research tool for academics and Trademarks were not a consideration in its development.

The domain name system includes two types of domains: national domains such as '.uk' and '.us', which are administered by a national authority, and the 'international' or 'three-letter' domain, such as '.com', that are currently administered by Network Solutions, Inc. under contract with the US government. The design of the domain name structure permits only *one* company to use the domain name 'apple.com'. Yet, under Trademark law, different companies can use the same Trademark so long as they do not confuse the public. More than 20 companies have registered and appear to be using the Trademark 'Apple' in the US.

The world includes more than 160 countries in which Trademarks may be protected. Many companies may have Trademark rights that could be infringed by a domain name. Many disputes have already arisen over the right to obtain various domain names. For example, a UK retailing corporation, Prince PLC, filed a suit against Prince Sports Group, Inc., an American manufacturer of sports equipment, over the rights to 'prince.com'. These disputes raise fundamental questions, such as how domain names should be treated under the law – as an address (thus, unprotectable) or as a source of origin like a Trademark (and thus, protectable)? Furthermore, how do you allocate the single domain name in the '.com' top-level domain among the different companies with legitimate Trademark rights to the domain name? These questions remain unanswered and difficult to answer.

Moreover, the informal nature of Internet governance has frustrated attempts to resolve these problems. As no person, government or company is 'in charge', such attempts need to obtain significant consensus. A recent attempt to form a coalition to help solve the domain name problem has raised significant objections from the US government, the European Union and Trademark owners.

These issues have made the selection of new brands much more complex. First, most brands must now be cleared internationally because any product sold over the Internet requires a Trademark available in numerous countries much earlier in its life-cycle. Second, the convergence of industries in electronic commerce-related activities means that companies with goods and services that would not previously have been considered potential problems may now block the adoption of a new brand. Finally, the availability of the domain name in the '.com' top-level domain takes on an important significance for many new products and services.

Conclusion

The GII poses fundamental challenges to the current structure of intellectual property law. As the GII grows in importance, it is likely to accelerate the harmonization of intellectual property law in major commercial jurisdictions. Because of the differing interests and multiple parties involved in all such international negotiations, this harmonization is likely to be very slow. In some areas – such as the relationship between domain names and Trademarks – the issues are especially difficult and only beginning to be addressed.

The conflict between national intellectual property laws and the borderless nature of the GII is unlikely to be resolved in the short term. The GII requires businesses to re-examine their intellectual property strategies to accommodate these new realities. For example, many media companies that do not 'own' sufficient rights in their properties (such as magazine articles or books) will exploit them through the GII. Media as well as other companies need to inventory the

> ... GII makes intellectual property a more important asset for companies, it creates fundamental problems for its protection and exploitation ...

current rights in their products in light of the GII and negotiate additional rights, if necessary. In the future, they need to obtain sufficient rights to new products to exploit them on the GII, if desired. They also need to reconsider the meaning of geographic exclusivity in distribution rights in the borderless world created by the GII. Most companies will find carefully drafted contracts the best way to hedge against this uncertainty. Finally, companies need to recognize the increasing importance of branding on the GII and the need to extend their current brands for GII uses (and the potential difficulty of such extensions). Companies should recognize that they need to actively participate in the revisions to intellectual property laws that will be necessary to realize the possibilities of the GII. Ironically, just as the GII makes intellectual property a more important asset for companies, it creates fundamental problems for its protection and exploitation of such intellectual property. ■

WIRED ORGANIZATIONS

contributors

The Rt Hon Peter Mandelson MP, was appointed Secretary of State for Trade and Industry in July 1998. Since the 1997 General Election, he had been Minister without Portfolio at the Cabinet Office. He was elected Member of Parliament for Hartlepool in 1992. He worked as a television producer for LWT before becoming Director of Campaigns and Communications for the Labour Party. Since being elected to Parliament, Mr Mandelson's political posts have included Opposition Whip (1994–95) and Opposition Spokesman on the Civil Service (1995–96).

Dr James Martin, business and technology consultant, lecturer and author, is Chairman and Founder of James Martin & Co, a prominent international management and technology consulting firm. After 19 years at IBM, Dr Martin founded several other successful companies. He is widely acknowledged as an authority on the social and commercial ramifications of computers and sometimes referred to in the press as 'The guru of the Information Age' and 'The father of CASE'. In its twenty-fifth anniversary edition, *Computerworld Magazine* listed him fourth among the 25 people who have most changed the world of computers.

Dr Martin earned an MA and D.Litt. from Oxford, a D.Sc. from Salford in England, and an honorary D.Eng. from Hokkaido Technical University in Japan for his work on information engineering. A Pulitzer Prize nominee, he has written 100 textbooks. Recent titles include: *The Great Transition* and *Cybercorp – the New Business Revolution*. In *Cybercorp* Martin discusses on a macro level the social, political, technological and educational implications of the technology revolution. On a micro level, he addresses topics such as international taxation, worldwide implications of government intervention of the Internet, deregulation and v-chip monitors.

Sir John Daniel, Vice Chancellor, the Open University, is a citizen of both Canada and the United Kingdom, and was knighted by Queen Elizabeth for services to higher education in 1994. He has been Vice Chancellor of the Open University since 1990. The success of his recent book, *Mega-Universities and Knowledge Media: Technology Strategies for Higher Education* (Kogan Page, 1996), has further enhanced his reputation in international university circles as a leading thinker and a thinking leader. He believes that only through the intelligent use of technology can higher education surmount its current crises of access, cost and flexibility.

In an extraordinarily varied academic career, which has taken him to eight universities in five political jurisdictions, he has known diversity on many dimensions. Sir John holds honorary degrees from universities in eight countries, serves as a trustee of the Carnegie Foundation for the Advancement of Teaching and is the President of the Open University of the United States.

Harald Norvik, President and Chairman of the Executive Board, Statoil, is an economist who started his professional career as a business consultant, before becoming involved in politics as an adviser in the Prime Minister's Office. He ended his political career as a Deputy Minister in the Ministry of Oil and Energy. He moved into business and became Finance Director of Aker, originally a shipbuilder, which was converted into a successful offshore contractor during the 1980s. In 1987 he was invited to join the supervisory board of Statoil. He has been Chief Executive Officer of Statoil since 1988.

by Anne Leer

SCREEN SOCIETY

How much time do you spend every day in front of screens, be it your computer or your TV set? And how much more time do you have to spend doing things via screens in the future if we believe the prospects of the Wired World? I have two very different visions of that day in the future when society is completely wired. I can see a world where the screens are the enabling interfaces to doing things better – whether it is governing or servicing a nation, educating people, running a business, doing our shopping or living our lives. The contributors in this section all feed this vision and that is exciting and comforting. However, I also have another vision tempering my usual enthusiasm for the Wired World. I can also see a world where screens become agents of dislocation, isolating people from direct human contact and social interaction, providing excuses for poor management, delivering escapism from dealing with the real world, creating cultural mismatches and communication breakdowns. We must take care when we wire up our organizations that we do not automate things that should not be automated, that we use technology wisely and put people at the centre of what we do.

The following chapters draw a picture of the real, practical process of building the Information Society. We will visit UK's Trade and Industry Minister, Peter Mandelson and see how the UK Government is responding to the challenges of the Wired World. We will hook up to the wired mind of Dr James Martin, who will educate us on what it takes to build a cyber-corporation. We will spend some time with Sir John Daniel, the Vice Chancellor of the Open University who will explain how a single university can effectively educate 250,000 students on-line. And we will travel north to see an example of how a large international organization is aiming to use the company's network to gain competitive advantage. The Chief Executive of Statoil, Harald Norvik will tell us about the company's investment in a multimedia network and how it works with strategic partners to create an effective learning zone for employees and their families.

Peter Mandelson, in line with Prime Minister Tony Blair's foreword, echoes the UK Government's strong belief in the benefits of the Wired World and in the strategic importance of ICT in building a competitive economy. Mandelson is quick to point out that there is no room for complacency. The European digital industries are not as productive as their US counterparts. In 1998, only 13 per cent of UK businesses with a web site used it for on-line trading, compared with 29 per cent in the US.

In his chapter he tells us that the UK Government's aim is for Britain to be the testbed for digital products and services in Europe, giving UK consumers and business early access to them. Mandelson points out how the government itself can be a model user and an early adopter of electronic commerce and other wired applications. He says, in the UK the target is for 90 per cent of central government's routine purchases of goods to be made electronically by 2001, and for 25 per cent of government services to be available electronically by 2002. The ambitious political agenda is to transform the UK into the world's foremost learning economy. Schools, libraries, colleges and universities are being linked up through the UK's National Grid for Learning. Business organizations and education providers are being linked up through the University for Industry initiative.

Mandelson sees the role of governments as absolutely crucial in terms of dealing with the barriers and market failures, which prevent take-up of digital products and services. He raises a series of key questions to do with developing the right policies and defining effective regulation for the so-called convergent industry. Do we need to move to a different kind of regulatory framework to facilitate growth in the networked economy, and if so, what shape would it take? Whatever the answer, both policy and regulation need to reflect the globalization of markets and economies. The aim of the UK Government is to regulate as little as possible – Mandelson believes in competition wherever possible and regulation only where necessary.

Dr James Martin is a pioneer in the business of enabling companies to make effective use of IT and communication networks. He has written a staggering 100 textbooks and works with companies around the world to find ways of improving organizational achievement and business performance. It is really good to hear such a great technology enthusiast say that what makes companies succeed is the quality of their people, not technology. He says technology itself is not a silver bullet, but in combination with people great things happen. Companies must take full advantage of technology if they want to compete in the future. In his chapter he explains why and how.

Like so many of the contributors in this book, Martin too refers to the massive process of rapid change that companies and individuals are being subjected to. The concepts of employment and education need to be different in the Wired World. Martin explains the job revolution, the disappearance of traditional notions of job security and describes the cyber-employees and employers of the future. He explains why education has become one of the most important issues for our economies and constant learning is essential for companies to remain competitive. He says the education revolution goes along with the technology revolution.

James Martin's chapter explains why Sir John Daniel is such a busy man these days. The demand for educational services and organizations like the Open University far outstrip the current ability to supply. Since the Open University was set up in 1965, its student base has grown from 25,000 to 250,000 people. The Open University has become what Sir Daniel calls a Mega-University. A quick count in 1998 showed ten other such Mega-Universities around the world enrolling around 2.5 million students at the time. In his chapter Sir Daniel describes just how enormous and complex the challenge of meeting the world's need for education is. Did you know that half of the world's population is under 20 years of age and that in some emerging economies that figure rises to three quarters of the population. He points out that higher education is in crisis even in the richest nations of the world, let alone the rest of the world. He argues that the only way we'll be able to educate the fast-growing numbers of students around the world at a sustainable cost is through the clever use of distance learning techniques and what he calls 'knowledge media', that is computing, telecommunications and learning sciences.

Statoil is an example of a company which recognizes the strategic importance of education and the need to invest in developing the skills and competence of its workforce. In 1996 Harald Norvik did something which really caught the world's attention. He sponsored the decision to give every member of staff the latest multimedia PC with an ISDN connection to the company network as well as the Internet, for installation in their homes provided they committed themselves to an IT training programme. Statoil has 17,000 members of staff in 28 countries – can you imagine the bill? In his chapter he will tell you all about it and whether or not he still thinks this was a good decision.

Clearly, if Statoil succeeds in this project, it has the potential to become a flagship example to business communities around the world. But it could also fail if management does not honour the original vision and commitment that was made. One problem for companies is that management changes and new leaders may come in who may not have the same understanding and ability to think beyond the immediate short term. Another problem is that if companies run into more difficult economic times with the consequent need to cut costs, education is often a vulnerable area and old-style managers may still see education as non-essential and a cutable expenditure. Whether or not the Statoil learning zone will materialize, it will be an excellent idea for other companies to build upon. ■

The Rt Hon
Peter Mandelson MP

Secretary of State for Trade and Industry

THE DIGITAL GOVERNMENT

We are living in a time of astonishing change, driven by technological and economic developments. Since the 1950s, automation and mainframe computers have underpinned nearly three decades of growth. In the 1980s, personal computers revolutionized the way we all work. In the 1990s, huge advances in computer power and its convergence with communications are continuing to spur growth.

For individuals, this convergence is bringing new ways of learning and communicating, changing how we carry out everyday tasks, such as shopping, and how we spend our leisure time. For businesses, it is changing working practices, opening up new markets, creating new products and new forms of distribution. Our aim is for Britain to be the test bed for digital products and services in Europe, giving UK consumers and businesses early access to them.

We start from a strong position. We have a top-quality skills base, world-class universities and a breadth and depth of intellectual capital that are the envy of many of our competitors. The UK also has a regulatory system that positively encourages innovation. The UK took the lead globally in introducing competition to the telecoms market. We now have over 125 licensed public telecommunications operators and competition between them is as developed as anywhere else in the world. Completion of the single market in telecoms throughout the European Union, which coincided with the start of the UK Presidency in January 1998, is a major step to improving the competitiveness of the whole European telecommunications industry. The UK continues to be at the leading edge, one of the few countries to abandon the idea that the local loop is a natural monopoly and setting the pace in Europe on standards for the third generation of mobile telephones. As a result, UK consumers have felt the benefits of greater choice, higher quality and reduced prices.

The way ahead

Although the UK is well placed to take advantage of the new Digital Age, there can be no room for complacency. Our digital industries are not as productive as their US counterparts, nor growing as fast. Constant effort is required if we are to succeed in markets that are driven by technological innovation and where the traditional business model can be turned on its head overnight.

There are plenty of examples where this has already happened. You only have to look at how mobile telephones transformed a previously unidentified demand into a mass market phenomenon or at the impact that telebanking and tele-insurance is having in those sectors. These are markets where innovation and entrepreneurial drive can take a business from start-up to global player in a matter of months, not years, and where the rate of change is exponential.

For the future, experts predict that Moore's Law – which states that computing power doubles every 18 months – looks set to hold true well into the next century. Internet providers estimate that the volume of Internet traffic doubles every 100 days, which is also the pace at which Amazon.com, the first Internet bookshop, doubled its turnover throughout 1997. Against this kind of background, businesses need to be constantly innovating if they are to succeed.

The same is true of nations. Government has to ask itself how it can hope to make an effective impact in such a fast-moving, dynamic and unpredictable global market. It is clear that our starting point has to be the marketplace itself. Underlying all the change and the leaps in technological innovation, there remain the three constants of any market – demand, supply and a framework within which these two factors can interact.

The UK's aim is to excel in all three – to have individual and business consumers who can provide strong and sophisticated demand for digital products and services; a supply sector that is innovative, dynamic and growing; and a market framework that both empowers consumers and encourages competition and innovation from the industries that serve them.

A world-class regulatory system

The role of government is most direct and influential in establishing and maintaining the regulatory framework. We are committed to keeping the UK's regulatory framework up to date – especially in the light of the convergence of telecoms, broadcasting and the other IT industries – which poses real challenges to our current system. There are several complex questions we will need to address, including the following:

■ How can we effectively regulate a converging industry using regulations and regulators designed for separate, distinct sectors? Should we move to a different type of regulatory framework and, if so, what shape should that take?

- How can we develop the international framework of intellectual property rights to protect adequately the intangible assets that will be the key drivers of the digital age?
- What are the implications of the digital economy for competition policy?
- How can we ensure that consumers are confident that the on-line world is as secure and safe a place for them to make purchases as the domestic high street?

Convergence is still at a relatively early stage, and the speed at which it will progress and the precise shape it will take are still unclear. What is clear is that the process is already underway and will continue apace. We also need to know more about the long-term implications of convergence for the wider economy if we are to exploit it to the full. The Future Unit in my department has recently published a report on this subject that is intended to be thought-provoking and to stimulate debate.

However, we can already set out four key regulatory principles that we need to apply if we are to meet the challenges of convergence. First, the regulatory framework should provide businesses with the clarity and certainty they need in order to invest in new infrastructure and services. Second, it must have the flexibility to evolve with technological and business change, and with new demands as they emerge in the marketplace, so that it does not stifle innovation. Governments cannot and should not attempt to second-guess the market, so it is vital that the regulatory framework can adapt to change. Third, the framework needs to be coherent, eliminating any gaps, overlaps and anomalies wherever possible. Finally, regulation must be enforce-able in a world where millions of transactions can take place instantaneously, and where the people involved could be anywhere in the world.

The UK will work with our European and international partners to ensure that these principles apply to all regulations affecting the digital economy. Above all, we will work to ensure that we regulate only where absolutely necessary and then with the lightest touch possible. To do otherwise risks suffocating rather than stimulating innovation. I believe in competition wherever possible and regulation only where necessary.

There will also be cases where we should be looking to empower the individual con-sumer by means of technology itself. Ratings systems and content filters, for example, may give parents the power to control the legal content to which their children have access on the Internet. The UK's Internet Watch Foundation is leading work to develop an internationally acceptable ratings system for Internet material, and their work is to be applauded. Similarly, the ability of consumers to control who has access to information about their purchasing preferences, via their own 'personal intelligent agents', may provide the key in the longer term to some major data protection issues.

Electronic commerce has the potential to become a huge driver of wealth creation. It was 38 years before radio users numbered 50 million; it has only taken 4 years to attract the same number to the Internet. However, there are barriers to be overcome before the full potential of electronic commerce can be realized. Some are technologi-cal, and many businesses are investing heavily in finding ways to overcome them.

Others are the responsibility of government, whether alone or in partnership with the private and not-for-profit sectors. These include ensuring adequate protection for intellectual property rights, the role of government as model user and early adopter of the technologies (especially through government procurement), the tax system, data protection, consumer protection and the legitimacy of electronic agreements. The potential prize for success in electronic commerce is enormous, but only if we get the regulatory framework right, both nationally and internationally. To help achieve this, we will be bringing forward legislation to promote the safe and successful growth of electronic commerce. During the UK Presidency, we also secured the adoption of a new mechanism that will require all Member States to submit any proposed legislation on Information Society services to collective scrutiny, to ensure that it does not create an unjustified barrier to electronic trade within the EU. This is an important step towards removing barriers to electronic commerce.

Strong and sophisticated demand

While the regulatory environment is essential, it is demand from informed and motivated customers that is the key to a dynamic market.

As Bill Gates argues in *The Road Ahead* (with Nathan Myhrcold and Peter Rinearson, rev edn, Penguin Books, 1996), it looks unlikely that a digital mass market will emerge on the back of a single killer application. Instead, for some years now, we have been seeing a steady increase in demand for a range of digital products and services. At some point, these incremental increases in supply and demand will explode into sudden, dramatic change – the creation of a true mass market. Such a market will be created by consumers and businesses, not politicians. Government, though, can help to move the process along.

> The potential prize for success in electronic commerce is enormous, but only if we get the regulatory framework right, both nationally and internationally.

Our most crucial responsibilities are for education and skills. In the knowledge-driven digital economy of the twenty-first century, a nation's key sustainable source of competitive advantage will be its people. That is why we are committed to transforming the UK into the world's foremost learning economy. We are linking up all schools, libraries, colleges and universities via the National Grid for Learning. Only a fifth were connected when we took over, but they all will be by 2002. We have already met our pledge that schools will be connected for free and pay-discounted call rates. We have also launched a £230 million programme so that all teachers who want training in IT – not just in how to use it, but how to use it to teach – are able to receive it. Also, the University for Industry we are creating will be capable of using IT to serve 2.5 million people and businesses with distance learning, focusing on IT skills.

We also need to make the best possible use of the Government's own market power. To this end, we want 90 per cent of central government's routine purchases of goods to be made electronically by 2001, and for 25 per cent of government services to be available electronically by 2002.

Government must tackle the barriers and market failures that prevent take-up of digital products and services. The major barriers are essentially cultural. Over a third of people in the UK say that they cannot see the benefits of digital technologies, more than twice as many as in the US. Moreover, only 49 per cent of UK employees work for firms with Internet access, compared with 73 per cent in Japan. Only 13 per cent of UK businesses with a web site use it for on-line trading, compared to 29 per cent in the US. This is a real threat to UK competitiveness that we are already addressing.

The DTI has 3000 IT for All access sites where members of the public new to IT can get hands-on experience in public places, such as libraries. Under the Government's Information Society Initiative's Programme for Business, we are rolling out a national network of local support centres aimed at giving Small and Medium-sized Enterprises (SMEs) impartial, expert advice. We are looking at how we can better market these initiatives and develop new and innovative ways to reach businesses, in particular SMEs. We aim to ensure that, by the end of this Parliament, the UK is leading demand for digital technologies from both businesses and individuals.

Dynamic supply industries

If we are to stimulate this demand, the Information and Communication Technology (ICT) supply industries need to anticipate and meet it, as well as playing a key part in generating it. The importance of these industries to the UK is enormous, with output of £90 billion, accounting for over 6 per cent of our Gross Domestic Product and directly employing nearly one million people. Furthermore, this is an industry that has frequently posted growth rates in excess of 10 per cent per annum in recent years. My goal is to ensure that this growth rate is maintained and improved, by government and business working together.

First on this agenda is skills. The converging industries represent a truly knowledge-based sector, which is dependent on advances in science and technology, both in academia and industry. This requires a strong skills base – in R&D, design, manufacture, customer services and a host of other areas. We will ensure that the Government's new initiatives on skills – the University for Industry and the Skills Task Force, to take but two examples – deliver results of real benefit to this vital sector. In particular, we need to turn around the UK's poor track record on electronics engineering, where the number of graduates has fallen in recent years. The total output of 2500 new graduates a year is simply not enough for an industry that employs over 260,000.

Second, together with business, we must support the development of networks to support knowledge-based industries. The Silicon Valley experience demonstrates that a healthy IT, electronics and communications sector thrives best when there are close links, formal and informal, between innovative companies, the science base, financial and other institutions. In the UK, we have the beginning of such networks, in particular in Cambridge, on the M4 Corridor and in Central Scotland, but we need to enhance them. In particular, business and government must work together to ensure that innovative SMEs have easy access to the mentoring, finance and any other form of practical assistance they need.

The third essential element is the effective transfer of knowledge. UK universities and companies do excellent research, but, all too often, it is exploited either overseas or not at all. The Government's comprehensive spending review has freed up welcome resources to invest in the UK's much neglected science base. We must ensure that this investment is exploited to the benefit of UK industry, for example, by giving universities greater incentives to collaborate with businesses; by ensuring that businesses have the skills and complementary assets

> ... business and government must work together to ensure that innovative SMEs have easy access to ... any ... form of practical assistance they need.

needed to transform scientific knowledge into successful innovations; and by enhancing the networks within which universities and businesses can come together.

Conclusion

This Government has a clear vision of the future in which the UK is the leading digital economy in Europe and a leading player worldwide. We will work with business to achieve that vision. I have set out targets against which our joint success can be assessed:

- achieving global recognition for the UK as providing the best environment worldwide for business to trade electronically
- ensuring that the UK leads in the use of digital technologies
- ensuring real improvements in the growth rate of the ICT sector in the UK, to see that we outperform our competitors.

I cannot guarantee that we will meet these targets. I *can* give my personal guarantee that the Government side of the partnership does its utmost to ensure that we will. ■

Dr James Martin

Business and technology consultant, and author

BUILDING THE CYBER-CORPORATION

The term reengineering may be inappropriate applied to business processes because the processes were never 'engineered' in the first place. They grew like ivy on a tree with a succession of changes motivated by internal economies of scale, empire building, corporate politics, computer software, tradition, geographical distance, use of unskilled people, and rarely a focus on how to please the customer.

Dr James Martin (Amacom,1996) *Cybercorp*

To position themselves for the future, companies must change the way they view their industry, competitors and selves. Companies can no longer afford the luxury of having inefficient and inflexible business operations. Businesses must react faster to the changes in the marketplace than ever before. No longer can the manager in one business unit clean up after the manager in another functional unit up the line.

To really compete in the future, companies need to have every advantage possible by taking advantage of all that technology has to offer. However, technology alone, in and of itself, is not a silver bullet. A company's people must use technology in the correct ways using straightforward processes. Its culture must support the innovation and harmonious change brought about by the integration of the technology into the everyday lives of the employees, commerce partners and customers. To achieve, companies must think 'Cybercorp' to reflect the characteristics and personality that a company needs to take on to be successful in the future.

Since the 1970s, employment growth shifted from manufacturing to the services and IT industries. As factory jobs went overseas, businesses hired a new type of employee – the knowledge worker. Instead of machine tools and rivet guns, knowledge workers used data warehouses and spreadsheets. Modern economies avoid using factories and cheap labour as their main means of production. Instead, they use information and knowledge – the digital bits and bytes of the new Information Age.

Figures show that two thirds of the United States' economic output comes from the services and IT industries. Only a third is attributable to traditional manufacturing industries ('Why Are We So Afraid of Growth', *Business Week*, 19 May 1994).

This change is quickening. As corporations adjust to the new marketplace, they shed the trappings of the industrial age. The massive corporate layoffs of recent years tell the tale. The jobs that disappeared were not on the factory floor or in the field, they were in the main office. Thousands of white-collar positions have gone – made redundant by advances in IT and communications.

The global job transition

Global corporations are slowly and painfully transforming themselves from 'old world' businesses to 'new world' businesses. Becoming a cyber-corporation means optimizing corporations for the information age and is characterized by massive automation, fluid organizational structures, dynamic intercorporate relationships using worldwide computer networks, electronic reaction times, virtual operations and intense global competition. Corporations must be designed for rapid change, continual learning and constant evolution and growth.

The growth and development of existing corporations will spark momentous change. The concept of employment will change dramatically, requiring new patterns of management, new organizational structures and new partnerships between humans and technology. When it has run its course, the technology revolution will have had a much greater effect on business and society than did the Industrial Revolution, and technology is driving this momentous change.

The global job market

Most corporations understand that, to be successful, they need the right types of employees. Cyber-corporations realize most employees can contribute much more than they have in the past and, in the process, make their jobs more exciting, enjoyable and fulfilling.

This 'jobs revolution' is based on the assumption that there is a horrifying waste of human potential in most corporations. Lower level employees who could be creative and productive spend their time on boring, repetitive tasks and quickly become uninterested in producing a quality product or providing excellent customer service. A Cybercorp must have process methodologies and extensive training courses that help corporations transform the skills of their employees.

The jobs revolution is closely interwoven with the IT revolution – changes in one support and feed the other. As cyber-corporations learn how to empower employees, make them more creative and build high-performance teams, IT helps put this new human capability to productive use. A recent survey of fast-growing small businesses by Coopers & Lybrand found that the average revenue per employee in companies with a high use of computers was 2.5 times higher than in companies showing limited use of computers ('Mom and Pop Go High Tech', *Business Week*, 21 November 1994). In order to maintain a competitive advantage, corporations require flexible, adaptive employees who can learn quickly and take advantage of IT.

A new paradigm for business education

There is a growing need for education and training in businesses that reflects the realities of the technology revolution. Most advanced corporations globally require employees to understand how to run a business, not function in a bloated corporate hierarchy. Employees must be computer literate, able to quickly adapt to changing markets and able to learn continuously. Business schools and training programmes must change their curriculums in order to produce the next generation of employees who can work and thrive in growing economies.

It is clear that most current educational systems cannot produce the calibre of employees competitive economies require for success. According to the National Education Goals Panel, an independent agency created in 1990 to assess and report on state and national progress towards achieving the National Education Goals, it was found that 84 per cent of twelfth-grade students cannot meet suggested standards in mathematics. The panel also reported that 88 per cent of twelfth-grade students could not craft a well-developed essay on a given subject ('What Kids Will Have to Know', *US News and World Report, March 1996*).

The concern about the quality of future employees was voiced during the opening plenary session of the 1996 National Education Summit – a gathering of educators, governors and business leaders to encourage the creation and enforcement of educational standards. In his opening remarks, the host, Lou Gerstner, Chairman and CEO of IBM, stressed the impact a poorly educated workforce has on a company. While businesses can educate and train employees how to create, market and distribute products, Gerstner stated 'What is killing us is having to teach them to read and to compute and to communicate and to think.' This thinking is mirrored by famed MIT economist Lester Thoreau, who estimates only 20 per cent of adults share the work skills or education to compete in the global marketplace.

> **... only 20 per cent of adults share work skills or education to complete in the global marketplace.**

A cyber-corporation takes a much more prominent role in the education of future employees and its customers. It is in a business' own self-interest to partner with other corporations to create new educational centres to prepare students and employees for the business realities of the information age.

The new global employment deal

Some of the changes the effects technology will bring about on Asian business and the economy can be felt already. Job security is a quaint concept of the industrial age.

Companies need to be flexible and adaptive, skills needed today might be obsolete tomorrow – that is why the cyber-corporation specializes in skills transfer. The days of annual pay rises based on seniority are gone. A Cybercorp compensates employees based on their contributions – or, more likely, their team's contributions – to the bottom line. According to a 1993 survey of 300 large corporations by the Association for Quality and Participation – a Cincinnati, Ohio-based professional group – 74 per cent of large employers have begun to dismantle their traditional pay systems ('The Wage Squeeze', *Business Week*, 17 July 1995). The use of temporary workers to augment or replace full-time workers has risen 50 per cent since 1990.

Most corporations are working according to a new deal for employment. They tell prospective employees, in effect, 'There is good news and bad news. The bad news is that your promotion prospects are low because our old hierarchy is gone. We cannot guarantee regular pay increases. You will have no job security. We have to be free to downsize, to lay off people whose skills are no longer needed, and to be able to trim back when business is bad. The good news is that this is an exciting place to work.'

Companies will train employees to do interesting jobs and coach them to become members of empowered teams – an approach that corporations must initiate and deliver on consistently. Employees' pay will be related to results, and each individual can earn big money if they add substantial value to the organization. Future corporations have to constantly challenge employees to find better ways to do their jobs, and will need to provide the resources they need to pursue that challenge. The cyber-corporation is a learning corporation, and the expectations are for individuals to constantly learn and help others learn. As employees learn more, they will become more valuable. In basic terms, the new employment deal says, 'You own your own employability. You are responsible.'

The cyber-employee

Cybercorp policies requires employees who can operate in completely new environments. A cyber-corporation recognizes that the knowledge and skills of their employees are their key resources. They look for individuals who are willing to learn, innovative, challenge the status quo and who can work in empowered teams.

Cyber-employees, in return, require a fundamentally different education and training. Gone is the emphasis on functioning in a corporate hierarchy – in this model, employees work in empowered teams. Gone is the emphasis on formalized higher education alone – employees must learn continually, gaining from the experience and actions of others. Gone is the emphasis on doing things 'because they've always been done that way' – employees must be flexible and able to continually change and adapt to new circumstances. Educating the global marketplace for the realities of the Industrial Revolution will be a challenge.

What transforms the old-world corporations into Cyber-corporations?

The value of knowledge

A key distinction of the Cybercorp is the recognition that information and knowledge are valuable. Knowledge is money. Cybercorps make every effort to use the knowledge, skills and experience of their employees to the fullest extent possible – as well as transfer that knowledge to their clients' employees. They construct a 'knowledge infrastructure' to capture, store and disseminate the skills and knowledge of cyber-employees. Companies realize it is more productive to learn from their experiences and mistakes than to recreate the wheel.

Enterprise redesign

Corporations also realize that they must redesign the business processes of their enterprises. Old ways of doing things should be scrapped. Outdated processes and useless hierarchies should be discarded. A detailed study at Ernst & Young's Centre for Information Technology found that 'in many companies the key processes were last "designed" (to the degree they were designed at all) well before the rise of information technology.' Computers and technology were used to automate ancient processes and fit into corporate structures designed in the Industrial Age. The processes and structures in most corporations were created before today's understanding of cross-functional teams, virtual operations and market demands for fast, fluid, flexible change. Many enterprises are still designed for an era of top-down hierarchical management, division of labour, inflexible mass production and rigid procedures.

> Corporations realize that there is a huge gap between the actual contributions of employees and their potential contributions. Cyber-employees are responsible for delivering results, not tasks.

By redesigning their processes, corporations demand new management structures that are intricately linked to IT. Most multinational companies know that bureaucracy slows down business processes, hinders the open exchange of information and hinders competitiveness. The goal of enterprise redesign is to tear down the boundaries that separate departments from interacting with each other and remove the barriers that isolate employees from their customers.

By means of enterprise redesign, a Cybercorp creates customer-focused value streams that replace vertical silos. Enterprise redesign makes it possible for companies to empower their employees in functional teams, freeing them from the burdens and restrictions of hierarchies.

Maximizing employees' potential

Corporations realize there is a huge gap between the *actual* contributions of employees and their *potential* contributions. They strive to maximize the contributions of all their employees by empowering them to take action, solve problems and add value wherever possible. Cyber-employees are responsible for delivering results, not tasks.

Hewlett-Packard (HP) gave its engineers the task of finding out how the defect rate in soldered connections could be reduced. The engineers succeeded in reducing the defect rate from 4 to 2 defects for every 1000 connections. Later, HP charged its production line workers with the same task. The workers made many small changes to the production process and eventually cut the defect rate a thousandfold, to fewer than two defects in every million connections. Cybercorps teach people to work smarter, not harder. They take advantage of the knowledge and experience of everyone. All employees are encouraged to use their minds to the fullest.

Constant learning

Traditional corporations must understand that, in order to remain competitive, they must strive to develop their human potential as fast as the potential of technology grows. In an environment of constant change and global competition, these corporations must challenge their employees to learn and insist on the steepest possible learning curves.

As Arie de Geus, the former head of planning for Shell, once remarked, the only sustainable competitive advantage a corporation has is its ability to learn faster than its competition. Corporations must be able capture and use the knowledge of its employees effectively. An increase in a company's productivity due to the introduction of technology typically follows a long gestation period where employees struggle to master unfamiliar skills and productivity temporarily dips ('Riding High', *Business Week*, 9 October 1995).

This relationship between innovation and productivity can be charted with an S-shaped curve. When critical advances in electricity were made in the 1870s and 1880s, there was not a corresponding increase in productivity. It took until the early 1900s for electricity to be fully adopted and its productivity enhancement realized. With multiple technologies – such as computers and communications – feeding off each other, it is crucial for corporations that they ensure employees learn as much as possible in as short a time as possible ('Why Are We So Afraid of Growth?', *Business Week*, 16 May 1994).

Without continual learning, the current global business community will lose its competitiveness. Good ideas or marginal productivity enhancements can be quickly copied and used by other corporations. Improvements in business processes only produce short-term competitive advantages. To remain competitive, companies must emphasize making their corporations learning laboratories.

Learning laboratories

For competitive corporations, the enterprise as a learning laboratory is the highest development of their employees' potential – and their key to competitiveness. In a learning laboratory, every employee is part of the R&D process. Cyber-corporations encourage employees to experiment, to find new ways to add value.

By constantly experimenting, corporations exposed to industry-proven methodologies are able to produce not incremental improvement, but breakthroughs. Experimentation is the only way to learn something fundamentally new and establish a lasting competitive advantage. The more experimentation that takes place, the more opportunities a global corporation has to improve its business. Experiments increase the speed of enterprise innovation.

An excellent example of a learning laboratory is Chaparral Steel in Midlothian, Texas. From its beginning, Chaparral was a learning laboratory, encouraging research and experimentation at all levels.

At a time when US steel productivity lagged behind Japan and Germany, Chaparral set out to make large structural I-beams for about half the cost of other steel mills. Endless experimentation went on in Chaparral to increase the efficiency of the process of casting these large beams. Employees were empowered to experiment and given the resources they required to do so.

By 1990, Chaparral succeeded. While Japan required an average of 5.6 worker hours per rolled ton of steel and Germany averaged 5.7, Chaparral's productivity was an astonishingly low 1.5. Constant experimentation helped Chaparral to make not just a marginal improvement in productivity, but a breakthrough.

To be effective, cybercorps create a 'knowledge infrastructure' to capture the knowledge and experience of their workers. Not only must small and multinational corporations be able to capture and store this valuable information, they must be able to disseminate it to their employees. Corporations around the world are learning the value of such experience warehouses, made possible with groupware and Intranets.

Preparing for the competitive economy
Education for the cyber-employee

For global corporations to succeed, they need employees who can run a business, not function in a corporate hierarchy. Companies require employees that have practical business knowledge about marketing, finance, distribution and so on. Beyond the basics of reading, writing and arithmetic, most employees will need to understand technology, be computer literate and able to communicate well and function in teams. Employees need to understand that their business education will never be 'complete' – rather, it will be continual.

The Cybercorp clearly communicates the types and levels of skills needed in their employees to meet the workforce requirements of the next century. A 1996 poll on school standards conducted by *US News and World Report* supported this statement, finding that 58 per cent of adult Americans believe employers should screen potential job candidates based on their exams and school grades (*US News and World Report* School Standards Poll, conducted by the Tarrance Group and Lake Research, 16–18 March 1996).

As students, employees must be prepared for the new employment deal. A practising Cybercorp helps its customers understand that they will be in charge of their own future and their own potential. They will be working in a constantly evolving business world where they will be expected to overcome challenges, cope with adversity and continue to learn.

Global education revolution

This means there should be a hue and cry for an educational revolution that goes along with the technology revolution. The work experience and foundation of employees determines the value and level of contribution they can make to their companies and to the overall economy.

Employees of competitive corporations will need to be much more involved than their Industrial Age counterparts. In order to be involved, they have to have the tools and proper educational background to think, function, learn and grow in a constantly changing business environment.

It is in the self-interest of companies everywhere for them to get involved with the educational system today. Without proper knowledge transfer, education and training, most companies will not be able to find the types of employees they need.

As companies transform themselves into corporations armed for global competition, the need for education and training will increase. Already, corporations spend large amounts of money on education and ongoing training for their employees. According to the Committee for Economic Development, a Washington, DC-based think tank, formal company training has increased 45 per cent from 1984 to 1993 ('Riding High', *Business Week*, 9 October 1995). The research firm International Data Corporation (IDC) reported that, in 1995, the worldwide IT training and education market stood at $13 billion, and was expected to grow to $22 billion by 1999.

> The rigid structures and processes of Industrial Age businesses are slowly giving way to the agile and flexible operations of Information Age companies.

Most global corporations require employees who can think and learn, who can adapt to the constant change they will face. It is critical that companies transfer these skills and attitudes instilled in the next generation of employees.

The role of technology in education

IT will play a central role in the education and training of future employees. The technology already exists to make education exciting and easy. By means of CD-ROMs, Computer-Based Training (CBT), remote education and virtual reality, future cyberemployees can benefit from the experiences and failures of today's corporations.

Technology will continue to have a huge impact on education, enabling students to learn at their own pace and explore topics that interest them. The market for technology products is vast. Already, companies are realizing the latent demand for educational products.

Conclusion

The business world of today is in the midst of a great transition. The rigid structures and processes of Industrial Age businesses are slowly giving way to the agile and flexible operations of Information Age companies. As global corporations change, so will their employment needs.

Employees must be highly educated and willing to learn and change constantly. These new skill sets will require a fundamentally new way to educate and train people – one that focuses on preparing students for a work world that is competitive, demanding and ever-evolving.

The same IT that made current successful businesses thrive will also help train and educate new workers. While corporations are now demanding more from their employees, adopting the cybercorp principles will offer business the promise of transfer of knowledge and skills to future employees and customers, providing a challenge and fulfilment rarely achieved today anywhere else in the world. ■

Sir John Daniel

Vice Chancellor, The Open University

THE RISE OF THE MEGA-UNIVERSITY

The technological turn in higher education

Higher education is in crisis in much of the world. What is the nature of the crisis and how can we resolve it? In Chinese lettering, the ideogram for 'crisis' is made by combining the signs for 'danger' and 'opportunity' – a tension that contemporary universities experience acutely. They often fail to live up to the hopes of the communities that support them. However, those same communities look to their universities for leadership in the knowledge revolution that is changing the world.

Technology – which has already had a transforming impact on many areas of human endeavour – is key to the renewal of higher education. The term 'knowledge media' has been coined for the new technologies emerging from the convergence of computing, telecommunications and learning sciences. It is a useful term – better than 'multimedia' or 'the information superhighway' – because it reminds us that these technologies mediate knowledge in ways not previously possible. Universities sense, almost instinctively, that the knowledge media are different. They suspect that the knowledge media do have radical implications for academic work.

Already the world's mega-universities have used technology to dramatic effect in changing the assumptions of higher education. Their methods are leading all universities into the wired world of the knowledge media, even in those countries where the wires have not yet been laid.

The aim of this chapter is to draw on the experience of the mega-universities to show how all universities can best use technology (meaning both systems and devices) to cope with the crises they face.

Universities in triple crisis

The ingredients of the crisis are:

- access
- cost
- flexibility.

These ingredients blend differently as you move around the globe. In the developing countries there is a crisis of access. At the end of the millennium in which the idea of the university has blossomed, population growth is outpacing the world's capacity to give people access to universities. Half the world's population is now under 20, and the figure rises to nearly three quarters in countries such as South Africa and Palestine. Our traditional concept of the campus university will deny higher education to nearly all these youngsters. We require one large, new campus to open every week, somewhere in the developing world, just to keep participation rates constant. New universities are *not* being created at this rate because countries cannot afford to build and staff them.

That is the second strand of the crisis. The traditional model of the university costs too much and its lack of affordability is not just a problem for the developing world. In most of the industrialized world, universities real costs have risen steadily for many years. For an American family today, the cost of sending a child to college – adding up tuition, room and board – is around 15 per cent of median family income for a public university and 40 per cent for a private one. Fifteen years ago, both percentages were only two thirds of today's levels. Americans are naturally asking whether or not this considerable personal investment in higher education represents value for money. In countries where the State bears most, or a proportion, of the costs of higher education, governments are asking the same question.

A lesson of this century is that any industry where costs increase faster than inflation over a long period is heading for trouble – either for complete collapse or unpleasant upheavals. If universities wish to avoid such turmoil, they must exorcise their hang-ups about reducing costs and accept the modern definition of quality as fitness for purpose at minimum cost to society.

> **The traditional model of the university costs too much and its lack of affordability is not just a problem for the developing world.**

The third strand of the academic crisis is a lack of flexibility. Are universities teaching the range of knowledge and skills that students need? Do our teaching methods match the habits of today's learners? Are universities confident about the quality of what they do? Bluntly, is the traditional campus model of the university appropriate in this era of lifelong learning?

Keys to competitive advantage

Fears that traditional universities will wither as commercial providers move into their territory are overdone. The bedrock function of universities is to inspire in their students that attitude of systematic scepticism known as the academic mode of thinking. Unlike the ideological mode of thinking, which starts from received dogma and works downwards, the academic mode of thinking starts with the evidence and argues its way to hypotheses that can be tested. The intellectual climate and egalitarian attitudes of systematic scepticism are unlikely to be congenial to the commercial sector.

However, to their core function of transforming knowledge and practice, universities have accreted a wider and simpler mission of transmitting standard skills and accepted orthodoxy to the next generation. This is a much more attractive activity for the private sector, which is already competing successfully with public universities in teaching uncontroversial skills and knowledge in areas such as business management and IT.

Enhancing competitive advantage in the face of such threats must be a central purpose of university renewal, and Michael Porter's analysis is apposite here. His approach to competitive advantage begins with the notion of creating value for buyers and lists three strategies for doing this:

■ lower costs
■ differentiate
■ focus on a niche market.

Clearly, success in these strategies in higher education would address some or all of the challenges of access, cost and flexibility. Porter also stresses that technology plays a major role in competition as a result of its effect on an industry as a whole. The higher education industry is no exception.

Technology and university renewal

Most attempts to use technology to enhance the competitiveness of universities miss the major opportunity for renewal by starting from a narrow definition of technology focused on devices. In contrast, the Open University teaches its students to define technology as 'the application of scientific and other organized knowledge to practical tasks by organizations consisting of people and machines'. This broader definition is much more helpful because it reminds us that:

■ there is more to technology than applied science – non-scientific knowledge (design, managerial, craft, tacit) is involved
■ technology is about practical tasks – as compared with science, which is mainly about understanding)
■ technology always involves people (social systems) as well as hardware.

This definition attaches as much importance to the softer aspects of technology (rules, systems and approaches to problems) as to the burgeoning array of hardware and software that the term more commonly evokes. Attention to systems and approaches is the key to the successful use of technology in university renewal. In particular, the combination of the notion of a learning system with the approach known as 'distance education' has proved to be revolutionary.

The rise of the mega-universities

By a nice coincidence, the seeds of the technological revolution in higher education were planted in 1969 shortly after the Apollo astronauts returned from the first landing on the Moon. That week, an inauguration ceremony was held to grant a Royal Charter to the Open University. In his address, the Chancellor, Lord Crowther, gave the new institution an ambitious and inspiring mission: 'to be open as to people, open as to places, open as to methods and open as to ideas'. The Royal Charter made it clear that the Open University was committed to new technology. Article 3 states, 'The objects of the University shall be the advancement and dissemination of learning and knowledge by teaching and research, by a diversity of means such as broadcasting and technological devices appropriate to higher education, by correspondence tuition, residential courses and seminars and in other relevant ways.'

Two years later, in 1971, the first cohort of 25,000 students began their studies with the Open University, and the revolution gained pace. A quarter of a century later, the Open University reaches nearly 250,000 people. Furthermore, there are now 10 other similar mega-universities around the world that enrol well over 2,500,000 students between them. Technology is being used successfully to expand access, cut costs and give students the flexibility that the era of lifelong learning requires.

I shall first outline the development of these mega-universities and then examine how the Open University's successful distance learning system has equipped it to lead academe into the Wired World.

The term 'mega-university' designates a unitary university that operates largely at a distance and enrols over 100,000 students in degree-credit courses. Table 1 lists the 11 universities presently covered by this definition. Several other open universities in Asia are likely to join the group in the next few years.

The mega-universities have addressed the challenges of access, cost and flexibility in a striking manner. Those listed in Table 1 now enrol over 3 million students between them. Each mega-university has made a major contribution to the expansion of its country's higher education system. The annual cost per student across all the mega-universities averages out at less than $400, compared to over $10,000 for conventional universities in the UK and the USA. When the cost per student at each mega-university is expressed as a percentage of the average cost for all the other universities in the same country, the figures fall in the 10–60 per cent range. This shows that the mega-universities have had a real impact on cutting costs. Finally, because they operate at a distance, they allow students much greater flexibility than campus universities in choosing the time and place of study.

The mega-universities are successful because they have established large distance learning systems. There are two approaches to distance learning. The first – which was adopted by the China TV University system and was fashionable for a time in the US – uses telecommunications to carry a live lecture to a set of remote classrooms.

Table 1 The mega-universities: basic data

Country	Name of institution	Est.	Students
China	China TV University System	1979	600,000
France	Centre National d'Enseignement à Distance	1939	185,000
India	Indira Gandhi National Open University	1985	350,000
Indonesia	Universitas Terbuka	1984	350,000
Iran	Payame Noor University	1987	120,000
Korea	Korea National Open University	1982[1]	200,000
South Africa	University of South Africa	1873[2]	130,000
Spain	Universidad Nacional de Educación a Distancia	1972	110,000
Thailand	Sukhothai Thammathirat Open University	1978	220,000
Turkey	Anadolu University	1982	600,000
United Kingdom	The Open University	1969	160,000

Notes:
1. As the Korea Air and Correspondence University.
2. As the University of the Cape of Good Hope.

This is a teacher-centred approach directed at groups and uses communications technology in a synchronous manner.

The second approach – used by all the other mega-universities – relies on a mix of media to bring the university to the students' homes. It is a student-centred approach directed at individuals and uses communications media in an asynchronous manner.

Comparison of the two approaches shows that the second approach provides a more powerful response to the challenges of access, cost and flexibility. It allows the process of teaching and learning to be reorganized in a way that allows division of labour, economies of scale, and robust quality assurance. Although the wired world now allows us to blend both approaches, it strongly reinforces the individually directed, asynchronous approach that is the essence of the World Wide Web. Reviewing the experience of the leading mega-university – the Open University – gives pointers to the future of distance education in the wired world.

The Open University – its mission and methods

The Open University is the world's leading example of a learning system that successfully combines scale, access, quality and knowledge. On the way, it has acquired unparalleled expertise in learning.

Scale is 160,000 students in degree-credit programmes and nearly 100,000 more in other educational and vocational programmes. Access means a flexible and efficient

Table 2 The mega-universities

Abbreviated name	Students in degree programmes	Annual intake	Graduates per year	Budget $ million	% of budget from[5]		Unit cost[6]	Academic staff		Total staff
					Fees	Grants		full-time	part-time	full-time
CTVU	530,000[1]	77,000	101,000	1.2[4]	0	75	40	18,000	13,000	43,000
CNED	184,614[1]	184,614	28,000	56	60	30	50	1,800	3,000	3,000
IGNOU	242,000[2]	91,000	9,250	10	42	58	35	232	13,420	1,129
UT	353,000[2]	110,000	28,000	21	70	30	15	791	5,000	1,492
PNU	117,000[2]	34,950	7,563	13.3	87	13	25	499	3,165	2,169
KNOU	210,578[3]	100,000	11,000	79	64	36	5	176	2,670	670
UNISA	130,000[2]	60,000	10,000	128	39	60	50	1,348	1,964	3,437
UNED	110,000[2]	31,000	2,753	129	60	40	40	1,000	3,600	2,023
STOU	216,800[2]	103,130	12,583	46	73.5	26.5	30	429	3,108	1,900
AU	577,804[2]	106,785	26,321	30[7]	76	6	10	579	680	498[7]
UKOU	157,450[2]	50,000	18,359	300	31	60	50	815	7,376	3,312

Notes:

1. 1994 figure.
2. 1995 figure.
3. 1996 figure.
4. Central (CCRTVU) unit only.
5. Student fees or government grants.
6. Unit cost per student as percentage of average for other universities in the country (approximately).
7. Open education faculty only (full-time academic staff figure for whole university).

learning system that has been consistently successful in taking people with weak educational backgrounds through to completion of a degree. Quality is shown in national assessments of teaching quality where the Open University ranks 10 out of 101 UK universities for the excellence of its programmes. Knowledge is central to the whole enterprise because, by bringing teams of faculty and specialists together for each course, academic paradigms are constantly driven forward. How successfully, though, has the Open University been in fulfilling its mission of being open to people, places, methods and ideas?

To make itself open to people, the Open University removed all academic prerequisites for entry as an undergraduate. In 1998, students without the conventional entry qualifications for UK universities accounted for a third of all new graduates of the Open University. This supported the conviction that, with proper learning systems, access to success in higher education can be greatly expanded.

In the spirit of openness to places, the Open University has become an increasingly international institution. In 1998, more than 25,000 students were taking Open University courses outside the UK, with the largest concentrations elsewhere in the European Union in the former Soviet bloc (where courses are available in local languages) and in Hong Kong and Singapore. There are also growing programmes in Ethiopia, Eritrea, South Africa and India. In 1998, the Open University created a new university, the Open University of the United States to foster activities in America. In its overseas operations, the Open University insists on reproducing the local tutorial support for each student that it provides in the UK. The new technologies of the Wired World – notably e-mail and computer conferencing – may now provide alternative ways of providing local support, but the jury is still out on whether or not they can be made to suit all tastes.

Openness to methods has caused the Open University's use of media and technology to evolve continuously. The 800 hours of TV programming broadcast annually on the terrestrial channel BBC 2 are still the most visible expression of the Open University's openness regarding methods to the general public. However, the newer media – such as VCRs and PCs – that Open University students have adopted over the years are of increasing importance. A growing number of Open University courses require students to have access to a computer at home. Today, over 40,000 students are networked from home and the 200,000 messages they exchange every day around the globe and around the clock must make the Open University the largest academic community of the Wired World.

... with proper learning systems, access to success in higher education can be greatly expanded.

The Open University implements its openness to ideas by means of a commitment to research and its practice of developing courses in teams. The course team gives the Open University's courses greater quality and intellectual vitality than most university teaching. The commitment to research partly explains why the Open University is part of the elite group of British universities where most programmes are rated as 'excellent'. This includes subjects such as music, chemistry and earth sciences, where distance learning would not appear to enjoy a natural advantage.

Into the Wired World

The scale of the Open University means that it is already the leading global university of the wired world, although most of its students are not yet on-line. The Open University learned long ago that there are no miracle technologies. It is not interested in technology for its own sake, but in technology for academic advantage. Its technology strategy addresses the same key challenges as most universities, namely:

- teaching effectiveness and learning productivity
- reinforcing the sense of academic community
- production and delivery of courses and intellectual assets
- scaleable growth and logistics.

Five developments are particularly important in taking the Open University's technology strategy forward in 1998:

- using CD-ROM technology in the new introductory science course
- expanding computer conferencing with students in a wide range of courses
- refining techniques for effective tutoring of students by e-mail and computer conferencing
- developing use of the World Wide Web, particularly in conjunction with broadcast television
- taking advantage of technology in the logistics and administration of the learning system.

CD-ROMs The 1998 version of the Open University's first-level science course – *S103 Discovering Science* – uses the full multimedia capabilities of CD-ROMs on a large scale. This course includes 11 CD-ROMs, which engage each of the 4000 students on the course in some 60 hours of work at home. For the next few years, CD-ROMs are the only technological means of bringing the advantages of interactive multimedia into students' homes. These CD-ROMs are proving enormously popular with students, who seem to be convinced that the highly interactive nature of the medium increases their learning productivity and challenges them to think by forcing them to answer questions.

Computer conferencing Computer conferencing has been the most successful large-scale application of the knowledge media in the Open University so far. Students enjoy being able to communicate with each other. They also like the ease and speed of communication with their tutors and with the university generally. In 1998, some 40,000 students were active in 6000 computer conferences, posting around 20,000 messages per day and reading about 200,000.

Apart from allowing tutors to assemble conference groups on the network, computer conferencing also allows students to create their own groups for various social and professional purposes. The Open University Student Association plays a very helpful role in moderating these conferences.

Tutoring The tutorial support system and the care with which tutors comment on student assignments are key elements in the Open University's success. This year, the 5000 students in the Open University's new introductory computing course, *Computing: An object-oriented approach*, which innovates in content as well as methods, are making intensive use of electronic tutoring. Pilot projects of increasing scale are being conducted to test newly developed techniques for handling the electronic submission of student assignments.

Each year, the Open University handles over a million student assignments and has sophisticated monitoring and quality assurance arrangements for this purpose. These are so central to the quality of the Open University's teaching that it will not switch over to electronic methods until they prove reliable to operate on a large scale and popular with students.

The World Wide Web The Open University is sceptical of claims that the World Wide Web provides a complete answer to the challenge of quality distance learning. In 25 years of successful teaching, the Open University has learned that there is no magic learning medium. Its plan, therefore, is to integrate the use of the Web into the Open University's broadly based multiple media learning system, not to move all teaching and learning activities on to the Web.

However, the Open University sees very exciting opportunities for combining the use of the Web with broadcast television. Broadcast television remains a core element of the Open University's academic strategy. It is the primary vehicle by means of which it achieves its Charter goal of 'promoting the educational well-being of the community generally', and the Open University is increasingly designing its TV programmes – which sometimes attract an audience of millions – with this wider general audience in mind.

Broadcast television is about to undergo a digital revolution that will increase the number of channels and offer possibilities for interactive programming. Together, the Open University and the BBC see exciting possibilities of combining the strengths of broadcast television (the ability to reach large audiences and create interest in a topic) with the advantages of the Web (to allow individuals to explore the topic inter-actively and in greater depth).

Logistics As with any large-scale distance learning system, the Open University relies crucially on the efficiency and effectiveness of its logistical and admin-istrative systems. These are areas where the wired world improves service levels by giving staff and stu-dents up-to-date information wherever they are. The Open University has just spent $16 million on a 5-year programme to redevelop its record and logistical sup-port systems and has taken advantage of this project to modernize many of its business processes. The pro-ject has been remarkably successful and staff are currently making 100,000 transactions per day on the new system. In the next stage, the benefits of access to these systems will be made directly available to students and tutors.

> ... the Open University and the BBC see exciting possibilities of combining the strengths of broadcast television with the advantages of the Web ...

The Knowledge Media Institute In all these developments, the Open University is greatly assisted by its Knowledge Media Institute (KMi). This was set up in 1995 with a mandate to combine leading-edge developments in the Web, the Internet and on-line communication generally with the scaling up of the resultant technologies to reach large numbers of students. The KMi has a special commitment to the develop-ment of enabling technologies for students with disabilities. It is constantly developing new applications of the Internet (such as its worldwide telepresence system, KMi Stadium). In a short time, the KMi has become a focus for the collaborative development of teaching technologies by all faculties of the Open University.

The promise of the Wired World

The Wired World presents exciting opportunities for all the mega-universities as they follow the Open University in using the knowledge media on a large scale. Their great asset – as well as the opportunity to make the investments that scale allows – is that they have learned what makes a distance learning system work well. The keys to success are:

- well-designed multiple media learning materials
- personal academic support to each student
- efficient logistics
- faculty members who do research.

The Wired World will facilitate further progress on all four fronts. ■

Harald Norvik

Chief Executive Officer, Statoil

HOME PCs FOR EVERYONE – THE STATOIL IT STEP

S tatoil was founded in 1972 and is fully owned by the Norwegian State. The core business is in the exploration, production, transportation, refining and marketing of petroleum. In 1997, the net operating revenue for the Statoil group totalled NKr125 billion, the company has over 17,000 employees and activities in 28 countries worldwide. The Statoil Group is one of the world's largest providers of crude oil, and is one of the most important suppliers of natural gas to continental Europe. Downstream, Statoil ranks as the biggest retailer of petrol and other oil products in Scandinavia. It has a 50 per cent interest in the Borealis petrochemical group and owns 80 per cent of the Navion shipping company. Navion owns the world's largest fleet of oil shuttle tankers.

For Statoil, 1997 will be remembered as the year when IT came home to their employees worldwide. Every Statoil employee was given the opportunity to receive a PC with an Internet connection in their own home, provided they committed themselves to an extensive IT training programme.

The programme is called the 'IT Step into the Future', and is part of a larger strategic programme 'Three Steps Forward to a New Millennium', which is designed to fulfil Statoil's corporate objectives and prepare the company for the year 2000 and beyond. The need to improve employee expertise in IT usage featured strongly in the decision to commit to this investment. All employees – from the top to the bottom of the organization (management, technical staff, office clerks, cleaners, cafeteria staff) – were included and all received an offer from Statoil during spring 1997 to take part in the IT Step project. The total cost of the project to date has been over $30 million.

The offer was well received, being accepted by 97 per cent of the workforce that was eligible. A year later, the IT Step had got about 14,500 participants – 10,500 in Norway and 3000 abroad. In return, they signed an agreement to complete, in their spare time, a training programme within a period of two years.

Statoil employees have great expectations of the IT Step, and experience so far has shown that they are being fulfilled. To be able to master IT, to see the opportunities it offers for sharing information and knowledge, both within and without the company walls and across organizational boundaries, enhances Statoil's competence, flexibility and competitiveness.

Many companies want a more digitally oriented workforce, but find that the pressures of existing workloads overpower the good intentions when rolling out a new desktop functionality. People cannot find the time in their busy schedules to attend classes, read manuals, explore the potential of Internet or experiment with a new PC to learn what IT can do. As a result, many employees use their computers at work mechanically, yet, at home, the employees may have more sophisticated equipment and usage patterns, thanks to the rise of home PCs, inexpensive Internet connections and cheap support in the form of teenage children and enthusiastic neighbours.

In the IT Step, Statoil's top management decided that connecting people via a home PC to the Internet is the way to create an infrastructure for computer-assisted learning at home. That learning should take place in the home is a signal to Statoil employees that responsibility for learning is not the company's alone, but that every individual has to accept a responsibility for their own learning. This will be increasingly important in the future.

The IT Step creates a working environment in the home that benefits the workplace, the employee and their families. Knowledge obtained via the training programme is increasing the level of competence both at work and at home. The result is a boost to the level of IT competency at Statoil.

In the fast-changing environment of the oil and gas industry, Statoil's ability to use IT in all aspects of business is crucial to long-term survival and success. This ability is dependent on the skills and competence of the workforce. The IT Step is our way of responding to this challenge.

The company has seen that work processes are changing and are increasingly more reliant on electronic support. At least 75 per cent of Statoil employees are already involved in work processes that use large amounts of information and it is believed that in the future everybody in our company will have to use corporate IT solutions.

Here are some examples of how it is more and more important to the oil and gas industry. For Exploration, IT is used for the analysis of seismic data; for Drilling, it is used for data analysis and drilling control systems; Reservoir simulation and production systems control; Construction projects, site models and partnering; Transport systems control – natural gas; Refinery optimization and process control; and Retail Marketing systems and oil trading information systems.

Another important trend is the way in which learning processes are changing. In the Information Society, a new basic competence is required, such as the abilities to acquire new knowledge, share experience and knowledge, communicate and work in teams and take part in the sharing of knowledge.

Statoil has recognized the need for significant competence development, both initially and as a continuous learning process. Continuous change means that we have to learn faster and be smarter. This means that the ability to learn becomes a competitive advantage for the individual as well as the company. As a company, we have to facilitate this in a way that is both motivating for the individual employee and effective for the company.

The idea of the IT Step programme originated back in the autumn of 1996, when a member of the trade union in Statoil suggested that the company should subsidize employee purchases of home PCs. A group of top managers decided the company should take an active role in developing the IT and business skills of its employees. The IT Step initiative was proposed to me as Chief Executive, and all of the management team enthusiastically agreed. In order to simplify administration (particularly of ownership issues) and increase the acceptance rate, it was decided that Statoil should invest in home PCs for all its employees, and that only employees (no contractors) should receive the offer.

The first stage of the project was kept a secret, both internally and externally for two frantic months as we determined the functionality of the computers and assessed the total cost. An independent project team determined that all employees should be included. It was seen as important to emphasize that the programme would be purely an initiative aimed at achieving the building of competence, not a device to coax more work out of people. Consequently, the home PCs would not be connected to any of the work-related Statoil systems, but, instead, to an independent Internet Service Provider (ISP). The networked Statoil employees would also have access to several 'Statoil-only' web pages.

The IT Step gained national and international attention when it was formally announced in October 1996. Some critics saw the IT Step, despite our efforts, as an attempt by the management to get more work out of employees, others as a way to reward employees without having to pay taxes. The employees, however, saw the project as a clear statement of the company's willingness to move beyond rhetoric and make an investment in them. The Norwegian tax authorities, after a careful evaluation, agreed.

> The employees . . . saw the project as a clear statement of the company's willingness to move beyond rhetoric and make an investment in them.

Eventually, the IT Step was received with enthusiasm by more than 97 per cent of those that were eligible to participate. It is also interesting to note that employees had to use the computer to sign up for the programme. Communication lines were installed during the early summer of 1997 and the PCs were distributed to the employees by August. The employees set up the PCs themselves, following installation instructions and signed up for the training programme by accessing dedicated web pages.

The technology is outsourced and the bid was narrowly won by Telenor – Norway's recently deregulated national telecommunications company. The specification included an ISDN telephone line and a large 17-inch screen. This equipment was chosen so that it could be used as a home office solution, connected to Statoil's internal data net, if this was wanted in the future.

The learning objectives of the IT Step in a world where free and open competition is 'the name of the game' are the ability to learn faster and develop and utilize human resources, which is also seen as the only way to sustain a competitive advantage. The most important input factor to Statoil's value chain is competence. The company wants to develop competence in its workforce in order to maximize the possibilities that IT offers, as well as to simplify the organization and its work processes.

The objective is to improve employee knowledge and skills in using IT in the new information society and to make the employees become 'cyberspace' literate. It is especially important to prepare for the challenges that the information society will bring as the world gets more and more wired up, as well as to provide training in Statoil's desktop software and give an understanding of Statoil's business activities.

It is an objective that employees shall be able to meet the challenges and explore the possibilities of the home computer. This means being able to operate in an 'information pull' environment instead of waiting for information to be pushed at you, and being able to work together with internal and external colleagues in a digital form. Sharing information and working together in new ways also requires security rules and principles to be turned around from the old view of 'Need to know' to make all information open and available unless it is necessary to restrict access.

The IT Step aims to improve employees' skills and abilities to change the way they work and improve their ability to apply the new functionality of modern desktop software to their work.

A CD multimedia presentation is included in the training programme to help increase and improve the employees' understanding of Statoil's various business activities and challenges. This CD – 'The Source' – was created for the IT Step and gives the viewer a broad interactive overview of Statoil's history, businesses, technological areas of interest, HES issues and programmes for change and improvement.

A PC-based three-part training programme was designed that covered three important areas:

- basic IT skills, such as using Windows '95, Lotus Notes and Lotus Office tools
- information society awareness, including Internet use, security and ergonomics
- Statoil business knowledge.

The training period is two years and the participant can complete the mandatory training modules using all this time. There are no formal exams, nor control of the actual learning process. The system is based on trust, and progress is reported based on each participant's conscience and values.

Employees receive the training modules on CDs and report their progress using the Internet. Individuals are not tested, but a mechanism for measuring success using random surveys run by affiliated academic institutions was set up before the IT Step was rolled out.

To communicate and distribute information to all the 14,500 participants living in 28 different countries, Statoil designed an Internet application including a large database to keep track of all its participants. This 'members-only' Internet home page won the 1998 Golden Alpha award for best Internet and network (Intranet) solutions in Norway – an award that is backed by Digital, Microsoft, Cap Gemini and Computer Associates.

The IT Step home page has proved to be a cornerstone in the day-to-day operation of the project, and is absolutely crucial to keeping in touch with all of its participants. The IT Step home page is used for a number of different tasks, including information about user support, feedback from participants, distribution of new training modules and software, individual progress reports on the training modules, Internet-based training, daily news flashes on subjects relevant to the IT Step, sharing of company- and job-related information at home and so on. The home page has become very popular and currently has an average of 4000 visits (hits) a day from IT Step participants and their families. The potential use of this communication channel, connecting almost all employees at home in a 'members only' Extranet, is vast, and Statoil has just started exploring the possibilities for innovative uses. For instance, Statoil is working together with Oxford University Press to create a lifelong learning zone that will provide interactive access to a range of mixed-media learning materials and educational resources via the Statoil Extranet. It is obvious that the potential for Internet-based training and marketing is extremely attractive.

The results so far show, in summary, that there are signs that people are learning quickly by using the home computer. The use of the Internet and the Lotus Notes software office package have increased. The surveys indicate that an overwhelming majority of the employees are very satisfied with the system and have taken the training programmes seriously. In particular, a number of employees, such as the oil platform personnel who work two weeks on the platform, then have three weeks off and are at home, communicate with Statoil via e-mail, either from home or from the oil platform. The unions have started communicating with their members using e-mail. 'Statoil-only' discussion groups on the Internet have been set up and used, and some experiments with home-based offices have been done.

The effects of the IT Step are mainly measured by noting employee use of Statoil's infrastructure, the individual progress reports on the IT Step home page and a set of surveys designed and executed by a dedicated group of academics working together with Statoil to evaluate the programme. The surveys were done on the same panel of 1000 participants in April 1997, October 1997 and April 1998.

In surveys, we have found that 90 per cent were satisfied with the delivery of the PC equipment and training material more than 60 per cent have been in contact with user support at some time and most employees are satisfied with the support system. The weakest point is follow-up when the problems cannot be solved on the phone. Help from colleagues and friends or family is very important. The three most popular CDs after one year are the general introduction, 'Getting Started', (95 per cent), Windows 95 and Internet (around 80 per cent), and Lotus Notes (around 65 per cent). The textbooks on IT and the Internet have been used by about half the participants. The use of the home PC increased strongly in the first six months of the programme. More than 90 per cent of the participants use the PC as anticipated with an increased usage by the rest of the family. The use of the Internet increased. When the programme started, about half the employees (42 per cent) had not used the Internet before. After the first year, only 4 per cent reported the same, so 96 per cent now master the Internet. Evidence based on the surveys indicates very strongly that the focus on the Internet in the training has made a huge difference. All expectations regarding training outside office hours were met. The number of internal training courses were dramatically reduced from earlier upgrades, and the load on the helpdesk was not increased more than experienced during previous upgrades. The in-house classroom training in the use of desktop software has almost disappeared, and the cost for this sort of training has been markedly reduced.

The fact that all employees of Statoil can have a home PC has become a powerful recruiting and retention factor ... In a time of shortage of skilled labour, we now have few problems hiring the people we want.

Statoil has also had some very positive effects as a result of all the unexpected media attention that the IT Step initiative has attracted. Statoil had not anticipated the effect on the company's public image when initiating the IT Step. The fact that all employees of Statoil can have a home PC has become a powerful recruiting and retention factor. Young, technically competent people are seeking work with Statoil because of the home PC – not merely because of the availability of a 'free' computer, but because the company has gained a reputation for innovation and progressive thinking. In a recent independent Norwegian survey ranking the most attractive company to work for, Statoil was ranked number one. In a time of shortage of skilled labour, we now have few problems hiring the people we want.

Statoil's reputation for innovation has been raised in the industry and other companies and foreign governments have noticed the impact of Statoil's IT Step. An American oil company told us that the IT Step 'hit the oil industry like a bomb'. Now our competitors have to consider doing the same for their employees.

Our conclusions so far are that it is too early to draw any definite conclusions about the effects of the IT Step, but early indications point to success. The employees, Statoil as a company and the unions are all very positive about the new Information Society with all its technology. The use of the Internet in the company is high and rising as people discover its usefulness and relevance to their work. Communication between the organization and its many shift workers has been vastly simplified. Something that has been dubbed the 'Statoil effect' has been observed in other Scandinavian companies, as they are debating whether or not to follow Statoil's lead in connecting their employees at home.

We believe that the IT Step has provided Statoil with a strategic advantage and the results so far confirm our original justification of the project. We have created a platform and an infrastructure for computer-assisted training at home. The IT Step home PCs have facilitated a gradual transition to 'home offices' for those who need it. We can see from the surveys that fear of new technology (the Internet) has been reduced and this makes way for faster organizational change. Also, last but not least, we believe that the IT Step has increased the probability of innovation or, as we term it, 'Somebody will do something smart'. ■

section 9

PUBLIC SERVICES

contributors

Edith Cresson, Member of the European Commission, is a graduate in business and demographics, and has led a political career both in France and at European level. Appointed National Secretary to the Socialist Party in 1974, responsible for youth and education issues, she was elected member of the European Parliament in 1979.

Elected to the French National Assembly in 1981, and mayor of Châtellerault in 1983, from 1981 to 1990 she carried out her ministerial duties in several governments, heading the departments of agriculture, foreign trade and tourism, industrial re-organization, and from 1988 to 1990, European affairs. From 1991 to 1992, she served as Prime Minister of the French Republic.

Mrs Cresson has occupied high positions in industry on several occasions in her career. Since 1 January 1995, she is member of the European Commission, responsible for research, innovation, education, training and youth. In this capacity, she promoted a new generation of European research and education programmes. In her most recent book, *Innover ou Subir*, Mrs Cresson presents her views on the economy, the role of the State, education and training, technological innovation and the relations between science and society.

Chris Yapp, ICL Fellow and Managing Consultant, ICL, is a specialist in Lifelong Learning and Information and Communication Technologies (ICT). He has more than 20 years' experience working on strategic implications of technology change. He is a frequent speaker on public platforms and has contributed to a number of books on the management and organizational aspects of technology. Chris Yapp has been working with a number of pioneering projects in multimedia and education. He is also active as a political adviser in the UK and to governments in other European countries. He is deeply involved in Information Society issues and a strong promoter of initiatives like the UK National Grid for Learning and the University for Industry.

Glenn R. Jones, Chairman and Executive Officer, Jones International, often referred to as 'the poet of technology', purchased his first cable television system in 1967 with $400 borrowed against his Volkswagen. Since then, his company Jones Intercable has become one of the ten largest cable television operators in the US, and has been the springboard for his creation of a number of innovative enterprises, among them, Knowledge TV, Great American Country, Jones Radio Network, Jones Entertainment Group, Jones Cyber Solutions, Jones Internet Channel, International University, and the International Community College. His pragmatic yet visionary approach to the telecommunications business has earned him the reputation of 'the entrepreneur's entrepreneur'.

Glenn Jones earned an undergraduate degree in economics from Allegheny College and obtained a Juris Doctor degree from the University of Colorado School of Law. He completed an Executive Programme at Stanford Business School in 1973. He holds Honorary Doctorates from Allegheny College, Regis University and Heidelberg College. He is a member of the Board of Directors and the Executive Committee for the National Cable Television Association (NCTA). Additionally, he has served on the Board of Governors for the American Society for Training and Development (ASTD) and the Board of Governors for the UCLA Center for Communication Policy. He is the author of the *Jones Cable Television and Information Infrastrugcard Dictionary, Make All America a School, Cyberschools, An Education Renaissance*, as well as several volumes of poetry.

introduction by Anne Leer

CITIZEN CARE IN A WIRED WORLD

What can we expect of our governments and public services in the future of the Wired World? Will citizens be looked after in terms of access to primary services such as education, healthcare and welfare? Will citizens enjoy the same degree of legal protection of their rights as citizens and consumers? In a Global Information Society, which government or public authority is responsible for what?

I wonder if the traditional divide between the public and private sectors is sustainable or indeed useful anymore. We have already seen many examples of privatization and outsourcing of public services. Some very successful, others not. There is an acute funding crisis in key sectors perceived to be the bedrock of Information Society. Schools, universities, libraries, museums, hospitals, social services are all struggling to fund their operations in an analogue world, let alone in a digital world. The growth of so-called public/private-sector partnerships is also evidence of the fact that governments are rethinking and reshaping the way public services operate. It is easy to blur the lines between what should be public and what needs to private, both with respect to roles and responsibilities, as well as down to who should be doing and paying what. There is need to develop sound models and guidelines for public/private-sector collaborations. Clearly, such partnership offers many opportunities to stimulate the development of new products and services for the benefit of every citizen.

In this section we will go to Brussels again and visit a colleague of Dr Martin Bangemann, namely Commissioner Edith Cresson who has special responsibility for education and culture within the EU. We will also meet Chris Yapp of ICL, a dedicated promoter of the Global Information Society agenda and someone who has been blamed for coining phrases like 'knowledge utilities' and 'national grids for learning'. Finally we will travel to America again, this time to meet a real veteran in the field of distance learning and education. Glenn Jones, the founder of Jones Education and Jones Knowledge Group, invented the term 'cyberschools' and wrote a book about it long before most of us had heard of the Internet.

Edith Cresson shares her enthusiasm for the many opportunities that the development of information and communication has brought about. She points out that the information revolution has already had profound impact on society and our lives. She says it is the duty of policy makers to raise questions about the impact this will have on citizens and their lives, to understand what the opportunities and risks are, and what the role of public authorities is in this process. Electronic commerce is one area with enormous potential. Edith Cresson sees it as essential that governments and businesses collaborate to establish the best conditions for electronic exchanges and achieve an environment of trust and security necessary for electronic commerce to flourish.

Teleworking is another major opportunity for industry to improve productivity and for citizens to enrich their working lives. It may even contribute to solving the problems of traffic congestion on our roads according to Edith Cresson. Although I wonder, whether there will be jobs for all, and if so, will people really want to work from home? And if there is only going to be jobs for the few smart cyber-employees out there that Dr Martin described in his chapter, the rest of us will have so much leisure time on our hands that we will definitely be out there cluttering up the road. ... Perhaps in the future what Edith Cresson and her colleagues will have to do is to come up with new public services to keep us entertained so we will stay off the roads.

There will be jobs for employable people with the right knowledge and the skills. Many of the contributors in this book have referred to the new job creations generated by the ICT industries. However, training and re-skilling, constant learning and need for effective education have been noted time and again. This is also emphasized by Edith Cresson, and Chris Yapp discusses this in more detail in his chapter.

Chris Yapp kicks off his chapter by stating that no country in the world has an education and training system that is fit for the future. He is probably right, but then it depends on what kind of future you are talking about. The future is always a moving target and to be able to create and deliver effective education, it is absolutely vital to have a very clear target with specific learning objectives. So who can tell us what the future looks like and how we need to design and develop our education systems. Chris Yapp makes a start and begins the process painting the future for us in his excellent chapter. Education concerns us all, regardless of where we are at in life. It is the lifeblood, it seems, of human existence. The day we stop learning we die, even if our bodies live on.

And in the corporate world it is essential that people are able to grow and learn continuously. Chris Yapp describes the acute skill problem of many industries and points out that in the ICT industries the shelf life of some core skills is down to two to three years. The need for re-training and education throughout people's working life is mounting. We should use the technologies of the Wired World to address the problem and deliver new effective learning systems designed to deliver the kind of skill sets and capabilities that industry needs from the workforce.

If you are interested in the notion of public/private-sector partnerships and want to find out more about how they can work, you will benefit from Glenn Jones' chapter. You may wonder what Free Market Fusion means and Jones will explain it all. He has invented this term to describe a new dynamic that he sees as being unique to the knowledge age, namely the emergence of hybrid public/private-sector partnerships. Successful business people, scientists, engineers and entertainment leaders are joining forces with non-profit organizations to develop new products and services. Glenn Jones says Free Market Fusion crosses the boundaries between corporate missions and public goals. He explains it has come about because of a new understanding that resources available for scientific and commercial purposes can be joined with less tangible assets of non-profit institutions to accomplish objectives beyond their separate capacities. ▪

Edith Cresson

Member of the European Commission

TOWARDS AN INFORMATION- AND KNOWLEDGE-BASED SOCIETY

In comparison with other features in the history of industry and technology, the development of information and communication technologies that we observe today presents two striking characteristics. The first is its fast pace: new generations of electronic components and products appear on the market every six months and these products spread at an unprecedented speed. The number of Internet users, for example, was estimated at 3 million in 1994. According to the latest estimates, the current figure stands at 115 million, and the number could reach 1 billion in 2005.

The second characteristic is the extent to which these developments have already affected our lives and the functioning of society, and how they will have even more of an effect in the future. There are almost no aspects of economic and social life that remain untouched. The word 'revolution' is often misused. In the present case, it applies perfectly: we are clearly in the middle of a true revolution – the information revolution – and we have to learn to live with it.

Faced with such a situation, it is the duty of the policy makers to ask themselves a series of questions. What effects could and will these developments have on citizens' daily lives? What are the opportunities related to them and the conditions that need to be in place to fully exploit these opportunities? What are the possible risks? What role do the public authorities have to play?

Reviewing the main domains where big changes and transformations can be expected, I will try to sketch some answers to these questions. I will focus on the European dimension of the issues, giving examples of European Union (EU) achievements in some of the fields concerned. To conclude, I will address a series of general and important issues.

The promises of electronic commerce

One of the sectors of high public interest today is electronic commerce, which has developed on a scale that very few people foresaw only a few years ago. From a relatively small base, electronic exchanges are growing dramatically. It is frequently stated that, in 2002, they will represent a market of several hundred billion dollars. Today, the bulk of this activity consists of business-to-business transactions, which represent about three quarters of the total. However, business-to-consumer exchanges are continuously

> The word 'revolution' is often misused. In the present case, it applies perfectly.

developing. At present, this activity mainly concerns 'intangible' goods, including information, data, consulting services and travel. The volume of physical goods exchanges is nevertheless expanding, starting with easy-to-deliver goods such as books.

This evolution will undoubtedly contribute to boosting the economy. The first sector to do this is that of information and communication technology itself, but all parts of the economy will progressively be affected. Together with wealth production, it could also lead to job creation. Electronic commerce has the effect of shortening the chain between producers and consumers (to the great benefit of the latter). However, it contributes equally to the generation of many new intermediaries and support services.

Two remarks have to be made here, of direct interest to public authorities. First, one of the pre-conditions for the development of electronic commerce is an environment of trust and security. Transaction, confidentiality, personal data protection and sender authentication are crucial issues. Here, public authorities have to satisfy opposite requirements. On the one hand, they have to contribute to ensuring the best conditions for electronic exchanges, in line with what both companies and consumers legitimately ask for. On the other hand, however, they have to take care that the means of protection – namely encryption technologies – will not be used for criminal purposes. The EU has recently taken numerous initiatives in this field, aiming to find solutions at an international level.

The second remark is that, today, nobody can foresee the exact extent to which the development of electronic commerce will transform the economy. Changes could be far greater than we imagine today. The move to 'de-materialization' can have effects and could lead to consequences that will not necessarily be totally positive or easy to manage. The dramatic development of the financial economy in comparison with the 'real' economy, for example, with a financial market working 24 hours a day, is often considered as an important potential source of destabilization of the economy, with all the dangers this implies.

New ways to work and produce in industry

Beyond commerce, the information revolution will affect the whole of industrial activity, as well as conditions of work. The development of an open network introduces big changes in the way companies work. Rigid, vertical organizations and structures will increasingly give way to flat hierarchies, with fewer hierarchical levels and networks at production levels, managed in a loose, flexible way. Flexible communication facilities will replace the vertical information flow of the past, increasing interaction and creativity. This is the case for a single firm, but on a bigger scale, it is worth mentioning the dramatic possibilities offered by the technology of 'concurrent engineering', allowing the design and manufacture of products from very remote locations. Europeans are directly concerned here. After all, they were the ones who made collaboration between companies, universities and research centres from different countries one of the main axes of their efforts in the field of technological development. As an example, I would like to highlight the large concurrent engineering project launched in aeronautics which is part of the framework of the EU research programme in this field. Collaboration is the key to European successes in research and technology. The information revolution gives us very powerful tools to achieve it.

Information and communication technologies also offer industry and services firms the broad range of possibilities related to teleworking. Teleworking has been (and is still often) presented as a source of possible gains for the firm, but at the same time as a source of risks for society as a whole, as businesses are tempted to use it to 'delocalize' activities in remote countries that pay their staff very little. On the other hand, I would like to underline all the possible benefits we can expect from clever use of this technology. While enhancing productivity by, among other factors, maintaining a high level of motivation among the employees, teleworking can contribute to solving the serious problems of traffic congestion European cities are suffering today. It can help to maintain and develop an important level of economic and social activity in suburbs and rural areas, and that means other jobs will be created. Here, too, we have to be careful in our statements and take into account all the possible unexpected negative effects. The net impact on transport, for example, will depend of the shape of the work schedules the employees will follow. Enterprises are also aware of the fact that, to maintain a high level of creativity, a certain level of physical contact between people is indispensable. While contributing to creating far more comfortable conditions for employees, teleworking could also lead to a blurring of the borderline between professional and private life, of which not all the consequences are necessarily positive. All in all, teleworking still represents an important source of opportunities for European economy and society. Fortunately, enterprises seem to have understood this.

A revolution in education, research and culture

A field that the information revolution will undoubtedly transform in depth is education and training. In our knowledge-based economy, education and training have acquired an importance they never had historically. They are directly linked to knowledge, as are information and communication technology. They can therefore provide very powerful instruments in education and training. First, they can open access to an incredible, quasi-infinite quantity of knowledge. The Internet gives reality to the dream of the Argentine writer Jorge Luis Borges: it works like a universal library, containing all human knowledge. Moreover, this knowledge is updated in real time.

However, the most important contribution of information and communication technology to education and training is that it opens up new possibilities for access to knowledge, new methods to process them, and new ways of learning, which are more autonomous and adapted to everybody's needs and pace. These possibilities can be exploited in the context of informal education as well as at home. However, they also have a key role to play at school. All over the world, great efforts are being made to equip schools with PCs and give them access to electronic networks. For Europeans, the list of tasks left to accomplish is still long. The situation is very unequal between countries, with the Scandinavian states clearly being the most advanced. On average, the level of IT equipment and connectivity is very low. To contribute to correcting this situation, and to stimulate European countries to invest at the necessary level, I am launching, together with my colleague Martin Bangemann, a programme called 'Learning in the Information Society'. This contains numerous measures, of which the first category is aimed at stimulating European schools to interconnect via electronic networks. To raise awareness among schools, public authorities and the wider public to the advantages of such an interconnection, *Netd@ys* Europe were organized in 1997 and 1998. The latter involved the setting up of about 120 projects involving formal and informal education establishments. The subject matters covered were extremely varied – mathematics, astronomy and space, history, the environment, the arts and so on.

Networks are, however, of little use without content to feed them. The 'Learning in the Information Society' programme therefore includes actions to stimulate the production of pedagogical content. In Europe, we have many rich sources of content that are important assets to use. The variety of languages and cultures characterizing Europe, as well as the quality of educational traditions existing on this continent can help European industry to develop original and diverse pedagogical products. Entrepreneurial resources are also present. As in many other fields, the key to the successful exploitation of these resources lies in collaboration. To stimulate this, and the production of material, the Commission is preparing the setting up of a European foundation for audio-visual and educational multimedia. This will rely on a strong partnership between private and public sectors at national and European levels. In fact, in this field also, as far as networking is concerned, nothing can be achieved without the framework of a strong and balanced private/public partnership.

> **Networks are, however, of little use without content to feed them.**

Transmission and use of knowledge are not the only fields that will be affected by the emergence of the Information Society. Knowledge production is also directly concerned. Information and communication technologies have already significantly modified scientific research. They will affect it on a scale difficult to completely assess today. The availability, in real time, of the totality of research results produced in the world contributes to the dramatic degree of acceleration of the production of new knowledge. The full exploitation of this opportunity requires the existence of an adapted infrastructure. In this respect, Europe has an important gap to fill. Networks at medium and high capacity do exist within the borders of some countries. They have to be upgraded and integrated at European level. To this objective, the European Union has launched a series of projects aimed at ensuring interconnection between national networks at, first, 34, then 155 and, later on, 622 megabits per second.

Beyond the increase of access to knowledge, information and communication technologies will affect research and technology, modifying the way the scientific community works. Working in 'distributed' mode opens totally new ways of collaboration between researchers. In this field, too, we are witnessing the 'death of distance', with the creation of 'virtual laboratories' beyond frontiers. Possible consequences of this development are, at this stage, difficult to determine. The traditional scientific publication on paper – a cornerstone of scientific activity – relies on a system of peer reviews guaranteeing the accuracy of the information. Will an electronic peer review system spontaneously develop? Does the scientific community have to organize such a system in a more formal way? Will equal access to databanks and databases be guaranteed to everybody? All these serious questions remain open and have to be addressed. They have been studied and discussed, among others, in the framework of several initiatives by the European Commission.

Administration and public services

Another sector that will feel the effects of all these developments is that of traditional public services, such as transport, environment, health and culture. The tools of the Information Society could help us improve the performance and quality of services in these fields. Navigation and positioning satellites, tele-medicine and surgery, databanks and simulations of various environments, and remote management in urban and rural planning are just a few examples of possible developments. I would like, here, to make two remarks. First, a large part of the programme 'Creating a User-friendly Information Society', in the EU's research and development fifth Framework Programme, is devoted to the development of applications in these fields. Projects will rely on a close collaboration of industry, public authorities and the 'user' community. My second remark is that, in the field of culture, very often presented as dominated by American products, Europe is not without powerful assets. It can rely on the richness and the variety of a cultural heritage, which citizens of other parts of the world are very keen to know and appreciate better. Europe is, in consequence, in a good position to take full advantage of the so-called 'convergence' between video and information technologies that we observe.

Public authorities are also directly concerned with the information revolution, as a result of the possibilities it offers for modernizing administration. The European Commission has tackled these possibilities, developing databanks and web sites covering the whole range of the EU's fields of activities. Information systems have been set up, for instance, in the field of research and technology, aimed at giving access to all potentially interested lay people and companies (SMEs in particular) to information on participation in EU research programmes and their results.

A comprehensive and global approach focused on people

To conclude, I would like to address some general issues of crucial importance to successful development of the Information Society. The first is equality of access. This issue, which arises very often, is among the ones we have to consider the most seriously. There is a real risk of seeing society split into two parts: on the one side, all those who have access to the possibilities offered by the Information Society, because they have the financial means to purchase the tools concerned as well as the skills to use them; on the other side, those who have neither. This borderline can divide a single country; it can also go through countries. The well-known argument that there are more telephone appliances in the Manhattan area than in Africa as a whole means a lot. The very unequal access to the resources of the Information Society between the regions of the world was at the centre of the ISAD (Information Society and Development) conference organized in 1996 in South Africa, with the support of the European Commission. The commitments made on this occasion should now be followed by concrete actions.

The second general reflection I would like to make is that all the problems related to the development of the Information Society are so inter-related that they demand a comprehensive and balanced approach. Contradictory interests and requirements have to be taken into account in the framework of a wide and open debate. In this context, the Ministerial declaration that concluded the conference jointly organized by the German authorities and the European Commission in Bonn in July 1997 can be considered as both a model and a source of inspiration.

We have to put people at the heart of the information- and knowledge-based society.

Third, it is clear that, despite – or, rather, due to – the existence of divergence of priorities and interests, and the constraints related to competition between companies, almost all the questions related to the functioning of the Information Society have to be addressed at international level. This is particularly the case in questions related to legal and ethical aspects, which can only be solved on the basis of close and fair international cooperation.

Finally, I would like to highlight the question of skills. The Information Society can contribute to the raising of the general skills level, providing tools for vocational training and the training of the jobless, opening new horizons of life to people who need new skills and so on. In return, it is clear that the Information Society requires a higher level of skills at all levels of activity and responsibility. The development of the Information Society is indeed one element of the broader evolution towards the knowledge-based society. This society cannot work without people – their cleverness, commitment, imagination and taste for innovation and change. This is good news. Our duty is to ensure that the building of this society will effectively rely on people. In other words, we have to put people at the heart of the information- and knowledge-based society. ■

Chris Yapp

ICL Fellow and Managing Consultant, ICL

LIFELONG LEARNING: THE RENAISSANCE OF EDUCATION

So much has been written about lifelong learning over the last few years that trying to separate the aspiration from the substance of the concept and creating policy frameworks to guide implementation is increasingly difficult. What I wish to argue in this chapter is that no country in the world has an education and training system that is fit for the future. It is a truism that the world is changing rapidly, unpredictably and discontinuously. For any nation now, it is recognised that the quality of education and training is key to long-term competitiveness. Far from being a frightening outlook, I believe that humanity is facing an historical opportunity for development on a global scale. In building the Global Information Society (GIS), if we are bold and imaginative, we can create a new renaissance with learning at its heart.

All these claims need to be justified and I am sure that any reader would like to see how the ideas can actually be made to happen in the real world. That is the challenge I wish to address in these next few pages.

The transition to an Information Society

Rapid developments in Information and Communications Technologies (ICTs) are facilitating globalization of an increasing number of industries, of which financial markets and airline travel are two visible examples. This combination of technological development and globalization is leading to restructuring of supply chains and the location and organization of work. What this means for the individual, for communities and, indeed, for nations is that the minimum skill set needed to earn a 'living' wage in the global economy is rising fast. Since the mid-1970s, we have seen across the developed world a situation where the top 10 per cent of adults have increased their income and wealth considerably, but the bottom 10 per cent have found incomes to be static or falling. I do not believe that this trend is either inevitable or desirable into the first decades of the new millennium. Concerns over a sharp division in society between the haves and the have-nots are a recognition of this increasing disparity in income and wealth.

What I will outline here is, I believe, an optimistic, but also a realistic programme to create a competitive economy and inclusive society. To understand how this might be achieved, we need to understand the changes we are facing from the viewpoint of the life patterns of individuals growing up in the emerging new economy.

In the aftermath of World War II, the reconstruction of the economies led to a period of relative stability. For those approaching retirement, or now in retirement, the conventional life pattern was a linear progression from education to training/ apprenticeship to work and retirement. For a significant proportion of the adult population, the skills acquired in youth and early adult life were adequate to secure employment over a working lifetime. The aims and objectives of public policy was to secure a skill base for full employment.

In building the Global Information Society (GIS), if we are bold and imaginative, we can create a new renaissance with learning at its heart.

By the late 1960s and early 1970s, authors such as Peter Drucker in *The Age of Discontinuity* (Heinemann, 1969) and Donald Schön in *Beyond the Stable State* (Temple Smith, 1971) were pointing to the breakdown of this pattern. Certainly, since the oil shocks of the 1970s, we have seen an emerging pattern of parallel and episodic life patterns. In this new model, life starts in education, moves into training and to work, but then to sustain employability individuals need to reskill themselves from time to time. What we are witnessing is a reduction in the period for which a particular skill set is adequate to sustain productive employment, a reduction in what we might call the shelflife or the 'half-life' of skills. In the ICT industries, this rate of obsolescence of skills is such that the shelflife of some core skills is now two to three years. That is to say, an individual faces the need for ten injections of skills to sustain a working career. This is not confined to ICT. In some areas of the biotechnologies and pharmaceutical industries, similar, or maybe even greater, rates of change can be observed.

For those who lose their jobs, we have witnessed an increase in the period of unemployment and the scale of unemployment, certainly in Europe, over the last two decades. Optimism about the creation of a leisure society in the 1970s has been replaced by the co-existence of increasing demands on those in work in terms of hours and an increasing pool of workless.

Alongside these changes, we have witnessed changes in society – with increased divorce rates, more single parents, an ageing population and increased female participation in the workforce being examples of common trends in many nations.

While these changes are of major importance, I believe that the reorganization of work is a factor of greater strategic significance. The days when 5000 men (it was mostly men) would enter the factory gates and work on a narrow range of tasks has gone. The truth is that the unit size of workplaces has declined and a common factor in the new jobs, firms and industries is the significance of Small and Medium-sized Enterprises (SMEs) as engines of economic growth. Big organizations have downsized in terms of direct employment, frequently by 50 per cent or more in many industries, most notably in telecommunications.

Combine this with general trends to casualization, increased self-employment and portfolio careers in many countries and the complexity of the changes is fully apparent. What is clear is that the optimum aim of public policy is now to secure full employability, as jobs-for-life and full employment become harder to sustain.

What is clear from the above narrative, is that technological developments are a major influence and cause of the turbulence outlined. ICTs, however, also offer a solution to the problems that they have helped create.

ICTs and re-engineering education

It is now 50 years since the creation of the first modern programmable computer. What we have learned in that period is important to reflect on before attempting to build a solution. First, ICT blurs the boundaries between what were previously discrete departments within an organization and then continues to blur the boundaries between different organizations and then between distinct industries.

Second, when looking at what separates organizations that 'win' with ICT compared to those disappointed with the outcomes, we see an important pattern. The key benefits of investment in ICTs come from increased organizational effectiveness – doing things differently – rather than efficiency – doing things better. This, in turn, leads to the observation that successful deployment of ICT is about organizational change management, not simply implementing ICT projects. The buzz word used to describe this process is 're-engineering'. To cope with the turbulence outlined above, I believe that the challenge we face is not to connect every school to the Internet or to get a computer for every teacher or pupil, but, rather, to re-engineer education to support lifelong learning. What exactly does this imply?

I believe that there are four key characteristics of a system of learning that is fit for the Information Society:

■ the creation of a culture of lifelong learning
■ access to lifelong learning on a socially inclusive basis
■ content and services to support the lifelong learner
■ a social context for learning.

At its heart, learning is a social and a socializing experience. My own observation is that ICTs greatly supplement and extend good teaching and learning practice. The role of teachers changes, certainly, but ICTs do not replace the skills of a good teacher. My argument is in favour of a socially inclusive approach because of the need to raise the minimum skill set to cope with the consequences of globalization. I will handle the issue of content in a later section.

What I have described in terms of a learning system can best be described as a system of learning on demand. Perhaps a little disingenuously, I could characterize the traditional organization of education and training as the last bastion of Fordism in the modern economy. A study of on-demand, user-driven systems, such as Just-in-Time in manufacturing shows some important characteristics:

- The ability to mass-customize products and services – in the context of the UK, I would prescribe a move from the National Curriculum to a national framework for personal curricula to international standards.
- Teamworking in teaching and learning – I foresee groups of teachers, lecturers and paraprofessionals working together to create learning environments optimized for individuals facilitated by ICTs.
- A move from supply-side quality measures to user-driven quality measures – the current examination systems and quality frameworks, I would argue, are there to meet the needs of the system rather than the learners' needs.
- Administration is built into, not bolted onto, the core processes of teaching and learning – this is an area where ICT can be of particular benefit.

Putting this altogether, I feel, leads to a new and dominant paradigm for learning in the Information Society.

Community learning networks and the knowledge utility

If we are to apply ICTs appropriately to learning, then what I foresee is the emergence of community learning networks in which the boundaries between the different social institutions of learning – such as schools, colleges, public libraries – are blurred by the technologies to create, at the community level, access networks for learning on demand from cradle to grave. I believe that this community approach can overcome the problems of the loneliness of the long-distance learner and create an environment for increased access to learning. There are many good working examples around the world of community learning approaches, so I will not develop the theme further here.

The problem arises when trying to scale up the community learning network to provide universal service at the national level. Four years ago, in trying to develop an approach to building community learning networks, I came to the conclusion that we need to see the 'Information Superhighway' as a set of information utilities, and to see the universal provision of this new infrastructure as a similar intellectual challenge to that of the earlier provision of water, gas and electricity networks.

What I believe is needed is the creation of 'knowledge utilities', and that the concept of a National Grid for Knowledge or Learning provides the policy framework – a means to facilitate the sustainable growth of community learning networks on a large scale.

> ... what I foresee is the emergence of community learning networks in which the boundaries ... are blurred by the technologies to create ... access networks for learning on demand from cradle to grave.

The experiences of other utilities demonstrates the ability to deploy both public and private investment and build open and competitive markets for provision, which I believe to be desirable goals in an open and democratic society.

How might a National Grid for Knowledge or Knowledge Utility work? In Figure 1, the conceptual model is outlined.

A utility can generally be separated into three core components – the customers' premises, distribution network and 'power stations'. We have experience of the regulation and development of utilities fitting this model, so the policies for competition, conditional access and vertical integration, for instance, are well understood.

The customers' premises for a knowledge utility would inevitably start with schools, colleges and libraries, although there is no reason for not developing home and other access points. At least by means of a community-based approach, some attempt to ameliorate the effects of a knowledge underclass can be made.

The distribution network needed to cover urban and rural areas can be composed of multiple technologies, such as fibre optics, satellite and microwave links.

A National Grid for Knowledge or Knowledge Utility

Customer premises	Distribution network	'Power stations'
• equipment • schools • colleges • libraries	• satellite • fibre • radio	• content • services

FIGURE 1

What this creates is an electronic distribution channel for learning content, which in this model is supplied by learning 'power stations'.

Some criticism of the model that I have outlined here has been along the lines that the Internet will do all this anyway, so there is no need for any policy action. My own judgement is different because, in discussions with publishers and broadcasters, museums and galleries, for instance, the economics of development of interactive learning materials, particularly the up-front costs are very different, and higher than in traditional materials. We have observed with ICTs in education that there is a vicious circle that needs to be overcome. In particular, you cannot justify the investment in the infrastructure without the interactive learning materials, but neither can you justify the investment in the learning materials without an adequate infrastructure. It is my contention that an entirely bottom-up, market-driven approach is unlikely to break this vicious circle and deliver universal access to learning in a rapid manner.

The technologies and ideas regarding school networks have been written about in many places and there is much research on the educational value-added of ICTs in learning. The area I think is least well developed and understood is the idea of educational power stations. It is this that I will now address.

Learning 'power stations' on the National Grid for Knowledge

Just as power stations on the electrical grid may generate electricity from various sources, such as coal-fired, nuclear and hydro-electric, different computer servers would provide different services to the National Grid, for Knowledge. For instance, different servers may support dictionaries on-line, virtual museums and galleries, interactive encyclopaedias along with courseware, teacher notes and access to virtual environments. Alongside these, administrative systems – including assessment, accreditation and planning tools – would provide a rich and supported learning environment.

There are several issues that need to be addressed in developing the processes and the business models for educational content in the digital era. The creation of multiple media and multimedia environments is frequently described in terms of technology convergence, but my own experience is that it looks more like a collision of different worlds. Let me explain.

The skills needed to create materials in the new digital environments come from different industries with different values, behaviours, processes. Film, music, animation, publishing, broadcasting and the software industries have very different business processes and economics from each other. Attitudes to authors' rights, publishers' rights and the economics of each industry are very different. It seems to me that the pace at which we can create groups with a 'digital culture', and develop appropriate processes for the new media will determine the pace at which the grid can deliver educational value-added rather than provide the infrastructure.

My own observations of a number of the existing media companies as they wrestle with evolving their existing businesses into the new media is that they miss one of the key aspects of the technology that I believe will impact the ultimate model/s that emerge.

Before the printing press, humankind had a largely oral and pictorial tradition. The transmission and development of stories and music evolved in the telling and performance – there was no 'definitive' version. With the coming of the printed word, the film, the CD, we have seen a move to a product that is 'complete' and 'definitive'. We have the book, the song, the film. We have moved from an evolving to a fixed entity. With modern technologies, I believe that we are creating a new hybrid that can have both a fixed and a developing component.

This is important because, in looking at the development of an electronic equivalent, there is frequently an assumption that a complete product has to be created to be useful. In fact, one of the ways in which the World Wide Web differs from the book is that, both as a whole and in parts, it is an evolving medium. Also, there is a clear separation between the author and the reader in the book, but in the new media the reader can be a participant in the creation rather than a recipient of its results. It is this that I feel has a major part to play in the creation of personalized learning and empowering the learner.

None of this is to suggest that I am in the camp of the 'death of the book'. For me, the book is still the most successful example of IT in human history and probably will remain so for many years and generations, certainly for the 'linear' novel. We have already seen, that, in reference works and 'non-linear' materials, CD-ROMs and Internet technologies have advantages over the printed book. Still, the real issue for those who wish to create 'power stations' is to identify the key educational value-added features of the new technologies that need to be exploited so that a CD-ROM or a web site is more than just an electronic book.

While I feel that we are in an era of experimentation and trial rather than having a clear picture to progress towards, there are some characteristics that I believe will emerge in the mature model. In comparison with the film industry, it often feels as if we are still on single-reel 8-minute silents, but with a glimpse of the possibilities of *Star Wars* or *Titanic* my ideas may well look ridiculous in time.

I have already referred to the technologies as 'participative'. In the trials I have observed, the educational value of the new learning technologies comes from giving the learner tools to manipulate material and create their own contexts for learning as much as from contexts created by the 'author'.

Also, it is commonly reported that individual learning styles and preferences can be accommodated by the new technologies. Consider, for instance, the ideas embodied in Neuro-Linguistic Programming (NLP). In NLP, three clear ways can be defined. Some people process information better from auditory, others from visual and others from kinaesthetic sources. Imagine a text on a computer as opposed to a book. One advantage of the digital medium is that a visual learner can read the book in its paper or electronic form, where an auditory learner can use technologies for turning the text into digital voice output. That is to say, we can improve the choices available to the learner. Certainly, for a blind person, a much wider variety of material could potentially be available in the new media than can be economically converted to braille.

Consider some of the difficult concepts in science and mathematics. The ability to create rich simulations that the learner can interact with can help abstract concepts come alive. We know from the biographies of some great scientists that they were often 'visual' thinkers. For some people, the formulaic notation of mathematics (and indeed music) can be quite hard. Thus the ability to create visual representations of mathematics can help overcome some difficulties. Einstein, for instance, was a visual thinker. The development of chaos theory in mathematics along with complexity theory has been greatly assisted by the visualization of mathematical ideas.

I have touched on the issue of disabilities briefly, but one of the great hopes for ICT is that we can overcome barriers to learning experienced by many classes of learning difficulty or physical and emotional handicaps. Stephen Hawking, the great Cambridge physicist, has been able, for many years now, to contribute to the increase in human understanding of the universe despite a terrible and debilitating disease. It has been the development of technologies that have enabled him to continue to communicate his ideas much longer

> **Technology thus offers the potential to take the 'dis' out of 'disability' for many people, which has many economic and social benefits for society at large.**

than would have been possible only a few years ago. Technology thus offers the potential to take the 'dis' out of 'disability' for many people which has many economic and social benefits for society at large. Are we ready to go for this, I wonder?

In the last few sections, what I have outlined is a model for developing the knowledge utility. To complete the story, I wish to turn now to the educational implications of the development of a National Grid for Knowledge.

The implications

There are many implications at many levels of the 'system' that I have outlined above. There are implications for individuals and nation states. There are implications for the curriculum for lifelong learning for the teaching profession and other actors in the learning environment. I cannot explore all of these here, but there are a number of core possibilities that I wish to explore.

Around the world, there are many patterns for State and private provision of education and training for children and adults, and I would not claim that this will be replaced by a converged model. However, the issues of competitiveness and globalization seem to me to cause a realignment of public and private provision. It seems likely to me that national governments, faced with difficult tax bases and the need to raise minimum standards as well as improve performance across the board, will find it necessary to focus public resources on children to ensure that an increasing proportion of their citizens can compete in the new economy. I would argue that this is economically sound and socially equitable. Above school leaving age, I believe that governments will seek to create markets in adult provision from both public and private learning suppliers. My own belief is that we will see an increase in the transfer from funding the institutions to funding the learner. This will facilitate the creation of learning markets as well as supporting learner-driven quality. The idea of individual learning accounts and learning banks is increasingly widely discussed. The use of smart cards for learning, carrying both money and also learning plans and records of achievement is widely discussed in the UK. If we are to create a culture of lifelong learning, the idea of a visa or passport for learning based on a personal learning account seems to me both desirable and practical.

Of central importance to the whole debate is a view of the skills and education needed to survive and thrive in the new economy – that is to say, the curriculum for the lifelong learner. There is a danger that the focus of lifelong learning is too much on the economic aspects of education. For myself, I believe that we need to separate out lifelong learning from lifewide and lifedeep learning. I use lifelong learning to focus on the skills and attitudes needed for economic life, for employability. I use lifewide learning to cover education for citizenship, for family, community and sense of self. Lifedeep learning is more for the spiritual aspects of human existence and for building bridges with other cultures and creeds. Learning for peace and cooperation falls into this part of learning.

If we are to create a global renaissance and competitive global economy, then respect and understanding of different cultures is not a 'nice-to-have' part of the educational process, but its core. What it is important to understand is that the costs and benefits of investment in each dimension of learning are different. Wrapping them up in one dimension may miss important goals for policy makers who wish to see the creation of open, tolerant and democratic societies as well as competitive economies.

However at its heart, we will not see optimal improvements unless the re-engineering of the educational infrastructure and the educational curriculum occurs alongside the re-engineering of the teaching professions. I stated earlier that I thought we would see the development of teamworking in teaching and learning. My own feeling is that the current structure of the teaching professions is too generalist and teachers are expected to fulfil more roles than is sensible. Adding ICTs into the mix will, I suspect, make the situation harder rather than easier. My own view is that we will see fewer, more highly rewarded master teachers and an increasing range of para-professionals working in teams. This will be hard, costly and time-consuming, but, ultimately without it I do not believe that we will see a real leap in the performance of educational systems.

Conclusion

Throwing technology at an ill-defined problem can, and often does, make things worse. ICT offers enormous potential to raise the effectiveness of educational systems around the world. Competitiveness with social inclusion is, I believe, the aspiration that we should aim for. At the end of the day, the optimal strategy can be summarized in a simple phrase: people first, technology second. ■

Glenn R. Jones

Chairman and Executive officer, Jones International

FREE MARKET FUSION: PUBLIC/PRIVATE COLLABORATIVE RELATIONSHIPS

The digital revolution's lexicon of technology innovations, applications and processes is indeed seductive. Groupwork, netware, bodynets, hyper-organizers, mass individualization, digital libraries, virtual neighbourhoods, personal Internet domains, Applets, augmented-reality surgery, automated tutors, cookies, portals, digitized animation, cyber-cafes and virtual classrooms are terms that stream across the attention span of consumers each day. They represent real products and services, originating in computer and software industries that, in anything resembling their current state, did not exist when anyone on the globe now over the age of 40 was born.

These same terms also represent billions of dollars in created wealth over the past 20 years for the companies and investors who have taken them to market. It's a new stream of wealth that is likely not to have existed without the meeting and convergence of amazingly adroit, perceptive and certainly opportunistic scientific and entrepreneurial personalities. Jobs, Wozniak, Gates, Allen, Kay, Berners-Lee, Cerf, Moore, Grove, Andreessen, Clark, Hewlett, Packard, Malone, Armstrong, Murdoch, Turner, Lucas and Spielberg are names mentioned so frequently in daily business conversations that their repetition begins to resemble a mantra from a religious litany.

Besides their technology and entrepreneurial successes, most of these personalities also have two additional common traits. First, each succeeded because there was an infusion of capital into their research or enterprise development that happened at a critical juncture. Second, each has gone on to share their material gains with others, both in their industries and in their wider communities of interest to accomplish business, societal and philanthropic goals.

Much of what these people have experienced and consequently contributed comprises an investment and innovation formula that I find unique. Carnegie, Rockefeller, Ford, Chanel and Renault were also famous for philanthropy, but primarily after their fortunes were secured and usually in the waning days of their careers.

Institutions: early examples of philanthropy and its evolution

English clergyman Thomas Bray in Maryland founded the first lending libraries in the US in the late 1600s. The US public library system was expanded exponentially when Andrew Carnegie funded the construction of 1689 community library buildings between 1881 and 1891, along with another 785 in Great Britain, Ireland and Canada. Today, US communities support some 5400 public libraries.

The Boy Scout movement, founded in the United Kingdom by Robert S. S. Baden-Powell was introduced in the US in 1910 and now involves well over 25 million members, in 142 countries. The YMCA, also with 25 million members in more than 90 countries, has been a pillar of thousands of communities since its inception in London in 1844.

The list of public initiatives and institutions that have been spawned or nurtured by the joining of private- and public-sector resources is indeed extensive. However, the late twentieth century has seen the emergence of a new brand of philanthropy/entrepreneurship that finds successful businesspeople, scientists, engineers and entertainment leaders becoming involved in hybrid public–private projects and causes while at the height of their careers, or sometimes even in the early stages. This represents a unique dynamic I call 'Free Market Fusion',

> **Free Market Fusion crosses the boundaries between corporate missions and public goals.**

and it is particular to what I call the 'knowledge age'. (This is the sequel to the Information Age, which passed largely unnoticed in October 1994 when Netscape released for free its first beta Internet World Wide Web browser. That event largely negated the question of how to give information access to millions of people and freed billions in intellectual capital to concentrate on putting the information to work in true knowledge applications.)

In the late twentieth century, much of our most important work in technology-based corporations has been in identifying meaningful applications of technology created over the past decade. The search for those applications extends into all sectors of society. It involves market constituencies large and small, and profitability can be considerable or not at all.

What Free Market Fusion Is

Free Market Fusion crosses the boundaries between corporate missions and public goals. It has come about not just as a result of the largess of individuals, but because of a new understanding that resources available for scientific and commercial purposes can be joined with less tangible assets of non-profit institutions and Non-Governmental Organizations (NGOs) to accomplish objectives beyond either's separate capacities.

Free Market Fusion involves the coming together of two or more entities – one or more of which is characterized as a for-profit enterprise and one or more of which is characterized as an institutional, non-profit, quasi-governmental or government entity. For purposes of illustration, we'll call them 'A entities' (for-profit) and 'B entities' (institutional, non-profit and so on). It is a process that culminates in the fusing of, typically, a portion, but possibly all, of the assets of one or more A entities with, typically, a portion, but possibly all, of the assets of one or more B entities. This relationship can be illustrated as shown in Figure 1.

FIGURE 1

Although Free Market Fusion may result in the formation of new enterprises, typically at the outset, existing organizations are the creators. Also, usually, there is a background of significant common need, concern or opportunity relative to the entities involved that generate support for resolution. In its ideal form, the collaborative process inherent in Free Market Fusion can engender the tremendous release of energies that comes from looking at the world not as a miasma of intractable problems, but as an arena of challenges awaiting exploration, initiative, resolution and reward.

How it works

In the Free Market Fusion process, each entity contributes its particular strengths to the project. For example, in a partnership between an entrepreneurial group or individual and an institution, the entrepreneur can contribute the initial innovative idea as well as technological marketing expertise, significant risk assumption and free market disciplines, such as accountability to shareholders and competitive strategy. The institution can contribute staff resources, physical facilities and familiarity with the existing market, credibility and stature.

Depending on the parties, some of the roles might be reversed. However, the purpose of the partnership is always to enable both parties to accomplish goals each would find difficult to attain alone – to create a new solution where seemingly there was none. As in a fusion process, that new solution is accompanied by a burst of energy as new possibilities and opportunities open up to everyone involved in the process – both those creating the solution and those benefiting from it.

The catalyst ingredient is leadership, the 'champion'. While some may be quick to reach the conclusion that leadership will be provided by the 'freewheeling' entrepreneur, this is not always the case. That an entrepreneur may be accustomed to operating in the public spotlight and in a robust competitive arena does not mean that person will assume the leadership mantle or that they should.

At the same time, leadership encompasses much more than just assuming the role of primary public spokesperson. The most critical leadership activities are planning, organizing, networking and acting as missionary within the organizations involved, persuading and recruiting supporters internally for a new concept. Often individuals with established credibility within an institution can do this most effectively if they are passionate about the project. The entrepreneur may assume some or most of this role or merely advise and be an 'outside' networker, promoting the concept to other organizations and individuals whose support is essential. This requires a special breed, an arguably 'new' brand of entrepreneur whose motivation to make a social contribution resides on the same pedestal with making a profit and wielding influence.

Risk-taking – a key role

One complementary relationship that can develop between entrepreneurs and partnering institutions relates to risk-taking. Often mis-steps within an institutional environment may easily spell the end of a promising career, a circumstance that has an obvious and understandably dampening effect on an institutional leader's willingness to take risks. In addition to identifying opportunities, then, another of the entrepreneur's key roles in a Free Market Fusion venture is to assume a substantial amount of the risk involved in any new undertaking, thus diverting a large measure of the 'exposure' from the institution and its leader on to the entrepreneur.

This imposes no unusual hardship, for although risk-taking is anathema to an institution, judicious and well-informed risk-taking is second nature to the entrepreneur. An entrepreneur has the freedom to respond to opportunity with a desire for gain rather than resisting it because of a fear of loss. Similarly, because entrepreneurs may not be part of the 'old guard' operating environment of the institution and have fewer vested interests in conforming to established ideologies, they are much freer to think outside the bounds of accepted practices, to envision radical alternatives and innovative solutions. It is something they are accustomed to doing. In at least one major study by MIT business economist David Birch, small businesses – usually entrepreneur-led – created eight out of ten new jobs in the US. Creating jobs is one of the most useful contributions any enterprise can make.

> **An entrepreneur has the freedom to respond to opportunity with a desire for gain rather than resisting it because of a fear of loss.**

In the US, Free Market Fusion has been made possible by the open economic markets available for companies operating there, but it is a dynamic increasingly evident in other countries as well.

My own most direct experience in applying the formula of Free Market Fusion has been in the field of education, where I first involved my company in 1987, following publication of 'A Nation At Risk', a 1983 report by the US National Commission on Excellence in Education. That report described a vastly underqualified and marginally educated generation of US high school graduates, who would eventually lower the calibre of college student bodies, and a rapidly declining primary and secondary education system.

While the conventional response from both government and the education establishment to 'A Nation at Risk' was to demand 'more' – more money, teachers, classrooms and computers – we decided innovation using existing technology might be at least part of the solution.

Our initial involvement was in video delivery of courses by cable TV and videotape, with one traditional university as a partner providing course content. Today, this enterprise has grown to include the Jones Knowledge Group (JKG) and an Internet-based, for-profit cyber-institution, International University, trademarked in its marketing materials as the 'University of the Web'. JKG includes E-Education™, Inc., which encompasses relationships and agreements with multiple universities and colleges delivering fully accredited courses, programmes, certificates or degrees via TV broadcasts and the Internet; E-Education software, which allows faculty to prepare their own courses for Internet delivery; and Knowledge TV, a for-profit TV channel delivering education, personal enrichment and business news programming on three continents and which regularly advertises the web addresses for the Jones educational sites.

Working with academic institutions that recognized a need but lacked the resources and technology, we were able to provide technology, seed funding and basic management expertise to put course content on TV and, more recently, on the Internet. The result was revenues for all concerned, years ahead of what individual organizational budget constraints might have permitted.

With over 7000 course enrollments, we, along with our university partners, are positioned to supply a growing demand for distance education, which more traditional education institutions eschewed as unthinkable just five short years ago.

In the early 1990s, we were also involved in another Free Market Fusion project entitled the Global Library Project with the US Library of Congress, giving funds, technology and expertise to help videotape portions of the Library's invaluable collection for dissemination to the rest of the world.

Separately and more recently, the Library of Congress, under the leadership of Librarian James Billington and a variety of private companies and individuals, is now pursuing the Digital Library Project. It is a prime example of Free Market Fusion that is digitizing five million items in the Library's collection by the year 2000. Once digitized, these materials can be available to anyone, anywhere.

It is an example of Free Market Fusion initiated on the non-profit side, and an important one from which potentially millions of public users around the world will derive benefit.

One of the most important aspects of these unique new relationships is the bringing of new technologies, to which entrepreneurial partners can often provide access, into the equation.

Business planners and would-be start-up enthusiasts often focus on where to 'get into' the computer or software industries and, in so doing, overlook non-technical opportunities that would benefit from a little technology and a lot of managerial innovation and energy.

As the Swiss physicist turned business forecaster Theodore Modis has projected, the market for new models of business computers will likely reach 90 per cent saturation around the year 2002. Taken at its most pessimistic, this could mean that the era of thousands of successful computer/software start-ups might already be drawing to a close. However, the era of successful applications of those products should easily eclipse it.

As we search for new opportunities and avenues to make contributions, we have to look beyond the end of product and business lifecycles and constantly ask, 'What if …?' Free Market Fusion is a business-planning process that helps do this.

Tools for identifying opportunities

Opportunities won't drop out of the sky, though they sometimes appear from unlikely quarters. For the aspiring team of entrepreneurs that wants to identify likely avenues, a regimen of scanning information media and societal indicators is essential. This involves a carefully structured process of reviewing both favourite and 'outside the box' news media for new ideas and trends, noticing what consumers are wearing and buying, and noting statistics – fluctuations in travel, car purchasing, incidences of illness, birth rates, marriage and divorce rates, and so forth. This should be done on a regular basis, including after a new venture is launched to stay in touch with outside-the-industry trends, which may indicate a change.

A further extension of this is to engage in futures research, including scenario development. Several good consulting firms offer this service, but it also can be done on a limited basis by individuals and small groups who have studied up on the practices. A scenario development project conducted by Global Business Network for the National Education Association in 1994 laid out several possible outcomes for the US public school system that went far beyond the doom prognosis of 'A Nation at Risk'. These scenarios also suggested at least a dozen new business ideas for the willing entrepreneur who was paying attention at the time (see http://www.gbn.edu for the scenarios).

Overall, the Free Market Fusion planning process can create new products, services or solutions and is associated with new, or highly modified, management concepts and organizations' goals. Portions of entire industries can be involved and the mix of participants can range widely, as evident in the examples mentioned above.

Structuring the Free Market Fusion relationship

Obviously, each project will have its own set of circumstances and concerns that need to be addressed and agreed on before other steps can be taken. However, the following areas can serve as a starting point from which to explore and negotiate further.

- *Goal issues* What broad opportunity or problem is addressed? What are the specific purposes and goals of this project? How will goals be measured? How and when will they be evaluated?
- *Inertia issues* Best-laid plans can easily be derailed by organizational inertia. How rapidly will both parties be able to respond to opportunities and/or crises? How rapidly are both parties willing to respond?
- *Structural and logistics issues* How will the project be undertaken? Where and how will it be located – centralized with one participant, headquartered at a project site, other? Who will implement what aspects of the project?
- *Timing is critical* What is a reasonable and mutually agreeable timeframe? This can become a key issue if both parties do not understand and accept how long it will take to accomplish key tasks. If the project will entail working with large institutions, government agencies or other bureaucracies, the standing rule that everything will take twice as long as predicted might be expanded exponentially. However, if the leaders fail to understand and commit to the importance of speed, including allowing for new processes and fast communications, the project may never succeed.
- *Long-term issues* Assuming the project is successful in meeting its goals and is profitable, what should become of it in the long term? Should the relationship between the participants continue as is or should it be reviewed on a specified basis? Should the project continue in its current form or be taken over by one of the participants? Be taken to the public as an established company? Move into other Free Market Fusion arenas?

- *Competition issues* How will you deal with competing players? Will you work around their established programmes, trying not to disrupt their 'market share,' or will you try to displace their 'product' with your own? When dealing with societal concerns, much care must be taken with regard to this issue. Society is rarely damaged when, in the rough-and-tumble competitive consumer market, a snackbar, laundry detergent or sportscar bites the dust. However, when addressing societal issues, often a less-than-terrific solution is worth keeping because it provides ancillary benefits.

  There are many areas where a Free Market Fusion approach is currently, or will soon be, enabling us to make more creative, effective use of the technological tools now available, including those below.

- *The environment* Almost 30 years have passed since the first Earth Day in April 1970 called the world's attention to the deteriorating state of the global environment. Since that first tolling bell of warning, we have become increasingly familiar with the challenges that confront us:
  - Global warming and its greenhouse effect have continued unabated as waste gases, primarily carbon dioxide released by the combustion of oil, coal, and gas, continue to spew into the Earth's atmosphere.
  - The world's waters and aquatic species are still being poisoned in even greater numbers by acid rain, largely the result of the sulphur dioxide released into the air by coal-burning power plants.
  - The Earth-circling ozone layer is less and less able to protect us from the life-threatening effects of the sun's ultraviolet rays as chlorofluorocarbons (CFCs) continue to eat away at this protective blanket.
  - In tropical regions of the less industrialized world, growing populations desperate to find a means of economic survival burn their forests to clear enough land to graze cattle or cultivate marketable crops, taking more and more tropical rainforests out of the increasingly precarious global ecological balance. The industrialized world's reliance on non-renewable resources simply guarantees the ongoing acceleration of these frightening trends. Technology has enabled a multitude of innovative environmental solutions across a broad range of targets. Alternative, renewable energy sources, such as solar photovoltaic cells, geothermal and solar-thermal generation, wind power, and hydrogen fuel cells are no longer dismissed as fringe thinking. 'Green manufacturing' is becoming an accepted manufacturing credo of the 1990s as more and more companies understand that by redesigning manufacturing processes they are able to use raw materials that are from sustainable resources and reduce toxic waste, and thereby avoid the costs associated with toxic material disposal or storage. Sustainable development is a goal we all must embrace. However, it is imperative to accept the fact that market-based environmentalism offers the most effective means of transferring technological advances into the areas of greatest need, ensuring that future generations will inherit land, not landfill.

- *Education, poverty and health* The list of challenges we face is long and daunting. A quick hit list of social concerns might include the high drop-out rate from education for minority ethnic groups, illiteracy, child poverty, drug addiction, a rising crime rate, AIDS, homelessness, overcrowded prisons and a sky-high recidivism rate, increasing the level of effectiveness and accessibility (financial as well as logistical) for our higher education resources, reincorporating senior citizens, with their skills and experience, into productive societal roles, mainstreaming the physically handicapped back into society, and adequate, affordable medical care for all.

The larger arena: tapping entrepreneurial talent

Why not go to the world's entrepreneurs and ask them for solutions? These are individuals trained to see the opportunities in change and the possibilities in dislocation. When not constrained by undue governmental structures and regulations or stifled by vested interests protecting sacred cows within corporations and other institutions, entrepreneurs are free to find the most effective ways to meet goals. Who knows what reordering of existing resources, what rethinking of current responses, we might achieve? We need to tap the creative energy and risk-taking spirit of those willing to operate in the late Buckminster Fuller's

Free Market Fusion offer[s] one avenue of solutions f[or] those who have technolog[y] at their disposal to he[lp] those who may n[ot]

'outlaw area' of untried solutions and no guarantees. The only constraint is the tendency of government to become involved and impede the processes and the individual's willingness to take on lawful risk.

I believe solutions are always possible. The key for us is to structure the circumstances that nurture creative, innovative thinking so that our most innovative thinkers can design new solutions. It is obvious that when a society faces a problem that has continually resisted traditional means of resolution, other solutions must be invented and tried. Free Market Fusion offers one avenue of solutions for those who have technology at their disposal to help those who may not. For those who do not and are, thus, left behind by the knowledge revolution, will also be left behind by the economy of the twenty-first century. ■

PEOPLE

contributors

Nicholas Negroponte, Director MIT Media Laboratory, is co-founder of the MIT Media Laboratory, and the Jerome B. Wiesner Professor of Media Technology. Established in 1980, the Media Laboratory is currently supported by more than 150 corporations worldwide, and has led in the development of now-familiar areas, such as digital video and multimedia. A graduate of MIT, Professor Negroponte was a pioneer in the field of computer-aided design (CAD) and has been a member of the MIT faculty since 1966. He is also author of the 1995 bestseller *Being Digital* (Hodder & Stoughton, 1995).

Professor Negroponte serves on the Board of Directors for Motorola, Inc., and as General Partner in a venture capital firm specializing in digital technologies for information and entertainment. He has also provided start-up funds for more than 20 companies, including *Wired* magazine. He helped to establish, and serves as Chairman of, the 2B1 Foundation, dedicated to creating an imaginative, global network of all the world's children.

Charles Handy was for many years a professor at the London Business School. He is now an independent writer and broadcaster. He describes himself as a social philosopher. He graduated from Oriel College, Oxford University with a first class honours in 'Greats', an intellectual study of classics, history and philosophy. He has said that this discipline gave him the ability to think. After college, he worked for Shell International as a marketing executive, an economist and a management educator, in South East Asia and London before entering the Sloan School of Management at the Massachusetts Institute of Technology. Having received his MBA from Sloan in 1967, he returned to England to design and manage the Sloan Programme outside the US at Britain's first Graduate Business School in London.

Charles Handy's main concern is the implication for society, and for individuals, of the dramatic changes which technology and economics are bringing to the workplace and to all our lives. His book, *The Empty Raincoat* (Hutchinson, 1994) (called *The Age of Paradox* in the US), is a sequel to his earlier bestselling book *The Age of Unreason* which first explored these changes. Other of his bestselling business books include *Gods of Management* (Arrow, 1995) and *Understanding Organizations* (Penguin, 4th edn, 1993). Handy has also contributed award winning articles to *Harvard Business Review*. *Beyond Certainty*, (Hutchinson, 1995), a collection of his articles and essays, was published in 1995, as was *Waiting for the Mountain to Move* (Arrow, 1995), a collection of his radio 'Thoughts' over ten years. Handy is known to many in Britain for his 'Thoughts for today' on the BBC's Radio Today programme. In his book, *The Hungry Spirit* (Arrow, 1998), he surfaces his doubts about some of the consequences of free market capitalism and questions whether material success can ever provide the true meaning of life.

Arne Fjørtoft is Secretary General of the Worldview International Foundation, a development organization with consultative status at the United Nations, implementing communication projects in 23 countries. Mr Fjørtoft is also President of Worldview Global Media – a TV network and multimedia group – and communications adviser to governments and institutions. He has written several books and received international awards for his achievements.

introduction by Anne Leer

READERS' INDIGEST

I n this section we will focus on what really matters – people, and what the impact will be on our lives as we move into the Wired World. An ongoing theme in many chapters of this book is the emphasis on the creative and meaningful use of technology, and not technology itself. So, just how much of the Internet is useful and how much of all that the Wired World offers do we want. I am reminded of Arthur C. Clarke's visionary analogy of man using the Internet – like he would open his mouth under the Niagara Falls to quench his thirst! There is much talk of information overload, of having too much choice and not enough time, of being bombarded by the media offerings and an avalanche of consumer electronic applications. Will the common cold be replaced by Wired Indigestion? Or will the readers of the Wired World get the right stuff digested to live happily ever after he or she got connected?

We will hear from Nicholas Negroponte of the MIT Medialab in Boston – if anyone has digested the prospect of wiredness, he has. He has been working at the cutting edge of technology development for decades and inspired people around the world with his innovative and thought-provoking work. In his chapter he describes how our lives and society will change. We will also travel to the English countryside and look for a teleworker who will share his deep insights of societal change. Charles Handy is the man who refuses to be bowled over by the benefits of technology, without thinking carefully about the long-term consequences. Our next and final stop is the beautiful island of Sri Lanka where we will look in on one of Arthur C. Clarke's good neighbours. Arne Fjørtoft is a most extraordinary and modest man of great achievements. For more than 20 years he has been dedicated to using media and technology to improve people's lives in the unprivileged parts of the world. It is appropriate that his thoughts are the concluding chapter of this book. He speaks for two thirds of the world's population and the Masters of the Wired World cannot afford to leave them behind. Our world and the lives of future generations are at stake.

Negroponte tells us that our highly structured and centralist world will morph into a planet full of loosely connected physical and digital communities. He says the Digital Age brings a new form of localism. The concept of neighbourhood will change in the Digital World as physical location will be less important. He describes the neighbourhoods of the Wired World as groups that evolve from shared interests like those found on mailing lists, in newsgroups, or in aliases organized by like-minded people.

Will all the people in the digital neighbourhoods of the global village speak English and will the global culture be an American culture, I wonder? Negroponte doesn't seem to worry about the supposed lack of cultural diversity and the dominance of the English language on the Internet. He says English as a second language, with or without computers, has become an international protocol and in the same way, English will continue to be the air traffic control language of the Net for the next ten years or so. But he expects English at some point to be superseded by Chinese and that other languages will flourish too.

Negroponte believes people who complain about digital lifestyles and cry wolf about the damaging social effects of the Internet are wrong. He says the evidence points to the opposite. People enjoy and benefit from being connected to the on-line world. Children learn and gain social skills through the Internet, they don't lose them. He refers to his own personal experiences of how being on-line has enriched his life and enabled him to travel more in scenic places and be with interesting people, because he can do his work anywhere.

Charles Handy agrees with him; there are many features of the Wired World which will liberate and enrich people's lives. In his chapter he points out that in the knowledge age individual differences will be important both inside and outside organizations. Like James Martin, he too believes, to quote him, that successful organizations will be built around talented individuals and that institutions will be less important as people will spend more of their lives outside formal organizations. But Handy warns us: a society founded on individualism could fall apart without the glue of fraternity, the awareness that there are others who are as important as oneself. Fraternity, he suggests, could be just the kind of new religion or fashion we need to save ourselves.

Handy describes how abundance of choice affects people and society, and argues that all this choice may lead to the erosion of any one dominant set of values. He also explains that people may choose to opt out of leadership roles in business and society, because talented people may find a life on the edges of organizations more fulfilling. This could have a serious impact on organizations, which would be left with the second best. Not everybody has this abundance of choice or any choice at all. Choice is for the privileged. And Handy points out that choice will seem a hollow mockery when someone is old and cold and poor.

Will the Wired World be a better world for people to live in? Will it make a difference to to the distribution of wealth and prosperity? Will it help us solve the biggest crises of humanity, poverty, unemployment, pollution and warring between regions? Arne Fjørtoft addresses these difficult questions in his chapter and his conclusion is that the choice is ours. We have an unprecedented opportunity to harness technology advancements for the purpose of making substantial progress towards a truly global economy and a real global society. However, it will not happen without strong leadership and joint efforts from both governments and businesses on a national and international level.

Hopefully the Human Rights Convention will count in networked economy; however, governments may very well say they can no longer afford to uphold it. The principles of equal access to education and knowledge in a Global Information Society beg the question of who will foot the bill.

Fjørtoft's chapter makes it very clear that the risk of a further widening of the existing gap between the haves and have-nots is prominent. It is a terrifying scenario that the great benefits of the Wired World would only be available to those who can afford it, which would rule out the majority of the world's population. But that is what will happen unless we come up with new models for economic development.

It is encouraging that in this book there seems to be unanimous agreement that the Information Society of the Wired World must be inclusive and provide an equal opportunity for all. There is equal agreement that people should be at the centre of the Wired World. The song started so eloquently by Al Gore at the very beginning of this book – Put People First – is singing throughout every section of this book. Let's hope we can really do it. ■

Nicholas Negroponte

Director MIT Media Laboratory

BEING DIGITAL IN THE WIRED WORLD

B eing digital has three physiological effects on the shape of our world. It decentralizes, flattens and makes things bigger and smaller at the same time. Because bits have no size, shape or colour, we tend not to consider them in any morphological sense. However, just as lifts have changed the shape of buildings and cars have changed the shape of cities, bits will change the shape of organizations – be they companies, nations or social structures.

We understand, for example, that doubling the length of a fish multiplies its weight no less than eight times. We know that suspension cables break after a certain length because they cannot support their own weight. We are almost clueless, however, about the fractal nature of the digital world and how it will change the shape of our environment. Yet the effect will be no less substantial than if we changed the force exerted by gravity.

The most astonishing part of the Net is that nobody is in charge. Everybody knows this, but nobody really wants to believe it. The buck must stop somewhere. Surely somebody is in control. After all, football teams have captains and orchestras have conductors. In fact, we take for granted some form of authority, some hierarchy, in almost everything. In childhood it comes from parents and teachers. In adult life it comes from bosses and government. While we may not always be pleased with where we stand in that hierarchy, at least we understand it.

However, sometimes the mere presence of a police car can cause traffic jams. The Net – a reliable system composed of loosely connected and imperfect parts that work because nobody is in control – shakes up all our centralist notions, and hierarchy goes away by example. Cyberspace is a lattice. If a part doesn't work, you go around it. The look and feel is suddenly much more biological, taking its character more from flora and fauna than the unnaturally straight-line geometry found in artefacts of human design. Picture the loose-V formation of ducks flying south.

Many pieces of our world – work and play – do have that centralism to them. Hierarchy has its place. Even the most conservative centralist will agree, however, that organizations have flattened, with considerably fewer levels between top and bottom. The Mitsubishi Trading Company, for example, summarily removed an entire level of middle managers, and other firms are doing the same. In part this is due to a competitive market economy that demands streamlining. In greater part, however, it is because modern communications allow people to deal with more than seven others (plus or minus one). Add current-day management doctrine and you get even thinner social forms. Leaders distinguish themselves by what they do, not by where they sit – something many politicians and industrialists have yet to note. The computer industry learned this with open systems, where competing with imagination proves far more profitable than doing so with locks and keys.

A libertarian view of the world adds flatness to decentralism and concludes that large organizations such as the nation state – are doomed. This is only half the truth. Instead, I would liken the digital world to indigenous architecture, where local and global forces make for individualism and harmony at the same time. Each house on a Greek island is totally its own design, reflecting the *ad hoc* needs of various individuals over time. However, common use of local materials – building in stone and applying whitewash to reflect the heat – results in a collective order. As soon as you use steel and air-conditioning, however, the only way to protect that harmony is to legislate, relying on zoning laws to do what nature did before.

My gripe with the nation state is that it is just the wrong size – it does not mesh with the digital form of the future. Most nations are too big to be local, and all nations are too small to be global. What the Net is doing is forcing all of us into a body of law we do so badly – international law. Law of the sea, non-proliferation treaties and trade agreements take forever to negotiate and are hard to maintain because nobody's primary self-interest is that of the world as a whole.

As soon as there is a means and mind-set to be global, governance should be pushed down into the village and up on to the planet. We see this happening to a limited extent if we look simultaneously at the business and political worlds. Economic forces are pushing towards a regionalization of commerce, and political forces are tending towards the break-up of nations. Bigger and smaller.

Businesses will do the same. Companies such as Time Inc., News Corp., and Bertelsmann keep getting bigger and bigger. People worry about control of the world's media being concentrated in so few hands, but those who are concerned forget that, at the same time, there are more and more mother-and-father information services doing just fine, thank you very much. The Wired World really does make everything bigger and smaller at the same time. The value of being big is twofold: size affords organizations the ability to deal with worldwide physical space and the ability to lose lots of money in order to make a lot more. The value of being small needs no explanation.

At this point in history, it is hard to imagine that our highly structured and centralist world will morph into a planet full of loosely connected physical and digital communities, but it will. For this reason, more and more attention needs to be paid to just how, and how well, we can coordinate this new mass individualization. It is, for example, easy to see who will build the road in my village. It is considerably harder to see who will connect our villages, especially if some have less wealth or control than others. It is also hard to see how we will agree on various standards. Think of it – we live in a world where we cannot even agree on which side of the road to drive.

> **It is hard to imagine that our highly structured and centralist world will morph into a planet full of loosely connected physical and digital communities, but it will.**

The need for new standards for standards

One of the biggest problems any traveller has with laptop computing, especially in Europe, is the plug. Europeans have more than 20 different formats, with the only semblance of a standard coming from that offered to power an electric razor. There is actually a committee addressing the so-called 'Europlug' – some estimates range upwards of a quarter century before such a standard can be implemented, if found, and then only at huge cost.

What the standards bodies need to do is turn their attention to some of the larger issues. The reason for making global standards is to enable global communications. This means people communicating with people, and people have the biggest standards problem of all – they often don't speak the same language.

If a Martian were to turn an ear towards our planet, conversations around the world would sound like modems unable to communicate with each other. In the face of today's digital globalization, it would be hard to explain the thousand-plus written languages and the scores of spoken dialects. On the other hand, people constantly question the digital dominance of English, yet, as I like to remind them, we are glad that a French pilot lands an Airbus at Charles de Gaulle Airport speaking English to the tower, as it means that other planes in the vicinity can understand. English as a second language – with or without computers – has become an international protocol of sorts and an accepted means of traffic control. In the same way, English will continue to be the air traffic control language of the Net ten years from now, but it will stop being the dominant carrier of content – English will be replaced by Chinese. Still, all sorts of other languages will flourish as well.

We had better learn a lesson – and quickly. That lesson, however, is not that we need to invent another Esperanto, but to realize that our bit streams will be in different languages, which need some standard headers. Making the Net multilingual-ready is even more important than setting the meta-standards for our modems and TVs. International bodies must recognize that a higher level of communications standard is needed to make sure that all languages are equally accommodated and self-descriptive. The 5 billion people not using the Net today have a lot to say.

The challenge of being local

The Net's envelope is the whole planet. Some governments and their regulators talk about curtaining their nations from the Net, monitoring bit streams and banning offensive Web sites – all essentially impossible tasks. Just about every conflict in cyberspace can be traced to a single phenomenon – the absence of locality.

Legal control is always local, and this is increasingly so. A country such as Switzerland, itself very small, gives its 20 cantons (states) and 6 half-cantons enormous power. The federal government keeps a low profile, so much so that I defy you to name Switzerland's head of state.

In many ways, the US is similar to Switzerland. Visitors marvel at our liquor laws, whereby, state by state and city by city, regulations change. While you may not be able to buy liquor in one town, you may in the next. Decency laws are similar in the range of views they reflect. An important part of the current political debate concerns increasing the control at local level because, we are told, people are more civic minded when they believe they will be held accountable and when control lies close to their doorstep.

When US Congress passed the Telecommunications Act of 1996, it included an absurd Communications Decency Act (CDA). This legislation makes transmitting digital material on abortion illegal and overlaps regulations already in existence. It is interesting to note that, even in the world of atoms, the practice has been not to enforce these regulations.

My point does not concern a violation of the First Amendment or the impossibility of enforcing such a law – although I believe the Act suggests both – it is that legislators made, in essence, a categorical mistake. Cyberspace is not geo-political. Cyberspace is a topology, not a topography. There are no physical constructs like 'beside', 'above', 'to the north of'. This is obvious. It is not so obvious, however, to the digitally homeless who govern most countries. The tragedy of the CDA is that countries less democratic than ours have already pointed to it and said, 'You see, even the Americans think the Net is smut,' failing to recognize that the Act was instantly enjoined. Sovereignty is an odd and maybe useless concept within the digital world. The real test of sovereignty, though, is not decency, it is money.

Excuse my apparent digression to a treatment of money as yet another issue of bits and atoms. What follows is an incident that caused me to think about digital money in a new way. In 1994, I was skiing in Klosters, Switzerland. On this occasion, the first ski day of the season, I found that the paper lift ticket had been changed to a smartcard, which, snugly nestled in your pocket, is read as you approach a turnstile – certainly convenient for the mittened skier.

As these smartcards contained electronics, the ski-lift company wanted them back and required a SwF10 deposit (approximately $8), which can be redeemed at any lift or railway station. I ended my first day near neither. Instead, I drove to the neighbouring town to visit my father in the hospital. On the way, I stopped to buy some chocolates and, while paying for them, reached into my pocket and pulled out a handful of coins, including the smartcard. Without my reading glasses, I squinted at the coins and must have looked like a struggling tourist. The cashier reached over the counter to take the exact change. First, she took the smartcard, saying that it was worth ten francs, followed by the few additional coins she needed. I was stunned. Then I noticed a pile of smartcards on the cash register behind her. 'What do you do with these?', I asked. 'We pay the baker,' she answered. This was too much. I visited the baker, and he had far more of these ski-lift cards, which he said he used to pay for milk, flour and delivery. Obviously, the lift company must be running out of cards. What does it do? It does what our government does. It prints more. I sure hope the cards cost less than ten francs!

Is this significant? Yes, because nobody cares and that's what is interesting. Nobody cares that these lift cards have become local currency because they are just that – local. This currency moves slowly and is restricted to a small section of a remote valley in eastern Switzerland.

Now, turn those atoms into bits. Suddenly locale has no meaning. I have a global currency as long as it's attached to a trusted entity – akin to the lift company – and that entity need not be a country. Most of us would trust GM, IBM or AT&T currency more readily than that of many developing nations because the 'currency' represented by those companies is more likely to remain convertible. After all, a guarantee is only as good as its guarantor.

The ski-lift currency moved by virtue of being in my pocket at the right time. As soon as currency becomes bits (dutifully encrypted), its reach is unlimited. In fact, while organizations such as the EU struggle to achieve a single currency, cyberspace may develop its own much faster.

> We are experiencing a new form of localism ... In the digital world, neighbourhoods cease to be places and become groups that evolve from shared interests.

We are experiencing a new form of localism. Neighbourhoods, as we have known them, are places. In the digital world, neighbourhoods cease to be places and become groups that evolve from shared interests, such as those described by mailing lists, newsgroups or aliases organized by like-minded people. A family stretched far and wide can become a virtual neighbourhood. Each of us will have many kinds of 'being local'. You can almost hum it. Being local will be determined by what we think and say, when we work and play, where we earn and pay.

Taxing tax in the Wired World

Cyberspace has enormous implications for tax laws and tax systems, which governments and tax regulators around the world are busy trying to come to grips with. The idea of taking a tax bite out of digital communications comes courtesy of The Club of Rome, specifically Arthur Cordell and Ran Ide's 1994 report 'The New Wealth of Nations'. More recently, the idea of redistributing the benefits of the Information Society has been championed by influential economist Luc Soete, Director of the Maastricht Economic Research Institute on Innovation and Technology. Despite their status, supporters of such a bit tax are clearly clueless about the workings of the digital world.

A typical book contains about 10 million bits, which might take even a fast reader several hours to digest. By contrast, a typical video – digital and compressed – burns through 10 million bits to produce less than 4 seconds of enjoyment. Thus, a bit consumption tax makes no more sense than tariffing toys by the number of atoms they consist of. Maybe the Information Superhighway metaphors have gone to the heads of digitally homeless economists who think they can assess value by something akin to counting cars.

Of course, collecting taxes can be tough enough without trying to assess something you can't see, especially when you don't know where it is going to or coming from. This helps explain why the Clinton Administration in February 1998 reaffirmed its commitment to making cyberspace a global free-trade zone. The policy's purpose, the brainchild of White House Senior Adviser Ira Magaziner, is both economic stimulus and practicable fairness. So, whether or not Congress has kept its promise to vote on the related Internet Tax Freedom Act, the legislation has the full force of careful deliberation – and historical inevitability – behind it. For these and other reasons, Europe abandoned the idea of the bit tax, but it still survived three and a half years of consideration, despite the growing awareness that bits, by their very nature, defy taxation.

Even so, the principled position taken by President Clinton and Congress comes, in part, because making the Net a free-trade zone works for the US federal government. The Treasury derives most of its revenues from personal and corporate income taxes. If the economy sees a boost from any form of free trade, the Feds will see a proportionate rise in their own intake. Simple arithmetic.

However, many countries and most states don't work that way. Instead, a sales tax is the means – often the principal means – of filling government coffers. Ohio Governor George Voinovich, Chair of the National Governors' Association, declared that the Internet Tax Freedom Act 'represents the most significant challenge to state sovereignty that we've witnessed over the last ten years'. Both he and the Act may be right.

The sales tax is also particularly popular among bureaucrats in developing nations, where collecting income tax is even harder because the poor make so little and the rich can avoid so much. Plus, the sales tax turns retailers into a nationwide web of tax collectors, and it is 'fair' because it's based on what you spend versus what you earn. Still, Voinovich and company would be smart to start looking elsewhere, because their receipts will plummet as we buy more and more on-line, especially if what we buy is bits.

While the sales tax is fairly commonplace, the value-added tax (VAT) is more or less unknown in the US. Loosely speaking, it taxes the various stages of transforming raw material into a finished product, the last stage of value added being what you pay at the retail counter (and get back at the airport's VAT refund counter). This kind of tax makes even less sense in a world of bits.

Assume that bits are my stock in trade and I use Microsoft Word to refine my raw material. Should I pay VAT on spellchecking each story? Should I pay VAT to have it encrypted and more VAT to have it decrypted, not to mention more for each of the layers of value added by various editors? In fact, as a cheerful taxpayer, if I have to pay taxes on bits – at least those that make up words – I would be willing to pay more VAT for the fewest possible bits – just the right ones, please. That would be value added indeed.

The most taxing aspect of cyberspace is not the ephemeral nature of bits, the marginal cost of zero to make more of them or that there is no need for warehouses to store them. It is our inability to say accurately where they are. If my server is in the British West Indies, are those the laws that apply to, say, my banking? The EU has implied that the answer is 'Yes', while the US remains silent on the matter.

What happens if I log in from San Antonio, sell some of my bits to a person in France and accept digital cash from Germany, which I deposit in Japan? Today, the government of Texas believes I should be paying state taxes, as the transaction would take place (at the start) over wires crossing its jurisdiction. Yikes. As we see, the mindset of taxes is rooted in concepts such as atoms and place. With both of those more or less missing, the basics of taxation will have to change. Taxes in the digital world do not neatly follow the analogue laws of physics, which so conveniently require real energy, to move real things, over real borders, taxable at each stage along the way. Of course, even analogue taxation without representation is no tea party.

The mindset of taxes is rooted in concepts such as atoms and place. With both of those more or less missing, the basics of taxation will have to change.

Looking ahead, taxes will eventually become a voluntary process, with the possible exception of real estate – the one physical thing that does not move easily and has computable value. The US has a jump-start on the practice, in that 65 per cent of local school funds come from real estate taxes – a practice Europeans consider odd and ill-advised. Wait, though, until that's all there is left to tax, when the rest of the things we buy and sell come from everywhere, anywhere and nowhere.

Get a digital life?

Any significant social phenomenon creates a backlash. The Net is no exception. It is odd, however, that the loudest complaints are shouts of 'Get a life!' – suggesting that on-line living will dehumanize us, insulate us and create a world of people who won't smell flowers, watch sunsets or engage in face-to-face experiences. Out of this backlash comes a warning to parents that their children will 'cocoon' and metamorphose into social invalids.

Experience tells us the opposite. So far, evidence gathered by those using the Net as a teaching tool, indicates that kids who go on-line gain social skills rather than lose them. As the distance between Athens, Georgia, and Athens, Greece, is just a mouse click away, children attain a new kind of worldliness. Young people on the Net today will inevitably experience some of the sophistication of other countries. In earlier days, only children from elite families could afford to interact with far-away cultures during their summer holidays abroad.

I know that visiting Web pages in Italy or interacting with Italians via e-mail isn't the same as ducking the pigeons or listening to music in Piazza San Marco, but it sure beats never going there at all. Take all the books in the world and they won't offer the real-time global experience a kid can get on the Net: here a child becomes the driver of the intellectual vehicle, not the passenger.

Mitch Resnick of the MIT Media Lab once told me of an autistic boy who has great difficulty interacting with people, often giving inappropriate visual cues (such as strange facial expressions) and so forth. However, this child has thrived on the Net. When he types, he gains control and becomes articulate. He's an active participant in chatrooms and newsgroups. He has developed strong on-line friendships, which have given him greater confidence in face-to-face situations.

This is an extreme case, but isn't it odd how parents grieve if their child spends six hours a day on the Net, but delight if those same hours are spent reading books? With the exception of sleep, doing anything six hours a day, every day, is not good for a child.

Adults on the Net enjoy even greater opportunity, as more people discover they can work from almost anywhere. Granted, if you make pizzas, you need to be close to the dough; if you're a surgeon, you must be close to your patients (at least for the next two decades). If, however, your trade involves bits (not atoms), you probably don't need to be anywhere specific – at least most of the time. In fact, it might be beneficial all-around if you were in the Caribbean or Mediterranean – then your company wouldn't have to tie up capital in expensive town centre offices.

Certain early users of the Net (bless them!) are now whining about its vulgarization, warning people of its hazards as if it were a cigarette. If only these whiners were more honest, they'd admit that it was they who didn't have much of a life and found solace on the Net. They who woke up one day with mid-life crises and discovered there was more to living than what was waiting in their e-mail boxes. So, what took you guys so long? Of course there's more to life than e-mail, but don't project your empty existence onto others and suggest 'being digital' is a form of virtual leprosy for which total abstinence is the only immunization.

My own lifestyle is totally enhanced by being on-line. I've been a compulsive e-mail user for more than 25 years as, more often than not, it's allowed me to spend more time in scenic places with interesting people. Which would you prefer: two weeks' holiday totally off-line or four to six weeks on-line? This doesn't work for all professions, but it is a growing trend among so-called 'knowledge workers'.

Once, only the likes of Rupert Murdoch or Aga Khan could cut deals from their satellite-laden luxury yachts off the coast of Sardinia. Now, all sorts of people from Tahoe to Telluride can work from the back seat of their car if they wish.

I don't know the statistics, but I'm willing to guess that the executives of corporate America spend 70 to 80 per cent of their time in meetings. I do know that most of those meetings – often a statutory one hour long – are 70 to 80 per cent posturing and levelling (bringing the others up to speed on a common subject). The posturing is gratuitous and the levelling is better done elsewhere – on-line, for example. This alone would enhance US productivity far more than any trade agreement.

I am constantly astonished by just how off-line corporate America is. Wouldn't you expect executives at computer and communications companies to be active on-line? Even household names of the high-tech industry are off-line human beings, sometimes more so than execs in extremely low-tech fields. I guess this is a corollary to the shoemaker's children having no shoes.

Being on-line not only makes the inevitable face-to-face meetings so much easier, it allows you to look outward. Generally, large companies are so inwardly directed that staff memos about growing bureaucracy get more attention than the dwindling competitive advantage of being big in the first place. David, who has a life, needn't use a slingshot. Goliath, who doesn't, is too busy reading office memos.

In the mid-1700s, mechanical looms and other machines forced cottage industries out of business. Many people lost the opportunity to be their own bosses and to enjoy the profits of hard work. I'm sure I would have been a Luddite under those conditions.

But the current sweep of digital living is doing exactly the opposite. Parents of young children find exciting self-employment from home. The 'virtual corporation' is an opportunity for tiny companies (with employees spread across the world) to work together in a global market and set up base wherever they choose. If you don't like centralist thinking, big companies or job automation, what better place to go than the Net? Work for yourself and get a good digital life. ■

The material in this chapter is based on several articles written by me for the *Wired* Column published by *Wired* Ventures between 1995 and 1998.

Charles Handy

Author

THE AGE OF UNCERTAINTY VERSUS THE AGE OF GREATNESS

My concern is that a world where individuals are left even more to their own devices as more of work and life moves outside the institutions of society, could be a world designed for selfishness.

Kingman Brewster, once President of Yale, then US Ambassador to Britain, once memorably asked a gathering of the British great and good, 'Who are the trustees of our future?' There was an embarrassed mumble, but no clear response. The question still holds good and my answer is that it has to be all of us, at least all of us who are capable of reading a book like this, and who have a concern for the world our children and our grandchildren will grow up in.

We may not, individually, be able to make their world safer from nuclear war or preserve the rainforests better or keep the ozone layer intact, but it is often the little things of life that matter most, the ways we work and love and play, the ways we relate to people and the manner in which we spend our days as well as our money. These things we can affect, we do not have to accept them as they are. The Wired World is inevitably going to be something of an exploration, but exploring is at the heart of learning and changing and growing. This is what I believe and this is what gives me hope.

The world that our parents knew is not the world we live in today; nor is our world any sure guide to the way our children will live and love and work. We live in an Age of Unreason when we can no longer assume that what worked well once will work well again when most assumptions can legitimately be challenged.

One thing is clear, however – institutions will be less important. More of us will spend more of our lives outside formal organizations. 'What,' I said to the chairmen of some large financial institutions, 'will your executives and your brokers be doing between the ages of 50 and 80 when, assuredly, they will not be working for you or with you?'. 'It's a good question,' they acknowledged, 'and one we ought to look at some time.' By the time they do, many of those 50-year-olds will have moved on and out.

> **'Who are the trustees of our future?' ... my answer is that it has to be all of us ...**

'I have ever hated all nations, professions and communities, and all my love is towards people,' said the poet Pope, 'but principally I hate and detest that animal called man, although I heartily love John, Peter, Thomas and so forth.' Pope would have been pleased with the way things are going, even with the chance to add a feminine name or two to the catalogue, for this is an age when individual differences will be important, both inside and outside organizations. The successful organization will be built around John and Peter, Mary and Catherine, not around anonymous human resources, while, in the world outside the organization, there will be no collective lump to hide under. We shall have to stand each behind our own name tag.

It should suit countries such as Britain rather well. Condemned for decades for the ineffectiveness of much of her industry, Britain has always been renowned, even celebrated, for her journalism, television and theatre, for skills of finance and consultancy, architecture and civil engineering, for medicine and surgery, design, photography and fashion. These are all byline occupations, meaning that the individual is encouraged to put their name to the work. They are all occupations where the organizations are more like a network than a pyramid, where hierarchy is minimal and individual talent of great importance. As more of industry and commerce become byline occupations, they will fit more naturally into the individual ethos of Britain and, indeed, of most Americans. The mass organizations of 'hands' and 'resources' never worked too well in the old democracies of either nation. It will be interesting to see how long they continue to work effectively in the newer democracies of the world.

This said, a society of individual differences has its problems as well as its undoubted opportunities. Liberty, or the right to be different, and equality have always been the two proud goals of democracy. Unfortunately, it has always proved difficult to have both at the same time. If people are encouraged to be different, they will not end up equal, and, if they are to be kept level, they will have to have their liberty curtailed. The equality of opportunity – normally defined as the right to go to school and hospital – is not quite the same thing as a full equality. A society founded on individualism could fall apart without the glue of fraternity that the French revolutionaries added to liberty and equality. Fraternity is the awareness that there are others who are as important as oneself.

The paradox of choice

People who are free to choose may choose wrongly. This is the age-old paradox. Sin is the other side of freedom's coin. A world without sin would be a world without choice.

All the forces I've been busy describing in my works seem designed to set the individual free to be more truly themselves. Choice is multiple for the fortunate ones. They can choose when to work, at home or in the office; what to eat, with irradiated foods coming fresh from all corners of the world; what to buy via electronic catalogues. They can choose to live richly or thinly in a material sense and even, perhaps, when to die. Within society, we may expect the abundance of choice to lead to the erosion of any one dominant set of values. No longer will we see some seeking to set or change the rules while others, the majority, wait to keep to the rules they set. 'Anything (or almost anything) goes' will be the message of the years ahead. It will be increasingly acceptable to do your own thing, provided that thing does not interfere with the choices of too many others. NIMBY (Not In My Backyard) has always become the plea, or bleat, of those who seek, at the same time, to promote individual liberty and defend their own islands of privacy – words once again heralding a change of tune.

Achievement and contentment in this society will have many different facets. It could be called a tolerant society, but it could also be a very fragmented society as an individualism rooted in personal achievement and material success replaces the mixture of institutional paternalism and dependency that we grew up with – good news for the strong, but not for the weak. Choice, in the end, is only good news for all if everyone has enough to choose from, enough information and enough inner resources. To put it more paradoxically, a society dedicated to the enrichment and enhancement of the self will only survive, and certainly will only prosper, if its dominant ethic is the support and encouragement of others. Proper selfishness is rooted in unselfishness.

There is a real possibility that those of the generation now in their thirties – the first generation to experience the full range of choice – may use it to opt out of leadership roles in business and society. For the talented ones, a life on the edges of organizations can be personally fulfilling, free and life-enhancing, but this might condemn organizations to be comprised of the second best and who will then run society? On the other hand, if the leadership roles are going to the talented ones, but also ones who want those roles for their own satisfaction rather than for the good of others, life will become a collection of private courts and courtiers – great if you are in, dismal and bleak if you are outside.

Choice in relationships now means that the extended family is not a collection of aunts, uncles and cousins, but of stepparents and half-brothers and sisters, or of stepbrothers and sisters with no blood connection at all. The courts may take care of the custody of the very young, but who will be responsible for an ageing stepgrandmother or for the lonely sibling fallen on hard times? There are some who hope that new communities, sharing their homes or their workplaces rather than their parentage, will replace the old networks of the family that were so often riddled with secret jealousies and ancient feuds. My own fear is that, in the end, shared bricks are not so reliable as shared blood, that these communities of common interest thrive as long as the interests are common, but fall apart when the interests diverge. Choice can seem a hollow mockery when someone is old and cold and poor; individual freedom can easily mean freedom not to care.

Organizations, for their part, need to think about their responsibilities in the midst of the pressures to maintain their flexibility and freedom of choice. Who, for instance, will train and retrain the contract workers if the organization chooses not to? Education and training definitely increase choice for those educated thereby giving them passports enabling them to move to greener pastures, but is this really a valid reason for not training one's executives? In the past it has been, and in many industries today it is still the complaint of the bigger institutions, that they lose their best people as soon as they have trained them and are therefore tempted to become poachers like the rest. Who, then, will train the game they want to poach? If organizations continue to think that way, then choice will become the enemy of progress. Too much emphasis on organizational choice, on flexibility, can look like a lack of commitment to your people, inviting a lack of commitment in return. Selfishness breeds selfishness.

> **Choice can seem a hollow mockery when someone is old and cold and poor; individual freedom can easily mean freedom not to care.**

Governments, in the meantime, having discovered that the market – the mechanism of choice – liberates initiative and penalizes inefficiency, are tempted to leave all to self-regulating choice. That would be dangerous. Markets do not look much beyond tomorrow, or at least next year. Markets are inherently selfish, disinclined to make investments the outcomes of which cannot be precisely predicted or the benefits of which cannot be claimed in advance. Basic research, for instance, in new sciences and new technologies has to be an article of faith. Who could predict in advance that the Science Research Council's investment in tracking down the structure of DNA at Cambridge would result in the whole new industry of biotechnology?

The education of the next generation, too, has to be an act of faith. Left to individual parents and competing schools, it would soon become a vocational rat-race for the few rather than a platform for growth for the many. Japan's government sees it as its responsibility, on behalf of the nation, to put national resources behind an infrastructure of creativity, building a new technopolis in nineteen locations and giving priority, in funding basic research and development, to seven emerging industry sectors. These long-term investments cannot be left to chance and the hope that individual firms will choose to do this of their own accord.

When Kingman Brewster asked who were to be the trustees of our future, his point was that governments tend naturally to think short term and that a national consciousness is needed that makes it permissible to spend our money today for the benefit of grandchildren yet unborn. It would be a reversal of the tradition that it makes good economic sense to borrow from those grandchildren to boost our standard of living today. Market forces will not produce the wherewithal or the political will to tackle the problems of the ozone layer and the possible global warming, yet if the Netherlands and East Anglia are not to be submerged in 50 years' time, someone must start spending money on finding solutions now. Making that decision requires choice to be exercised by a few on behalf of the many, with the consent of the many – leadership on a big scale.

The new ethic

In a world of individualism, the dominant ethic can so easily become 'What harms no one is OK' or 'What the others do and get away with has to be all right' or even 'If no one knows, then you're fine'. At the height of the insider trading scandals of 1987, a leading London banker called insider dealing 'a victimless crime', implying that it was more a legal nicety than a sin, rather like taking an extra bottle of whisky through Customs. What is wrong, some athletes say, with the odd drug to boost your stamina – it harms no one save yourself. What is wrong with receiving welfare payments and doing work on the side – the State can afford it. If that ethic were to prevail then any attempt by governments or organizations to spend money today to benefit people in 30 years' time or to spend more of our money on other people in need would be futile – voters, shareholders and employees would shout them down.

The new freedoms and choices will only survive if those who exercise them take time to look over their shoulders, if they genuinely have a care for others as well as for themselves, others beyond their families and their own institutions. Just as businesses today invest in their local communities out of a sense of enlightened self-interest, because good communities mean, in the end, better recruits and better customers, it is in the long-term interests of us all to make sure that choices are not rationed in our society because any rationing of choice might cause it to self-destruct. It is, however, for companies and individuals a calculation that has to be built on faith instead of genuflecting to the spirit of the times, talking the language of proper selfishness.

We need a new religion to save us, or at least a new fashion. Fraternity – caring for others as much as for oneself – must be our guiding ethic. First, learn to love yourself, then your neighbour, but don't forget the neighbour. Hubris, the Greeks called it, when overweening pride or excessive enthusiasm for your own achievements aroused the irritation, even envy, of the gods. Nemesis, or downfall, would follow. It was a way of putting a moral embargo on improper selfishness. It can't be done by laws, by institutions or taxes, for fraternity is one thing that cannot be contracted out or outsourced. It is a core value, and it is established by the example of the people at the core, by the new élites, the fortunate ones.

The signs are not all that encouraging, but I am hopeful. Conspicuous consumption – German cars, the electronic gadgetry, houses that cost more than most people earn in a lifetime – is often the outward and visible sign of greed made respectable. When a company chairperson, better nameless, boosts their salary by 37 per cent while their company's profits have declined by 7 per cent, and sees no reason for explanation or apology, it can seem that private exploitation of public responsibility has become the norm.

On the other hand, there are other signs:

- **The Bob Geldof effect** More people, particularly young people, are prepared to give to good causes than in the past. More companies, too, recognize that good causes have a legitimate claim on their budgets and give less grudgingly than just a few years ago.
- **The willing taxpayer** Nearly 80 per cent of Britons, in many surveys, would like to pay more taxes if doing so resulted in better education, healthcare and social welfare.
- **The young crusaders** Many young people want to spend at least part of their youth working overseas or helping out in places of adversity. The knowledge that they themselves will probably never be destitute seems to give them a new sense of freedom.
- **The Third Age** As more and more middle-aged people discover that there is life beyond retirement, that there is real work to do, their values will often shift. Having proved themselves in their work, they now want to improve the lot of others – by helping in education, voluntary organizations, sports and community associations. Helping others becomes a way of giving new meaning to their lives.
- **Institutional tithing** More organizations are encouraging their employees to lend their talents and/or their time to charitable causes, often in the firms' own time, but sometimes by means of secondment, sometimes by corporate support for individual initiatives.

More needs to happen

True fulfilment is, I believe, vicarious. We get our deepest satisfaction from the fulfilment, growth and happiness of others. It takes time, often a lifetime, to realize this. Parents know it well, as do teachers, great managers and all who care for the downtrodden and unfortunate. We need to give more public expression to what is a deep human characteristic, so that we are not ashamed to be seen to care for others as well as for ourselves, for the future of all as much as for our own, for everyone's environment as well as our own.

My hope is that as more people have more time outside organizations, they will discover that portfolios are always enriched by work done for others. I believe that the intensification and the rationing of paid work will, ironically perhaps, encourage more gift work or unpaid work as people realize that it is the 'contribution' element in work that they miss most, and that contribution can be found in a wide variety of work, most of it outside organizations.

My hope is that, as more people can choose where to live, they will live in places more like villages than cities, places where your neighbours have names and faces, where their concerns gradually become part of your concerns. It is always more difficult to care for strangers or for people in the abstract. In a society of smaller communities, there should be fewer strangers and more time to stop and talk as well as stare.

My hope is that life is now the right way round. Our wants are hierarchical, as Abraham Maslow pointed out long ago. To put it more simply, life is largely a matter of crossing things off the list until you get to the bits that are really quintessentially 'you'. Success, money and achievement should now, to many, come earlier, leaving them free to be different while there is still time and energy. In the past, there was neither the time nor the energy – too many died without discovering their full portfolio of possibilities.

My hope is that a society of differences will produce many models for success. Achievement will not be measured simply in terms of money and possessions, but by creativity in the arts, social invention, lives of dedication to the care of others, political leadership in small places as well as great, writing and acting and music of quality. We need to make sure that the whole variety is honoured, by press and politicians alike.

My hope is that our various religions and faiths will be more outward-looking than inward-looking, realizing that to strive towards a heaven, or something like it, in this world, is the best guarantee of one in the next world, wherever and whatever that may be. Britain's countryside is dotted with ancient churches and they are important symbols. They should be symbols, not of spiritual escapism, but of God's and man's involvement in the world around them.

My hope, finally, is in the nature of humankind itself. I believe that a lot of our striving after the symbols and levers of success is due to a basic insecurity, a need to prove ourselves. That done, grown up at last, we are free to stop pretending. I am conscious that we each have our quota of original sin, but I also believe in original goodness. The people I admire most have grown up soonest and become their own people. That seems to happen more easily outside the constricting roles of institutions. The world I see emerging, with its looser organizations, has many threats and many dangers, but it should also allow more people to stop pretending much earlier in their lives. If that is so, then the Wired World and Age of Unreason may become a better world and an Age of Greatness. ∎

Arne Fjørtoft

Secretary General, Worldview International Foundation

CHALLENGING THE DIGITAL DIVIDE

The gap between the information rich and the information poor

New opportunities in a divided world

The gap is widening. Disparities in the global society are fast increasing. The world is becoming dramatically divided between the haves and the have-nots. The gap has traditionally been one of basic need issues, but the communication revolution is dramatically increasing the gap as it represents the very foundation of development – access to information and knowledge, the raw material for sustainable growth. Those who have much will get more, much more, and those who have little will get less, or nothing. The whole world of information and education – of stored knowledge during the history of mankind – is increasingly available at our fingertips. However, millions of people with no access to information will continue to live in the past, in information darkness. In these societies, the basic need is not for computer literacy, but for a much more fundamental literacy, acquiring the magic skills of reading and writing.

There are, it is estimated, 880 million adults who can neither read nor write in the developing countries and well over 200 million adults in the industrial world who cannot use what little they have learned in these areas. This is so 550 years after Gutenberg invented the art of printing. If the current trend continues,1 the lack of such fundamental skills will remain a major international problem well into the twenty-first century.

With this in mind, the dream of a harmonious world with equal opportunities for all seems further away than ever before. With the communication revolution rapidly transforming many countries into knowledge-based societies, the less-developed countries will be left out of the process, light years behind the rest of the world. It is an irony that the cradle of mankind, Africa, will fall further behind in the wake of the communication revolution. Our oldest known ancestor, Lucy, lived in Ethiopia 3.4 million years ago. The recent explosion in new technology and information-based knowledge have passed by Lucy's birthplace and other less-developed countries. The prospect for human development is not very encouraging in a country such as Ethiopia, with 75 per cent of its women and 55 per cent of its men not being able to read or write.

Making sure people are able to read and write is a formidable challenge in bridging the information gap, but it is not impossible. There are many examples of successful literacy programmes. It is, first and foremost, a question of political priorities, and it is high time development agencies concentrated their efforts in the development of people. No country can prosper without basic education for all. Proper use of new communications technology provides a very cost-effective opportunity to do this that should not be missed. The consequence of ignoring these opportunities will be a world split further apart.

Media for human development

The historic gap we feel between Lucy and our modern world is odd in that most of the high-tech gadgets we take for granted today emerged only during the last 50 years. Human society was at the zero point for a very long time. The agricultural society lasted only 10,000 years, and the industrial age 300 years. Today, we are entering the communications and knowledge age – a new and unknown era is just around the corner. Any limitations to technological development are those that stem from our own way of thinking, our own visions. We have certainly reached the gates to the brave new world, as further development will take place at lightning speed, a pace unknown in human history, beyond our own imagination. Do we know, though, where to go, what to achieve in terms of real human development?

The affluent part of the world is hit with an unprecedented overflow of information that is fast increasing day by day. It is not humanly possible to consume all the bombardments from the Internet, e-mail, CD-ROM, video, discs, radio, TV and print – and this is only the beginning of the new era. By the year 2000, it is estimated that western European satellite transponders will have up to 4500 TV channels. The Astra satellite system can today boast of only 2000 digital channels. The problem is not any longer how to get information, but to select from the information coming at us. This development is breathtaking, but the corresponding lack of access to information in the poorest countries represents a growing world problem of dramatic dimensions.

Millions of people have absolutely no effective communication links with the outside world. This is a human tragedy as even a tiny amount of information can save lives, especially in relation to preventable diseases. A case in point is diarrhoea, which is one of the main child killers in the world, causing approximately 5 million deaths per year. Most of these precious human beings could have been saved if their parents had had the knowledge that a glass of water with salt and sugar added should be given to children suffering from diarrhoea. Unfortunately, many parents have inherited the tragic belief that children with diarrhoea should have nothing to drink, and so they unconsciously worsen their condition. This is a dramatic example of unnecessary ignorance, as there are ways and means of communicating life-saving messages today, if properly used. UNICEF's media campaign on the oral rehydration solution mentioned is an example of a cost-effective life-saving intervention, but much more could have been done.

There is an urgent need to disseminate simple, practical knowledge that will save lives, increase awareness and stimulate development. When this need is set against the heavy downpour of all kind of information hitting us daily in the more affluent part of the world, it is a large human tragedy that the world is so gravely unbalanced. If just a fraction of the resources used in countries with information overload had been channelled into the development of communication in the poorer parts of the world, millions of people could have been provided with important knowledge that could empower them to solve their own problems. There are more than enough channels already that could be used in this way.

> **There is an urgent need to disseminate simple, practical knowledge that will save lives, increase awareness and stimulate development.**

Radio breaks the barriers of illiteracy and is reaching most of the population on earth. It is an effective, low-cost communication medium for national audiences or local communities. In some parts of the world, radio transmission is still under strict political control, being an instrument of propaganda and brainwashing. The opposite of this is commercial radio that has no social responsibility. There is certainly more than enough radio around, but its usefulness in bringing high-quality journalistic content to enlighten and inspire people's development has, to a great extent, been lost. The most promising concept in this regard is community radio, which provides a voice for the people and helps preserve their culture and values. There is great potential in radio broadcasting – it could be used much more constructively than is generally so today. One example is the experience of Worldview Foundation, which has mobilized disadvantaged people in Bangladesh to create more than 2 million home gardens by using cost-effective media, with radio as an important provider of information. This has greatly improved the nutritional standard of more than 10 million people and significantly reduced child mortality and nutritionally related blindness.

In a larger context, digitalization of radio technology will overcome many technical limitations and globalize the airwaves further, making it easier to break up propaganda monopolies from outside in support of democracy and human rights. This will improve the efficiency of the present shortwave radio transmissions by the exiled Burmese Government and other groups in reaching their people from outside with alternative information. Dictators and their henchmen will find it increasingly difficult to poison the minds of people with lies and political propaganda.

The greatest challenge for radio is that of introducing knowledge-based participatory concepts, using the medium as a tool in support of sustainable development. By opening the airwaves for people in general, new and low-cost transmission technology will greatly contribute to democratization of the media. Its largest impact could be in developing countries, if decision makers are ready to empower their own people to speak for themselves.

In spite of radio being an affordable medium, there is no doubt that TV has become the most dominant global mass medium. According to a survey in 1997 by the London-based Television Trust for the Environment, channel expansion – including hours of TV watched and the increase in TV ownership – has been truly astonishing. There has been a 100 per cent increase since the end of the 1980s. The single best-selling consumer product in the world is the colour TV set. According to Philips, 105 million colour sets were sold worldwide in 1995. There are an estimated 1.6 billion TV sets in use today, reaching more than 75 per cent of the world's population.

In 1995, the average American spent more time watching TV than listening to the radio, surfing the Internet, reading newspapers or listening to recorded music put together. This is not exceptional – a Pole spends more time watching TV than an American, a Malaysian as much as a Dane, an Italian as much as a Turk.

TV has become a large, global business. The industry generated a world total of $300 billion in 1995, with 60 per cent derived from advertising. Nearly all the top 20 companies by turnover are multimedia conglomerates operating from the US, Europe or Japan. Some of their programmes are screened in more than 100 countries – a truly global industry. However, with more than 40 per cent of the total value generated by US companies alone, the cultural and social aspects bring about serious concerns. In some parts of the world, this has been labelled as a cultural war. The massive flow of foreign programmes has a large impact on a global scale, specially among youth in traditional societies that have become sandwiched between old and new lifestyles. In some societies, the new media penetrate deeply. Even in some of the most remote areas in the world, TV has become a part of the daily lives of people. A study in isolated villages in Indonesia concluded that 64 per cent of the people got most of their information from TV, compared to 70 per cent in Great Britain. While access to TV has narrowed, the gap in communicating cultural and social diversities has widened, as a few Northern conglomerates dominate the visual airwaves all over the world.

New digital technologies could, to a certain extent, change the scene as the communication process becomes simpler and more cost-effective. This new development creates space for new actors and for alternative networks. Many of the world's broadcasters are planning for the new era, for Internet TV and other network solutions that can bring thousands of TV channels to each customer. We are fast approaching the multimedia age where everything is coming together in one, single technology. There is no doubt that this new development could strengthen the process of democratization, accessibility and active participation by the viewers. Experience has shown that people prefer to watch programmes in their own language with quality content that is related to their own cultural identity, if possible.

Today, there is great potential to create knowledge-based networks with social and cultural values. It is up to us to make use of the new opportunities. Several initiatives have been taken, among them is Young Asia Television, which has a value-based content, is produced by Asian youth and reaches satellite and terrestrial networks with more than 150 million viewers in ten countries. Among its partners is the Asian Development Bank, which supports the project 'Media for the disadvantaged', the aim of which is to reach disadvantaged groups with useful information and knowledge via the Young Asia TV network. This is a new concept in reaching large audiences with development programmes.

With the cost of production decreasing, more and more people will not only be able to get access to a variety of programmes, but also organize themselves and create their own networks. The recent introduction of small, low-cost digital cameras and PC-based editing units will fuel the change in video and TV production. This could further democratize media and bring about a colourful variety of various TV programmes and participatory video/group media, which could hopefully be supportive in maintaining cultural diversities and, in addition, bring the world closer together. Ultimately, we are all neighbours in the global village.

A lesson from Bangladesh

The population of Bangladesh is one of the poorest in the world, with $220 per capita GDP (compared to the US with $28,600). It is a disaster-prone country, too, plagued with yearly floods and tidal waves, regarded as having some of the worst and most intractable problems in the world. Its rapid population growth (which doubles every 35 years) is seen as the largest threat to its own future. However, the population can also become a formidable resource, if properly mobilized.

The establishment of Grameen Bank, for example, has given new hope to millions of disadvantaged people, not only in Bangladesh. The idea of micro-credit has so far spread to more than 60 countries. The man behind it is Professor Muhammad Yunus, who left his position at Chittagong University to practice economic development for the benefit of the poor. Dr Yunus has turned a concept into reality and it has become an ideal tool to provide credit to the poor on a sustainable basis. His bank has, during the last 25 years, reached more than 2.1 million households (more than 10 million people) with a total of more than $2 billion in cumulative lending and a repayment rate of 97per cent! This stunning success has been achieved in spite of scepticism among the banking and economic development sector at the start of the project. Only Dr Yunus believed it could be done and he did it!

Grameen Bank has developed into a sizeable institution, with its network of 12,000 grass root bankers/development workers and has become a social invention. The Bank is ready to continue to undertake new and daring projects. Among its new ventures is a company called Grameen Phone. Dr Yunus wants to bring the age of the telephone, of communication, to the poorest of the poor. He has aligned himself with Telecom Norway (Telenor), which is introducing the latest in mobile phone technology for the benefit of Grameen Bank borrowers. It has become a new business in a number of villages. Loans to buy a mobile telephone are given to people in the village (mostly women, whom the Bank regard as the most socially responsible) and they operate the telephone on a commercial basis. For the first time, the villagers have access to modern means of communication, and can reach relations and friends without travelling for days to deliver information and messages of importance to families (funerals, weddings and so on) and also receive valuable information on market prices of agricultural products, which prevents them being cheated by traders and middlemen. For the first time, they can instantly reach decision makers far away and argue their cases. From their own villages, they can now talk to sons, daughters and other relations abroad, as Bangladesh has a large population of workers in other countries. The introduction of the phone system is a development that brings the villages of Bangladesh at least 100 years forward. It is also a technology that they can manage themselves, giving the village telephone operators a new way of earning a living and meeting urgent human needs.

Another dimension is that the project is breaking the state monopoly on telephone services. It represents cheaper connection costs than was possible with the old copper wire system and faster connection as well – the waiting list to get a telephone with the old system is more than 5 years, in a country of 130 million people with only 300,000 telephones.

The Grameen Phone system is a new and promising revolution that brings the world to the fingertips of the isolated villages in Bangladesh. The wonder is that it is designed to put a communication tool in the hands of the poor, those who have earlier been totally deprived of any access to modern means of communication.

There are, sadly, still some people in positions of influence who do not understand the potential of bringing access to communication to the disadvantaged. Some have questioned the project by asking why people who don't even have enough to eat should have access to mobile phones. This is an old-fashioned concept that results in no improvement being brought to people's lives. It is time that is was understood that information and education are the most important raw materials in building a sustainable society, and that modern communication is the most cost-effective tool to

> There are, sadly, still some people in positions of influence who do not understand the potential of bringing access to communication to the disadvantaged.

bring about the necessary change. This is the lesson that has been learned in the more developed parts of the world and, without proper recognition of this, millions of disadvantaged people will be left totally outside the development process. It is necessary to realize that development is a human exercise and until people get access to information and knowledge, no real development will take place.

The new communications technology, the digital world, opens up unparalleled possibilities for rapid human development. Grameen Phone in Bangladesh is just the beginning of a very exciting process. The next step is to develop an interactive system that will be available to every villager at an affordable price. The Grameen Bank and Telenor have invited the Worldview International Foundation (an international organization with 20 years' experience in development communication) to join them in a project to develop the ultimate learning system using the latest digital technology. The Grameen Bank will provide the economic and social network, Telenor the technology, and Worldview the content. This is an ideal example of fruitful cooperation between various organizations in building a common project on the particular strength of each partner. Research and concept development is already in progress, with the aim of utilizing the latest and most appropriate technology in designing and operating a village-based interactive learning and information system.

Taking into consideration that the communication revolution accelerates the speed in creating new and exciting technology, some of the systems planned to be used by the project have still to be properly developed and tested. Based on this futuristic approach, the project will be launched in the year 2000, at the dawn of a new millennium. By then, the various components will be in place and the practical operation of the system will be ready to start.

The fact that the cost of the new technology is rapidly becoming more and more affordable gives it great potential. This is the ultimate advantage for the poor, the less privileged, who will finally reap the largest benefits. And with new and effective learning systems, the cost of the operation can be met by small contributions from the users. With a sustainable concept, the communication revolution may gradually bridge the gap between haves and have-nots in the global society. This will, to a certain extent, depend on the decision makers and their ability to accept new visions. If not, the process will take more time, but it will still ultimately materialize, in spite of ignorance and old-fashioned thinking, as people want to assert themselves in a world of new and challenging opportunities. Projects like the new Bangladesh learning system and others will, regardless of political or bureaucratic brakes on the wheels of development, show the way to a new tomorrow.

Example of the digital revolution

The development of IT technology has moved faster than anyone could imagine. As a result, a number of industrialized countries are short of qualified manpower and capacity. Many of these jobs need to be given to those with creative brains. The suddenness of the developments is another example of this being a revolutionary change no one planned for. Less well-developed countries with a resourceful population (creative brains) have already benefited. India has developed a new export industry with more than $3 billion in export earnings per year. Interesting and relatively well-paid jobs are created in the country, thus partially preventing the damaging brain drain, as opportunities are created locally.

The beauty of the new technology is that it is global and can be applied nearly anywhere in the world. It is the professional skills, the creativity and the commitment to the professional challenge that count. Operators in India and other developing countries have proved that they are equally good, if not better, than many others. With further advancement in this industry, new potentials for great export are on the verge of taking shape.

A case in point is virtual reality products, such as three-dimensional architecture walk-ins, which today can be produced on low-cost PC-based technology. This type of creative, labour-intensive work can be done anywhere in the world. With skilled people readily trained and available, countries with low production costs will be very competitive on the world market. This can be a new growth industry in developing countries that have readily available human resources. It could that up human and technical capacities that will be a valuable asset for the country's own development, with high-level technical competence. It is another example that the development of new digital technology does not need to bring along with it a possibly negative impact on the poorest countries. On the contrary, it is a question of grasping the opportunities, of being in line with the new developments instead of becoming a victim of events. It needs visionary and brave leaders who are committed to the wellbeing and progress of their people. Instead of cursing negative aspects of new technological development, successful leaders concentrate on the opportunities.

A case in point is the Multimedia Super Corridor in Malaysia. This is the brainchild of the country's Prime Minister, Muhammed Mahathir. As a visionary leader, he had enough strength and determination to get the whole country behind this large and prestigious project (an idea that would have been killed off in other countries with less dynamic and visionary leadership).

The Multimedia Super Corridor is not only a 15 by 50-km geographical area with a digital optic fibre cable of an unprecedented 2.5–10 gigabit per second capacity, it is a comprehensive concept of a new development strategy bringing Malaysia well into the twenty-first century. The project is being developed in partnership with several of the world's largest players (Bill Gates is among the members of the Advisory Council). More than 120 world-class companies have already decided to establish operations in the Corridor. The project has been developed with lightning speed at a former palm oil plantation outside Kuala Lumpur. It is linked to the new airport and the new capital, which will house the world's first paperless government. It is also linked to a new and brave plan to provide all the schools in the country with Internet connections, and create 'smart schools' – a new and modern school system that is the first of its kind in the world. The centre of the new development is Cyberjaya, the world's first major Multimedia Super Corridor (MSC) designated cybercity. This pioneering effort will bring together all the elements needed to create an environment that engenders mutual enrichment for all kinds of IT/multimedia companies, with the ambition of being in the international forefront of new communication development.

The ultimate aim is to transform the whole country into a MSC. Dr Mahathir and his government colleagues have realized that the future depends on proper use of new communications technology, and have taken bold steps to bring Malaysia into the twenty-first century, becoming a beacon for development opportunities in the South. The Malaysian story is a practical example, showing that the world does not need to be further divided due to the new technology, and that developing countries can equally benefit, or reap even more gains with a large quantum jump into the future.

> **The tool to achieve a more balanced world society is available; it is the very technology that is today threatening to tear the world further apart. The choice is ours.**

With new communications opportunities, the political and social challenges in bringing the world together are within reach. Even the poorest countries do not need to be left out. On the contrary, the benefit could be the most rewarding, with a quantum leap for countries like Ethiopia, the cradle of mankind. However, in order to bridge the growing gap between rich and poor, a new vision with a modern development approach has to be implemented as soon as possible. It is a question of political priority and utilization of professional skills and knowledge. The tool to achieve a more balanced world society is available; it is the very technology that is today threatening to tear the world further apart. The choice is ours. ■

afterword

by Marjorie Scardino

Chief Executive, Pearson Plc

The Wired World is exciting, but no single approach can define it. The best and the brightest thinkers, congregating to share their thoughts in this book, give a range of perspectives on the expanding digital frontier.

Some themes emerge. Speed is one: both the infrastructure and the dynamics of the 'Global Information Economy' are developing at their own dizzying pace, but predictions about the real impact of the pace differ. Regulation is another, and there is some consensus. Governing bodies should err on the side of less rather than more to allow competition rather than bureaucratic prescription to shape the market.

The *laissez-faire* bias falls away over the issue of infrastructure, however. The commentators agree that the development of a 'Global Information Infrastructure' runs into issues of national sovereignty. Electronic commerce in particular disregards national boundaries and creates what Donald Johnston has described as 'global stewardship issues'. To cope with them, we will need global institutional frameworks that deal with intellectual property, taxation, encryption, consumer protection, and any other cross-border issues that may arise.

Policy makers in each country also agree that the digital revolution must be inclusive and not create a divided society of information 'haves' and 'have-nots'. To do that, they say it is essential that the infrastructure is extended to all corners, and that people in the developed and the developing world are trained to make the most of the Internet and encouraged to use it to talk to each other.

It's hard to argue with this urge for even-handed, democratic distribution. There have already been many initiatives to make the digital revolution more inclusive. Governments from the UK to Malaysia have developed Information Superhighways and made computers and the Internet available in schools. Regulators have tried to provide competitive structures. Global institutions such as the OECD are well down the road to creating new, worldwide economic frameworks.

But achieving universal access and training, if it can be done, is only half the battle to use information technology effectively. The larger challenge is what to use the technology *for*. How do we make the users and their needs more important than the tools?

Connectivity is vital, but connection without conversation, without content, has no value. The PC hooked to the Internet can be revolutionary, but as Esther Dyson says, 'it's not a new art form; it's only a tool.' Its interest is in what it means to the people who are using it. As more of us begin to focus on this, the next phase of the development of the Wired World is the creation and management of the content that can take best advantage of the benefits of the digital revolution.

For those creating the original content, this revolution opens up a variety of new distribution channels. Those delivering the content may be different from the creators (maybe not), and will need creatively to adapt existing skills into richer, more innovative formats and will need the flexibility to create and distribute across a variety of media.

There will be more competition for everyone in the chain. The term 'the content industry' itself indicates the collapse of the traditional boundaries between publishers, filmmakers, television producers, music labels, educational enterprises advertising agencies and even retailers. All may now be 'creators' of content, or intellectual property, that can be owned, traded, exploited or distributed across a variety of media. Or, indeed, they may provide only the raw material – the real 'creators' may be those who make it relevant – the users themselves, who will select, massage, reformat, add to and have it all their own way.

Of course, these changes are not happening at the same time everywhere in the world. Countries and cultures are still different. The globalization of communications infrastructures will not automatically lead to the globalization of content. Some content, just as some culture, will keep certain distinctions of genre and nationality, and suppliers will adapt. The Global Information Society will lead to inclusion, but not homogeneity.

Education is a good example of the power of new media when combined with effective content and made to suit a special, sometimes individual purpose. The Internet and electronic publishing allow coursework to be customized to the needs of a particular culture, curriculum, teacher or pupil, transferring power into the users' hands. Students are no longer passive absorbers of material presented to them by teachers; they choose their own ways to learn.

This, in turn, leads to another change in education – the importance of form as well as substance. Education has to compete for students' attention and imagination with digital television, computer games and the Internet, so it will adapt to the expectations created by those media. No more grey, uninviting text-only pages. Content has to be clear, engaging, entertaining and capable of making use of all media, from print to web site, to combinations. And it has to do it all with style and quality. Unless content is compelling, students won't be excited by an Internet site any more than they are by a textbook.

As form and distribution improves for educational materials, the audience grows. The waning of passive and the waxing of interactive media are revolutionizing the learning process, and the opportunities. Hooked up to the Internet, students, teachers and authors can 'talk' to each other on-line, anywhere in the world. Interactivity releases education from the traditional boundaries of the classroom or university campus and frees it from the world of under-25s: distance learning and lifelong learning become commonplace. Creators from universities to publishers can attract and motivate a wider audience than merely those who 'have to' study.

Technology gives curiosity and imagination a vehicle, a tool. But however new and exciting it is, what counts is what we do with it. The new communications infrastructure will continue to evolve; but the focus of the next phase of development of the Information Society will be on what we use the infrastructure *for*. As the facilities evolve, so must the content and its form. So long as the market is left free – from regulation, national boundaries or exclusionary economic models – to explore using these new tools, they will help foster intellectual discovery and invention. That is what matters.

November 1998

index

Welcome to the wired world

Key strategic agendas for commerce in the digital age

Anne Leer

ISBN 0 273 63560 3 Price £29.99

Do you know what impact the information superhighway will have on your business?

Do you know what the key commercial factors are in the Digital Age?

The companion volume to this book, *Welcome to the Wired World*, will help you master the key strategic issues and enable you to propel your organization forward in our Digital Age. It provides further background information, a description of market changes, an explanation of new business models, and includes a comprehensive glossary of terms, bibliography and subject index.

For further information or to order the above title, please contact your local bookseller or telephone +44(0) 1704 508080.

All prices quoted in sterling. Prices are recommended retail price for the UK; they may vary from country to country. Although rare, prices are subject to change without notice.

FINANCIAL TIMES
PITMAN PUBLISHING